KU-431-281

PENGUIN BOOKS
2637

I, CLAUD...

Claud Cockburn was born in Peking, China, in 1904 and educated at the Universities of Oxford, Budapest and Berlin. In 1929, he became a correspondent of *The Times* in New York and Washington. But after four years he resigned from *The Times* in order to found his news-sheet *The Week*, which attained a high degree of notoriety. During the same period he fought for the Republic in Spain and was Diplomatic Correspondent of the *Daily Worker*. Since moving to Ireland in 1947, he has written three novels and three volumes of autobiography, besides innumerable short stories and articles for the *New Statesman*, *Punch*, the *Saturday Evening Post*, *Hibernia*, and *Private Eye*. His novel *Beat the Devil* was filmed under the direction of John Huston. This book is taken from the three well-known autobiographical volumes, *In Time of Trouble*, *Crossing the Line* and *View from the West*, together with a final section bringing his autobiography up to date.

I, Claud...

THE AUTOBIOGRAPHY OF CLAUD COCKBURN

*

PENGUIN BOOKS

Penguin Books Ltd, Harmondsworth, Middlesex, England
Penguin Books Inc., 3300 Clipper Mill Road, Baltimore, Md. 21211, U.S.A.
Penguin Books Australia Ltd, Ringwood, Victoria, Australia

—

First published in three volumes:
In Time of Trouble published by Rupert Hart-Davis 1956
Crossing the Line published by MacGibbon & Kee 1958
View from the West published by MacGibbon & Kee 1961
Revised edition published in Penguin Books 1967

—

Copyright © Claud Cockburn, 1956, 1958, 1961, 1967

—

Made and printed in Great Britain
by Cox & Wyman Ltd, London, Fakenham and Reading
Set in Linotype Pilgrim

This book is sold subject to the condition
that it shall not, by way of trade or otherwise,
be lent, re-sold, hired out, or otherwise circulated
without the publisher's prior consent in any form of
binding or cover other than that in which it is
published and without a similar condition
including this condition being imposed
on the subsequent purchaser

CONTENTS

*If God lived on earth,
people would break his
windows*

I

WAR GAMES

In our little house, the question was whether the war would break out first, or the revolution. This was around 1910.

That period before the World War I has since got itself catalogued as a minor Golden Age. People living then are said to have had a sense of security, been unaware of impending catastrophe, unduly complacent.

In our neighbourhood, they worried. They thought it was the Victorians who had had a sense of security and been unduly complacent.

There were war scares every year, all justified. There was the greatest surge of industrial unrest ever seen. There was a crime wave. The young were demoralized. In 1911, without any help from Television or the Cinema or the Comics, some Yorkshire schoolboys, irked by discipline, set upon an unpopular teacher and murdered him.

Naturally, alongside those who viewed with alarm, there were those who thought things would probably work out all right. Prophets of doom and Pollyannas, Dr Pangloss and Calamity Jane, all lived near us in Hertfordshire in those years, and I well remember being taken to call on them all, on fine afternoons, in the open landau, for a treat.

At home, the consensus was that the war would come before the revolution.

This, as can be seen from the newspaper files, was not the most general view.

At our house, however, people thought war was not any nicer than revolution, but more natural.

It was in 1910 that my father desired me to stop playing French and English with my tin soldiers and play Germans and English instead. That was a bother, for there was a character, on a white horse, who was Napoleon – in fact, a double Napoleon; because he was dead Napoleon who fought Waterloo, and also alive, getting ready to attack the Chiltern Hills where we lived.

It was awkward changing him into an almost unheard-of Marshal von Moltke.

Guests came to lunch and talked about the coming German invasion. On Sundays, when my sister and I lunched in the dining-room instead of the nursery, we heard about it. It spoiled afternoon walks on the hills with Nanny, who until then had kept us happy learning the names of the small wild flowers growing there. I thought Uhlans with lances and flat-topped helmets might come charging over the hill any afternoon now. It was frightening, and a harassing responsibility, since Nanny and my sister had no notion of the danger. It was impossible to explain to them fully about the Uhlans, and one had to keep a keen watch all the time. Nanny was no longer a security. (An earlier Nanny had herself been frightened on our walks. She was Chinese, from the Mongolian border, and she thought there were tigers in the Chilterns.)

One night, at hay-making time, when the farm carts trundled home late, I lay awake in the dusk and trembled. Evidently they had come, and their endless gun-carriages were rolling up the lane. My sister said to go to sleep; it was all right because we had a British soldier staying in the house. This was Uncle Philip, a half-pay Major of Hussars whose hands had been partially paralysed as a result of some accident at polo.

His presence that night was a comfort. But his conversation was often alarming, particularly after he had been playing the War Game.

In the garden there was a big shed or small barn, and inside the shed was the War Game. It was played on a table a good deal bigger, as I recall, than a billiard table, and was strategically scientific. So much so, indeed, that the game was used for instructional purposes at the Staff College. Each team of players had so many guns of different calibre, so many divisions of troops, so many battleships, cruisers and other instruments of war. You threw dice, and operated your forces according to the value of the throw. Even so, the possible moves were regulated by rules of extreme realism.

The Game sometimes took three whole days to complete, and it always over-excited Uncle Philip. The time he thought he had caught the Japanese Admiral cheating he almost had a fit – not because the Japanese really was cheating, as it turned out, but because of the way he proved he was not cheating.

The Admiral and some other Japanese officers, on some sort of goodwill mission to Britain, had come to lunch and afterwards played the War Game. As I understand it, they captured from the British team – made up of my father, two uncles and a cousin on leave from the Indian Army – a troopship. It was a Japanese cruiser which made the capture, and, at his next move, the Admiral had this cruiser move the full number of squares which his throw of the dice would normally have allowed it. Uncle Philip accused him of stealthily breaking the rules. He should have deducted from the value of his throw the time it would have taken to transfer and accommodate the captured soldiers before sinking the troopship. He found the proper description of this cruiser in *Jane's Fighting Ships* and demonstrated that it would have taken a long time – even in calm weather – to get the prisoners settled aboard.

The Admiral said, 'But we threw the prisoners overboard.' He refused to retract his move.

Uncle Philip hurled the dice-box through the window of the shed and came storming up to the house. Even in the nursery could be heard his curdling account of the massacre on the destroyer.

'Sea full of sharks, of course. Our men absolutely helpless. Pushed over the side at the point of the bayonet. Damned cruiser forging ahead through water thickening with blood as the sharks got them.'

Even when the Japanese fought on the British side in World War I Uncle Philip warned us not to trust them.

His imagination was powerful and made holes in the walls of reality. He used to shout up at the nursery for someone to come and hold his walking-stick upright at a certain point on the lawn while he paced off some distances. These were the measurements of the gunroom of the shooting lodge he was going to build on the estate he was going to buy in Argyllshire when he had won £20,000 in the Calcutta Sweep. Sometimes he would come to the conclusion that he had made this gunroom too small – barely room to swing a cat. Angrily he would start pacing again, and often find that this time the place was too large. 'I don't want a thing the size of a barn, do I?' he would shout.

Once, some years earlier, his imagination functioned so powerfully that it pushed half the British Fleet about. That was at Queen Victoria's Diamond Jubilee in 1897, when the Fleet was drawn up for review at Spithead in the greatest assembly of naval power anyone had ever seen. Uncle Philip and my father were invited by the Admiral commanding one of the squadrons to lunch with him on his flagship. An attaché of the Admiral Commanding-in-Chief was also among those present.

Half-way through lunch Uncle Philip began to develop an idea. Here, he said, was the whole British Fleet gathered at Spithead, without steam up, immobile. Across there, was Cherbourg. (At that time, the war, when it came, was going to be against the French.) Well, suppose one night – tonight, for instance – some passionately Anglophobe commander of a French torpedo-boat were to get the notion of dashing across the Channel in the dark and tearing between the lines of the great ships, loosing off torpedoes. The ships helpless, without steam up. In twenty minutes, half of them sinking. In an hour, Britain's power reduced to the level of Portugal's. By dawn, the Solent strewn with the wreckage of an Empire. Before noon, mobs crazed with triumph and wine sweeping along the Paris boulevards, yelling for the *coup de grâce*.

He spoke of this, my uncle said, not as an idle speculation, but because he happened to have recalled, on his way to this lunch, that in point of fact a French officer, just mad enough to carry out such a project, was at this moment in command of a torpedo-boat at Cherbourg. (His voice, as he said this, compelled a closer attention by the Admiral and the attaché of the Commander-in-Chief.)

Certainly, he said, he had met the man himself, a Captain Moret, a Gascon. Hot-blooded, hating the English for all the ordinary French reasons, and for another reason, too: his only sister – a young and beautiful girl, Uncle Philip believed – had been seduced and brutally abandoned by an English Lieutenant, name of Hoadley, or Hoathly, at Toulon. A fanatic, this Moret. Had a trick of gesturing with his cigar – like this (Uncle Philip sketched the gesture) – as he, Moret, expatiated on his favourite theory, the theory of the underrated powers of the torpedo-boat as the guerrilla of the sea.

'And there,' said Uncle Philip, in a slightly eerie silence, 'he is.' He nodded ominously in the direction of Cherbourg.

On the way back to Cowes in the Admiral's launch, my father upbraided Uncle Philip. A nice exhibition he had made of himself – a mere Major of Hussars, lecturing a lot of Admirals and Captains on how to run their business. Also they had undoubtedly seen through this yarn, realized that this Moret was a figment of Uncle Philip's imagination, invented half-way through the fish course. Then, and during the remainder of the afternoon and early evening, Uncle Philip was abashed, contrite. After dinner that evening they walked by the sea, taking a final look at the Fleet in the summer dusk. Silently my uncle pointed at the far-flung line. Every second ship in the line was getting up steam.

People told Uncle Philip that if he would employ his gift of the gab in a practical way, not spend it all in conversation, but take to writing, he would make a fortune – like Stanley Weyman or someone of that kind. It seemed a good idea, and while waiting for the Calcutta Sweep to pay off, he wrote, and published at the rate of about one a year, a number of historical romances. They included *Love in Armour*, *A Gendarme of the King*, *The Black Cuirassier*, and *A Rose of Dauphiny*. It was unfortunate from a financial point of view that he had a loving reverence for French history, which he supposed the library subscribers shared. The historical details of his stories were to him both fascinating and sacred. He refused to adjust by a hair's-breadth – in aid of suspense, romance, or pace of action – anything whatsoever, from an arquebus to a cardinal's mistress. Once you were past the title, you were on a conducted tour of a somewhat chilly and overcrowded museum.

However, he did make enough out of these books to feel justified in buying a motor-car in the days when that was a daring and extravagant thing to do. He reasoned that since the Sweep would ultimately provide a motor-car as a matter of course, it was foolish to spend the time not having a motor-car just because the Draw was still nine months off.

He was not its possessor for long. He was superstitious. The car was of a make called Alldays. He showed it to my father. My father was against motor-cars. Some people of his age were against them because they went too fast. My father disliked them because they did not go fast enough. He took the view that if people were to take the trouble to give up horses and carriages and go about in these intricate affairs instead, it was only reasonable that the machines, in return, should get them to wherever they wanted to be in almost no time – a negligible, unnoticeable time. The fact that even with one of these vaunted motor-cars you still took hours and hours to get from, say, London to Edinburgh, struck him as disgusting and more or less fraudulent. Later he felt the same way about aeroplanes. He was thus not enthusiastic about Uncle Philip's motor-car, and when he saw the maker's name on the bonnet, he unkindly murmured the quotation, 'All days run to the grave.'

Uncle Philip took fright and sold the car immediately at a heavy loss. Of this I was glad, not because I thought the car would run him to his grave but because I thought it would get him into a dungeon. He had a chauffeur called Basing, and I once heard somebody say, 'That man Basing drives too fast.' He had been known to exceed the speed limit of twenty miles per hour. In those days when people spoke of motor-cars they spoke also of police traps. My idea of the police was simple and horrifying. I thought they would soon manacle Uncle Philip and leave him to rot in a cell. We should never see him again.

Real life, like curry, which he ate Anglo-Indian fashion – so hot it would have charred an Indian's stomach – was never quite sharp enough for Uncle Philip. The weary present he made endurable to his taste by a sort of incantation. He recited old French ballads aloud as he walked to the village, or simply shouted agreeably sonorous words. You asked him where he was going and he peered through his monocle and shouted, 'I am on my way to the headquarters of his Supreme Excellency the Field-Marshal Ghazi Ahmed Mukhta Pasha.' When the past tasted a little flat, he peppered it artificially. No one was safe from his cookery. He was talking to me once about his grandfather, a worthy officer, I believe, of the Black Watch who had died peacefully but at a rather early age. Finding the story dull, Uncle Philip told me that in reality, though it had been hushed up, his grandfather had shot himself in melodramatically scandalous circumstances. I think that at the time he actually believed he was really doing the deceased a good turn – making him more interesting than he had, in fact, managed to be. Uncle Philip was my mother's brother, and I asked her about it. She was in a dilemma. She wished to deny it as authoritatively as possible. On the other hand, she hesitated to tell a child of seven that his uncle was a monstrous liar.

As for the future, Uncle Philip seasoned it with the Calcutta Sweep and the imminence of a very interesting war. As things turned out, he never did win the Sweep, and the war was no fun either. He got himself back into the Army, despite his crippled hands, but the cold and damp undermined his health and laid him low.

The theoretical basis of Uncle Philip's belief that war was coming soon was quite simple. He thought any Government which supposed itself to have a reasonable advantage in armaments and manpower over its neighbours or rivals would go for them as soon as it was convinced that this was the case and provided the weather was suitable for the type of campaign its armies preferred. In this view he had the concurrence of my Uncle Frank, my father's elder brother, who in other respects was so different from Uncle Philip that he might have been brought up on a different planet. But he did enjoy the War Game, finding it more sensible than cards, and even made, in collaboration with Uncle Philip, some suggestions for changes in the rules which were sent to the Staff College, or whatever the strategic institution was that used the Game, and I believe adopted there.

He was a banker and a Canadian, and he took, uninhibitedly, the view that the world was a jungle, and civilization a fine but flimsy tent which anyone would be a fool either not to enjoy or to treat as a secure residence. Compared to the rest of the family he was rich. Enormously so, I thought at the time, for there seemed to be nothing he could not afford, and I was told once that he actually had a lot more than Uncle Philip would have if he drew the winning ticket in the Sweep.

During those years, when we were moving about southern England looking, my father kept assuring me, for somewhere to settle down permanently, Uncle Frank was a frequent visitor, fleeting, but as impressive as a big firework.

His headquarters were at Montreal, but the place where he felt at home was Mexico. He spent a lot of time there, helping to organize some kind of revolution or counter-revolution – nominally in the interests of the bank, but mainly because that was the kind of work he liked. The details were never fully revealed to us. This was due partly to discretion, partly to the fact that the precise lines and objectives of the undertaking – which once had been a quite simple business of violently overthrowing the Government – had become year by year increasingly complex and uncertain.

Nobody seemed to know just whose side anyone was on, which generals and politicians and rival financiers and concessionaires were good – that is to say, pro-Uncle Frank – and which bad. Not, I think, that he cared much about that. He enjoyed a colourful kind of plotting for its own sake, regardless of the monotonous aims of the fogies back in Montreal.

People would say, 'But I thought So-and-So was the man you were supporting? Wasn't he the one who was so good and was going to save the country?' And Uncle Frank would say vaguely that that had been before that business when Whatsisname shot up that bunch of Thingummies that time in Vera Cruz. There would follow a story full of sunshine and pistols and oil – very exciting and even intelligible, as far as it went, like a single battle-scene from a Shakespearian drama.

It seemed to be wonderful to have a job where that sort of thing was your business, and you were praised for your hard work doing it. The banking business attracted me a good deal – a banker, evidently, was something between Long John Silver and the Scarlet Pimpernel, and rich, too, and respected. The clerk at the local branch of the London, County, Westminster and Parr's became a figure of romance. I made up stories about his secret life.

Uncle Frank proclaimed himself a 'reactionary'. This piece of news went around among the neighbours and was applauded. They were deep-blue Conservatives, but already nervous of calling themselves, uncompromisingly, 'reactionaries'. Yet they found it comforting when someone else was unashamed to do so. My mother, active in the Women's Conservative Association and the Primrose League, did not care for the word at all. A devout and serious Christian, she was often bothered by what she read of socialists because she could not, instantly and absolutely, see where they were so wrong. To her horrified ear, they kept sounding as though they had ideas rather like Christ's.

This hesitancy of mind ashamed her. She felt it to be a kind of betrayal of Mr Bonar Law and Lord Balfour. She would steady herself by thinking about the atheistic opinions of socialists in France.

Uncle Frank was, in his way, more disturbing, as a fellow-traveller in the Conservative caravan, than the Christian-looking socialists roaming the desert. He treated all politics as some kind of sordid Mexican brawl about money and land, and took for granted that anyone pretending to a different attitude was merely practising a cunning hypocrisy, deceiving simpletons for the sake of votes. To listen to talk about patriotism, the good of the community, progress and the imperial ideal, except when the words came from a platform for a practical political purpose, bored him shockingly.

He was in constant fear of having people bore him, and carried antidotes about. He was a big man, and his clothes bagged on him under the weight of financial reviews, stock-market reports and similar documents which were in some of the pockets, and fat little volumes of Homer or Herodotus which he carried in others. He must have had an idea that when he wished to abstract himself from company he became, by virtue of his wish, invisible. He would go to some local gathering and, at tea or after dinner, slide a paper or book on to his knee so as to read it while people were talking to him. 'I don't think anyone noticed,' he would say afterwards.

His period of popularity among the local gentry as a visiting imperial lion from the Great Dominion did not endure. He was taken to some garden party held in the Conservative interest, and there introduced by the Vicar to a young barrister who had political ambitions and was popular for his renderings of 'Yip-I-Addy-I-Ay'. This person said to him, 'I must say, Mr Cockburn, I do admire your courage – I hear you are not afraid to call yourself a reactionary.' He then, according to my father, who was present, neighed.

Uncle Frank, who had been in a trance, looking at the back view of the village church and meditating on episodes of the Trojan War, or the current price of hogs in Chicago, or whatever it was, took a moment to focus on this remark, and the musical barrister filled the pause by stating that he himself was a bit of a reactionary, too.

Uncle Frank shouted his approval. 'You're absolutely right,' he said; 'everything since ancient Greece has been a mistake. Of course, the real trouble is Christianity, don't you agree? My idea of a real, dangerous damn fool is the Emperor Constantine. What an ass!'

My father remarked gently that the Vicar quite possibly did not agree with him. Uncle Frank, when he was talking to one person, often forgot that anyone else was present, and he now turned to the Vicar, with an apologetic bow. 'I don't,' he said, 'mean to say a word against Christianity as a religion. It's fine. But it's unsuitable.'

'Unsuitable?' said the Vicar.

'To the human race,' said Uncle Frank. 'That's where Constantine was a damn fool. Another hundred years of steady persecution and they'd have had the Christians licked. They could have got right back. After all,' he said to the Vicar, 'as a God there wasn't much wrong with Zeus.'

The story went around that he had sworn at the Vicar and insulted the Church of England, but he was not there to hear it, for next morning he succumbed, once again, to what my father referred to as 'Frank's deplorable weakness for this fellow Aitken'. He went off to London to see the Canadian financier, Sir William Maxwell Aitken, afterwards Baron Beaverbrook, who had lately embarked on the English stage of his career.

They had been financial associates, and later close friends in Canada, and all his life Uncle Frank secretly thought that Max Aitken was practically the only man in England who approached things realistically. Secretly, that is, so far as our household was concerned, because my father, although he had never met the future Lord Beaverbrook, and insisted he had nothing against him personally, thought he was a portent – boding no good.

After the first war, and the rise of the newspaper proprietor to immense power, my father was more than ever convinced of this.

My uncle, when he was in England, liked to go and talk about money, and imperial politics, and – on occasion – religion and poetry with Rudyard Kipling and Bonar Law and Lord Beaverbrook at the latter's Surrey home. One day, when he was planning such a visit, my father said to him that if he went from our house to Lord Beaverbrook's, he need not bother himself to return. Thereafter, when he wanted to make such a visit, Uncle Frank pretended he was only going to London for a couple of days on business. But since he needed an intermediary who could forward urgent cables to him if necessary, he had to take me into his confidence.

'It's a pity,' he said, 'your father should feel this way about Max. Your father,' he added sadly, 'doesn't understand about Max.'

Though he found such an association shocking, my father felt sorry for Uncle Frank, considering that he should be pitied rather than censured.

'No doubt,' he would say in extenuation of his brother's choice of friends, 'a banker has to associate a good deal with financiers and people of that kind. Naturally. Your Uncle Frank has had a hard life, you know. You see, ever since he was a young man, he has had to deal with *money*.'

This, to his mind, melancholy fact, explained a great deal. It explained why his brother, of whom he was very fond, should have developed a view of life which seemed to my father lacking in delicacy and understanding of reality.

Each of them had been initially propelled along their widely divergent roads by the same force – namely the high principles of my grandfather, a younger son of Lord Cockburn, the great Scottish Advocate and Judge who shone so brightly in the Golden Age of Edinburgh society. The adults surrounding my grandfather's youth were gay, civilized and earnest. They would not have understood how, later, earnestness became a term of disdain, and was supposed to be incompatible with gaiety. They took life, as the saying goes, seriously. To take it any other way would have been, in them, a sign of despair.

When my grandfather was about fourteen he liked to make explosions by pouring gunpowder out of a horn into the kitchen furnace. Then his hand slipped, the whole of the gunpowder slid down the stone funnel into the furnace, and the explosion blew off his right arm. It was a horrid disaster to which relatives near and far reacted immediately and in the same way: before the week was out he received from uncles, aunts and cousins all over Scotland eleven separate presents of writing-desks, to encourage him to lose no time in learning to write with his left hand.

He learned not only to write but to drive a carriage and pair in a dashing manner. He went to India in the service of the old East India Company, lived in an oriental splendour which caused remark even in those unbridled days, became a Judge in the Administration of the new Indian Empire, and retired to Edinburgh intending to spend the remainder of his days in reasonably rich comfort. He lived, in fact, well, and was astonished at the comment of the son of some Rajah who came to visit him. The young man had seen my grandfather only with the trappings of a high British official in India. After what in Edinburgh was esteemed a rather magnificent dinner, the Indian asked permission to pose an indiscreet question. 'Sir,' he said, 'after your life in India, is it not irksome to exist in this state of indigent obscurity?'

Later, the indigence became, comparatively speaking, a fact. The cost of living rose. So did the number of relatives who for various reasons had to be supported by grandfather. Many of them were young women, more or less distant cousins whose parents had left them penniless. It might, even then, have been possible for them to support themselves by some kind of work, but they said, 'Our dear mother would not have liked it,' and that, in the circumstances of the time, was undeniably true. In the end, grandfather had to get a second house in Edinburgh to put some of them in. Seeking to ease the financial strain, he took his own immediate family to Bonn, on the Rhine, which was cheaper and warmer.

Frank, eldest male among seven children, was to go to work – in Canada, because friends said it was a fine place for a young man, particularly a Scotsman. Arrangements were made to get him, for a start, a good job in an engineering concern there. It was a new and prosperous concern and prospects were said to be fine. Just before he sailed, it was discovered that the managing director of this firm was a friend of an intimate friend of grandfather. The mutual friend had actually written to him asking him to keep a favourable eye on Uncle Frank. My grandfather was appalled. He felt at once that this necessitated a change in the carefully laid plans. As he pointed out to Uncle Frank, there was now, as a result of this deplorable turn of events, a distinct possibility that this director in Canada would feel obliged to show special consideration and favour to the lad – advance his interests by various means, give him preferential treatment. This would be morally wrong. In the circumstances, the only proper course was for Frank to write, withdrawing from the job in the engineering firm, and – on landing in Canada – simply do the best he could. That was how he happened to start working for a moribund bank at Quebec. He worked sixteen or seventeen hours a day and ate only at breakfast-time. Late at night he drank cocoa, which he tried to make more interesting and long-lasting by each night decorating the cocoa-jug with elaborately painted Greek verses and proverbs. The largest inscription he made on the jug was the Greek text of 'For the night cometh when no man can work' – *Nux gar erchetai*, etc. Years later, the jug stood prominent on the study mantelshelf in his big house in Montreal, and was referred to by the staff – bidden to treat it reverently – as 'the Nuxgar Jug'.

The period of penury and cocoa did not, in fact, last very long. Thousands of miles from Bonn, and exhilarated by the atmosphere of Canadian business, Uncle Frank soon pushed his way out of the torpid bank for which he had originally gone to work and into the Bank of Montreal which was booming and brimming with opportunity. But at Bonn, in the meantime, another crisis had occurred.

For more than a year it had been understood that my father was to enter the Indian Civil Service, an ambition which had been his since he was fifteen. Indeed, to a young man brought up on Plutarch's *Lives* and the history of Rome, the Indian Civil Service in those days seemed to offer limitless scope for the realization of boyhood dreams – a subcontinent to be organized and governed, power to be exercised over millions of people, a game with whole kingdoms and principalities on the board.

At that time the examination for the Indian Civil Service was the most rigorous and the most highly competitive in existence – the prospects and prizes of that Service attracted hundreds of the more brilliant and the most ambitious. The age limits within which candidates were eligible were such that you could make, if necessary, three attempts in three successive years. Almost nobody expected to be among the winners at his first attempt, which was regarded chiefly as a trial run, a way of getting, so to speak, to know the course. If you did fairly well then, you could make your serious attempt next year.

My father at his first attempt failed by only two places. It was considered a spectacular achievement. His success at the second attempt seemed certain. But, perhaps made over-confident by this achievement, he was rash enough, in the course of a theological discussion with grandfather at Bonn, to disclose that under the influence of German philosophy he had become an atheist.

Grandfather was distressed, but felt that his first duty was to the Indians, whom he had so long helped to govern, and to the British Empire in India. He still had some influence at the India Office and with the Government of India. He travelled to London, saw influential and authoritative friends holding power in that branch of Government and disclosed the unpleasant situation which had arisen. It was obviously monstrous, inadmissible, that an avowed atheist should get into the Indian Civil Service, particularly as the young man concerned was evidently of exceptional ability and might quickly rise to a position of power and importance. Grandfather believed strongly in the value of the Christian religion as an ideological instrument of imperial rule. An atheist in such a position might cause havoc and wreckage. He therefore desired those in authority to take whatever steps were necessary to ensure that, however brilliantly he might perform in the examination, my father should not be admitted to the Service.

He then returned to Bonn and reported his actions to my father, who knew quite enough about the working of what is nowadays called 'The Old Boy Net' to realize that as things now stood he had considerably less chance of entering the Indian Civil Service than he did of entering the Church of England and becoming a Bishop. Enough strings had been pulled in London to keep an Archangel out of Delhi if he were caught disbelieving in the Thirty-Nine Articles.

He was bitter about the way things had turned out and wished he had kept his mouth shut about atheism. But he liked and admired people who knew their own minds and had convictions upon which they really acted, and he did not quarrel with grandfather.

'After all,' he said to me long afterwards, 'a person ought to carry his beliefs to their logical conclusion. I think I should have been rather dismayed if father had done anything else. It would have seemed so feeble. Given his opinions on religion and government, it was the only sensible thing for him to do.'

'He might,' I said, 'at least have tried to convert you.'

'But you see,' said my father, 'he took for granted that everyone else's views were as unshakeable as his own. And he would have thought, too, that I might be tempted to make a false pretence of conversion – which would have been bad for my moral character; and then, later, when I was Lieutenant-Governor, I might have come out in my true colours and started massacring the missionaries, or forced them to give readings from Feuerbach from their pulpits.'

It was, however, clear that life at home had reached an *impasse*, and, not wishing to take any further chances with grandfather's convictions, my father sold all his books and all except one suit of clothes and disappeared to London. When his family next heard from him, he had secretly sat for, and passed, his entrance examination for the Eastern Consular Service, which was then a kind of half-way house between the Diplomatic Service – for which you needed a lot of money – and the ordinary Consular Service which dealt mainly with commercial affairs and was confined to Europe and the western hemisphere. The point about the Eastern Consular Service was that it functioned east of Singapore, and that it was possible to pass from it into regular diplomatic service in the Far East.

He went to China and never left it until he was thirty years old. From his nineteenth to his twenty-second year he was

British Vice-Consul at the then awfully remote city of Chungking. It was the most isolated British agency in Asia. The city had three hundred thousand inhabitants and was the pivotal point of trade along the Yangtze between central China and the south-east. But foreign trade was officially barred. In the whole of those four years he saw only half a dozen Europeans – none of them, as he remarked with satisfaction, 'unduly obtrusive'. Since there was almost no trade, there was no tiresome routine work. His duties, in fact, were vague. He was simply an outpost. His life was full and happy, gay and studious by turns. There were at Chungking excellent professors of philosophy, poetry and calligraphy. The political intrigues in which as British agent he became involved were intricate, dangerous and delightful. Once a month he conducted a public exercise in imperialism.

At that time it was forbidden for foreigners to reside on or even visit that part of Chungking lying on the right bank of the Yangtze. Rightly, the Chinese believed that if you gave the foreigners an inch they would take an ell. Once a month my father – designing to establish precedents and break down this ban – used to send a formal notification to the Governor, who resided on the right bank, that the British Vice-Consul proposed to call on him on a certain date. The Governor, not wishing to make a formal breach of relations, always acceded. On the day fixed, my father was transported across the river, and was met on the opposite bank by the Governor's litter, with a heavy guard of soldiers. The steep streets to the Governor's residence were lined with furiously hostile crowds – their natural hatred of the intruder encouraged and stimulated when necessary by agents of the Governor. They pelted the litter with stones. Every couple of hundred yards the litter was halted while the soldiers battled with the populace.

At the Governor's residence the Governor entertained the Vice-Consul and they talked for a couple of hours. At some point during the conversation, the Vice-Consul took occasion to remark with satisfaction that it was now evidently the policy of the Imperial Government to permit an Englishman to visit the right bank of the river at Chungking. At some other point the Governor would take occasion to express his satisfaction that in this single instance it had been possible for the Imperial authorities to suspend for a few hours the inviolable rule against the presence of foreigners on the right bank, and that the efficiency of the troops had sufficed to curb, on this particular day, the profound indignation of the people.

The parting ceremony was also a somewhat elaborate manoeuvre, it being necessary for the Vice-Consul to take his leave in words carrying the general sense of *au revoir*, whereas the Governor must give to his courteous parting remarks the unmistakable nuance of an adieu. Then came the progress back to the river, with stoning, battles and occasional bloodshed.

When I was a little boy I thought it must have been a very grand feeling to be carried thus in a magnificent litter, an outpost of Empire with hostile thousands roaring for one's blood. 'Didn't you,' I asked my father, 'feel grand and triumphant?'

'A little, sometimes,' he said. 'But then I tried, too, to remember that to those people I didn't look grand at all. I reminded myself that to them I was physically an evil-smelling monkey, and in character and status a vulgar barbarian thief trying to break into China. An excellent spiritual exercise.'

Much later, when I was sixteen or so, I bothered him with another sort of question.

'Were you always absolutely sure it was a good thing to try to extend British power in China?'

'Absolutely.'

'But you don't much like English people. You prefer Chinese.'

'Hang it, I like some English people.'

'Not many.'

'True.'

'You don't care for their attitude to life. You know they bore you to death. Secretly, everything they say seems to you platitudinous or else untrue.'

'A lot of Chinese are awfully silly, too.'

'And you spent more than half your life working to help the English dominate the Chinese.'

'It's nothing to do with people. It's a question of realizing an idea.'

'"The Imperial Idea"?'

'I hope you're not getting that deplorable habit of picking

25

phrases out of newspapers and using them without knowing what they mean. A good thing to do is to read two pages of the *New Oxford Dictionary* every day. You get the exact derivations of all words and their differing shades of meaning at different periods. An excellent habit.'

'You seem to be changing the subject.'

'Let's play a game of chess.'

He seemed unaware of any contradiction in his attitude. He did not care to argue about it. He did say once that talking to me about it was like trying to explain music to a deaf child. It was tedious to make clear to a person who did not grasp it immediately how one could deplore almost every material and spiritual manifestation of the Empire and still dedicate oneself to its expansion and consolidation as the highest Good.

Between leaving Bonn and retiring, he spent more than thirty years in China and Korea, and less than that number of months in England. Except for the countryside in spring-time, he did not care much for anything about England. About the personalities and forces – political, financial, commercial – which motivated and directed the imperial machine, he had, as they say, no illusions. He found them comical, subjects for savage ribaldry. Or pathetic. Or sordid. And often simply ignoble. The machine, on the other hand – that was admirable and good: a fine bit of work, satisfactory and even inspiring to tend. Perhaps his reference to music was the clue. He was listening, perhaps, to some strange symphony. The rest was as irrelevant as would be the fact that the composer took dope and the conductor lived on the immoral earnings of women.

He moved into the Far Eastern Diplomatic Service and as 'Chinese Secretary' at the Peking Legation was for a long time the principal liaison between the British Government and the foundering dynasty of the Manchus. Secretly he intrigued on behalf of an immense scheme which he thought might ensure British domination of Asia for generations. The idea impressed him – others, I suspect, had the same motives earlier and independently – while watching the special Legation Guard of Punjab Lancers sent up from India. Suppose, as a gesture of friendship and courtesy, the British Government were to offer to lend certain trained Indian troops to the Imperial House as a reliable bodyguard against the subversive elements which seethed around it? He knew, from discreet soundings, that important officials in the Palace would be favourable. They would like to have troops who would be safe from contamination by revolutionaries and throne-seekers. Over a period of years, such a Guard – corresponding, he pointed out, to the Scottish Archer Guard of the French kings – would be developed from a toy to a real instrument of power. In a dozen or twenty years these Janissaries would become indispensable. As such, they would work for the Dynasty, but also, in the last analysis, control it and its policies. And the Guard, in turn, would of course ultimately be controlled by the Government of India.

At a suitable moment somewhere along the line – there could easily be 'trouble' in India – the Chinese Government would offer to 'facilitate' the recruitment of Chinese troops for 'garrison service' in India. Within a half-century or so, the trained manpower of China – under British control – would be on tap to hold India against any possibility of successful revolt, and the manpower of India – under British control – would be the decisive military force in China. 'The beauty of it is,' he would say, 'that the Chinese and the Indians really hate and despise each other even more than they hate and despise us. And of course that would be something that could be fostered – there would be very little danger of fraternization. Occupying forces are bound to be thoroughly unpopular.'

By hindsight the scheme appears merely preposterous. In reality there was a kind of crazy feasibility about it. He worked at it for years, and in the days shortly before and after the Boxer Rising, when on terms almost of intimacy with the sinister old Empress Dowager, he used to discuss it in an abstract, allusive kind of way with her. When he felt that it was ripe enough to be presented, cautiously, to British 'official circles', he found that they did not by any means have the courage of his convictions. They professed themselves dreadfully shocked. Perhaps it was his method of presentation they found unpalatable. In dealing with British officials he sometimes left behind the wrappings of tact and double-talk he could employ so naturally and successfully with the Chinese, because the Chinese regarded double-talk as a courtesy and did not expect anyone even to pretend to believe in it. Apparently in outlining his plan to the British he forgot, until it was too late, to make the indispensable statement that the aim of the whole thing was of course to uplift, spiritually and materially, both the Indian and Chinese peoples, offering them greater and greater opportunities of self-betterment, guiding their steps along the path to ultimate self-government.

Large phrases of this kind about the Empire were received by him with derision or an unpleasant silence. He said he liked to feel, when taking part in an all-night, whisky-drenched poker session at the Shanghai Club, that the long-term purpose of the gathering was to elevate the cultural standards of the Chinese. He caused offence at a public dinner at Amoy by declaring his belief that the true function of our business community in China, with its fine appreciation of the good things of life, was to bring some modicum of civilization to the missionaries.

But talk 'justifying' the Empire on account of its 'good works' annoyed him in another way, too. It was as though someone were to find it necessary to 'justify' the symphony by proclaiming that the composer, conductor and members of the orchestra were all people of the purest moral character.

Just before the Nationalist outbreak of 1900 he went briefly to England, married and returned with my mother in time to be besieged in the Legation quarter by the Boxers. Because of the official acceptance of reports that the Legations had fallen and the besieged all been killed, he had the pleasure of reading his own obituary notice in the newspapers. He had always been in grave trouble with the finance-controllers in London on account of his heavy and ingeniously contrived over-spending of a special 'entertainment' allowance. He wrote to the Foreign Office, noting with pleasure that these difficulties were not mentioned in the obituary notices, based on official information, and were therefore evidently recognized as of a trivial nature. Dr Morrison, the famous China correspondent of *The Times*, who was also among the besieged, simply cabled the paper saying, 'Have just read obituary in *The Times*. Kindly adjust pay to suit.'

I was born at Peking, on the day the Japanese blew up the Russian flagship *Petropavolsk* at Port Arthur, and spent the first few weeks of life at Wei-hai-wei, which until a couple of years before had been the headquarters of the British-officered Chinese regiment which my father had seen as a primitive instrument of the Sino-Indian plan. People used to stare northwards across the sea at night and claim they could see the flashes of great naval battles in the Port Arthur direction. My Chinese amah, who had seen the looting of Peking by the foreign troops, expected the Japanese or the Russians to land at any minute and massacre everyone. She was glad to take me to England, but there the boys shouted and threw stones at her in the street because she wore blue trousers, and she longed to return.

My father became Minister to Korea while it was still nominally independent, and then Consul-General as the Japanese progressively took over control. He thought the whole British agreement with the Japanese on the Korean issue disastrous. He was offered another ministerial post. Quite suddenly he announced he was weary of the whole business and retired, saying that at forty-nine it was high time to start leading an entirely new sort of life.

We rented four or five different houses in four years. Each of them was discovered, after a few months, to have some intolerable defect. Secretly, as he admitted to me later, my father had come to the conclusion that it would really be more satisfactory to buy a house in the hills west of Peking, but he wanted to give England every chance. According to my mother, the house in Hertfordshire lasted longer than the others only because it had this shed or barn which was so suitable for housing the War Game.

I had played Germans and English with the tin soldiers for a couple of years when I thought I, too, would like to learn to play the War Game. I was disappointed. Neither my father nor my uncles would teach it to me. They had given up playing it themselves. They said that to learn it now would be not only pointless but actually misleading because very soon now there would be a new war which would make all strategy, tactics and rules of the War Game obsolete.

2

HOLES IN THE FENCE

VIRTUS LAUDATA CRESCIT, or 'virtue grows with praise', was found, at the last moment, to be the motto of the school I was to go to, and if arrangements had been less far advanced I believe my father would have changed his mind and sent me somewhere else. It was symbolic, he felt, of a state of mind – a lax state. All very well to take the view that a pat on the back could occasionally make goodness better; but very improper, he opined, for a school, of all places, to turn this notion into an official motto. To do so was virtually to flaunt a conviction that people cannot be expected to be any good *unless* they are patted on the back for it.

It was one of those small pointers that suddenly indicated to him the extent of the gulf existing between his own ideas and those of the age in which his children were to grow up. Useless to point out that the motto was not modern – had, it was understood, been the family motto of the school's founder, in the mid sixteenth century. What, might one ask, was known of *his* character and achievements? But it was too late to back out now. We had already taken a house in Berkhamstead so that, at any rate to begin with, I could attend the 'Preparatory' section of the school as a day boy rather than a boarder.

However, he took it for granted that a school which prided itself on a motto like that, and had a headmaster who apparently supported the Liberal Party, would likely be incapable of teaching me the rudiments of Latin and Greek in a sufficiently thorough way. He therefore coached me himself for a couple of hours a day in term time and an hour a day in the holidays. These hours were happily astringent.

In the school they seemed to want us to believe that Latin was on the whole fairly easy provided one took it slowly without undue exertion of the brain. My father told me sharply that to learn Latin correctly, and at a respectable rate of progress each week, was exceedingly hard, and that unless I exerted myself to the utmost I should fail miserably. These exhortations turned the undertaking into an agreeably challenging and arduous enterprise.

Some months after war broke out – I was then between ten and eleven – I told him proudly that I had been second out of fifteen in my Latin class for three weeks running, though most of the boys in it were older than myself. He was unimpressed. 'But why not be top?' he said. 'If you can be second, you can be first. This war is going to make things uncomfortable for any one of our sort who doesn't get to the top and stay there all the time. Don't take your pace from other people. I doubt if the people at the school realize what things are really like.'

The school – with its Preparatory, Junior and Senior sections – was one of those institutions where you could spend all your life from the age of eight to the age of nineteen and a half; except, that is, for the years 1916–18, when you were liable to spend your eighteenth birthday packing for the journey to the training camp, and your nineteenth, if you were lucky enough to have one, in a Flanders dugout.

By the time I went to Berkhamstead the school had five hundred boys, and was poised somewhere between Stalky and Co. and the Welfare State. The Rugby Tradition, the standards of the barrack-room, and intimations of modernism and 'progressive' education overlapped or struggled confusedly for supremacy.

Since the 'free scholars' from the elementary schools came, in the main, not from the town itself but from homes in Watford and Tring and other towns of the area, they were known to us collectively as 'train boys'. It was a term of disdain, and quite often hatred, and in the derision and repugnance for the train boys expressed by the sons of parents who could afford to pay for their education, several of the teaching staff openly, or *sotto voce*, joined, for they felt that the presence about the place of so many of these uncouth fellows with working-class accents detracted from their own social position as masters at a distinguished school for the sons of gentlemen.

The train boys had got these free places by intelligence and hard work, in competition with hundreds of others in the elementary schools, and now many of them continued to push ahead with their work in a harsh, ostentatious, menacing sort of way. These we either feared or patronized.

Among ourselves – though not often, as I recall, to their faces – we parodied and loudly condemned their unseemly Hertford-shire intonations and pronunciations, which, however, were satisfactory as being a badge of evident all-round lowness. The amusement and disgust that could be extracted from these accents were not, however, inexhaustible; but it was satis-factory, too, to be able to conclude, on first-hand evidence, that the standard of manners and general behaviour among the lower orders was low indeed; for thus to conclude gave an agreeable sense of superiority, and showed that everyone had the advantages he deserved.

Even quite earnest members of the staff, who in theory and on public occasions welcomed the train boys as demonstrating the breadth of our democracy, were privately uneasy lest, in-stead of the train boys being elevated to the moral and cultural level of the rest of us, they might drag us, and the school, disastrously down. Conferences on this disturbing subject were actually held between members of the teaching staff and senior boys.

The conclusion was that what was wrong was that the train boys did not live under the conditions that are necessary to make for *esprit de corps*.

What did these fellows do? They came from their homes, they got into their trains, and they then arrived at the school, where they received the tuition which had been paid for; after which they got back into the trains and went home. Some of them brought sandwich lunches in paper bags, and others – even lower – went to small cafés in the town to get something to eat at the lunch-time break.

The official view was that this meant that the train boys were in reality being defrauded of the full advantages of Public School education, and were not even being properly shown what those advantages might be. The rest of us were organized in Houses which intensified *esprit de corps*. Some big progressive came up with the suggestion that the way to overcome the train-boy difficulty was to organize them into a House, too, and that was what was done. At frightful inconvenience to themselves they were organized in this way and made to leave their paper bags behind and abandon the cafés where they had formerly met at lunch. Instead they were compelled to eat in a little house on a piece of marshy land between the back of the school and the canal which ran along the railway bridge, and they were forced also to organize themselves into House teams, so that a good deal of the leisure they had formerly had after their school hours was now gone. All the other Houses in the school had names. The two School Houses, for instance, were called Uppers and Lowers, and there was a House called St John's and another called Incent's, and the day boys were called 'Bees'. There was another day-boys' House called 'Wasps' – their shirts were pink and white.

It took a little while for the authorities to find a suitable name to give the train-boys' House so as to raise it to a proper sense of equality with the others. However, they did get it named at last. It was called Adder's. Incent's was called Incent's because there had been a man called Incent who had founded the school. But none of us had ever heard of anybody called Adder who had founded Adder's House. It meant just snakes.

This English genius for harmony stayed with us all the way, and it was nearly at its best when it had to harmonize the view of life expressed by such ancient and uninhibited Levantines as Euripides with the way we ought to feel now.

It was taken for granted that any boys left alone and un-occupied for more than a few minutes were going to get up to vicious mischief, with the result that efforts were made to fill every interstice of every day with public and communal acti-vities – many of them conducted, like the drill of the Italian bersaglieri, at the double. Paradoxically, Sunday was the moral danger zone, because to work would have been to break the Fourth Commandment and to play games would have been shocking to local opinion. Even two Chapel services could not be stretched right across the gap, and there were a couple of hours on Sunday afternoons when we had to be allowed to go for walks, in couples or groups.

On Mondays, Wednesdays and Saturdays in the summer we played compulsory cricket from two in the afternoon until dusk, and on the other days from noon until lunch-time, and

33

again in the evenings from five o'clock – when school ended – until the light mercifully failed. The playing-fields were at the top of a steep hill about half a mile long, and to get from one end to the other of it on time one usually had to do it at a brisk jogtrot. During all the years I was there I made a total of only seven runs.

In winter and spring there was nothing between us and the perils of leisure except football, running and the school Cadet Corps. With most of us the Corps was unpopular, but I liked it. I had been brought up in expectation of a war, and there was a war going on during a good deal of the time I was at school. The thing seemed to make sense. It was a game with a visible point to it. It seemed realistic. You would be out one day on a field exercise, firing blank ammunition under command of a prefect who was also your platoon commander, and a few weeks or months later you would hear how he had been killed in genuine battle in France. I, too, became a cadet officer in the end, and used to enjoy explaining, in elaborately military terms, to elderly and diffident officers of the Brigade of Guards who came to inspect us, what we imagined we were up to.

All the other games seemed to me terribly like hard and, on the whole, uncongenial toil. On the other hand, the teaching was so stimulating that what was described as 'work' often seemed an entrancing game.

Regimentation of the kind we were subjected to is supposed, I believe, to destroy individuality, and conduce to the development of a conformist attitude. I have no notion whether this is a general truth or not. I can only say that, as a direct result of all this supervision and ordering about, one of the most valuable lessons my school taught me was how to break other people's rules. And at sixteen I read and profoundly appreciated Bernard Shaw's invaluable advice to 'get what you like, or you'll grow to like what you get'.

Relief from our routine was provided by the accident of our headmaster being a chess addict. When the craving for chess came on him, he had to play; in the fire of this passion rules, regulations and routine were reduced to ashes. As I was supposed to be the best chess player in the school, I was often invited to play with him, and at such times I would sit securely, and for hours on end, at one side of a table by the fire in his study, listening contentedly to the imperious, but temporarily innocuous, jangle of bells summoning people to get on with something or other, and the shouts of prefects driving others along cold corridors without.

Charles Henry Greene, this headmaster, gave the impression of conducting the affairs of the school and viewing life in general with the same smouldering, sometimes explosive intensity which he brought to the chessboard. He was a man of powerful and vivid reactions. Certain events, sometimes major, sometimes quite trivial, seemed to strike his mind with the heat and force of a branding-iron, and for a long time would remain in the forefront of consciousness, to be referred to, commented, brooded upon aloud in a singularly sonorous voice, and with occasionally florid eloquence.

His history lessons to the Sixth Form were not so much history lessons as comments on a state of affairs in which history had taken a distinct turn for the worse. For the most part he treated history simply as a series of signposts to the probabilities and possibilities of the present. Most of them pointed to ruin. For Charles Greene was, in the widest as well as the party-political sense of the word, a Liberal, and in the crack-up of Liberalism he saw the mark of doom.

When he looked at the Treaty of Versailles, his slightly bulbous grey eyes rolled, shone and started from his head, and his yellow moustache bristled. It reminded him of every disaster in the history of treaty-making since the errors committed by Pericles. As he spoke of it he sank back in his chair, pulling the mortar-board farther and farther down on his forehead as though to shield his eyes from the sight of so much folly and horror. 'When I gaze,' he said, 'upon the activities of Mr Lloyd George, when I consider the political consequence of Mr Clemenceau, my mind, abdicating its intellectual function, shrinks, half-paralysed, from the very attempt to contemplate the abyss which opens, inevitable but unregarded, before us.'

Reading the news from Moscow and from the various fronts of the war of intervention, he would sink into an almost luxurious awareness of impending doom. The spirit of Bolshevism, he said, was permeating everywhere, and the most ordinary events and *contretemps* of everyday life confirmed his view.

Bored at the fact that they were mobilized months after the ending of the war, the soldiers camped outside the town became drunker and drunker, and once rioted, breaking into the school itself and threatening to throw the headmaster into the canal. It was Bolshevism.

Prefects neglected their duties; a French master turned pacifist and started teaching his pupils that the whole war had been a monstrous mixture of crime and blunder in which people had been slaughtered for nothing; and a conspiracy was uncovered among the older boys to wear dark-blue serge suits to chapel on Sundays instead of the short black coats which were required by regulation.

All these were manifest indications of the bolshevistic way things were tending.

And then death-watch beetles were found at work in the timbers of the high roof of the Elizabethan Hall. It was horrifying, but in its awful way satisfactory – a climactic symbol of decay and violent collapse. 'Once again I have reports of slackness and indiscipline, everywhere I detect a falling off in keenness. The pernicious and destructive doctrines of Marx and Lenin are tapping away at the foundations and at the roof beams of civilization like the death-watch beetle which even as I speak is carrying out up there, invisible to us but none the less menacing for that, its work of voracious disintegration.' Since he said all these things with a vivid sincerity, and these extravagances were the product of genuine and agonized beliefs, the effect was not at all grotesque, but as vividly impressive as a revivalist meeting.

He worried sometimes about my political future. He wanted me to have a political career so that I could take a hand at halting the general decline, and possibly reversing the trend. I held strong Conservative views, and he, though a Liberal, thought that on the whole that was probably a good thing – I should enter the Conservative Party and so stimulate its moral sense and moderate its crassness. At lunch in the schoolhouse, when no one could leave the table until the headmaster had stood up and said the Latin grace, our arguments on the origins of the Boer War, or the policy of Palmerston, used sometimes to be prolonged for as much as a quarter of an hour after the last crumbs of the suet and treacle pudding had been eaten. The discussion was conducted amid a rising shuffle of impatient feet and the rebellious tinkling of spoons on empty plates. Sometimes he would use his initiative of the Grace to cut short an argument which displeased him or to which perhaps he did not see an immediate rebuttal.

'Well, well, Cockburn,' he would say, getting slowly to his feet, 'I don't see how civilization's going to be saved Benedictus Benedicat.'

Disruptive tendencies were at work even in the circle of his own family. As was the custom of many old-fashioned people at the period, the Greenes used at breakfast innocently to describe to one another anything interesting, bizarre or colourful they had had in the way of dreams during the previous night. Mr and Mrs Greene were unaware that their third son, Graham, had at about this time discovered Freud. He would leave the bacon cooling on his plate as he listened with the fascination of a secret detective. When necessary he would lure them on to provide more and more details which to them were amusing or meaningless but to him of thrilling and usually scandalous significance.

'It's amazing,' he said to me once, 'what those dreams disclose. It's startling – simply startling,' and at the thought of it gave a low whistle.

Since my father viewed the British Public School system with increasing uncertainty and distrust, I probably should have remained in the semi-detached position of a day boy to the end if the War had not ended when it did. During it my father had returned to government service in some job so hush-hush that neither then nor subsequently did I find out what, exactly, he was up to. When it was over he retired again, intending at last to pursue that new life which he had envisaged on his first retirement in 1908. But it soon turned out that he had miscalculated the rise in the cost of living – or, rather, its permanent character – and was now in a state of acute financial embarrassment.

A friend told him there was a good job going as chief of some inter-allied financial mission to look after the finances of

Hungary. Perhaps he would like that? My father asked whether the circumstances of his knowing almost nothing about Hungary and absolutely nothing about finance would be a disadvantage. His friend said that was not the point. The point was that they had had a man doing this job who knew all about Hungary and a lot about finance, but he had been seen picking his teeth with a tram-ticket in the lounge of the Hungaria Hotel and was regarded as socially impossible. My father said that if such were the situation he would be prepared to take over the job.

Fortunately it turned out that the work did not, after all, consist in running the finances of Hungary, merely of helping to sort out the financial claims upon Hungary of British, French, Italian and other Allied nationals. He bought a Hungarian grammar and a small book on money, arranged for me to become a boarder at the school, and got into the Orient Express.

3

HUNGARIAN GOULASH

BUDAPEST in 1920 was a battlefield where everyone has come to a bad end, where all the heroes are dead and all the great causes are betrayed. 'Freedom from fear' was one of 'the Four Freedoms' very noticeably lacking there. It was a city where everyone was frightened – frightened of being arrested, frightened of being murdered, frightened of just being ruined.

In my father's view we were very soon going to settle down in a nice house on the hills just west of Buda. This being so, it would be foolish to spend time and trouble looking for anything in the way of economical accommodation in the city. It would all be so temporary. For such a short time it was foolish to run the risk of being poisoned by inferior food or wearied by bad service, and therefore the prudent thing to do was to move into the best hotel in the town and take a fairly large number of rooms there so as not to be cramped. Also, in case anyone objected to this course as rash, it must be recalled that it would not look very well for British prestige to do anything else. We lived in that enormous suite at the Gellért approximately eighteen months, at the end of which it turned out that so far from any money being saved for the third and ultimate retirement, we were actually spending a good deal more than we had made. Facing facts, we moved upstairs to another suite on the top floor. This was cheaper, but the rooms were a good deal smaller. Observing that there was no point in being cramped, my father took a couple of extra ones and the top-floor suite in the end turned out rather more expensive than the one we had originally lived in. We were there for another eighteen months.

Sometimes we drove or walked about the hills west of Buda looking for a nice little house. There were a lot of them, but objections to all. The specific objections raised in each case were really unimportant, all of them had one defect in common – none of them stood on the hills west of Peking.

It seemed to my father, surveying Central Europe in the early 1920s, that human nature had deteriorated considerably. And he thought that this deterioration was unnecessary, self-inflicted, self-willed. He startled people sometimes by saying in moments of indiscretion that in his opinion everyone was taking the Great War and its consequences a great deal too seriously. Since he rarely bothered to explain exactly what he meant by this, he gave offence. In the eyes of quite a number of younger men he was a walking embodiment of that type of cynical old man who was supposedly 'responsible' for the war and for the consequent misfortune of the younger generation.

What he really felt was that, after all, he had, so to speak, lived with this war for years before it happened; for years before it happened he had said that it was coming, that it would be terrible, that in his view we should survive.

Since he had never supposed that the war would do anything but incalculable harm to the fabric of civilization, he simply could not understand the frustration and bitterness of the young men who said, 'You told us this was a war for civilization, and now look.' To him the results appeared to be just what anyone in his senses would have expected, and he therefore was suspicious of people who seemed to be taking the war and its results as an excuse for every kind of intellectual, moral and political extravagance.

Why, he asked, should people take this war which, when all was said and done, was simply a larger, more extensive, more destructive war than the ones we had had before, as an excuse for demanding, as they so constantly did, 'a radical reappraisal of moral values', a 'reassessment of our entire attitude of life'?

Because he had never taken seriously any of the high-toned propaganda slogans of the war period, he never came near understanding the rage of those who had believed in them and now felt themselves betrayed. During the war itself he had never for a moment imagined that the battles were being waged in the interests of democracy or civilization, or even of freedom; he found quite adequate inspiration in the conviction that we were fighting to prevent the German Empire from doing us down.

One year, on the way from school to Budapest, I sat, at Oxford, for a scholarship examination. At that time the colleges were grouped for scholarship examination purposes, so that a candidate could compete for a scholarship at five or six colleges at the same time. You could, so far as I remember, state in advance that you would accept a scholarship at only one chosen college of the group, or you could indicate that you were prepared to enter any college of that group which would pay you to do so. Friends of the family, many of them military men who had never been near Oxford, said emphatically that there were only three or four colleges which it was really possible to go up to. They named them. Other friends of the family who had been at Balliol said there was only one possible college.

I had to disregard them. I cared very little what college I went to provided that I went to it almost immediately and thus got away from school. I was sitting on the terrace of the Hotel Gellért drinking iced beer when a telegram was brought to me. It said, 'Are you member Church of England?' After a momentary mystification I realized that I must have won a scholarship to Keble College and that membership of the college must be confined to Church of England members, or at least that only Church of England members were eligible to hold scholarships there.

I was downcast. It seemed to me extraordinarily improbable

that I was any such thing. Bitterly annoyed that one's movements should be hampered by what seemed to me an irrelevant obstacle, I took the telegram to my father and said despondently that it seemed that my first raid on the scholarship front had failed. He immediately asked me whether at any time I had secretly but formally been converted into any other faith? Had I, for example, been received into the Roman Catholic or Mohammedan Church? Since most of my ideas at that time appeared to him strange and even perverse, he would not have been surprised to hear that I had secretly become a Buddhist. When I told him 'No', he said that in that case everything was in order. It seemed that once one has been baptized a member of the Church of England, one automatically retains membership for the rest of one's life unless one is formally received into some other faith. Profoundly relieved, I telegraphed to Keble saying, 'Yes.'

4

OXFORD ACCENT

AN aunt of mine once sent me a dead scorpion as a birthday present – she was travelling in the West Indies at the time. It fell out of a little box on to the breakfast table and the letter that fell out with it explained that she had chosen it because it was characteristic of the fauna of those parts and thus, in her opinion, more interesting and instructive than the kind of souvenirs ordinarily sold to tourists. She never sent me anything else and I thought that in the years that followed we had entirely lost touch.

However, an incident which occurred after I had been a couple of years at Oxford showed that this was not the case. Evidently she had been following my movements and career with keen family interest. By this time she had a little house in Hampshire, and once a year on the lawn she gave a small garden party or fête, in aid of sick, aged or homeless cats. The objective, as I understand it, was to organize lodging for the homeless, to provide medical attention for the sick, and to popularize the use of lethal chambers in extreme cases. My aunt had a couple of these lethal chambers in her own possession, and at the garden party these were displayed as a centre of interest and attraction on the table beside the tea-urn. Quite a number of people stayed away from the garden parties because they were horrified and disgusted by the name and purpose of these devices. Newcomers, suddenly confronted with them over the tea-cups, sometimes trembled and turned sick. My aunt said that the people who stayed away were obviously no good to man or beast anyway, and that for the others it was an educative experience.

My aunt, who looked rather like the well-known bust of Julius Caesar except that she had a lot of white hair and wore on top of it a hat in the fashion of 1911, used to march about among the guests in a military manner, carrying a mauve parasol which she did not open but used to emphasize points she was making in the interests of cats, waving it to draw inattentive people's notice to the lethal chambers, or prodding the lawn with it as she spoke of statistics and atrocities. She felt that hardly anyone was properly alive to what was going on, and sometimes in her indignation at apparent lethargy and indifference she would prod their feet with the parasol.

On the occasion I speak of a clergyman living in the neighbourhood brought to the garden party a young friend of his, a nondescript, rather solemn undergraduate who was down from Oxford for the long vacation. This young man took it into his head to chat knowingly and at length about the character and what he called the 'tone' of post-war Oxford. He said that of course the vast majority of undergraduates were sober, hardworking and well conducted, but one could hardly overlook and must certainly deplore the behaviour of certain flamboyant and thoroughly undesirable elements, who, because of their vulgar capacity for self-advertisement, were often treated as though they were typical of the Oxford of our day, and were getting the place a bad name in some quarters as a consequence. He knew of course, he said, that there were people who, no doubt deceived by meretricious display, thought that such persons as that awful man Evelyn Waugh, who etc. etc. etc., and an equally frightful fellow called Harold Acton, who used to shout his own poems through a megaphone and etc. etc. etc., and

Robert Byron and Christopher Hollis and Basil Murray and a lot of others were 'brilliant' figures really carrying on – as they falsely pretended – the basic tradition of some older Oxford. One heard, said the nondescript young man, really hair-raising, almost unbelievable, stories of the goings-on at the club – called so appropriately the Hypocrites Club – which these elements seemed to have made their headquarters.

The group around the tea-urn tutted and listened with keen interest. The young man was happy to say that at length the authorities had taken action and suppressed the Hypocrites Club. Disgraceful scenes, he believed, had accompanied this suppression. The Club had given a funeral dinner at an hotel in Thane, and leading members had driven back to Oxford riotously in a glass hearse.

Delighted with the attention of his audience the young man was replying to eager questions, and repeating most of what he had already said, when the group was suddenly joined by my aunt, who had been only half listening, while she demonstrated the working of the lethal chamber. The undergraduate was now astounded to receive a violent prod from the point of the parasol which my aunt, coming on him from behind, jabbed painfully into his heel above the top of his shoe. Turning he found himself confronted by a pair of wobbling pince-nez through which she glared at him as furiously as though she had detected him advocating cat torture. She always had a formidable, explosive kind of stutter, and now, in her rage, she stuttered more formidably than ever.

'I don't,' she said, 'know who you are, and I don't want to know. I do know that you are a nasty little tittle-tattler and a disgrace to your university.'

The young man stared in stupefaction, the circle of other guests expanded, drawing away from the storm centre.

'I happen to know,' said my aunt – though from what source she had this information she never revealed, even to myself – 'that a number of the people you mention are not only people of distinguished talent and ability, but are also friends of my nephew, Mr Claud Cockburn, a person whom you probably have not been privileged to meet.'

'Heard of him,' mumbled the young man miserably.

'About all you're likely to do,' sneered my aunt, giving him a slight bump on the side of the calf with the parasol. 'Furthermore,' she said, 'I should advise you to be extremely careful in what you say about the Hypocrites Club of which I imagine you know absolutely nothing, for the very good reason that if you were to attempt to become a member, you would, I should say, quite certainly be b-b-blackballed.'

The young man made a feeble attempt to recover the initiative by saying something to the effect that he hoped he would never sink so low as to seek membership of the Hypocrites Club. My aunt shouted him down.

'All I need to tell you,' she shouted, 'about the Hypocrites Club is that my nephew is a member of its Committee.' She paused in an attitude of expectation and the young man goggled at her. My aunt hammered the lawn with the point of the parasol in a frenzy of impatience. 'Well,' she said, 'in the light of what I have just told you, surely you do not propose to remain on this lawn?'

Utterly confused, he looked vaguely around at the other guests, seeking apparently some kind of explanation or support.

'Are you daring,' said my aunt, 'to try to remain here? Get out!' And with that she lifted the parasol and hit him quite hard with it on the side of the head.

He started to run and ran right out on to the road – with the expression, as my informant at the party told me afterwards, of one who has just realized the truth of the saying that there is nothing quite so terrifying as a mad sheep.

Naturally when I heard, some time later, of this incident I was very grateful to my aunt and took an early opportunity to go down to Hampshire and see her. The episode with the young undergraduate she took as a matter of course, but being thanked for it she found a little embarrassing.

'He was,' she said, 'obviously an ignoramus. He obviously had no understanding of the quality of Oxford. Oxford has the quality of –' Here her conversation began to meander somewhat, and she spoke vaguely of places which, in their physical aspect, had struck her by their quality. She floated verbally from some night scene in Jamaica to another night scene in Venice, and concluded at the corner of a street in Amsterdam. 'But I

44

don't,' she said, 'of course mean simply a physical quality. I mean a total quality like' – she jabbed her finger towards a bowl which was, I believe, part of the exquisite loot of the Temple of Heaven at Peking – 'that.'

Characteristically, since she knew Latin but no Greek, my aunt expressed particular interest in my Greek studies and begged me to expatiate upon them. In the same manner she, who in the way of philosophy had been brought up on Locke and Hume and nothing else, was almost humbly anxious to know what had gone on in the philosophical line since then. I told her truthfully that my own philosophy tutor was a man who appeared to take the view that philosophy was something like alcohol – amusing and possibly stimulating if taken in moderation, but no use as a sustaining food. Of any philosophical idea less than two hundred years old he would say, 'I think you'll find that it's pretty well been exploded.' Once, straight back from Budapest with a volume of philosophy which had just appeared there, and which he could not possibly have read, I hurried to him saying that I thought this was something really worthy of all our attention. He kept the book for a few hours and on returning it to me remarked, 'I rather gather that the man is likely pretty soon to be exploded.'

'That,' said my aunt, truthfully, 'is very Oxford.'

In my aunt's tiny drawing-room, which smelt of tea and warm hay, I was overcome by the nostalgia which at that time I felt more and more strongly for Central Europe, and in consequence spoke wildly and harshly. In the crudest fashion I sought to depict the contrast between what I considered to be 'the realities' of Hungary and Austria and the 'artificiality' of Oxford. I did it badly, partly because I did not in the fullest sense of the term know what I was talking about.

There was some truth in it all the same. Despite everything, despite even the casualty lists of the war years, it would have been just possible at Oxford to imagine that the First World War had not taken place – or at least that it had been merely a big, ugly, necessary episode, in the sense envisaged by my father. Above all it was a fact that for most of us the Bolshevik Revolution remained a nearly irrelevant event. People who regarded it with horror, and those who looked upon it with at least a tepid enthusiasm, were unconsciously at one in viewing it with a more or less comfortable detachment, rather in the mood of people going to see a novel play or a technically revolutionary film. I took the same attitude myself. I told my aunt violently that Oxford was a place where everyone was complacently waiting the moment when any new idea would be 'exploded', whereas in Budapest it was only the old and the traditional which people expected at any moment to blow up. I thought I was speaking rather eloquently on the political and social situation, but my aunt said suddenly, 'It's all a question, you know, of the light.'

'The light?'

'Yes,' she said. 'It's a matter of the way in which the nerves of any given person's eyes react to different qualities of light. All the rest – politics, people and so on – are relatively unimportant. It is one's reaction to a particular quality of light which makes one happy or unhappy in a place.'

I had told her that the valley of the Danube was the first area in which I had ever felt immediately and completely at home, not after months or even days of living there, but immediately – within an hour. And this was true at the time, although since then I have twice experienced this same sense of being immediately at home in an entirely strange place – once in New York and once in Oklahoma City.

My aunt said there was nothing unusual in my feeling about the Danube valley, it was simply that the quality of the light in that particular area happened to be the one which I found simultaneously most stimulating and soothing to the nerves. In the same way, the light quality of the Thames valley was evidently unsuited to me.

I believe now that there really is something in this theory, although at the time it appeared to me bizarre. My aunt seemed to be treating as mere secondary trivialities the factors in the situation which I regarded as most important. After discoursing for a short time on this theory of light, she remarked casually, 'And of course having enough money is so important too. I don't suppose you have enough.'

I said that nobody had. She said, 'I should very much like to

46

give or at least lend you some. It is a pity that the cats take all the spare money I have.'

I said that naturally I entirely understood, and I did, although it did seem rather a pity that there was not enough for all of us. For by this time my debts were relatively enormous – enormous, that is, in relation to any prospect there seemed to be of ever meeting them. They seemed to rise uncontrollably like flood water, without any reference to my efforts to increase my income. For a while I edited the Oxford University weekly paper the *Isis*, I wrote a weekly column during term time for one of the Oxford City papers, and occasionally I sold articles or a short story elsewhere. None of it seemed to make any difference, and the situation was the more harassing because, having for more than two years done almost no work of any kind which could be considered useful for the purposes of my final examinations, I now found myself compelled to get up at 6.30 to start reading, to read intensively most of the day and to dose myself with caffeine tablets so as to keep awake and working until two or three in the morning. I had never been able to attend lectures because they, like public speeches, drove me to a frenzy of boredom and impatience. I never could understand why the lecturers could not spend the time writing down what they had to say and distributing it in convenient pamphlet form. Gibbon took the same view. But, although not having attended lectures was supposed to be disastrous, and was naturally regarded with great disfavour by one's tutor, I did not myself find it much of a handicap, particularly as most of the lectures which I had missed a year or so before had by now dropped into print somewhere. All the same, the amount of reading to be done was prodigious and the repeated irruption of duns distracting.

Also at about this time my father had finally retired for the last time. The Financial Commission had completed its work, and in any case it became more and more apparent that the whole conception of the job in Budapest being an economy, a means of actually saving money, was an utter illusion. In these circumstances it was natural that my family should begin to hint, although in the simplest and most tactful possible way, that perhaps I really ought to be starting to think what I was going to do for a living when I came down from Oxford.

A few days before the end of my last term, I went – hesitantly – to say good-bye to my tutor. Hesitantly, because he was a man who shunned humans even when they were absolutely calm. Excited or emotional ones affected him like asphyxia. I tried to remain absolutely calm.

Naturally he was always glad to see the last of anyone, but he dreaded the potentially emotional business of an actual 'good-bye'. Wearing a russet-coloured suit, he lay as though camouflaged on a russet-coloured sofa. I saw him groping for some seemly valediction. He looked despairingly at the ceiling and then along the bookshelves all round the room, all full of works by philosophers who either had been, or were just about to be, exploded. 'Hitherto,' he said, 'your life has been neatly criss-crossed by school terms and school holidays, university terms and vacations. Now you are going down from Oxford and you have – well one may say that you have a straight run to the grave.'

Driven by extreme distaste for committing myself at this stage to any particular career, a thought which gave me a kind of claustrophobia as though one were entering a tunnel, I sought almost frantically for possible means of evading such a commitment, and at length discovered the existence of a Travelling Fellowship offered by Queen's College to anyone who had secured first- or second-class honours in the final examinations. Apparently there was a rich man called Laming who had come to the conclusion that British representatives abroad, diplomatic and otherwise, were below par, and he had endowed this Fellowship so that people intending to enter the Foreign Service, or to function more or less permanently abroad in some other capacity, should be enabled, after coming down from Oxford, to reside for two years in any country or countries of their choice on an annual income of £250. And although in most countries of modern Europe this sum would hardly keep a person in cigarettes, at that time there were a number of places where a student without financial obligations to anyone but himself could live in comfort and freedom on that amount.

In preparation for the Fellowship examination I went, for the study of French, to the cheapest section of France I could hear of – a gaunt village in the Cévennes. By a bizarre concatenation of events I even became, briefly, a French Government official – Receveur d'Enregistrements, the only Englishman I believe, ever to hold that position. With a strong Meridional accent, I left for Vienna. But passing through Venice I had rashly sold most of my clothes to raise cash. In the summer suit, adequate for the Cévennes, I trembled in Viennese snowstorms and had still no money for fuel. I moved for a couple of weeks to Luxembourg which was cheap, comparatively warm and bilingual. Back in London, I was lent a flat in Bloomsbury but it, too, was cold. When I tired of reading in bed, I took a penny ticket on the underground and went with my books to sit on a little bench on the platform of the Warren Street tube station.

I forget how many people competed for the Travelling Fellowship that year – I think a couple of hundred, or perhaps more. They looked to me horribly intelligent and some of them I gathered had spent a good part of the past month at expensive coaching establishments in Tours or Hanover. More alarming, however, was the fact that so many of them seemed so well dressed, so well groomed. The reason this was alarming was connected with the purposes of the Fellowship as defined by its Founder. It was quite understood that the sort of person he wanted to benefit by his Foundation ought to be not only an efficient scholar, not only have, if possible, the 'right' sort of accent, but also be the type to make a good impression at, for example, a diplomatic luncheon party. In order to examine the qualifications of candidates from this point of view, each in turn had a brief but vitally important personal interview with the Provost and dons of Queen's College.

An attempt was made to give this interview something of the character of an informal social occasion. One was expected to sit at ease in a comfortable chair and was offered sherry.

When I sit at ease I like to cross the calf of one leg over the knee of the other, but unfortunately in the course of my wanderings my shoe leather had worn through utterly, and where the soles of my shoes should have been only my socks were visible. Indeed, having had to walk some distance from my rooms in the college to the place where the interview took place, I could not be sure that my exhausted socks had not given way too, leaving the bare flesh showing. In any case, either socks or flesh would create an abominable impression, so that throughout the conversation I had to sit rigidly in an entirely unnatural position trying to remember, while chatting in an easy manner, to keep my feet flat on the carpet. Also I am in the habit of gesticulating a good deal when I talk; but since the cuffs of my shirt were almost spectacularly frayed and had to be kept out of sight, this habit too had to be abandoned for the duration of the interview, and I sat hunched like some semi-petrified gargoyle, my hands gripping my wrists so as neither to display the frayed cuffs nor even to suggest to the minds of the examiners that the cuffs could not be shown.

Candidates had been required to fill up a form showing where they had been during the period between the end of the last summer term at Oxford and the date of the examination. Simply to keep the record straight I had put down that I had spent a couple of weeks in Luxembourg. After some more or less light-hearted conversation and casual questioning, the Provost suddenly remarked that he observed I had spent some time in the Grand Duchy of Luxembourg. I said I had been there for a bare fortnight.

'And what,' he asked 'did you gather of conditions there?'

I got off a rather sapient piece about the operations of the International Steel Cartel, which had its headquarters there, together with some observations upon the possible effects of a recent Luxembourg decision to hitch the Luxembourg currency to the belga rather than to the franc. Meaty stuff, I secretly opined, after only a fortnight in the country. The Provost tapped the table impatiently, and his expression was that of a man who does not relish having his time wasted by chit-chat about trivialities.

'Yes, yes, yes,' he said, 'very interesting, no doubt, but what I would really like to know is what you gathered about the varying systems of land tenure in the north and south parts of the Grand Duchy?'

All this was harassing enough, but still more disconcerting was the fact that my Oxford creditors had chosen this moment to make an attack in force. Whether this was an unhappy accident, or whether they had somehow learned that I was sitting for this Fellowship examination and considered it a suitable moment to turn on the heat, I have no idea. For whatever reason, they became suddenly implacable and menacing. (In fairness I should say that there were some noble exceptions.) Several of them threatened legal action, and it was grimly evident that although a man with bare feet and frayed cuffs might possibly still clutch at the Fellowship, one who had just been served with several writs could not.

I interviewed the fiercest of the creditors and begged them to hold their hand until after the results of the examination had been announced. They refused. Maddened by their short-sighted folly, which threatened not only my career but the prospect of their ever getting paid at all, I decided that only a bold policy could save the situation. The result of the examination was scheduled to be announced a couple of weeks or so after the written part, which lasted several days, was concluded. I gave them all post-dated cheques for sums adequate to satisfy them temporarily, dated for the day the results were due to be announced. Personally I had no doubt that I should win one of the Fellowships, and of course in that case the bank would be quite happy to advance the money. But I could see that the creditors probably would not be entirely satisfied with this security, and I did not mention to them the fact that the cheques would be payable only as and when I was successful in the Fellowship examination.

Although as the written examination proceeded I became more and more confident, I was undoubtedly aware of a sense of tension and excitement which probably was not shared by candidates in more comfortable circumstances. The examination ended and a week or so passed, and then something happened which made me feel that fate was deliberately hitting out at me.

My father had told me long ago that if one wished to be lucky one should always believe in luck – that people who cursed their luck suffered for it. I did my best to carry out this policy now, but it was difficult because what had happened was that one of the examining dons had caught a cold, or contracted some other minor ailment, and the announcement was made in a notice to the candidates that declaration of the results would be postponed by a week beyond the scheduled date.

It was only after a half-hour of despair that a possible solution occurred to me. I wrote a letter to one of the principal examining dons – a charming man who had already showed me great kindness – saying that I had just heard that a relative of mine, who had helped me greatly throughout my academic life and took a passionate interest in my career, was dangerously ill. In fact it was doubtful whether this relative could survive for more than a few days. Surely, it would be tragic if, on account of this accidental change of schedule, my relative should pass away without knowing whether I had succeeded or not – particularly tragic if I had succeeded and this news came too late to cheer the last hours.

The good-hearted don wrote to me immediately – I had of course taken the precaution of going to London before sending him my letter so that his reply, if any, would be in writing – saying that he could not in any way officially anticipate the result, but that, speaking as an individual, and purely on the basis of his own personal estimate, he would say that I would not be deceiving my relative if I indicated that I had obtained the Fellowship. With this letter I dashed back to Oxford, interviewed the bank manager, who fortunately was aware of the position of the don in question on the examining board, and asked him whether on the strength of it he would meet the cheques which were now due to be presented within a matter of three or four days. He agreed.

Naturally I had to sign documents which in fact meant that in the course of the next couple of years something like half the whole of the Fellowship payments would have to be handed over to the bank.

The prospect did not much bother me. It seemed to me that these were rivers that could be crossed when we came to them.

Also those early years in Budapest during the inflation time, when the value of money in your pocket could be halved between breakfast and lunch, and halved again before dinner, had made it hard for me to focus at all steadily on any financial problems, or to treat such problems otherwise than as entirely fluid and impalpable.

And when it was indeed officially confirmed that I had gained the Fellowship, all this optimism seemed fully justified.

Months before, I had told my tutor that I vaguely planned to start my 'run to the grave' by connecting myself with *The Times* newspaper. My tutor thought it a fate considerably worse than death. Did I realize I would probably have to speak to comparative strangers, and write about events as though they were important? But being very properly uninterested in my future he made no other attempt to dissuade me.

At the outset, before I had heard of the existence of the Travelling Fellowship, a job with *The Times* had been a mainly negative ambition, formed to avoid the Foreign Office which had been so long and so highly recommended that I could think of it only in the words of the songster as 'a wonderful opportunity for somebody – somebody else'.

To the advocates of a Foreign Office career the notion of 'going in for journalism' was pitiably degrading. 'And mark you,' as a friend of my father told me sternly, 'split what hairs you will, mince words as you may, in the last analysis *The Times* is nothing more or less than *sheer journalism*.'

It seemed certain that journalists had the choice of being absolutely servile (as reported by another very old friend of the family who had the latest information from Germany under Bismarck), or corrupt (the conviction of another who had personally known Caillaux), or intolerably vulgar (the view of a fourth who had always said Lord Northcliffe should have been hanged).

I discovered very soon that these hesitations and *hauteurs* were paralleled at Printing House Square. Applications for employment poured in, sometimes producing a kind of *folie de grandeur*.

Brilliant and sound I grant you. But brilliant and sound enough for The Times? *This one mentions his triple First, his double Blue and his uncle the Bishop. Estimable, but the dear good chap does only speak four languages. Is one justified in giving him a trial when some nearly perfect aspirant may already be on his way from Winchester to Balliol? Is, indeed, anyone, anywhere, truly worthy of* The Times?

This was the awfully solemn thought which at that time sometimes oppressed Printing House Square, and if held long enough, could have led to a total depopulation of *The Times* offices everywhere. For even correspondents of the London *Times* sometimes perish or lose all sense of values and seek other employment. I had myself already met one who had resigned – for a reason which, though uncommon, seemed sufficient. He had formed the opinion that his appointment as a part-time correspondent had been a Parthian act of malicious sabotage by a retiring foreign editor with a grudge against the paper. 'My having the job,' he said with candour, 'was intended simply to discredit *The Times* in the eyes of the world.' His resignation was a touching gesture of loyalty to the paper's best interests.

In these circumstances I had been warned, back in the previous summer, that to fill up one of the regular application forms for a job with *The Times* would be worse than useless. To begin with it would reveal the fact that one was actually in need of a job, a state of affairs which could be regarded as ignoble. However, before entering the Fellowship examination, it had been necessary to state in an application form what exactly one proposed to do after the two years' period of the Fellowship – in what capacity was one going to take advantage of the benefits received from the Fellowship and fulfil the wishes of the Founder.

Most people said that they were aiming for the Diplomatic Service; a few whose fathers or uncles controlled businesses operating abroad indicated they would be ambassadors of commerce. I had been warned, indirectly, that merely to say that one had an idea of being a journalist, a foreign correspondent of some kind, would be absolutely fatal. There were bound to be several among the examiners who would instinctively feel that the fewer British journalists there were running about the world the better. Also they would take the view that any man of birth and education who deliberately announced his intention of becoming a journalist probably was beyond salvation, even by the exceptional facilities afforded by the Travelling Fellowship. 'But *The Times*,' I said. 'Surely if I say I am going to be a correspondent of *The Times*? Think,' I said, 'of Russell! Think of Dr Morrison! Think of Wickham Steed!'

My adviser agreed that *The Times* would possibly pass muster, 'Although,' he said dubiously, 'it *is* journalism, you know.'

Thus, unknown to *The Times*, I was forced to commit myself to becoming at some future date one of its correspondents.

The residential conditions attaching to the Fellowship were elastic – you could spend the whole two years in one town or country, or you could keep moving about. The only absolute condition was that you must be in a town with a university. I wanted to get back to Central Europe, and just after the results were announced I met a man who said he was a good friend of *The Times* correspondent in Berlin and would give me a letter of introduction to him. Up to the last moment I had been wavering somewhat between Berlin and Vienna, but this decided me. I bought, on that wonderfully long Oxford credit, some suits which more than adequately expressed the gaiety and even flamboyance of my mood. To compensate for the distress experienced at the interview, I had four pairs of shoes very expensively made for me and had a lot of silk shirts made for me too. When all these garments had finally been constructed, I took off for Berlin.

When I got there it emerged that the man to whom I had the letter of introduction had been transferred – had not been in Berlin for nearly two years. But by that time I was there, and the smell of Central Europe had a new tang to it.

5

UNTER DEN LINDEN

TOADS used to come out of swampy ground in the Tiergarten and sit looking out of the backs of their heads at the packed buses, the racing taxis and the limousines and the huge German touring cars, roaring eastwards and westwards on the Charlottenburger Chaussee, which strikes unswervingly across the green heart of Berlin.

The toads, motionless except for the slow blink of their eyelids, were the only immobile creatures in sight, and gave an impression of cynical watchfulness. Their performance was corny but impressive; by hindsight even more impressive than it seemed at the time.

The sight of these squat, old-looking observers, gazing backward at everything that happened, sharpened the sense of impermanence, of foolish vulnerability in the face of inimical and indifferent forces of destruction, which could always be felt so strongly in Berlin. In Berlin you felt that the deluge was always just around the corner. There is a book or short story (well known but I have forgotten who wrote it), about a city which establishes itself in the sandy desert, defeats the desert, and just when things seem safest is – at first almost imperceptibly – attacked by the desert, defeated by it and finally engulfed. Similarly in Berlin you could without difficulty believe in a day when the toads and perhaps worms and snails would, after so long awaiting their opportunity, note that the human defences had collapsed, and take over.

I have known scores of people who have lived in Berlin most of their lives and always had this sensation about their city. It would be oppressive or stimulating according to one's mood or temperament. What caused it I do not know. It cannot have been, as some people have suggested, the relative newness of Berlin compared to, say, Vienna or Paris, for great areas of Paris and Vienna are no less modern than most of Berlin, and in any case neither Chicago nor Kansas City produces this sensation. Perhaps my aunt was right and it is a trick of the light playing on the nerves of the retina. I think it is a character of Jean Giraudoux's *Siegfried et le Limousin* who remarks that there is more mystery and terror in a single pine tree in the streets of Berlin at midday than in an entire French forest at midnight.

After discovering on the first day I was in Berlin that the man whose presence there had been the whole reason for my coming to this capital was no longer present, I got the name and telephone number of his successor as *The Times* correspondent and the next morning rang him up – at 8.30 a.m. so as to create a good first impression of alertness, not one of those slouching Oxford decadents.

This might have been disastrous, because the correspondent had only just reached bed after one of those tiring journalistic evenings in the Berlin of those days, which used to start about 6 in the afternoon and rarely ended until 6 or 7 in the morning.

However, Mr Norman Ebbutt was a man of warm-hearted goodness and this he displayed immediately, pretending that it was
time for him to get up and behaving in general as though I
really were an old friend and had come with a letter of introduction to him. He even pretended to believe that I might
actually be of use to him in *The Times* office in Unter den
Linden. With extraordinary tact he somehow managed to suggest that I might be doing him positively a favour by coming
and 'helping'. He must have known that he, of course, would
have to spend hours teaching me to do things he could have
done himself in a tenth of the time.

It was true that he was alone and grievously overworked,
because at that period a mild manpower crisis, starting in remote
parts of the world, but developing by a kind of chain reaction,
was afflicting the foreign organization of the paper. Two correspondents had acted vexatiously and had to be transferred to
other posts.

In those days it was nearly impossible to be sacked by *The
Times*. You just got a less important and less interesting job at
about the same pay. This civilized policy worked excellently
and removed the root cause of many journalistic crises. This
cause is fear of the sack. It is fear more potent and menacing
in journalism – at least in foreign correspondents' journalism –
than in most professions, because in so many cases the foreign
correspondent has through no particular will of his own been
suddenly whisked on to a standard of living obligatorily high on
account of the paper's prestige, and has often inadvertently
convinced some girl that this is the standard of living to which
she may confidently become accustomed, and then found himself involved in a fearful rat-race of competition, pursued – at
least in his nightmares – by other young men who want to live
on that standard too and will put him off it unless he quickly
and repeatedly does something that will impress the London
office. As the London office frequently does not know what is
really impressive about the events in the country to which its
correspondent is accredited, and is thinking only about what it
imagines will impress Birmingham or Newcastle tomorrow
morning, the correspondent is tempted into vicious journalistic
ways.

One of the two unfortunates of *The Times* who had to be transferred had developed 'views' on something or other – and in *The Times* language 'viewy' was a dreadfully damaging epithet. Another had embarrassed the British Legation in a capital city in Latin America, where he was a part-time correspondent. He had turned up with a girl to whom everyone was quite prepared to believe him married. But he was painfully high-principled, and he publicly disabused them of this idea. For valid reasons he was not, and could not be, legally married to her. He wanted to make that perfectly clear. On the other hand he must insist that she be invited with him to all official functions as though she were indeed his wife. Otherwise he would feel obliged to boycott such functions and make scenes.

The Legation in the foreign capital wrote to the Foreign Office, and the Foreign Office wrote to *The Times* asking them to reason with their man. Could he not, *pro forma*, and to avoid affront to stuffy foreign diplomats, courtiers and ecclesiastics, pretend he was married to the girl? Or at least cease to deny it? Or else leave her at home?

The Times wrote to the part-time correspondent, so reasoning. Much later one of the foreign editorial staff who had been in charge of the delicate negotiations told me the outcome. 'He simply wrote that she was his wife in the eyes of God. Surely,' he said, sighing, 'he couldn't have expected *The Times* to see eye to eye with God, could he?'

Norman Ebbutt was intelligent and courageous, and he needed to be, for he was a man of goodwill. He even believed that one day he would go to the British Embassy in the Wilhelmstrasse and find out what the policy of the British Foreign Office was, and perhaps that would turn out to be intelligent and courageous too.

Politically he was, I suppose, what could be described as a Left Wing Liberal, which meant, at any rate in his case, that he hoped for the best in everyone. He used to take me to drink beer with Herr Stresemann, who was Foreign Minister, and in whom at that time Liberals believed. Personally I found that Stresemann was entertaining provided that you did not believe in him. He was one of those Germans who had at a fairly early date, discovered that the way to get away with being a good

German was to pretend to be a good European. He had a wonderful act in which he pretended to be not only fat, which he was, but good-hearted and a little muzzy with beer into the bargain. In reality he was as quick and sharp as a buzz-saw, and if being a sharp, fast-moving buzz-saw was not enough, he would hit you from behind with a hammer. We used to sit in the late spring in the garden of the Foreign Office drinking beer and playing a kind of diplomatic chess game which would have been risible if it had not been serious.

I think it was Stresemann, sitting under a fruit tree, talking about European unity, who first sowed in my mind the doubt as to whether my warm-hearted enthusiasm on behalf of the victims of the World War, my romantic belief in the Nationalist movements of Central Europe (Nationalist even when they were disguised as the resurgence of Central European democracy), and my conviction that the Treaty of Versailles had been a disastrous diplomatic crime, really covered all the facts.

I do not mean to imply that I cleverly saw what the old boy was really up to. I simply had an impression; an impression, that is to say, that if this was the kind of old boy I had been feeling sorry for and enthusiastic about all this time, I probably had been making a mistake. I think, although here I may be doing Ebbutt an injustice, that Ebbutt, just because he longed so much for European unity, for people to be reasonable and blissful, believed a shade more in Stresemann than he should have. If that were so, he certainly erred in the company of several million other people of goodwill. Stresemann's eulogies of peace, in the then militarily vulnerable condition of Germany, came back to my mind years later when I was talking to the British Military Attaché at the Washington Embassy who had just returned from a visit to Cuba where he had inspected the Cuban army. He said, 'I have taken a very careful look at the Cuban army, and my tour of inspection has convinced me that, for the moment at any rate, the adherence of Cuba to the Kellogg Pact outlawing war as an instrument of national policy is absolutely sincere.'

These encounters with Stresemann produced, in fact, a jolting dissatisfaction with a whole body of 'liberal' political ideas which, in the sixth form at Berkhamstead, at Oxford, and in Budapest had seemed to me axiomatic. This sort of liberalism was still, basically, nationalist. The nation States were still the determining factors. The questions it posed concerned their proper relationships and policies. It could be said to be a strictly vertical view of the situation, hardly taking into account the horizontal divisions – that is to say, the social, class divisions existing within those States and prolonging themselves beyond their boundaries.

And soon I came, in Berlin, into contact with an attitude to life and politics which immeasurably increased the dissatisfaction engendered by Stresemann and the friends of Stresemann. The contact was not gradual but sudden. It occurred at a party – the first of many – given (in this case at the Kaiserhof Hotel) by a Viennese baroness comfortably equipped with advanced political views and a banker for a husband. She also had wide philanthropic interests, and her parties were given to promote these causes.

6

THE NEW VOICE

I HAVE forgotten which of these causes this party in the Kaiserhof Hotel was in aid of, but in any case the people I met – the Viennese bankers, the diplomats suspected of undue brilliance by their Foreign Offices, the industrialists suspected of improper relations with socialist politicians, and the socialist politicians suspected of improper relations with industrialists, the painters, film directors, publishers, writers, dancers and musicians – would have been present whatever the object of the Baroness's party, because they were all members of a kind of perambulating salon which functioned sometimes in Berlin, sometimes in a huge chalet, formerly an hotel, on the shores of a lake in the Austrian Alps where she went for the summer.

Naturally I cannot remember now just what was said or done at the party in the Kaiserhof Hotel and what was really said and done much later in Vienna that spring or in the summer by the lake. But I do remember that after a few hours of conversation at the Kaiserhof I had that sensation you get when you look with an inexperienced eye into a microscope, seeing nothing on the slide below but a confusing blur, and then someone adjusts the instrument to an effective focus.

Ever since I returned to Central Europe, the slide which earlier had been so clear had become increasingly blurred, and now it seemed that I had only been waiting for someone to make the adjustment. The Viennese essayist Polgar wrote that the Café Central in Vienna 'is not a coffee house like other coffee houses, but rather a way of looking at life'. And that could truthfully have been said about the people who at various times and places frequented the Baroness's travelling salon. Their opinions, of course, were diverse and usually passionately conflicting. Yet they had more in common with one another than any of them had with, let us say, the Oxford Liberals, or Norman Ebbutt and the corps of foreign correspondents in Berlin.

Although people who disliked the Baroness referred to her circle of friends as a 'set', a 'circus' or even a 'menagerie', all these epithets, kindly or hostile, were wide of the mark, because in reality the salon was a fluid affair and – which was more important – was very far from unique. You could have found replicas of the same people all over Central Europe, and even in Paris. And it was precisely this fact of their being not unique, nothing special, which gave them their significance.

Probably I had met them – them or people like them, I mean – often before, but inside some cocoon of sentimental Hungarian nationalism or Oxford Liberalism, had been impervious to the contact. This, in other words, was a noise which had been going on all the time but to which I had never been attuned. And this was true although neither at the Kaiserhof nor afterwards was there as much political conversation in the ordinary sense of the word as one could hear at any gathering of Anglo-American journalists in Berlin. But in politics, in the wider sense, these people were drenched, steeped, dyed.

They were for the most part Austrians, Hungarians, Poles or Russians, and some were Bulgarians or Rumanians. Most of them, too, were between the ages of twenty-five and forty-five.

That is to say, all of them had been inescapably involved in the social upheavals and conflicts of the years after 1916 and had thus been involved at an age when they were still young enough to adjust themselves to those conditions. Also, being people of energy and intelligence, they were able to accept the facts of life as they knew it and, where others saw chaos or defeat, to see a pattern; a pattern, moreover, which people of energy and intelligence could take hold of, to perfect or change.

What all of them, despite their curious differences of view, shared and could not help sharing, however much it might irk them, was – to put it with a bluntness which would have offended many of them by its lack of subtlety – a recognition of Communism as the central dominating fact of our generation and indeed of our century. A platitude of course. To people nowadays such a recognition may seem a somewhat limited achievement, but I am speaking of the year 1927.

I dare say that before then I had often nodded 'yes' to this platitude myself, but it had not in any way affected my attitude to life – to, for example, the Treaty of Versailles, or the policies of either Herr Stresemann or the London *Times*. But these people had been impregnated by their experiences. They could no more ignore the facts of revolution and class conflict than they could the facts of astronomy. And the views of those who deplored these facts were as deeply coloured, and as pervasively informed by them, as were the beliefs and attitudes of those who continued to look upon them with enthusiasm.

When some direct references to current politics did occur, it was immediately borne in upon me that whereas I had been aware almost exclusively of the, so to speak, vertical divisions between peoples and policies, to my new acquaintances the horizontal divisions were more absorbing and in the end more important.

People who believe that the earth is round do not keep asserting that it is so, yet their attitude to everything is profoundly affected by that assumption. And the assumptions of these people were apparent even when the talk was farthest from politics. There were often moments in our early acquaintance when, after I had made some statement which seemed to me simple and even self-evident, I would be asked to repeat it as if it had been some astounding paradox, and I presently found that the reason for this was that people could not believe that I had really said what I had said, because to them so many of my assertions sounded like assertions that the earth is flat.

'Perhaps,' I said to Madame T., the Viennese draughtswoman and painter 'they think I am merely idiotic.'

'No, no,' she said, 'they expect anything of an Englishman.'

I began to be irked by my own ignorance of the events and particularly of the writings which had so profoundly affected these people's lives. Reluctantly, because I felt sure it would be tedious and utterly wrong-headed and mistaken, I bought in Vienna on my way to the chalet in the Austrian Alps a volume – nicely printed now and freely displayed in the bookshop – containing all those pamphlets and manifestos of Lenin and Zinoviev which eleven years before had had to be smuggled dangerously across Europe, and were now collected under the general title *Against the Stream*.

'The Stream' was of course the current of majority socialist opinion in most of the belligerent countries in favour of the prosecution of the war. In the intervals of canoeing or boating on the icy, brilliantly blue waters of the Grundlsee, climbing to high places to see the shining or shadowy panorama of the Alps, chattering lazily under the fruit trees with fellow guests, or walking over the grassy hills by moonlight to drink freshly distilled plum brandy in the kitchens of upland farms, I set myself to examine in a rather desultory fashion those hysterical polemics, packed tight as shell-cases with high explosive. I found them shocking, repugnant, alien. They pricked and tickled like a hair shirt. They seemed to generate an intolerable heat. They existed in a world of notions with which I had no contact, and, exasperatingly, they dared totally and contemptuously to disregard most of the assumptions to which I had been brought up and educated, or else to treat them brusquely as dangerous delusions peddled by charlatans bent on deceiving the people.

I was bewildered, too, and shaken by a mysterious and violent quality of style, as though some intellectual masseur had got one's brain down on a slab and were twisting and pummelling it. 'As to that,' said the poet Ezra Pound, 'in the style of Lenin the space between word and action is less than in that of any other writer I know.'

Accompanied by the composer George Antheil, Pound had turned up in Vienna, and having read a fiction story of mine which he liked in the New York *Dial*, sent me– the first and only written communication I had from him – a note written apparently on lavatory paper in blue chalk saying, 'Hail. Dial story great. Can we meet? What chance you coming this city jolly month June?'

By his own writings I had been more profoundly affected – 'changed' one could almost say – than by anything else I had read during the previous few years, and I hurried to Vienna to meet him. I could afford only a couple of days there, but we spent several hours of them together. At that time Pound had the idea of establishing himself in Vienna and thereby, as he said with his characteristic mixture of arrogance and irony, turning the place into the cultural centre of Europe.

I returned to Berlin to find that *The Times* which, a few weeks before, had repeated its insistence that I was not to be allowed to write anything – they were afraid, Ebbutt gathered, that I was trying to chisel myself into a position where I would suddenly demand a job or a quantity of back pay – had suddenly reversed itself. Despite their injunctions I had written an article about the Hugenberg Trust, the vast newspaper, advertising and cinema combine controlled by the extreme Nationalist, Alfred Hugenberg (later a patron of Hitler), and particularly about the use of the German films of extreme Nationalist propaganda. *The Times* published it, and now had written to suggest that the best thing for me to do was to leave Berlin immediately, return to England and start going through the hoops which, by what *The Times* like to consider an unbreakable law, had to be negotiated before one could hope to become a foreign correspondent.

Theoretically, candidates deemed worthy of trial were sent first to serve an apprenticeship on some newspaper in Liverpool, Newcastle or Nottingham. If they survived that, they did a spell in the home room of *The Times* occupied with domestic reporting, and were then – assuming that worthiness was maintained – transferred to the Foreign Room. After that all was uncertainty.

Some people, who had entered the Foreign Room in the belief that they would be out of it again in a year or so and on the way to *The Times* bureau in Vienna or Buenos Aires, remained there for years and years, and in the end often lost any inclination to be anywhere else.

The prospect of abandoning for Nottingham or Newcastle the Berlin which I was just beginning to discover presented itself as both distasteful and ridiculous. In particular, the violent voice I had heard for the first time by the Grundlsee kept exasperatingly ringing in my head. It was a low insistent drumming, and annoyed and disconcerted me, but it had the effect of an assurance that there existed unknown territories and horizons, which, if I were now to involve myself in regular 'gainful employment', would never be visited or viewed by me. Just then my father died, and England seemed more distastefully, more drearily alien to me than ever.

I wrote rejecting *The Times*'s offer. I thought that probably this meant I should never be a Correspondent of *The Times* at all, but Ebbutt, on information received from London, said that on the contrary the people at Printing House Square had been shocked but rather pleased – for years nobody had actually refused a job on *The Times*; they thought this showed originality. It was agreed that I might occasionally write short items of news for the paper under the strict supervision of the regular Correspondent, which was, in fact, what I had been doing for weeks past.

Then, towards the end of a blazing afternoon, tornados of rain rushed suddenly down on Berlin, and there were reports of a cloudburst on the borders of southern Saxony. The reports in the evening papers had that curious smell about them which suggests immediately that somebody somewhere is trying to conceal something. Ebbutt was away on a couple of weeks' leave and his place was being taken by a Mr Barker. He and I both had this curious impression that something rum, and possibly sensational, had taken place in the mountains down there beyond Dresden.

I went there at my own expense – an alarming speculation. I got there at dawn, observed with satisfaction that there were no other journalists about, and found that, in one of the strangest small-scale catastrophes of the decade, the cloudburst had poured unheard-of quantities of water into mild little mountain streams, which tore down trees formerly far above their beds, jammed the broken trees against the bridges until they formed high timber dams, and, pushed higher than ever by the dams, rose and rushed along the streets of sleeping villages on the valley sides, peeling off the fronts of houses like wet cardboard, and killing more than a hundred people in a few minutes. Half a mile of that little valley smelled of death. There were corpses in the mud and in one house the table in an upper back room had been laid for breakfast. In several other houses canaries were singing or moping in their cages.

No other newspaper in London had had a man on the spot, and their stories were scrappy compared to the column *The Times* had next day. After that *The Times* wrote again, suggesting that perhaps I might be permitted to cut out the period of apprenticeship in the English provinces and go straight into the Foreign Room in London. And, when I refused this offer too, they presently wrote a third time proposing that I should cut out the Foreign Room, too, and simply stay where I was as Assistant Correspondent in Berlin. This blithe disregard of the hoops which I had always understood it was necessary to pass through quite worried me. It seemed to me almost as though the Church of England had told someone that he could be ordained without bothering to get confirmed first. Finally I asked a visiting High Priest from Printing House Square about it. His reply was an exhilarating example of what perhaps may be called *The Times* spirit.

'That,' he said – referring to the traditional hoops – 'is our rule. Unwritten, but I hope you take it no less seriously for that.'

'Not at all,' I said hastily. 'I just wondered. . . .'

'And a very sound rule it is,' said the High Priest, sternly. 'Very sound indeed. Remember that.'

I never, as a matter of fact, heard of the rule again.

However, with every day that passed my claustrophobic distaste for immuring myself in a regular job increased, and again I refused. My resolve was strengthened, no doubt, by the fact that I had recently sold a few articles and short stories to German and American newspapers.

Even Ebbutt, always optimistic on my behalf, thought that this third refusal might have put an end to my beautiful friendship with *The Times*. However, nobody seemed to mind my continuing to occupy the centre room at the Berlin office, working there as I chose without pay except for special articles, and without any definite obligations.

A little later in the summer, rioting broke out in Vienna on a scale which caused many quite serious observers to believe that the second wave of East European revolution was beginning; the Chief Correspondent – either Ebbutt or Barker, I forget which at the moment – had to rush off at a moment's notice, and nobody seemed to find it odd that I should be left in sole charge of the office in Unter den Linden.

Quite a number of my friends and acquaintances from the party at the Kaiserhof had dashed to Vienna to see the revolution if that was what it was really going to be, or to observe at close quarters this extraordinary explosion in the midst of a relatively calm European summer. When they returned, their circle had been enlarged to include, temporarily, a lively section of the United States in the shape of Mr Sinclair Lewis.

German friends begged me to take them to a party to meet this great Voice of America. Their earnest intention was to spend an hour or so happily cross-questioning Mr Lewis on such matters as Americanism, Babbitry, and the Philosophy of Main Street. Lewis, however, was tired and turned up rather drunk. From beneath his jacket hung the ends of two towels clearly marked with the name of his hotel. He had them knotted round his waist to keep his trousers up. Some German at once thought this significant of something or other – the American revolt against convention, perhaps. But when he mentioned it to Lewis, the novelist looked at the knotted towels with an air of surprise as if he had only just noticed them and merely said he supposed his belt must have got broken or lost.

The German guests wished to start a discussion of trends in modern world literature. Lewis, for his part, was anxious to give a rendering of a song he had just heard or just composed, a parody of 'I didn't raise my Boy to be a Soldier'.

'I didn't raise my boy,' he chanted loudly, 'to be a bourgeois, I raised him to be the Third International's pride and joy. But the son of a bitch has gone and gotten rich, my boy! my boy! my boy!'

I undertook a forlorn and stumbling attempt at explaining the joke – starting with the origins and political character of the original song. Probably it was hopeless from the start, and in any case I had hardly begun before we were all attacked by a dog which Lewis had with him, but did not have under control. This dog was the property of the future Mrs Lewis – better known as Dorothy Thompson – who was at that time either still married to, or just divorced from, her first, Hungarian, husband. The dog, an ungainly Airedale which looked like the Mock Turtle in *Alice in Wonderland*, had apparently esteemed the first husband and did not thus esteem Lewis. Or else he regarded Lewis as the breaker of a home to which the dog had become comfortably accustomed. However that may have been, this Airedale followed Lewis about like an angry detective, literally dogging his footsteps, in what at first sight looked like devotion but was really hatred. Every now and then, exasperated possibly by the man's vigour and well-being, the dog would lose command of its temper, and bite either Lewis or one of his friends. The situation got so bad that in the end the dog was given to the biologist, Dr Wiesner, but it broke loose in the Schering chemical laboratories, where some vital experiment was in progress, and dashed about smashing things, setting back the course of science by several months before it was recaptured. Wiesner then gave it to Madame T., who, when she went to Vienna for the Christmas holidays, left it in my care.

It was a horrible Christmas for the dog, because just at that time I had run entirely out of money, and was living chiefly on expectations of a cheque from the United States which never came. To begin with, the dog fed fairly well because the butcher round the corner always had a pile of scraps – offal, bacon rind and the like – which he gave me free when I bought meat for myself. But on Christmas Eve when everyone I knew had left town for the holiday I found, distressingly, that I had only just enough money to buy a couple of drinks and some tobacco.

Feeling very low mentally and morally, I went round to that butcher and told him that I myself was, of course, invited to eat my Christmas dinner with friends, and therefore did not wish to buy anything for myself, but was anxious that the dog should have a particularly good Christmas dinner. The kindly butcher made up an unusually large and nasty-looking parcel of scraps, which I took home and cooked. The dog watched me with satisfaction. But the next day at noon, when he saw me carefully dividing the mess into equal portions and putting only half of it on his plate, his disappointment and indignation knew no bounds. At first he watched me with an expression of sheer incredulity. Then, when he saw me actually digging my fork into that portion of his dinner which I had reserved for myself, he got up on his hind legs with his forepaws on the table, and threw back his head, howling in astonishment and despair at the pass things had come to.

In the spring I was waiting anxiously for the last instalment of my Fellowship payment to arrive, and at length wrote urgently and rather irritably to Queen's College to inquire about it. The reply was disconcerting. It pointed out that the instalments had all along been paid in advance, and I had had the last one a month ago. There was nothing more to come at all. In these circumstances I wrote to *The Times* saying that although I had previously rejected their offers, I had now finished the period of my Fellowship, and would like to work as a *Times* correspondent provided, however, that I could do so in New York.

The reason for this was that by now I had widely extended the studies I had begun beside the Grundlsee, had read *Das Kapital* and the *18th Brumaire* and *Civil War in France* and other works of Marx; read Lenin's *State and Revolution*, and *Imperialism*, and *Materialism* and *Empirical Criticism*, and been particularly impressed by Bukharin's *Historical Materialism*. Yet at the same time highly informed books continued to appear in quantity, proving that what was happening in the United States in that year of boom, 1929, was making the sheerest nonsense of Marx, Lenin, Bukharin and everyone else of their way of thinking. The United States hung over my thoughts like an enormous question mark. I felt that I should never be able to make up my mind about anything unless I went there and saw for myself.

Mr Geoffrey Dawson, then Editor of *The Times*, did not have the reputation of a particularly warm-hearted or sympathetic man, but his response to my letter was a gesture which indicated a quick sensibility to my situation, and a realization that maximum speed might be of very considerable importance to me, as indeed it was. He did not write, he simply telegraphed. 'Have no fear for tomorrow. Return at once. Job waiting.'

7

PRINTING HOUSE SQUARE

NOTHING sets a person up more than having something turn out just the way it's supposed to be, like falling into a Swiss snowdrift and seeing a big dog come up with a little cask of brandy round its neck.

The first time I travelled on the Orient Express I was accosted by a woman who was later arrested and turned out to be a quite well-known international spy. When I talked with Al Capone there was a sub-machine gun poking through the transom of the door behind him. Ernest Hemingway spoke out of the corner of his mouth. In an Irish castle a sow ran right across the baronial hall. The first Minister of Government I met told me a most horrible lie almost immediately.

These things were delightful, and so was the first view of *The Times* office in London. In the Foreign Editorial Room a sub-editor was translating a passage of Plato's *Phaedo* into Chinese, for a bet. Another sub-editor had declared it could not be done without losing a certain nuance of the original. He was dictating the Greek passage aloud from memory.

That very first evening I saw the chief sub-editor hand a man a slip of Reuter's Agency 'tape' with two lines on it saying that the Duke of Gloucester on his world tour had arrived at Kuala Lumpur and held a reception. It would run to about half an inch of space, and on some newspapers I dare say might have been got ready for the printer in a matter of minutes. I was glad to see nothing of that kind happen here.

The sub-editor, a red-bearded man with blazing blue eyes, who looked like a cross between John the Baptist and Captain Kettle, had at the age of twenty or thereabouts written the definite grammar of an obscure Polynesian language and gone on to be – a curious position for an Englishman – a professor of Chinese metaphysics in the University of Tokyo. He took the slip of paper into the library and then to the Athenaeum, where he sometimes used to go for a cold snack during *The Times* dinner hour.

His work on it was completed only just in time for the ten o'clock edition. It had been a tricky job. 'There are,' he explained, 'eleven correct ways of spelling Kuala Lumpur, and it is difficult to decide which should receive the, as it were, *imprimatur* of *The Times*.'

All foreign correspondents believe sub-editors to be malevolent troglodytes, happiest when casually massacring the most significant lines of an informed, well-balanced despatch. Sub-editors believe foreign correspondents to be flibbertigibbets, uselessly squandering enormous expense accounts, lazy and verbose, and saved from making fools of themselves in print only by the vigilance of the staff in the Foreign Room.

Sharing, myself, the correspondents' views of people working at the London headquarters, I was naturally nervous. However, *The Times* people proved genial and made kindly efforts to put me at my ease. One told me that, although the London climate was lethal, one could prolong life by getting up very early three times a week and travelling to Southend for a brisk twenty minutes' walk on the sea-front.

'And of course,' he said, rather mysteriously, 'being in the train so much gives one more time for thinking and reading.'

(He was, I need hardly say, a Fellow of All Souls.)

I said I hoped to be leaving shortly for New York. He was sincerely sorry for me – such an awfully long way from healthy Southend.

This conversation took place at tea, a rather serious function performed round a large oval table in a room on the ground floor of Printing House Square. We reached the office at about four in the afternoon and went straight down to tea and a half-hour's conversation before going up to the Foreign Room, a big, well-lighted place overlooking Queen Victoria Street, furnished principally by a long narrow table, extending from the inner wall almost to the windows. Junior members of the Foreign staff like myself sat at the part of the table nearest to the Chief Foreign Sub-editor. The seniors at the far end barricaded themselves with volumes of the *Encyclopaedia Britannica* or other large books and thus were able, as one of them remarked to me, to 'get on with our work without being disturbed'.

I did not at first see why this type of protection should be necessary, but later learned that several of them were engaged in writing historical works of their own, or authoritative treatises for various learned reviews, on the subject in which they were particularly expert. Mr Scott Moncrieff, the translator of Proust, worked there at one period, and I was told that the business of *The Times* was often held up for as much as a half-hour at a time while everyone present joined expertly in a discussion of the precise English word or phrase which would best convey the meaning and flavour of a passage in *La Recherche du Temps Perdu*.

For further entertainment in the long evenings, someone had invented a game – a competition with a small prize for the winner – to see who could write the dullest headline. It had to be a genuine headline, that is to say one which was actually printed in the next morning's newspaper. I won it only once with a headline which announced : 'Small Earthquake in Chile. Not many dead.'

From five until about eight o'clock work continued without a break, and then people went to eat at their clubs or the *Times* dining-room or the canteen. Unless you were on late duty you finished work at about eleven o'clock.

At first I was fascinated by the work, but after a few weeks I became bored and rather nervous because I was still afraid that someone would notice that I had not gone through any of the proper hoops, and pack me off to Newcastle instead of New York. Sometimes it seemed to me that I caught one or other of the High Priests looking at me somewhat askance, as though, perhaps, I were not, after all, worthy of *The Times*. My alarm was increased by the discovery that everyone already knew the story of something which had happened in Berlin one day when

Ebbutt was on holiday and his place had been taken by a man called Pugge or something similar. Extensive unrest and street fighting were going on in Berlin at the time – I think it arose out of a demonstration on May Day. It was a confused situation and many people opposed to the unemployed demonstrators also thought the Prussian police were acting trigger-happy. Pugge, the newcomer, had no doubt that it was a straight fight of law and order versus the licentious mob. Any hesitant angels caught loitering were apt to get a sharp pushing around when Pugge rushed on to the scene.

Irked somewhat by his attitude I wrote, one afternoon when he was out watching the shooting, the despatch which I conceived Pugge would have written – From Our Own Correspondent in Jerusalem – had he been covering events there approximately two thousand years ago. It was a level-headed estimate studded with well-tried *Times* phrases. 'Small disposition here,' cabled this correspondent, 'attach undue importance protests raised certain quarters result recent arrest and trial leading revolutionary agitator followed by what is known locally as "the Calvary incident".' The despatch was obviously based on an off-the-record interview with Pontius Pilate. It took the view that, so far from acting harshly, the Government had behaved with what in some quarters was criticized as 'undue clemency'. It pointed out that firm Government action had definitely eliminated this small band of extremists, whose doctrines might otherwise have represented a serious threat for the future.

I put it on Pugge's desk. Glancing rapidly through it after a tiring day and seeing familiar *Times* clichés – small disposition to attach undue importance, Government acting with firmness, band of extremists – all bowing and scraping at him from every paragraph, Pugge did not bother to read it properly, and passed it, together with his own despatch, to the telephonist.

By a piece of ill-luck it chanced that *The Times* had recently reorganized its European telephone system, with the result that the Berlin office was used as a relay centre for despatches from a number of smaller capitals which formerly had communicated direct with London.

The telephonist was already vexed by the extra work

involved. Now he came rushing back from the switchboard waving my despatch in a mauve fury.

'What's all this?' he shouted. 'Are we taking flaming Jerusalem now?'

Mr Pugge was abominably shocked. I had always hoped to hear someone use the phrase 'in the worst possible taste'. Pugge did. He did his best to bring home to me the appalling character of my action.

'Do you appreciate,' he said, 'that what you have done is to attempt to play a *joke* on *The Times*?'

This he obviously felt was the most blasphemous aspect of an altogether blasphemous bit of work. And in my present state of anxiety it seemed to me that there were several people around Printing House Square who would probably share this view. I began to wonder whether the job that had been waiting for me was really the New York job or something quite different and, from my point of view, unsuitable.

It was difficult to find out, because Mr Geoffrey Dawson had perfected a technique for not telling people anything much, and yet appearing all the time both approachable and communicative. His room had two doors. When you had been announced, and had entered, you found him standing in front of his desk, poised always on the same mark on the carpet, both hands slightly outstretched and his whole attitude that of one who has been unable to prevent himself bounding from his chair and rushing forward to meet you. Already touched and impressed, you were further overwhelmed by the warmth of his greeting and the voluble geniality of his conversation as he put his hand on your shoulder or took your arm.

There you were, pacing the floor of the sanctum of the Editor-in-Chief of *The Times*, and he concentrating on you while his secretary, you could imagine, told anxious cabinet ministers and bishops over the telephone that the editor was in conference. The effect was practically hypnotic, and in this state of partial hypnosis you were scarcely aware that with one arm across your shoulders the Editor was with the other hand opening the door at the far end of his office and pushing you gently into the corridor, bidding you a warm farewell after an interview which had lasted approximately eighty seconds.

74

Nothing had been promised, nothing decided; but for several hours you certainly felt that you had accomplished something or other.

As things stood I need not have bothered about my position because, without my knowing it, Sir Campbell Stuart, at that time one of the most energetic directors of *The Times*, and the man who had played a major role in preventing the paper being acquired by Lord Rothermere after the death of Lord Northcliffe, had been kindly watching over my interests, for he was a Canadian and a friend of my Uncle Frank. I had told my uncle that I wanted to go nowhere but New York – though I had concealed from him the full reason for so wishing. My Uncle Frank, who looked upon Europe as little more than a fascinating museum in which it was good for people on holiday to pass a certain amount of time each year, was enthusiastic about my decision, and he enlisted the help of Sir Campbell Stuart to ensure that I was not disappointed.

Sir Campbell Stuart lived with his mother in his suite at the top of the Hyde Park Hotel, and when I finally went to call on him there, he lay almost flat on his back in an armchair, and with his extremely long and angular legs extended to the fire, smiled at the ceiling in a whimsical manner as he explained to me the real reason for the delay in my appointment and the apparent inability of the Editor to make up his mind.

'They are afraid,' he said, 'of Louis Hinrichs.'

This character, of whom I had never previously heard, immediately assumed formidable proportions in my eyes. To be a man of whom *The Times* was statedly afraid was sufficiently imposing. Who and what was Louis Hinrichs? And why was *The Times* afraid of him?

Well, it appeared that Louis Hinrichs was the New York Correspondent of *The Times* and had formerly been the Wall Street Correspondent of *The Times* and the *Daily Mail* when the two papers were in the same ownership. *The Times*, said Sir Campbell Stuart, was afraid of him because he knew about finance, Wall Street, stocks and shares, things like that. Sir Campbell spoke of *The Times* with a mixture of respect and affectionate derision, as though of a distinguished but elderly uncle having venerable abilities and a good many more or less ludicrous quirks of character. Or, as I sometimes suspected, he felt himself rather in the position of the able butler when the entire family of aristocrats is marooned on a desert island and the butler, despite his comparatively lowly colonial origins, is the only one who knows how to deal with reality and pull them through.

Smiling at the ceiling, Sir Campbell Stuart explained to me that *The Times* had a certain awe of anybody who in fact understood finance. 'They think, in fact,' he began to giggle at the idea, 'that Hinrichs is a holy terror.'

The Times, in fact, liked its Correspondents to be familiar with history, archaeology, the classics and the higher reaches of diplomatic society in whichever capital they happened to be established, but it was bothered by people who knew too much about money and economics and even tended to regard these subjects as of greater importance than the personal relationship existing between a cabinet minister, member of political Party A, with a politician, member of political Party B. The idea that they had a Correspondent who really understood Wall Street and positively regarded Wall Street and its problems as essential in the affairs of the world, was to *The Times* awe-inspiring. Hinrichs, in fact, was to them a Man from Mars. And in consequence one had to act pretty gingerly in deciding whom to send him as his office mate and Assistant Correspondent. Therefore everyone had to mark time until Hinrichs, in the late spring, arrived in London and could be confronted with the candidate for this office – that is to say myself.

Since I was determined to go to New York in any case, and the question of whether I went there with a comfortable amount of money and prestige as *The Times* Correspondent or had to struggle off again under my own inadequate steam, depended upon this Louis Hinrichs, I was naturally in a nervous state of mind when I went to call upon him at the Waldorf Hotel at tea-time one afternoon. I can still recall more or less clearly the brutal figure I had expected to meet, and during the first ten minutes of conversation with Louis Hinrichs I was tormented by the fear that some appalling mistake had been made and that I was talking to the wrong man.

He was one of those people whose physical appearance more

or less expresses their entire personality. He was unusually tall, stooped a little, and could have been considered emaciated were it not that the fineness and delicacy of his bone structure conformed perfectly to this almost spectacular leanness. His head was small but the face exquisitely aquiline, his eyes rather more luminous than the rest of him had led to you expect, and these eyes and his sensitive mouth prepared you for the otherwise disconcerting variations in the gestures of his enormously long hands and fingers, which sometimes were dryly decisive, and at others fluttered in movements of philosophic bewilderment.

English people, or people at least with English upbringing, were apt to make him nervous. And this, considering his experiences, was not surprising. As his subordinates or colleagues in New York, he had viewed a whole string of English newspapermen and had of course met on more or less intimate terms large numbers of British financiers and industrialists. Most of them had asked him to tell them what he knew, from his vast experience, of the situation in the United States, and after listening to him for an hour, a day, a week or a month, had begun to lecture him on the situation in the United States and the character of the American people.

Because he had that diffidence and capacity for genuine self-criticism which Americans of his type have in a much higher degree than English people, they would leap to the conclusion that being an obviously civilized and cultured man he must share all British prejudice about the United States. He was capable of criticizing America savagely, but none of these people seem to have caught the peculiar intensity of his intonation when, very occasionally, he would use the phrase 'my *dear America*'.

Few of them seem to have understood – or so at least I gathered from him even in our first conversation – that he loved America in the way Europeans once used to love their countries, and the way a person might his family. At our first meeting he peered at me over a cup of China tea with a mixture of hope and despair. By an extraordinarily courteous piece of acrobatics he managed to reverse our true positions.

'I do hope,' he said, 'that after this meeting you will not reconsider your wish to come to work in New York.'

As we drove down Fleet Street he said, 'You know, I wish I did not have to go to *The Times*. I wish one could simply telephone them to say that everything is all right and that I hope to see you in New York soon. *The Times* frankly terrifies me.'

Recalling vividly that he terrified *The Times*, I could think of nothing to say. He added, just as the taxi swung into Queen Victoria Street, 'You know, sometimes I feel that I really ought to write a letter to *The Times* explaining to them that I am not at all the sort of man they imagine I am.'

In Printing House Square he interviewed Mr Dawson, who was as usual delighted to find that 'everything was all right' and therefore required no supervision or attention on his part. We then went together to see Mr Ralph Deakin, entitled Foreign and Imperial News Editor. Mr Deakin was believed to be the originator of the statement that nothing was news until it had appeared in the columns of *The Times*, and at that period he gave – from his shining shoes to the beautifully brushed bowler hat on the rack behind him – an impression of mental and physical discretion and complacency which could have been offensive had it not been, in its childish way, touching. Certainly nobody could have guessed from his manner that he was the sort of man who would saddle himself with an employee of of whom he so clearly disapproved.

Deakin had never made any secret of the fact that he was dubious as to whether I was the 'right type' for *The Times*. I think that he, who was a friend of Pugge, had been seriously influenced by the affair of the Special Correspondent in Jerusalem. He was obviously a little surprised that Hinrichs should accept me. He would have expected him to stand out for something a little more svelte, or else a little more businesslike in appearance. Resignedly he turned from the immediate topic of my impending journey to New York to discuss the fate of one of my predecessors, a former assistant to Hinrichs, who had been brutally murdered by the hangers-on of some Chinese war-lord under the walls of Peking. Hinrichs expressed his sorrow.

'Nevertheless,' said Deakin, 'he had his reward.'

Hinrichs and I, simultaneously startled by this observation on the death of that distinguished young man, exchanged rapid glances, each of us wondering what comment one could possibly make on such a statement. Also it occurred to each of us at the time that this could only imply the existence of some bitter feud between Deakin and the victim of the banditti, and each of us was horrified to realize that Deakin apparently was prepared to continue this feud beyond the grave. There was a moment of danger during which either of us might have made some extraordinarily ill-placed remark had not Deakin added with a note of extreme satisfaction in his voice, 'Yes, he had his reward. I mean a column-and-a-half obituary in *The Times*.'

'You see,' said Hinrichs as we left the building, 'what I mean about *The Times*.'

During this period I had seen very little of my Uncle Frank who, although in London, was constantly busy. But about half a minute before the boat train for Southampton was due to pull out of Waterloo Station I heard my name called, and saw my uncle's huge figure lumbering noisily along the platform, his hand waving some kind of document. His face expressed intense concern and anxiety. 'I am so glad,' he gasped, 'to have caught you. This is important. I want you to take good note of it.'

He thrust the document at me as the train actually left, and when I had time to examine it I found that it was a list of names – names of people, some of them known to my uncle personally, others taken simply from newspaper reports, who had either died or gone blind as a result of drinking impure alcohol in New York. To this list my uncle had added only two lines, which said, 'Do remember, my dear Claud : at *all* costs secure a *reliable* bootlegger.'

Already the Southampton boat train and the liner *Homeric* were ringing to the roar of the great bull market in New York. Only a few weeks before, the market had staggered momentarily in its advance. The Federal Reserve Board had attempted to get the boom under some kind of control. Now it had been defeated by the action of speculative bankers led by Charles Mitchell of the National City. Now this ship, heading past the Isle of Wight for Cherbourg, throbbed with the rhythm of Wall Street, and the people on it seemed all to be dancing to the same distant tune. There were brokers' offices aboard, and some people sat in them all the time the market was open, looking at the changing prices going up, up, up again as though they were pilgrims listening to hymns and incantations on the road to a promised land. When the broker's clerk made a special announcement, there was that kind of hush which otherwise you hear only at solemn services for the dead, or at the moment when on a race-course they announce the runners in the succeeding race.

The ship was alive with messenger boys taking telegrams from passengers to their brokers in New York, or bringing telegrams of advice and exhortation from the men on the spot.

There were Americans who had cut short their European holiday, and were dashing back because they could not bear the thought that they might, by not being on the spot, miss the chance of doubling the paper fortunes they had already made. They were British and Europeans, some of them rich already and determined to get richer, others with strained, gaping faces, half-incredulous, yet half-convinced that at last the impossible-seeming thing was really happening – they, too, were going to be rich and happy for ever after.

At Cherbourg the American tide engulfed us altogether. I was supposed to have a stateroom to myself, but just before we sailed from Cherbourg the purser informed me apologetically that owing to an emergency he had had to put an American gentleman in the other berth in this cabin. I found him, a man about thirty years of age, sitting on the other bunk between a bottle of Scotch and a bucket of ice. He was dressed as though he had that minute walked off some expensive bathing beach. He looked at me with gloomy intensity.

'You'd think,' he said, 'on a boat of this size they'd have more space. But it isn't so. Well, naturally, on account of the market. People getting back, people going over. Listen – want a drink? Did you see what Cities Service opened at this morning? Can you imagine that?'

It was late afternoon at Cherbourg, but only around midday in New York, and the morning's quotations from the market were already available. My companion tossed off his drink and mixed himself another, looking from time to time cautiously around the cabin as though he were uncertain of its material existence.

'So,' he said, 'we finally made it.'

'You only caught the boat,' I asked, 'at the last moment?'

He gave me a long appraising stare and then hitched himself forward on the bunk with his forearms on his knees, thrusting his head towards me and speaking slowly as though this were something that it was of the highest importance for me to understand.

'Look,' he said, 'there we were at Biarritz. There I was. My name's Louis Genser, and there were Tom Holt and the Wertheims. And then Laura, she died. I'd had a little drink, and I hadn't been down there on this what they call the *plage* more than half an hour, three-quarters maybe, when they came down and told me what had happened. She'd died, see?'

'What a terrible thing. Laura was . . . ?'

'I don't get you.'

'I mean she was a friend of yours, one of your party?'

'Now listen, I've known Laura five years – more. I'm talking about Laura Nehring. Well, of course when I first knew her she was Laura Price.'

'Terrible for you.'

'Well, of course first thing we did we rang up Gleneagles and we rang up the Danieli in Venice – places like that. And then there was a lot of difficulty about the mortician too. It seems in France if you die you have to go through a lot of regulations. And the casket. That was a problem too. How were we to know what sort of a casket Jack Nehring wanted her put in? Hell of a problem. And then when we had a nice casket all picked out it seemed the man had that one sold already and if we'd waited while he made another one like it we'd have missed the first boat home. That was what we wanted to get, the first boat home.'

'Naturally.'

'So we got this cheap old box and when we got to Paris we had it on the top of the cab, and we stopped off at the Ritz to get a little drink, and the first thing you know there's Jack Nehring right there in the bar having a little drink with Jack Benstead. Works in the Guaranty Trust over there in Paris. And Jack looks at us and first thing he says is, "Where's Laura?" God!'

His gaze wandered round the cabin again and he actually touched the bunk tentatively with the tips of his fingers, seemingly to assure himself that it was there and he was sitting on it.

'Well, naturally we went on up to the Majestic to see the porter there. After all, it was quite a situation. And Jack Nehring and Jack Benstead and Jack Wertheim they got in touch with the American Express and our Embassy and they all said that the boat was loaded down already, but one way and another they got it fixed, and here we are. Well, that's it, fella. Have another drink?'

The door of the cabin opened and a big man came in with a spray of orchids in one hand and a highball in the other and said,

'Say, Louis, have you seen the way Cities Service is acting this morning?'

'Certainly have,' said Mr Genser, earnestly.

A second big man with a spray of orchids and a highball was fighting his way into the cabin, and behind him there was a woman; and out in the corridor, pushing gently but purposefully, as though they believed the small stateroom was made of indiarubber and would presently expand, were another man and another woman. Through the crowd, which in that space seemed enormous, I could see that they too were calling out comments on the performance of Cities Service stock.

Mr Genser got to his feet, backed himself against the porthole to make a little more room, and said,

'Want you to meet . . .'

He waved his highball glass in introduction.

He had already, it emerged, obtained my name and profession from the purser.

'This,' he said, 'is Mr Cockburn, the distinguished British journalist and writer. Mr Cockburn, I want you to meet my friends, Mr Jack Wertheim, of Wertheim and Driscoll, Mr Jack Nehring, I told you about him, and this is Mrs Wertheim, and over there that's Jack Benstead of the Guaranty Trust Company and Mrs Benstead.'

For a while we stood or squatted on the bunks, drinking highballs and talking about the stock market. Mr Benstead started with the air of one who has remembered important and urgent business.

'Listen, Ethel,' he said, 'did you bring that spare orchid spray along for Louis?'

Mrs Wertheim produced an extra spray and it was handed to Mr Genser. Mr Wertheim looked at me with concern.

'I am afraid,' he said, 'we don't have an orchid spray for you, sir. We just have so many of them for each day of the voyage in the refrigerator. . . . But if you'd care to join us all the same?'

'Yes, indeed,' said Mrs Wertheim.

'We're going to see Laura,' explained Mr Genser helpfully. 'They finally got her fixed up all right.'

'And I just want to say,' said Mr Nehring over his shoulder to Mr Benstead, 'that we'd never have made it, Jack, if it hadn't been for you. It was on account of that thing you said at the Embassy. I want you to know I'm grateful, Jack.'

'Anything I can ever do, Jack,' said Mr Benstead. 'And don't forget it was you . . .'

As we moved in single file along the corridor he could be heard reminding Mr Nehring of some stock-market operation in which Mr Nehring had been of service to Mr Benstead.

'But I thought,' I said in a low voice to Mr Genser, who was walking immediately in front of me, 'I thought this Mrs Nehring – Laura – I thought she was dead?'

'Certainly she's dead,' said Mr Genser loudly over his shoulder. 'I told you that. That's why we're taking her these orchids.'

And indeed, in a distant part of the ship, there she was, in the 'cheap box' that had been obtained with such difficulty in Biarritz. The orchid sprays were laid reverently on the coffin and we spent a quarter of an hour standing round drinking a number of toasts to her memory. Mr Jack Wertheim happened to have a big flask about him, and was able to refill our glasses as required. Then the bereaved Mr Nehring made a little speech, and we went back to the main deck to get the latest news about the day's performance of Cities Service.

8

GRAND SLAM

In New York, you could talk about prohibition, or Hemingway, or air conditioning, or music, or horses, but in the end you had to talk about the stock market, and that was where the conversation became serious. Unless you understood this, and it took me quite a while to understand, you caused that shadow to fall. There was a 'mystique' about the market. You could argue about the merits of this stock or that, you could analyse earnings, you could consider rationally the effects which the weather in, say, Missouri was liable to have upon the stocks of companies producing agricultural machinery. But what you could not with impunity do was to suggest, not by words only but by so much as an intonation, that there was any doubt about the fact that the market as a whole was going on up and up, that every 'recession' there might be in the near future would be 'temporary', 'technical', 'an adjustment', after which the new era of American life would resume its swift, inevitable progress towards a hardly imaginable stratosphere of prosperity. To hint that you regarded such an assumption as in any way questionable was – whether you were talking to the Italian who kept the nearest speak-easy or to your hostess at dinner in the East Sixties – to put yourself in the unpleasant position of making some vulgarly ironic reference to the Holy Father in the house of devout Roman Catholics. There was an element of sacrilege about it, but it was worse than that. For in this 'mystique' of the market there was an element of sympathetic magic too. Deep in people's consciousness there was an instinct, like that of a primitive African, that to speak ill of the market was in itself unlucky, a proceeding capable of bringing upon not only the speaker but all associated with him the wrath of the Market God.

Most people are capable of carrying more or less incompatible ideas in their head at the same time, and the same man who had convinced himself, by a study of innumerable market reports and statements by economists, that the level of stocks was fully justified by the underlying economic situation, and that a rise was predictable in the light of factors which could be analysed and calculated, also often believed in his heart that the whole thing was a kind of marvellous subjective trick; a séance where the table moved, and the spirits spoke, by virtue of the combined will power and capacity to believe of all present – a beneficial atmosphere which could be dissipated or seriously affected for the worse by the presence of an unbeliever. Perhaps that was only another way of stating the simple fact that if enough people started to disbelieve in the future of common stocks, common stocks would cease to have a future, but that was not the way in which most people put it to themselves. If they had, the existence of just one unbeliever would not have alarmed and wounded them so gravely.

In cold blood, and by hindsight, these attitudes can sound childish, and furthermore can support that tediously erroneous Anglo-European view of the Americans as people who are unduly – in the vulgar sense of the word – 'materialistic'. If the attitude of the Americans to the stock-market boom in the summer of '29 proved anything, it proved the opposite – for it showed that they believed in miracles. Myself I find this an endearing quality. The idea that two and two can never make anything but four is in itself depressing and limiting, and turns out, in the higher mathematical regions, to be probably untrue. This belief in miracles is simply an expression of the notion that if you try hard enough you can make wonderful things happen. The chief trouble with the Americans of 1929 was that they had their money on the wrong miracle.

The situation was no doubt absurd, and after the ball was over there were plenty of people to point out just how 'crazy' the country had been at that period. But to see it as merely absurd is to miss the pathos of what was happening there and, in the welter of greedy gamblers, to lose sight of what was tragic and even noble in this grotesque scene. For it was a scene which could have been enacted on that scale only in America, and this was so because it was a brief re-enactment of what was essentially an old American dream. They had dreamed that if you could get away from the principalities and powers of old

Europe you could found a free and noble society. And when the eastern seaboard become an area oppressed by new principalities and powers, they dreamed that in the Middle West and the Far West the miracle could still happen. From the harsh necessities of millions of emigrants in the mid-nineteenth century was distilled a new and heady component of that dream-liquor, a faith that there was still room on earth for the kingdom of heaven. And the people to be pitied were perhaps not those who had that faith, however naïve, but those who had lost it. Even the most superficial student of our day is familiar with the fact that the American Civil War was an affair of inextricably confused motives, of gigantic political swindles, of meanness masquerading as patriotism, and avarice disguised as love of liberty. Yet it would be a pity to forget that there really was more to be said about John Brown than that his body was mouldering in the grave, and that the sentiments expressed later in the Battle Hymn of the Republic are not invalidated by the fact of political intrigues, however sordid. The eyes of the corrupt army contractors and later of the carpet-baggers had not 'seen the coming of the glory of the Lord', but the eyes of a lot of other people had seen something like that, and the fact that the glory of the Lord did not in the end turn up did not make the hope of it ridiculous. What it did do was to add something to the sometimes overpowering American sense of frustration.

The Big Bull Market, as Frederick Lewis Allen wrote later in *Only Yesterday*, was a compensation for innumerable disappointments and disillusionments of the past. And it was this which gave the atmosphere of the summer of 1929 its peculiar quality. There were moments when you said to yourself that this was just a casino. And then you had to admit that at the same time it reminded you of a revivalist meeting and even of the starting of some kind of crusade. It seemed like the pleasantest kind of crusade – one in which the whole world was going to get happy by getting richer and richer. It would start of course with people who were gambling in American stocks getting rich, and then the rest of the Americans would become prosperous too, and pretty soon the whole world. America felt kindly towards the world that summer – when it had a moment to think of it at all. In any case, there was no need to think of it much, because America was going to solve all the world's problems automatically.

The atmosphere of the great boom was savagely exciting, but there were times when a person with my kind of European background felt alarmingly lonely. He would have liked to believe, as these people believed, in the eternal upswing of the big bull market, or else to meet just one person with whom he might discuss some general doubts without being regarded as an imbecile or a person of deliberately evil intent – some kind of anarchist, perhaps.

I did not at all wish to be regarded as any such thing, and I kept my doubts pretty carefully under wraps, especially as they did not, after all, arise from any expert assessment by me of the immediate factors in the situation, but simply from the 'academic' theories of the Marxist and Leninist writers whom I had studied in the apartment on the Kurfuerstendamm and my studio in Paris.

From Louis Hinrichs I was particularly anxious to conceal my schizophrenic frame of mind, to hide from him the fact that as I read the market reports, the innumerable expert predictions of the financial writers, or listened to the talk of brokers and financial editors, I was only a little more than half-persuaded that those Marxist philosophers were wrong. I thought it would be a confession that would shock and perhaps alarm Hinrichs. I did not at that time know him very well. In any case, my comprehensive ignorance of the factual details of the present situation, as distinct from some general theory of economic movements, made it easy to avoid generalizations. I had too many questions to ask. Naturally Hinrich's knowledge of the stock market and of the 'over-all picture' of American business conditions was encyclopaedic, and in addition to that he had a fascinating sort of physical intimacy with the financial district of Manhattan. Most days we used to walk about there, going from office to office to see people who, he thought, might be useful to me later on. I had arrived with a preconceived notion of Wall Street, and that whole area, as a roaring, pulsating jungle, but under Hinrich's gentle guidance one had, surprisingly, rather the impression of going on a conducted tour of a village; a largish village and one full of oddities and unexpected situations or characters, but still a place where you could soon learn to find your way about, and one which you could hope, after not too long, actually to comprehend. This impression was curiously deepened by the physical qualities of the financial district itself. As one approached this hub of the world's largest city one subconsciously expected a crescendo of mechanized noise. But the fact was that here traffic congestion had reached its logical paradoxical conclusion.

There was a time, I suppose, when everyone tried to drive along Wall, Pine or Cedar Street in a motor car, but what had happened by now was that since there was not conceivably room for all the mechanical wheeled traffic which wanted to use those streets, mechanical traffic had virtually abandoned them, and the crowds padded about their business on foot.

The result was that when you turned out of Lower Broadway into one of these side streets you were conscious of a kind of hush, and the noise of tens of thousands of people moving about on their feet without engines reminded you of Venice.

This powerful, towering village, the activities of whose inhabitants could tilt whole nations, was familiar to Hinrichs in all its aspects. He knew who was who now and who had been who when, and as you toured it with him you thought that here as much history had been packed into a couple of decades as had occupied a century elsewhere. We had just passed, one day, the bomb-scarred offices of the House of Morgan, its windows now heavily protected in case anyone should want to throw a bomb again – that earlier bomb had been in itself the violent expression of an earlier American dream – when Hinrichs stopped in a disconcerting manner he had when he wanted to make an important point, and spreading his fingers in the fluttering motion which expressed uneasiness and a certain bewilderment, he said.

'All the same, Claud, I don't believe it.'

In New York at that moment there was only one 'it' of which you could say that. I was as astonished as a member of some underground movement in an occupied country who discovers that the local Captain of Police is of the same opinion as himself.

Strangely, for it was quite unnecessary, yet significantly – for it was an indication of the hypnotic effect of the climate we had been living in – we both of us, I noticed, as we walked along, lowered our voices. In the sixty-six-storeyed shadow of the Manhattan Bank Building Hinrichs began to explain to me what he felt about the bull market, and why he believed not only that it would not continue, but that it was a possibly monstrous delusion which could do serious harm to 'my dear America'.

We had many such conversations and from these emerged, paradoxically, the fact that, although we had reached a somewhat similar conclusion, we had reached it from premises which were diametrically opposite. Apart from the fact that I had acquired my doubts on a purely theoretical basis, whereas Hinrich's were the result of expert practical knowledge, mine had their roots in revolutionary soil, whereas his grew from the most orthodox conservatism. He knew the form book and he went by it. He could see nothing in the history of American development to suggest that, on behalf of the American Joshua of 1929, the Lord God was going to suspend the laws of economics.

Excited by the extraordinary disclosure of Hinrichs's scepticism, I drew exaggerated conclusions.

'Then you mean,' I said, 'that you believe that the capitalist system won't work?'

But this was not what he meant at all. He meant simply that the capitalist system – a phrase he somewhat disliked, I think, because it implied the existence of other, equally valid, systems – would proceed as usual by a series of jerks frequently interrupted by catastrophes. To 'defend', so to speak, the catastrophes seemed to him unnecessary, for he considered them as inevitable as sunrise. There was not, in his view, a 'system' to blame; if one had to blame anything, then it was just life. The capitalist system was life, and therefore attempts to substitute any other type of 'system' were both nonsensical and dangerous. You could not step out of life.

He was a warm-hearted man, generous and sympathetic towards all individual miseries, but he saw no cure for the general miseries of the human race – such as want and war – and thus, at least in conversation, took the view that people who proffered such cures were mentally defective or else quacks.

Our theoretical discussions in *The Times* office were frequently broken in upon by one who might be said to have been the embodiment of the Spirit of the Boom – namely, Mr Frederick Bullock, correspondent of the *Daily Mail*. In Northcliffe's day the *Daily Mail* and *The Times* correspondents in New York had naturally shared offices, and after the papers separated no one had thought it worth while to change the layout of the office. Thus we had, on the floor above the *New York Sun*, three fair-sized rooms of which the centre one was occupied by our joint secretary, and those on either side of it by *The Times* and the *Daily Mail* respectively. It is hard to imagine how more comparatively incompatible elements could have been jammed into so small a space.

The communicating doors were usually left open, and behind Hinrichs's most delicately learned exposition of some point in the past policy of the Federal Reserve System could be heard the rising bellow of Freddie Bullock's Rabelaisian laughter, or the cheerful bark of his bullish orders being shouted into the telephone to his broker.

He was a short, enormously muscular man of sixty or so, and when you first saw him you saw a huge cigar, a pair of tufted eyebrows and hairy muzzle, combined in a face which seemed designed for durability rather than elegance. You were just deciding that what you had to deal with here was a somewhat roughly constructed cannonball, when the cannonball would come to sudden rest, the cigar smoke would cease to swirl, and you were being examined hopefully by shrewd, alertly sparkling eyes, which brimmed with amusement, eagerness and goodwill. Their expression said that if you were a member of the human race you would certainly get from Mr Frederick Bullock the benefit of any doubt your conduct might occasion. He had the candour and exuberance of a twelve-year-old schoolboy, and the theatrical instincts of a first-class clown. He smelt rather than understood Hinrichs's scepticism about the market, and as a result regarded Hinrichs with a kind of derisive compassion. He would come steaming into our office behind his cigar, launch a general discussion on the state of financial affairs, listen impatiently for a few moments while Hinrichs attempted in the most meticulous fashion to explain his point of view, and then with something between a bark and a guffaw go steaming out again, pause for a moment to tell, or attempt to tell, an indecent joke to the handsomely blonde and strictly respectable secretary, and dash into his own office where the telephone was ringing. We would hear him shouting and laughing into it, and a few minutes later he would come rushing back again, sometimes executing a burlesque dance step as he did so, and – thrusting his half-smoked cigar under Hinrichs's nose by way of emphasis – shout out the news which his broker had just given him, to the effect that some stock in which he was interested had already risen four points that morning. In his estimation this was momentarily conclusive proof that the sceptics were a lot of nervous old women who, pusillanimously, or as a result of academic inhibitions, were letting slip the opportunity to make a million dollars.

A million dollars or thereabouts was in fact the sum which Freddie Bullock had made, on paper, by gambling on the stock market during the past couple of years. He used to tell with glee, and at the same time a touch of melancholy, the story of his most recent visit to Europe where, in Paris, he had had breakfast with the then Lord Rothermere. For a time, under Lord Northcliffe, Freddie Bullock had been, so far as I recall, a director of the *Daily Mail*, and had been on intimate terms with Lord Rothermere. He had looked forward to seeing him in Europe after a separation which had lasted several years. Lord Rothermere asked him to breakfast at his hotel in Paris. There were a lot of people there, and as Bullock came into the room Lord Rothermere bounded through the crowd and gripped him by the hand, shouting, 'How much did you make? How much?' By this Bullock was somewhat vexed and disappointed – he had expected at least an inquiry after his health, or an expression of gladness at seeing him again. He shrugged.

'In your terms, nothing worth writing home about,' he said.

Lord Rothermere became almost violent in his impatience. 'I'm asking you,' he shouted, 'how much did you make?'

'But I tell you,' said Bullock, 'in your terms it's the merest bagatelle, nothing.'

'I'm not asking you for that kind of answer,' said Rothermere. 'I want the figures.'

Bullock paused to make sure that he had the full attention of the roomful of editors, financiers and politicians. 'I tell you,' he said airily, 'it's nothing – peanuts. In fact I can say that during the past three months I have not made more on the market than about six times the annual salary of a first-class man on the *Daily Mail*.'

He was a real Anglo-American. You could say that he was Americanized, yet you had to admit that he was as English as an Orange Pippin. In this Englishness of his he profoundly believed, and was proud of it. As an Englishman (he came, I think, from the West Country) he took the view that, unlike Americans, who are prone to hysteria, English people sternly control their feelings, never display emotion. In a roomful of American friends gambling like himself on the market, he would bound about shouting with excitement and begging everybody to keep perfectly calm. At dinner one day at his home – a costly penthouse apartment just off Washington Square – the talk turned on the sufferings of Great Britain following World War I. Everyone present, except myself and Bullock, was American. Bullock gave them a patriotic little lecture on how to face adversity. 'Don't think, you fellows,' he said, 'that because we English ride our feelings on a tight rein we don't feel these things deeply. It simply,' he said, his voice trembling, 'means that even when we are thinking most deeply of all our country has been through, we never show it.' His voice trembled more and more, and the glass of wine shook in his hand. 'We never,' he sobbed, 'show a trace, not a trace of emotion.' He drank deeply and two large tears rolled from his eyes.

Together with journalism, stock-exchange gambling and women, medicine shared his keen interest. He believed that almost any time now medical science would come up with some gadget which would enable people of nearly sixty to live at top speed without the slightest ill-effect upon their health and in a general way prolong life more or less indefinitely. He was thus the victim of countless expensive quacks.

His attitude to modern medicine resembled in some respects my father's attitude in the old days to the motor-car. For years, when he was younger and poorer, Bullock had pooh-poohed new-fangled medical notions, as being certainly decadent and probably fatal. He spoke of 'nature's remedies', and implied that what was good enough for his father's body was good enough for his. When, however, he did start to take an interest in it his position reversed itself: his objection now was not that its pretensions and achievements were too great but that they were not great enough. Just as my father had thought that if you were going to have a motor-car at all it ought to be capable of taking you from here to there in virtually no time, so Bullock felt that if you were going to pay to have the wonders of science let loose on you, you ought to get something spectacular in the way of health and vigour for your money.

Though nobody formulated it quite like that, this was a notion quite common in the subconscious minds of people in New York at that time. Quacks of every description from half-trained psychiatrists to golden-tongued doctors with multi-purpose hobby-horses throve upon it. One of them, franker than most, told me that, in his opinion, this obsession with health, this nervous preoccupation with the possibilities of disease on the one hand, or of prolonging life on the other, was simply an inevitable symptom of the gambling fever and the gambling boom itself. How horrible to think that Anaconda Copper might go to 150 and you would be too ill to care; how dreadful to die and miss the universal Utopia which was just coming up. He drew my attention, this psychiatrist, to the theme in the story by Leonid Andreyev called *Grand Slam* where a man dies of a seizure at the card table just as he is about to play a grand slam in No Trumps.

An idea terrifying in its simplicity struck the emaciated little body of Jacob Ivanovitch [the dead man's partner] causing him to leap from his chair. Peering round, as though the thought had not come to him of its own accord but had been whispered by someone into his ear, he said aloud: 'But he will never know that the ace was in the pack and his hand contained a certain grand slam. Never, never.'
And it seemed to Jacob Ivanovitch that he had not understood until this moment what death really meant. Now he really understood, and the thing he saw plainly was senseless, awful, irrevocable.
'Never, never,' Jacob Ivanovitch said slowly, to convince himself that such a word existed and had meaning. The word existed and had meaning, but the meaning was so strange and so bitter that Jacob

Ivanovitch again fell into a chair and wept helplessly. He pitied Nikolai Dmitrievitch in that he would never know, and he pitied himself and everyone, since this senseless cruel thing would happen to him and to everyone alike.

When Bullock was not chiding or commiserating with Louis Hinrichs for his stiff-jointed inability to grasp the opportunities offered by the stock market, he was upbraiding him on medical grounds, pleading with him not to pass up, too, the opportunities offered by modern medical science.

Significantly his feelings on this score were if possible more passionate than those he had about the stock market, and it was evident that here, too, lurked a belief in sympathetic magic – he manifested an obscure fear lest Hinrichs's lack of faith, not to mention his open derision, might be actually weakening the power of the doctors.

9

THE CHIPS WERE DOWN

THE morning of Thursday, October 24th, was like the morning of a battle which people are beginning for the first time to realize may be lost. Until soon after the opening of the market on the previous day, nobody had thought of such a thing. It was assumed, as it had been assumed on each previous occasion when a break in the market had occurred, that this was a temporary setback, a 'readjustment' – the bulls were losing a skirmish or two but they were not going to lose the battle.

But by the close of Wednesday's market the *New York Times* averages for fifty leading industrial stocks had lost over eighteen points, and long after the close Freddie Bullock, in the intervals of trying to reach his brokers on the jammed telephone lines, kept coming into our office talking, arguing and listening for the first time to Hinrichs with a kind of nervous awe. Bullock came across from his apartment to have breakfast with me that Thursday in the café of the Hotel Lafayette. He needed company, and I dare say, too, he needed the peculiar atmosphere of the Hotel

Lafayette which took you a little bit out of this world. It was owned by Raymond Orteig, who had put up the original prize of twenty-five thousand dollars for the non-stop flight between New York and Paris ultimately won by Colonel Charles Lindbergh. The Lafayette was no mere curiosity, a French hotel in New York. It was, on the contrary, a first-class hotel and one which was simultaneously as French and as American as the French district of New Orleans. The food was the best in New York, and if you were a resident and took your meals in your own apartment you could get the benefit of one of the best cellars in New York too – the management of the Lafayette taking the view that prohibition did not apply to resident guests.

We had breakfast at a marble-topped table in the café at the end of which there was a ticker machine. Bullock kept jumping up and walking over to it by force of simply nervous habit, because at that hour the ticker could tell us nothing that we did not know already. Yet that morning there was a stream of men trotting up to the ticker and standing for a few minutes gazing at it in an unusual silence.

It takes nothing less than a major air raid to produce any visible change in the social 'atmosphere' of London, but New York lives more externally, and on the subway to the City Hall Square the change was as evident as a notable change in the weather. At the *Sun* office there was just that nip in the emotional air which you get on the day after a big air raid, when people have grasped that the bombers really did get through last night and may do so again today. It was a situation in which nobody says much but everyone knows what everyone else is thinking and knows that everyone else is a little frightened too.

As the electric clocks ticked off the minutes until the opening of the market, the tension was nearly intolerable. I do not mean that any of us had much idea of what was really going to happen except perhaps Louis Hinrichs. None of us, I am sure, thought, 'This is a turning-point one way or another in the history of the twentieth century.' None of us was sapient enough to reflect, 'Upon what happens today hangs the fate of nations. A way of life is going to survive or is going down the drain. After today, either everything will be as it was, or else nothing will ever be quite the same again.'

There were some very smart people hanging over the ticker at the opening of the market that morning in the *Sun* office, but none of them was quite smart enough to know that, as they saw in those first few astounding minutes shares of Kennecott and General Motors thrown on the market in blocks of five, ten and fifteen thousand, they were looking at the beginning of a road which was going to lead to the British collapse of 1931, to the collapse of Austria, to the collapse of Germany, and at the end of it there was going to be a situation with Adolf Hitler in the middle of it, a situation in which no amount of get-togethers on a log at Rapidan was going to do much good, a situation in fact which was going to look very much like the fulfilment of the most lurid predictions of Marx and Lenin.

I kept being reminded of the old story about the enthusiastic American who took his phlegmatic British friend to see Niagara.

'Isn't that amazing?' said the American. 'Look at that vast mass of water dashing over that enormous cliff!'

'But what,' said the Englishman, 'is to stop it?'

There was nothing much to do that morning except just to watch Niagara. It seemed pointless to go through the usual routine of telephoning to 'contacts' and informants and asking for their comments on the situation. There was no sensible comment that anyone could make, and furthermore you had the feeling that there was no question you could ask which would not strike the man at the other end as some kind of affront. Even so I scarcely began to guess how bad the situation really was until Hinrichs, in a low voice, said to me: 'Remember when we're writing this story the word "panic" is not to be used.'

At length we left the crazy-looking ticker and started to walk through the bright streets towards Wall Street, walking in silence because, in the light of the enormity of the event, anything that one could say seemed intolerably trivial. Thousands of other people were streaming towards Wall Street and they were walking in silence too.

In the Street itself there was an enormous murmuring crowd, and the people pressed close around us were talking, when one listened to them, almost in whispers. Every now and then you could hear quite distinctly a hysterical laugh. As time passed, the crowd grew thicker and noisier, and then there was an eddy in the middle of it and a man in shirtsleeves was pushing his way across the street in the direction of the Morgan offices. Hinrichs nudged me sharply. This was an easily recognizable denizen of the Village, namely Charles E. Mitchell, Chairman of the National City Bank, the leader of the bull market and the champion of the 'expansionists' against the 'restrictive' efforts of the Federal Reserve Board. He pushed his way into the offices of the house of Morgan and a little later we learned what he had gone for. He and the other leading bankers of Wall Street had been summoned there to establish a multi-million-dollar pool in an attempt to steady the market.

Silver-haired Mr Lamont received us with a manner so reassuring that, upon me and many others, it had the same effect as Hinrich's warning against the use of the word 'panic'. It was like the manner of the man who comes on the stage of a burning theatre and urges everyone to keep perfectly cool, stating there is no cause for alarm. He made soft, soothing gesticulations with his pince-nez as softly, gently, almost stammeringly, he deprecated anything in the nature of sensationalism. His first sentence has been aptly described as one of the most remarkable under-statements of all time.

'There has been a little distress selling on the Stock Exchange,' he said, 'and we have held a meeting of the heads of several financial institutions to discuss the situation. We have found that there are no Houses in difficulty and the reports from brokers indicate that margins are being maintained satisfactorily.'

The pince-nez gently waved away ill-informed rumours of the disaster, moving to and fro in the dim light from the high window heavily covered with anti-bomb steel netting. Nothing fundamental, he said, had changed. There was nothing basically wrong with the country's economy. What had occurred was due simply to 'a technical condition of the market'.

Since becoming a journalist I had often heard the advice to 'believe nothing until it has been officially denied'. But, despite this, even the ominous blandness of Mr Lamont did not shake me into full awareness of what was going on. The shake came a little later at lunch with the Edgar Speyers.

'Edwardian' was the adjective which inevitably occurred to you in the presence of Edgar Speyer, and equally inevitably he recalled to me the Rothschilds as I had seen them in my boyhood days at Tring. He was an American now, had been an American for years, and he and his brother were not only millionaires but had made themselves powerful figures in the cut and thrust of Wall Street, but the aroma of Edwardianism still hung about him like the scent of a good cigar. This was natural enough since it was in Edwardian England that this originally German Jew had risen to wealth and prominence. He had been Sir Edgar Speyer then, and a Privy Councillor. Then he was caught in the storm of indignation against Germans in high places in England which at the beginning of World War I swept even Prince Louis of Battenberg out of the Admiralty. He could afford to recall what for many people might have been a disaster with an amiable shrug. His enforced good-bye to all that had by no means been disastrous for him. He just got on a boat and went to Boston and made a couple of million dollars. Later he advanced triumphantly on New York and, at the time I knew him, lived in one of the lovely rose-coloured houses on the north side of Washington Square. It housed, not in any special gallery but as part of its furnishings, a small but luminously beautiful art collection composed chiefly of Chinese paintings and porcelain. The atmosphere was one of elegant calm in which the rich odour emanating from pots and pots of money was naturally, but not disagreeably, perceptible. It was at that time one of the few houses I visited in New York where you did not have to talk about the Stock Market or any other form of business, and the food and wine were so good that nobody thought it odd if at lunch or dinner you were perfectly silent for minutes on end. There were a middle-aged English butler and a youthful English footman, but, except for their age, one might have supposed that they had been trained in Edwardian England and come over with Speyer on the boat to Boston in 1914. Their only departure from an older tradition was that they both of them left the room as soon as each course had been served by the footman under the butler's supervision.

Leonora Speyer was a writer. She had, as I recall, recently published a volume of poems, and on this October 24th of 1929 the Speyers and their four guests were talking about modern American poetry. I was eating pompano and listening to somebody telling something about some poet I had not yet heard of, when I perceived to my astonishment that some kind of disturbance was going on at the other side of the dining-room door, which faced me as I sat at the table. Something had certainly bumped against the door. I heard a very faint thump, and I saw the door shiver slightly. The idea of anything, as it were, untoward occurring in the Speyer household was nearly inconceivable. I concluded that they must be the owners of some large dog which I had never seen, and that this dog had escaped and was probably at this moment being hauled off to its proper place by the footman. And then just as I was about to give full attention again to the conversation, something else happened.

The handle of the door turned very very slowly, the door shuddered again and moved an inch or so inwards. Then it closed again, and again the handle very very slowly turned in the direction opposite to its direction before. There was no longer any doubt about it. Either somebody in an ecstasy of indecision was trying to make up his mind to come into the room, or else, as seemed more likely, two people were struggling over the handle of the door, one of them trying to open it and the other to keep it closed.

In any other house there might have been a dozen explanations for this – children loose in the passage, for instance. Perhaps children playing with a big dog. But in the Speyer household things were so ordered that a disturbance of this kind was as startling as it would have been to find the dining-room too hot or too cold, or to have a draught blowing down one's neck. Fascinated by the mysterious struggle behind the door, I found myself gazing at the man who was talking intelligently about this poet with an expression, as I could see from the surprised look he gave me, of absolutely idiotic vacancy. I was so placed that I was the only one at the table who, when the door opened, could see right down the corridor outside, and what I saw, when the two manservants came in to put a saddle of lamb in front of Speyer, was that at the end of the corridor either four or five maidservants of various ages were grouped together in what seemed to be an excited attitude and one of them – unless I was under some kind of hallucination – had actually shaken her fist at the footman as he came through the door.

Within a few minutes the butler and footman had again withdrawn, but we had swallowed no more than a mouthful or two of lamb when the noise in the passage became so loud that nobody in the dining-room could even pretend to ignore it. A woman shouted, 'Go on – or else ! – ' and then the door was burst open and the butler, very red in the face, nearly bounced into the room as though he had been pushed violently from behind at the last moment.

He closed the door and as collectedly as possible marched across the room to Speyer and in low apologetic tones begged him to come outside for a moment. Listening with an air of astonishment, Speyer, after a few seconds' amazed hesitation, left the room with him. Almost immediately Speyer came back again looking a little dismayed. He begged us to excuse him. The staff, he explained, had of course their own ticker-tape in the kitchen premises and of course they were all heavily engaged on the Stock Market. And now the ticker was recording incredible things. In point of fact the ticker was by that time running just over an hour and a half late, owing to the enormous volume of trading, so that the prices which the Speyer staff were reading with horror at a quarter to two were the prices at which stocks had changed hands at the very worst moment of the morning before the bankers had met and the formation of the bankers' pool had been announced.

The staff saw their savings going down in chaos; since they were certainly operating on margin, they might at this moment already have been wiped out. Among the stock in which all of them had speculated was that of Montgomery Ward, and that had dropped from an opening price of 83 to around 50 before noon. And all this was going on before their eyes while their employer, reputedly one of the shrewdest financiers in New York, was calmly sitting upstairs eating pompano and saddle of lamb. They absolutely insisted that he go at once with them to the kitchen, study the situation, make telephone calls if necessary, and advise them what to do for the best.

Speyer left the rest of his lunch uneaten, and his wife and her guests finished the meal under conditions of confusion and makeshift which probably had never been seen in the Speyer household before. I left as soon as I decently could and did not see Mr Speyer to say good-bye. He was still in the kitchen. I hurried to the office to write my story, beginning at last to be aware of what the great crash meant.

By this time everyone else was beginning to be aware of it too, most of them more fully than myself. Whereas in the morning the atmosphere had been in the main one of incredulous excitement, now there was a strong smell of fear in the air too.

Our office had begun to look as though the waves were going over the bridge. Naturally we all of us had to write several thousand words to London describing the great crash. But at the same time everybody was either emotionally or financially so deeply engaged that there were constant little conferences in the corners, where people were trying to figure out what really had happened. Every now and then forlorn telephone calls came in from other people who were also trying to figure that out. And, as always happens at times like these, the element of low farce walked in in the shape of a little man whose name I remember so poorly that I can only describe him as Colonel X. Colonel X was some kind of dilapidated British peer who had spent years of his life in the Intelligence Service in India. He was now in New York, had been in New York for some time and had repeatedly come into *The Times* office suggesting that we buy from him for a large price a story he had, which told that a new anti-British revolution in India was being planned among the Indian students of Columbia University. He was a dirty little Lord, and it was obvious to the least experienced observer that he was reeking with heroin. However, he had at one point somewhat endeared himself to me by showing a really extraordinary knowledge of the English hymn-book. He could at any moment recite any hymn in the English hymn-book of which you gave him the number, and this seemed to me a very remarkable accomplishment. He had also once borrowed from me a sum of money after I had determined never to lend him any more money at all. He had said to me, gazing into a battered straw hat which he wore, 'You know, laddie, what I need is five thousand dollars.'

I, who had been so sure that I never would lend him any

money at all, had said laughingly, 'Well, that is unfortunately too bad. I don't have more than ten dollars available.'

To which he had replied, 'That will do, laddie. That will be sufficient for the moment.' And of course there had been nothing to do but to give him the ten dollars.

He stank so badly that normally one did not care to see him otherwise than on the public street, but on this occasion, on the day of the great crash, one stench seemed no worse than another. I could not at first focus upon the little man. I could not make out what on earth he was doing in this *galère*. Then I realized that he was standing on his bow legs with his little cane and his busted straw hat on the side of his head, looking at everyone with an air of enormous superiority. At last he, so to speak, 'cut me out' in the way that a cowboy cuts out a cow, and he said to me, 'You know, all these people are worrying, worrying, worrying. They are worrying about the crash in America, about some crash they think is going to happen in consequence in Britain; they think that we shall all go off the gold standard or something of the kind. And what I want to say to you, laddie, is just simply this. Don't worry, don't worry, don't worry.'

I said to him that there were grounds for worry. He said, 'I thought you would say that, laddie, and that is why I am going to tell you something. Let me tell you that to me, and just a very few people in the Intelligence Service, is known the fact that in the heart of Africa, right in Zululand, we have a mountain of gold. Yes, laddie, a mountain of gold. And that gold – that mountain of gold – is patrolled day by day and night by night by a great troop of the finest Zulus in the world. Loyal chaps, laddie, yes, loyal chaps.'

At this point his voice had risen to such a screech that even the Financial Editor of the *New York Sun* was peering to see where it came from.

'And these Zulus,' he said, 'splendid physical specimens, magnificent men, they go round and round this mountain once at dawn and once at night. At dawn they run up the Union Jack on the mountain, and the chief of this magnificent tribe drives in a carriage round it, with, laddie, cream-coloured ponies – cream-coloured ponies like Queen Victoria had. And if any one of the magnificent Zulu guards is not in his place, that guard is taken out and lashed – lashed practically to death, laddie, because these are loyal fellows. And that means that whatever happens – whatever happens to America, whatever happens to Germany or Russia or this kind of nonsense, we've got this mountain of gold and we are going to survive. Do you see what I mean, laddie?'

I saw just what he meant, and it was the end of that day.

IO

WHILE THE ROOF FELL IN

THE next week was just the same and every day people said that everything was going to get better, and every day it got worse. Things reached a point where it became almost impossible to face one's friends or acquaintances in New York because everything that had happened or was happening seemed to make them out to be fools, and just because at one time or another one had questioned their judgement in the grand old times of ten days ago, one seemed to be swaggering with superior knowledge. Superior knowledge which of course one did not possess.

I was thus both happy and tremulous when I suddenly received the news that *The Times* Correspondent in Washington, Mr Wilmott Lewis, had been summoned to London to attend some international conference or other, and the plan was that I should immediately go to Washington and take over his job. I was elated because I was glad to get away from the gloomy atmosphere of New York at this period, and to get also to the political centre of affairs. On the other hand, I was nearly unnerved by the thought that I was suddenly, at so brief a notice, and with such minimal knowledge and journalistic experience, to take over what by this time had become the major political bureau of the London *Times*. I left for Washington on the night of December 31st, 1929.

Sliding into Union Station, Washington, in the darkness of New Year's Eve, I reflected momentarily that the last member of my family to visit the American capital was Admiral Sir George Cockburn, who had burned the White House and the Capitol, and much else of Washington besides, in 1814. Not, I had always thought, a very nice kind of man. For example, when he was in command near Annapolis before the assault on the city, he considered the food and drink available in the camp not up to the mark. He had also heard that there was an excellent restaurant on Pennsylvania Avenue in the enemy capital. Sensibly enough, he made arrangements to visit this restaurant every evening in disguise. However, no memory of these pleasant little soirées prevented him later from cantering up and down Pennsylvania Avenue on his horse urging the soldiery to further acts of rape and arson. The proprietress of the restaurant is said to have been very much wounded by his behaviour.

As I left Union Station there was a considerable glare in the sky. The dome of the Capitol had just burst into flames.

Startled, I drove to the house of Wilmott Lewis where I was to stay. It was our first meeting. He was entranced by the occurrence at the Capitol. Holding both my hands in his he beamed upon me and, 'Now,' he said, 'one sees at once that you have been born under the right star. You have luck – and that is the most important thing in life.

'Even with your outstanding abilities – which I may say I have for some time been noting from afar with admiration – it might have taken you weeks to make your mark, to become any kind of a lion in the Washington Zoo. Now, as a result of this happy concatenation of events – call it luck, call it destiny, call it what you will – you will be at least a lion cub no later than tomorrow morning.'

Before he had even finished speaking he had lifted the receiver of the telephone in the hall and communicated the story, decorated with some remarkable grace notes of his own, to all the columnists in Washington, and to two in New York. In the brief intervals between the calls he gave me a little lecture on the values of publicity in facilitating one's serious work, and smoothing the path towards one's real objectives.

'Do any of the people you have been talking to,' I asked, 'know what actually caused this fire tonight?'

'They suppose,' he said, 'that it was a painter. The inside of the dome is being redecorated. One of the painters, no doubt drunk, since it is New Year's Eve, probably dropped a cigar among the paint and varnish and so on. However, it is what one may call the "Cockburn angle" that really makes the story.'

Still talking, he led me into the drawing-room, where an exhilarating symphony of noise and almost overpowering volume of sound proved after a time to be composed of the Philharmonic Orchestra playing something rowdy on an enormous radiogram, about thirty of the best-informed people in Washington rattling the tall windows with their gossip, and the yells and incantations of two senators, a Congressman, several journalists, and the then Mrs Lewis, daughter of the owner of the Associated Press, who were on their knees shooting craps in the middle of the carpet.

'Curiously enough,' said Lewis, towards five in the morning when the party was beginning to break up, 'I feel a little tired. I must be getting old.'

He was then in his early fifties. For all these hours he had 'conducted' that party of star performers as a conductor conducts a band. Reeling to bed when the last guests had gone, I passed the open door of his study and saw him in his shirtsleeves, his dinner-jacket draped over the back of his chair, thoughtfully beginning to tap out two or three pages of notes recording impressions, potentially significant pieces of information, dropped into his attentive ear in the course of the evening.

'There are a million pieces in the jigsaw,' he said. 'At any moment you may unexpectedly find that you have just picked up the one you need.'

I had met a lot of colourful and impressive personalities that evening, but before I finally got to bed I could not feel that any of them was quite as impressive as my host. Nothing in the years that I knew him altered that opinion.

Strangers thought he must be a famous actor or Envoy Extraordinary of some very civilized state. In the grey dawn of an all-night poker session he seemed, rather, the phantom of the original Mississippi Gambler, so sardonic, debonair and quick on the draw. Or smiling thoughtfully in the inner circle round the President at a White House reception, he suggested an angularly handsome Mephisto, wondering whether or not to wave a conjuring hand and transform the company into swans and bullfrogs.

High-placed Americans insisted he was the secret Chief of the British Intelligence Service in the United States, and, years before he became officially 'Sir' Wilmott Lewis, American colleagues recognized the panache of his personality by referring to Wilmott Harsant Lewis as the Knight of New Hampshire Avenue, where his big house was situated. When he was knighted they asked him whether they should address him in some new way.

'You will continue,' he said, 'to address me as "You old s.o.b.", but from now on you have to smile as you say that.'

Up-to-the-minute as a portable voice recorder, he yet had about him a flavour which evoked Europe of the late nineties. In his teens he had been at the universities of both Heidelberg and Paris, and one of a group of *avant garde* poets and critics who met at the Closerie des Lilas. He admitted occasional nostalgia for the continent he had scarcely seen in twenty-five years.

'Nevertheless,' he said, in his habitual style of faultlessly elaborate parenthesis, 'Washington – which Viviani, when he led the French delegation to the Disarmament Conference, was tactless enough to describe as *"un Versailles nègre"*, thus (for you figure to yourself the reactions of Southern senators to whom his ill-timed if apt remark was, I need hardly tell you, instantly communicated) stabbing himself in the back, a performance singularly otiose in a city where so many stand only too eagerly ready to do it for you – Washington has many amenities and compensations, not least among them the fact that it is the last world capital still resisting Americanization.'

Among the amenities he enjoyed were the rare, perhaps unique, local prestige and international influence his ability had achieved for him during his first years in the capital. He had come to be regarded generally as more important than most Ambassadors most of the time and always much more fun. It was a situation he appreciated without illusions.

'The advantage,' he remarked to me once, as we sat eating enormous oysters in a tiny yacht on the Potomac, 'of having spent a good deal of one's early life on – not to put too fine a point on it – the bum, is that one learns never to take even a square meal entirely for granted.'

As a very young man he had been for a time an actor, down and nearly out. He had sat up at night in an Eastbourne lodging-house writing fresh material for the bankrupt troupe, himself among them, to act next day. It was presumably during this period that he had acquired a kind of barnstorming fruitiness and floridity of tone and gesture which sometimes disconcerted the stolid.

'As you gaze, Mr President,' I once heard him say to President Hoover, 'into the future, as you peer down the grey vista of the years, do you not apprehend, sir, that the problems of the United States are problems not only of growth, but' – the voice sank to a vibrant whisper – 'of decay?'

The President seemed bemused alike by the question itself and by the sudden extension of arm and hand which accompanied it, the index finger pointing menacingly down the grey vista. The incident must have disturbed him, for later he made a speech in which he said the problems of the United States were those of growth only – not of decay.

Lewis would describe as poignantly as though it had happened yesterday the occasion when after starving for nearly four days in London he had found a shilling or so in the lining of his jacket and rushed out to buy a tin of beef or something of the kind. When he got it back to his room and had hacked it open, with the saliva running down his chin, he found that the beef was hopelessly maggot-ridden.

'It is a good thing,' he said, 'to remember, that, however nicely we may be doing, to millions and millions of people all over the world, privations and disappointments of that kind are happening all the time.'

He told me when I came to know him well that he thought probably the most 'formative' influence in his early life had been the occasion when as a very junior reporter he had been assigned by the *Daily News* to write a preliminary 'feature' story about the Diamond Jubilee Review to be held at Aldershot by Queen Victoria in 1897.

'I went to Aldershot and viewed the sand-dunes, the broad driveway where the Royal cortège and the whole pomp and panoply of empire, the Kings and Queens and Princes, were to be assembled, where troops from twenty races and from every continent were to pass in view. As my mind's eye envisaged the superb spectacle, my physical eye detected an unexpected movement among the sand-hills on the other side of the reviewing place. Mildly curious, I moved in that direction. I soon saw that the movement was caused by human figures.

'Approaching still nearer, I perceived these to be the figures of women in rags and horribly decayed. At that time, you know, there was in the British Army no proper system of education and instruction on the subject of venereal disease – it was thought that to introduce such a system officially might be offensive to the "respectable" public, and perhaps to the Queen herself. These women, then, were former prostitutes of Aldershot, so diseased as now to be unable to pursue the practice of their profession and living in the most miserable shacks and shanties among the sand-dunes. One must admit, of course, that they were excellently placed to enjoy the prospect of the great Diamond Jubilee Review.'

An abruptly switch-backing course took young Mr Lewis from London to the Far East, where he was alternately on top of the world and reduced to helping to manage a tough bar at the Shanghai racecourse. Soon after that his astounding energy shoved him to a point where he was internationally recognized as one of the most ingenious and brilliant war correspondents in the Russo-Japanese War.

He edited a newspaper in Manila, worked as a sports writer in San Francisco, was 'hard pressed' again in New York, emerged penultimately in Paris at the moment of the Versailles Conference. Deeply impressed, Mr Wickham Steed, then editor of *The Times*, introduced him to Lord Northcliffe. The meeting was in a sense a failure. Apparently Lewis, as was his habit, illustrated his conversation with rather frequent quotations from the French minor poets. Lord Northcliffe complained that the man was a damned foreigner. He compromised by agreeing that he be hired, provided he was sent somewhere far off. They thought first of Tokyo, finally agreed on Washington.

By the time I met him his prestige was alarming, and his dispatches were misleadingly described as models of what such things should be – misleading because anyone trying to imitate these superbly individual works of art would have come a nasty cropper. Sometimes he spent three or four days or even a week preparing and polishing a dispatch on some aspect of American affairs which would be filed to London at a moment when an event, foreseen by Lewis, occurred to form the 'news peg' upon which the rest of the carefully prepared message was to be hung. More often he wrote his dispatches or articles very fast, but this was only because he was, so to speak, permanently 'in rehearsal'. He was always rehearsing, mentally or in conversation, the formulations or comments which would be appropriate to this or that development of the situation, so that when the development actually occurred, the polished phrases and considered judgements poured from the typewriter at a pace which, but for the unending 'rehearsals', would have been incredible.

I was to have only forty-eight hours with him in Washington before he left for London. Considering my ignorance of this vast and complex stage, the experience would have been very alarming had not Wilmott Lewis, by a kind of courteous hypnosis, succeeded in creating for myself and almost everyone else the illusion that I was a person of such enormous experience and ability that – with a hint or two, probably unnecessary, from him – I could effortlessly take charge of the situation.

Comment flowed briskly as he hurried me on a conducted tour of personalities and situations. ('In fairness to Senator Cole Blease, old boy, it must be said that he has the unique distinction of combining in his sole person *all* the disadvantages attaching to the democratic form of government.' 'One should perhaps avoid being hypercritical of acts of high policy. Take the charitable view, bearing in mind that every government will do as much harm as it can and as much good as it must.' 'He is one of those American politicians who believe that the women of his country are more virtuous and its diplomats more stupid than those of any other. Since he is wrong on both these counts, it is reasonable to assume that he is wrong on every other, too.' 'Do not under-estimate his capacity for snatching defeat from the very jaws of victory.' 'Inspiring, is it not, to see eyes so ablaze with insincerity?' 'He will always be happy to advise you. You may rely upon him to maintain a firm grip on the obvious.')

Just before leaving, he suddenly presented me with the first of two pieces of journalistic advice which were the best I had ever had.

'I think it well,' he said, 'to remember that, when writing for the newspapers, we are writing for an elderly lady in Hastings who has two cats of which she is passionately fond. Unless our stuff can successfully compete for her interest with those cats, it is no good.'

Months later, when he was back in Washington, I once submitted to him a two-column article for *The Times* on which I had worked hard and of which I was extremely proud. Lewis read it with close attention. As he nodded appreciatively my pride and pleasure increased. He read it for the second time. Then, holding it between his finger and thumb, he said, 'Old boy, this piece is not only informed but erudite. Its material is solid and accurately observed; its style polished – and, in my estimation, witty. In fact it is everything which one imagines to oneself an article in *The Times* should be. Yet I'm afraid – my instinct tells me – that,' he opened his finger and thumb and the pages dropped into the wastepaper basket, 'the cats will have it.'

Despite the intensive forty-eight-hour course in Washington affairs which I had gone through under his guidance, I was uneasy. Left to myself, I thought, I should write something terribly mistaken, causing panic in London and upsetting the empire. Sensing my emotion, Lewis pushed head and shoulders out of his departing taxi and gave me the second piece of admirable advice.

'Whatever happens,' he shouted, 'don't be nervous. Remember, old boy' – the taxi was moving faster now and he had to shout through the driving sleet – 'whatever happens, you are right and London is wrong.'

He had been away many weeks, was in fact just returning, before I grasped the full extent of his own faith in this statement. He had invited me to stay in his house and also use it as my office. He had omitted even to mention that there was in fact a *Times* office in Washington. I found it by accident one day when I was wandering through a downtown office building looking for something else. It was locked. I obtained a pass-key. The door moved with difficulty. When I did get inside, I found the door had been jammed by a cascade of cablegrams and letters pushed daily for weeks and weeks through the letter slip.

Most of the cables were from *The Times*, some of them sent since I had taken over, most of them of earlier date. They said 'Urgently require 700 words on . . .' and 'Please cable most urgently full coverage of . . .' 'Must have tomorrow latest . . .'

Appalled, I met Lewis on his return with the dreadful news; I supposed it to be due to some ghastly mistake by the Cable Company. He looked at the cables distastefully.

'Ah yes,' he said, 'perhaps I should have told you about that office. London, you know, *does* these things. I've always found it best to maintain a certain distance. Better to decide for oneself what to send and when to send it.'

I found out later that a couple of years previously *The Times* really had made a determined attempt to get him to respond to their cabled inquiries and demands. When he was in London on a brief visit they waited until the last day of his stay in order to make the *démarche* the more impressive and memorable, and then a number of the High Priests cornered him in a small room somewhere in the labyrinth of Printing House Square, and Mr Deakin, Foreign and Imperial News Editor, made an impressive statement. It was, he said, intolerable that *The Times* should launch urgent cablegrams across the Atlantic and hear no more of them than if they had launched their messages upon the bosom of the ocean. He depicted movingly the distress and confusion thus occasioned. Could not Lewis promise solemnly, here and now, that, in future, cables sent at urgent rates, and signed personally by the editor, would at least be acknowledged? He went so far as to suggest that in return for such a promise *The Times* might be inclined to consider a bonus or a rise in salary as compensation for the trouble involved. While Deakin was speaking Lewis had got to his feet, and seemed to be beating his breast and to be making other mysterious gestures with his hands.

'I am,' he said, the moment Deakin concluded his remarks, 'a sinful man, my dear Deakin. I feel like a San Sebastian – every word of yours is an arrow in my heart.'

By now everyone's attention was concentrated on Lewis's theatrically trained hands plucking imaginary arrows from his heart. As he plucked, he strode about the room. For about five seconds too long his audience sat bemused or hypnotized by the performance, and too late saw the door closing behind him, and heard the words, 'arrow in my heart, my dear fellows' floating down the corridor outside, as Lewis hastened towards the exit and to the taxi which would hurry him to the Southampton boat train, still uncommitted to answering even urgent cables signed by the editor.

Relieved by his explanation of the business of *The Times* office in Washington, I asked him why he had refused the Foreign Editorship of *The Times*, which I knew had been offered him during his most recent visit to London.

'I am too scabrous an individual,' he said, 'to survive for long the rarefied air of Printing House Square. I did, however, offer to become their *London* Correspondent – reporting, you know, on the motives and personalities of political activity in England with the same interest and detachment that one seeks to display here. Would it not, I suggested, be an excellent idea for *The Times* to be as informative, and when necessary as candid, about people and events in Westminster, Whitehall and the City as it is about goings on in Washington or Paris? They didn't,' he said, looking happily out at Washington, his expression more Machiavellian than usual, 'seem awfully keen on the idea. I wonder why not?'

The roar of the Press Club dining-room engulfed me. Lewis, listening to a fierce political discussion, seemed a little tired. He said he kept remembering the dream a French poet friend of his had once had, in which he saw the whole world covered by an inundation. Only the tops of the highest spires and steeples peeped above the flood, and the only survivors were some parrots which perched on these and, taught by man, kept screeching out 'Justice, Progress, Freedom!'

Somebody said, 'Bill, you're a nasty old cynic.'

Wilmott Lewis looked at him shortly. 'Cynic? Not at all, old boy. If humanity leaves such memories to the birds, it will have been a considerable achievement, something of which we may all be proud.'

During the first two and a half years of that decade, when I was in Washington, sometimes for months at a time, sometimes only for a few weeks or even hours, things to take pride in seemed to be what we were rather short of. First we had a crisis which no one would admit officially existed, so that – somewhat like the prostitutes at Aldershot who became diseased because the army did not dare officially to admit the existence of syphilis – unemployed men in Chicago had to fight one another for first grab at the garbage can put out at the back doors of the great hotels because a full and proper system of unemployment relief would have been 'socialistic', and above all would have been an admission of the existence of a crisis of scarcely believable proportions.

Later the crisis was admitted all right, and what we had then was something very like chaos. It was one of those situations in which deterioration and collapse are so rapid that even quite sensible policies always seem to be put into operation too late. There were flashes of hope and optimism which as they flickered out only emphasized the surrounding gloom. It seems odd, almost ludicrous, perhaps, by hindsight, that the so-called Hoover moratorium – the suspension of payment on all international government debts – should have appeared to enormous numbers of people as equivalent to an announcement that salvation after all is just around the corner, that God, after some agonizing stumbles, is once again marching on. Yet it was so. The atmosphere of those sweat-soaked summer days when the moratorium was announced throbbed anew with the electric impulses of American evangelism, of that enthusiasm for the crusade which in America can be touched off so easily because the American heart feels so deeply the need of it.

Austria was going to be saved from financial collapse and Germany from Communist revolution and Hitler. All Europe was to be saved from financial collapse, or from the preventive war which it was then commonly supposed in Washington the French were about to undertake. For a few days Washington felt itself the headquarters of salvation. The New World was going into action to put the Old World on its feet. America was going once again to assume its natural leadership as the champion of peace, unity and common sense – its policies could be seen by all to be far-sighted, generous and altruistic. And since Heaven must surely be on the side of the good, and the good need to eat, Heaven would certainly see to it that the idealism of the good paid off pretty damn quickly, rewarding America by ending its depression, restoring its prosperity and getting things back to normal before the hire-purchase men finally came to repossess the car.

I saw President Hoover several times at that period, and if ever a man was transfigured with pleasure and a sense both of rightness and righteousness, it was he. Secretaries used to run in and out of his office with the latest quotations from stock markets all over the world – Berlin, New York, Chicago, London, New Orleans, Tokyo and Sydney. For long years Mr Hoover had accepted the view that the way things look on the ticker is as important as the way things really are, or, rather, is the same as the way they really are. Now everything was going up. The depression was over. If it was not over, why was everything going up? I noted at the time that 'it was just the sort of public mood that the President liked best: *carte blanche* and no maddening interruptions from the blundering crowd. He is the Great Executive again, the Great Engineer of modern society, and he has pulled the right lever at last.'

The shock was naturally all the more severe when it became evident that the declaration of American policy had solved almost nothing, and the optimism and enthusiasm petered out in a long and violent wrangle over the exact terms of the moratorium between Washington and Paris. When 'agreement in principle' was finally reached, M. Paul Claudel invited a number of American officials and others to the French Embassy to celebrate the event. Worn out with quarrelling and heat, the guests looked forward to the ceremony with gloom. There would be rhetoric and platitudes, speeches dripping with false optimism like the leading articles in the newspapers.

In the drawing-room at the Embassy M. Claudel greeted them.

'Gentlemen,' he said simply, 'in the little moment that remains to us between the crisis and the catastrophe, we may as well take a glass of champagne.'

II

MR CAPONE, PHILOSOPHER

In Chicago the Director of the Illinois Central Bank, to whom I had been putting solemn questions on the subject of car loadings, commodity prices and the like, said moodily, 'Hell, boy, the capitalist system's on the skids anyway, let's go and get a drink.' I was glad of this attitude on his part because I had not really come to Chicago to discuss commodity prices in the Middle West, but to report the background to a murder. A couple of days before, we in New York had read the news of the killing in broad daylight of Jake Lingle, then crime reporter of the *Chicago Tribune* and – as emerged later – an important liaison officer between the Capone gang and the police department. It was one of the most spectacular and, for many reasons, looked like being one of the most revealing Chicago killings of the period when Al Capone was at approximately the height of his power. From a friend in New York who knew Chicago I learned enough of the background of the crime to make me very eager to go to Chicago myself. Hinrichs, who thought it would be a splendid story, was nevertheless hesitant. He explained to me that whenever *The Times* published a crime story from the United States somebody from the American Embassy or the English-Speaking Union or some other agency for promoting Anglo-American relations would ring up or would attack the editor at dinner, saying how much he had always previously admired *The Times*'s treatment of American affairs, and could there not be at least one British newspaper which did not represent the United States as a land dominated by gunmen and hoodlums? Hinrichs thought we had better cable London asking whether they wished me to go to Chicago.

As an assignment to report a murder the reply from *The Times* was probably a classic. 'By all means,' it said, 'Cockburn Chicagowards. Welcome stories ex-Chicago not unduly emphasizing crime.'

By the time I was in the air over Cleveland the difficulty of carrying out this directive successfully had notably increased. Ex-Ambassador Charlie Gates Dawes had impetuously been 'drafted' or had drafted himself to act as 'strong man' of the situation, to put himself, it was stated, at the head of 'the better element' and to 'clean up' Chicago. Before I touched down at Chicago Airport he had arrested nearly six hundred people and a number of others had been wounded in indiscriminate gunplay. I drove to the Criminal Courts Building and sought the advice of the dean of Chicago crime reporters, the original, I believe, of one of the central characters in Ben Hecht's play *The Front Page*. I showed him my cable. His deep laughter shook the desk. What, he asked, did I want to do? I said I supposed the first thing to do was to interview Mr Capone. He suggested that I listen in on an extension while he telephoned Mr Capone at the Lexington Hotel where he then had his offices. Presently I heard Capone's voice on the wire asking what went on. The crime reporter explained that there was a Limey from the London *Times* who wanted to talk with him. They fixed up an appointment for the following afternoon and just before he rang off the crime reporter said, 'Listen, Al, there's just one thing. You know this bird's assignment says he's to cover all this "not unduly emphasizing crime".' Bewilderment exploded at the other end of the line. 'Not what?' Capone said. 'You heard me,' said the crime reporter. 'Not unduly emphasizing crime.'

The Lexington Hotel had once, I think, been a rather grand family hotel, but now its large and gloomy lobby was deserted except for a couple of bulging Sicilians and a reception clerk who looked at one across the counter with the expression of a speakeasy proprietor looking through the grille at a potential detective. He checked on my appointment with some superior upstairs, and as I stepped into the elevator I felt my hips and sides being gently frisked by the tapping hands of one of the lounging Sicilians. There were a couple of ante-rooms to be passed before you got to Capone's office and in the first of them I had to wait for a quarter of an hour or so, drinking whisky poured by a man who used his left hand for the bottle and kept the other in his pocket.

Except that there was a sub-machine gun, operated by a man called MacGurn – whom I later got to know and somewhat esteem – poking through the transom of a door behind the big desk, Capone's own room was nearly indistinguishable from that of, say, a 'newly arrived' Texan oil millionaire. Apart from the jowly young murderer on the far side of the desk, what took the eye were a number of large, flattish, solid silver bowls upon the desk, each filled with roses. They were nice to look at, and they had another purpose too, for Capone when agitated stood up and dipped the tips of his fingers in the water in which floated the roses.

I had been a little embarrassed as to how the interview was to be launched. Naturally the nub of all such interviews is somehow to get around to the question 'What makes you tick?' but in the case of this millionaire killer the approach to this central question seemed mined with dangerous impediments. However, on the way down to the Lexington Hotel I had had the good fortune to see, in I think the *Chicago Daily News*, some statistics offered by an insurance company which dealt with the average expectation of life of gangsters in Chicago. I forget exactly what the average expectation was, and also what the exact age of Capone at that time – I think he was in his early thirties. The point was, however, that in any case he was four years older than the upper limit considered by the insurance company to be the proper average expectation of life for a Chicago gangster. This seemed to offer a more or less neutral and academic line of approach, and after the ordinary greetings I asked Capone whether he had read this piece of statistics in the paper. He said that he had. I asked him whether he considered the estimate reasonably accurate. He said that he thought that the insurance companies and the newspaper boys probably knew their stuff. 'In that case,' I asked him, 'how does it feel to be, say, four years over the age?'

He took the question quite seriously and spoke of the matter with neither more nor less excitement or agitation than a man would who, let us say, had been asked whether he, as the rear machine-gunner of a bomber, was aware of the average incidence of casualties in that occupation. He apparently assumed that sooner or later he would be shot despite the elaborate precautions which he regularly took. The idea that – as afterwards turned out to be the case – he would be arrested by the Federal authorities for income-tax evasion had not, I think, at that time so much as crossed his mind. And, after all, he said with a little bit of corn-and-ham somewhere at the back of his throat, supposing he had not gone into this racket? What would he have been doing? He would, he said, 'have been selling newspapers barefoot on the street in Brooklyn'.

He stood up as he spoke, cooling his finger-tips in the rose bowl in front of him. He sat down again, brooding and sighing. Despite the ham-and-corn, what he said was quite probably true and I said so, sympathetically. A little bit too sympathetically, as immediately emerged, for as I spoke I saw him looking at me suspiciously, not to say censoriously. My remarks about the harsh way the world treats barefoot boys in Brooklyn were interrupted by an urgent angry waggle of his podgy hand.

'Listen,' he said, 'don't get the idea I'm one of these goddam radicals. Don't get the idea I'm knocking the American system. The American system. . . .' As though an invisible chairman had called upon him for a few words, he broke into an oration upon the theme. He praised freedom, enterprise and the pioneers. He spoke of 'our heritage'. He referred with contemptuous disgust to Socialism and Anarchism. 'My rackets,' he repeated several times, 'are run on strictly American lines and they're going to stay that way.' This turned out to be a reference to the fact that he had recently been elected the President of the Unione Siciliano, a slightly mysterious, partially criminal society which certainly had its roots in the Mafia. Its power and importance varied sharply from year to year. Sometimes there did seem to be evidence that it was a secret society of real power, and at other times it seemed more in the nature of a mutual benefit association not essentially much more menacing than, say, the Elks. Capone's complaint just now was that the Unione was what he called 'lousy with black-hand stuff'. 'Can you imagine,' he said, 'people going in for what they call these blood feuds – some guy's grandfather was killed by some other guy's grandfather, and this guy thinks that's good enough reason to kill the other.' It was, he said, entirely unbusinesslike. His vision of the American system began to excite him profoundly and now he was on his feet again, leaning across the desk like the chairman of a board meeting, his fingers plunged in the rose bowls.

'This American system of ours,' he shouted, 'call it Americanism, call it Capitalism, call it what you like, gives to each and every one of us a great opportunity if we only seize it with both hands and make the most of it.' He held out his hand towards me, the fingers dripping a little, and stared at me sternly for a few seconds before reseating himself.

A month later in New York I was telling this story to Mr John Walter, minority owner of *The Times*. He asked me why I had not written the Capone interview for the paper. I explained that when I had come to put my notes together I saw that most of what Capone had said was in essence identical with what was being said in the leading articles of *The Times* itself, and I doubted whether the paper would be best pleased to find itself seeing eye to eye with the most notorious gangster in Chicago. Mr Walter, after a moment's wry reflection, admitted that probably my idea had been correct.

Even so, when I did start writing my thesis from Chicago – not unduly emphasizing crime – I became aware, really for the first time, that about fifty per cent of what seemed to me to be the truth about the situation in Chicago would certainly be unpalatable and perhaps in parts unintelligible to *The Times*. I struggled with the article, produced a couple of readable pieces, and *The Times* wired me quite a large and much-needed bonus on the strength of it.

As for Capone, one could say of course that he was politically a buffoon, and the fact that his views coincided with those of the leader writers on the paper was a clownish and insignificant accident. But I knew then, and I felt more deeply still in the time that followed, that the incident had only expressed in terms of farce a genuine situation and a genuine problem. *The Times* of the early 1930s was of course a great deal farther to the Right than it is today. It is hard to recall so many years later the tenacity with which people hung on to notions and principles which their successors might still consider theoretically desirable but have come to recognize as untenable for any practical purpose. I remember the disconcerting feeling that myself and nearly every serious person that I met in the United States were growing up under the tremendous pressure of the great crisis much faster than the people in Printing House Square. It is true that in many respects *The Times* was a good deal more open-minded, or at least more prepared to consider possible novelties in the situation, than many of the other London newspapers. I can recall very few occasions indeed when it would have been possible to have accused *The Times* of deliberate distortion, suppression or invention of 'favourable' news by means of pressure upon the correspondent.

Once in New York when I was covering for a colleague on another paper who had gone off on a more or less illicit holiday, I was astonished to receive a cable from London in the following terms: 'Good woman story today.' (This in the jargon of the Foreign Editor meant alternatively a story about women likely to interest men, or a story about women for women.) 'Send sensational story today illustrating futility Hoover's efforts arrest market decline emphasizing possibility bottom imminently outcrash.'

When the colleague returned he was quite annoyed to find that I had failed to respond to this directive. I asked him why I should help to make money for somebody in London who was evidently short of the market in a big way, and trying to use the paper to accelerate the decline in stocks. Somebody responds to a request like that and what happens? The dispatch under the date-line New York appears on the front page of the paper in London, and somewhere in the financial columns, or perhaps even in a leading article, there is a reference to it. 'Our New York correspondent in his exclusive and significant story today,' etc., etc. And that section of the public which pays attention to such things starts to unload.

'What beats me,' I said, 'is why they bother to have an office in New York and a correspondent, and pay the rent and your salary, when they could just as easily write the whole stuff in London and simply put "from our New York correspondent" on top of it.'

My colleague, a thoughtful man who understood the form better than I did, said, 'They would never do that. They wouldn't think it at all honest.'

The Times never did anything like that, and to tell the truth I should not have been shocked or startled if they had. It seemed to me that a newspaper is always a weapon in somebody's hands, and I never could see why it should be shocking that the weapon should be used in what its owner conceived to be his best interest. The hired journalist, I thought, ought to realize that he is partly in the entertainment business and partly in the advertising business – advertising either goods, or a cause, or a government. He just has to make up his mind whom he wants to entertain, and what he wants to advertise. The humbug and hypocrisy of the Press begin only when newspapers pretend to be 'impartial' or 'servants of the public'. And this only becomes dangerous as well as laughable when the public is fool enough to believe it.

Such 'pressure' and 'guidance' as *The Times* did attempt to exercise were usually of a subtle and more amusing sort and caused me neither trouble nor vexation. The pressure of events in the United States – where the prophecies of the Marxist classics were being fulfilled with the punctuality of minute guns – was of a different kind. (When I speak of 'prophecies' I am not of course referring to the quick-firers of contemporary day-to-day controversy who necessarily and for obvious morale-building purposes prophesied that the current crisis in America was the final crisis of American capitalism, and that a revolution might confidently be expected in a year or two. I knew the United States fairly well by that time and I agreed with Mr Capone that the American system would get by for a lot longer than that.)

But the American 'way of life' of the past decade was changing before one's eyes, and the exhilarating sense of change, of history on the march, of new possibilities opening, was all-pervading. There was nowhere you could go in the United States and feel that things were as they had been or as they would be again.

I was privileged to view what I suppose might be called 'the dawn of social consciousness' in the mind of a Middle Western millionaire who had the reputation of being what was then called an 'economic royalist', a political troglodyte, a foe to progress. He was known to his friends as 'Mr Pop', on account of the way in which he had made his first pile of money. At that time – at the time, I mean, when Mr Pop was a fairly young man – big developments were taking place in the popcorn-vending industry. There was a continuous effort by inventors and manufacturers to modernize and streamline the machines in which popcorn was visibly popped and sold to the onlookers. As he went about the streets and occasionally stood watching corn being popped in one of these machines, Mr Pop was aware of a sense of disappointment. Ruminating, he at last got his finger on the cause of it – these machines were not like the machines used to be when he was a boy. There were not so many wheels, not so many lathes, not so much to watch. Being evidently a man of humble mind, Mr Pop decided that, if he felt this disappointment, millions of other people must be feeling it too. Acting on this assumption, he went around buying up the patents on the old types of machine -- the patents could of course now be had for a song, since the machines, totally unfunctional, were supposed to be obsolete. Mr Pop manufactured these machines by the thousand and put them on the streets, and pretty soon the news came in from the street vendors that the public was flocking to them, happy indeed to watch all those nostalgically whirring wheels and writhing lathes and to buy their corn from the vintage models rather than from the modern types. With the packet of money he made out of that Mr Pop went on and made a lot more, and now he had a big house in Southern Indiana with a stream and a road bridge, with towers, which was a model of something he had seen on his travels about the world, I think in Southern Germany.

As a result of some muddle in the instructions given to the architect, the house had, as a matter of fact, got built the wrong way round, with its back to the stream. This was unfortunate, but Mr Pop reasoned that it was no ground for piling one misfortune on another, and losing his bridge. In consequence, when one approached the house, one did so by a mile or so of perfectly flat driveway which suddenly humped itself up between the towers of the bridge, and from the top of the bridge you looked down and saw the green grass growing beneath you. Inside, the house was full of 'finds' of archaeological and artistic interest made by Mr Pop on his world travels. Beside each of them was fixed an elaborate bronze plaque describing the nature of the object, its age, and so on. One of them was a tile from the Summer Palace at Peking, which was described on the plaque as being three thousand years old. Rather oddly, when I visited Mr Pop he explained emphatically to myself and the other guests that there was no doubt whatever that this tile was a fake – manufactured probably strictly for the tourist trade.

The guests on this occasion were for the most part politicians – there was a Republican senator from Washington and a couple of Republican congressmen, the Republican governor of Indiana or his deputy – I forget which – and two or three members of the Indiana legislature. At dinner the talk naturally enough was all of the crisis, of unemployment, of threatened hunger marches, of the bread lines, and of the need for the organization and extension of relief measures. It was the kind of talk which Mr Pop hitherto had supposed was only to be heard among anarchists, socialists, and the long-haired agitators of one kind and another. Coming from leaders and fellow-members of the Republican Party it hit Mr Pop like a blow on the head. After dinner he was sitting with me a little apart from the others, and he presently began to move about uneasily and peer at me with the air of a man preparing to propound a question of supreme importance. At last, peering into his glass, he said: 'Mr Cockburn, may I ask you something?'

I bowed.

'Would you,' said Mr Pop, 'see anything wrong in being the fourth richest man in Indiana?'

I made some incoherent reply.

'Well that,' said Mr Pop, 'is what I am. I am the fourth richest man in Indiana.'

I had sympathized with Capone in his human and social predicament, although I had not found him a particularly likeable man. And I sympathized now with Mr Pop, whom I had grown to like, at the moment of his confrontation with the possibility that there might be some snag, something historically or morally not absolutely nice, about being the fourth richest man in Indiana in the year 1931. I sympathized with *The Times*, too, but it did not make the situation any easier or solve any problem.

In a sense *The Times* entered into the matter only incidentally – in a sense, I mean, that we were all engaged in the newspaper business. Had *The Times* been a firm of automobile exporters, and I their salesman, the problem would not have arisen in the same form. An automobile salesman can go about – mentally speaking – in disguise, and I believe many of them do. He can believe passionately that the earth is flat without causing a drop in sales. He can even secretly hold, and secretly propagate, some unpopular political or religious opinion without going to pieces and without – if he is careful – being caught at it. For the journalist things are more difficult.

Essentially, the late Lord Northcliffe was right when he said to some intellectual who thought himself so very smart that he could 'write popular' and get away with it, 'You can never successfully seek to put upon the table of Demos what you would not put on your own table.'

A lot of people, perhaps influenced directly or indirectly by the late C. E. Montague's book *A Hind Let Loose*, where the same man writes the leading articles for two newspapers of fiercely opposed opinion, believe that newspaper offices are full of successful journalists who write with their tongue in their cheek. When such people get journalists alone, they say, 'I know that's what you wrote, but what do you really think?'

It is of course possible to write for two newspapers of opposed opinions at the same time, I have even done so myself, but for the writer – and I am talking here of the journalist who is really a writer, and not a failed politician, diplomat or lawyer, or defrocked clergyman – it is a dangerous business. It turns him from a creative writer into a lawyer. Lawyers can be creative writers too, but there is no identity between the two sides of their activity. Or else this kind of double game – the kind described in *A Hind Let Loose* – is only an expression of the writer's probably genuine scorn and derision for both his clients and for all their readers too. And that also is a risky attitude.

Naturally the aeroplanes and sleeping-cars are filled with people who have 'journalist' written on their passport, but are really only secretly prospecting for uranium, or going to assassinate the Chief of Police, or filling in time until they can meet such interesting people as will marry them and let them settle down. But these are not writers either.

Evidently there are plenty of people in journalism who have neither got what they liked nor quite grown to like what they get. They write pieces they do not much enjoy writing, for papers they totally despise, and the sad process ends by ruining their style and disintegrating their personality, two developments which in a writer cannot be separated, since his personality and style must progress or deteriorate together, like a married couple in a country where death is the only permissible divorce. It is a fate which through incompetence or economic necessity may overtake anyone, but one does not wish to start out by accepting it as one's own.

Although by the beginning of 1932 I was secretly bootlegging quite a number of pieces of news and articles to various extreme Left American newspapers and news services, I was conscious that my style – in the narrow and in the wider sense of the word – was deteriorating.

I decided to make a change. The relief of having taken this decision was such that I probably should have dithered about for months without actually doing anything had not my elbow been jogged by an external event.

What had happened was that Wilmott Lewis, whose doctors had at last succeeded in causing him some mild anxiety about the state of his heart muscle, was beginning to entertain the idea of a partial retirement. He had suggested to *The Times*, and *The Times*, he told me, had agreed *en principe*, that I should be transferred from New York to Washington and there take over the ordinary or day-by-day and week-by-week operation of the Washington bureau. He would retreat to a beautiful winter residence he had his eye on in Georgetown, and in the summer he would live on the Blue Ridge Mountains. He would be 'available for consultation', and occasionally, perhaps once a month, write an article for the paper. He would also read all the books he had never had time to read, and write, he surmised, at least one of the books he had never had time to write. It was a wonderful prospect and his eyes shone with enthusiasm as he first unfolded it to me. Particularly characteristic of Wilmott Lewis and particularly moving was the fact that a great part of his pleasure in this plan was that, as he saw it, the scheme would be as splendid a thing for me as it would be for him. His excitement and his solicitude for my career were so touching that for a moment I felt that it might even be humanly better to abandon my own plans and fall in with his. However, short of that, there was not a moment to be lost in disillusioning him.

He sat for a few seconds in an aghast silence, watching the house in Georgetown, the summer place on the Blue Ridge and all the books fade into thin air. I asked desperately whether somebody else could not take over the role proposed by himself and *The Times* for me. He said it was quite impossible, and I knew that this was in fact the case. Within a minute or two he had entirely recovered himself and with his native and extraordinary delicacy was consoling me as though it were I whose plans had been upset and not himself. He guessed, of course, that I felt a certain sense of guilt *vis-à-vis* himself, as though I had betrayed the years during which he had taught me so much of what I knew about the United States.

'My dear boy,' he said, 'any small debt you may have owed me has been long ago repaid over and over again. And if you insist on regarding yourself as my pupil, reflect how far more agreeable it must be for me to have produced one who now moves freely under his own steam rather than being stuck, my dear boy,' he made the last words sound like death, 'in the mud.'

After an equally melancholy explanation to Hinrichs, who tried to take the sadness out of our parting by remarking that for several months he had expected that something of the kind must happen, I wrote to *The Times* announcing my decision. To my vexation they treated my big gesture simply as a sign of a slight over-strain, and wrote back suggesting that I take a couple of months' paid holiday in Mexico. I had to write again in more vigorous terms, explaining, by way of putting an end to any discussion, that my motives were largely political. I was horribly disconcerted to find that *The Times* did not take this very seriously either. Mr Dawson wrote me a letter in which he said that it was foolish in his opinion to give up working for *The Times* simply on account of one's political views. *The Times*, he said, was a vehicle which could be used by people of the most varied opinions. 'For myself,' he concluded, 'I have always regarded *The Times* as something of an organ of the

Left.' There followed in brackets a classic qualification. 'Though never,' wrote Mr Dawson, 'I hope of the extreme Left.'

I had to abandon my naïve belief that however difficult anything else may be, the one thing that is easy, and makes everyone happy, is that you resign. Resigning was proving a lot more difficult than I had expected. A short while after the exchange of letters Mr Dawson, Mr Deakin, the Foreign and Imperial News Editor, and one or two other of the High Priests who had been to Ottawa for the Conference, came down to New York and took it in turns to explain to me the folly of my attitude. One view was that the thing to do was settle the whole business quickly on a cash basis, and there was talking of something in the way of a bonus, plus an early rise in salary. I was humiliated to find that my important decision had been interpreted in these quarters as an act of vulgar blackmail. Others, probably reflecting that they had to do with a wild-eyed intellectual, thought that a more spiritual approach would be the right ticket. They spoke of the good which a first-rate correspondent of *The Times* could do to mankind. When these and other suggestions, which had been made separately, had all failed, we gathered one morning in *The Times* office in New York and were joined by Wilmott Lewis, who admitted to me privately that he had not been able to resist coming up for the final scene. Sitting at what until now had been my desk, Dawson swung his tortoiseshell spectacles lugubriously and remarked, looking at me with a puzzled frown, 'It does seem rather bad luck that you of all people should "go red on us".' His voice put audible inverted commas around the phrase 'go red on us'. At this point Wilmott Lewis, his sense of the theatre overcoming any discretion he may have had, moved to the centre of the stage, or rather of the office, and with a gesture which in some indefinable way suggested that he was flaunting the black cloak of a magician, gazed down upon Dawson and raised his hand in a familiar gesture.

'You speak, my dear Dawson,' he said, 'of luck. Speak rather of history. Throw your mind forward along the path of history. Envisage, my dear Deakin, with the eye of imagination the not too distant future. The time will come, my dear fellows, when you will hire as correspondents elderly men who will be conservatives. But many of them, mark you, may well be suffering from heart attacks when the great story breaks. Or, my dear fellows, you may hire young men who will also be conservative but, note this! many of them may well be too stupid even to know when the great story is breaking. Or you may hire men who are both young and intelligent, and quite a lot of *them*, my dear fellows,' his voice dropped to a menacing whisper, 'will be Reds.'

Dawson, who had put on his spectacles to watch the performance, now peered up at Lewis over the top of them. He gave a small acid-sounding laugh.

'I'm afraid,' he said, 'you have been talking too much to your *ex*-assistant.'

Then I knew that I had resigned at last.

12

DAY OF THE WEEK

MY intention had been to walk out of *The Times* office on to a boat, tour Europe, and then see what was best to be done. There was a hitch at the very outset. I had supposed – reasonably enough considering the amount of money I had been making during the past two and a half years – that I must surely have enough money in the bank to finance me for at least the next three or four months. This was a miscalculation, for there was an amount in the bank of only about a hundred dollars.

Fortunately there happened to be at this time a boom in books about the 'inside' of Washington politics, and a leading American publisher offered me an advance of five or six hundred pounds, plus expenses, to write anonymously such a book on condition that the manuscript was completed and delivered within six weeks. I had to go down to Washington in the heat of one of Washington's hottest known summers to do it, but at the end of six weeks it was ready and I could collect the money and sail for Europe, and return to Berlin.

To come to Berlin just then, after New York, was to be whisked down suddenly from the gallery of a badly lit theatre and pushed against the flaring footlights to see that what you thought you saw from back there is really going on. The act is coming to its horrible climax, and furthermore the man who is playing the part of the murderer really is a murderer. His knife is not a familiar stage property but a real one and he is going to kill people with it.

Already the Storm Troopers were slashing and smashing up and down the Kurfuerstendamm, and there were beatings and unequal battles in the city streets. The toads beside the Charlottenburger Chaussee looked more menacing than ever. The newspapers and the 'thoughtful observers' and the pro and con men went humbugging along, but no one with any feeling for the situation believed them. I several times met Herr Willi Muenzenberg, who was popularly believed to be the real brains and driving force of the German Communist Party, and once I had the opportunity for a short private conversation with General Schleicher, then Chancellor. Each spoke in terms of reasoned optimism, and each gave the impression that he did not give a damn whether you believed a word he said because he did not believe it himself. (Schleicher was murdered sooner than Muenzenberg, who survived until the early 1940s, when he was strangled – on suspicions of being a secret Nazi agent – in the forest of Fontainebleau.) A situation in which even the professional humbugs cannot keep a straight face is always somewhat exhilarating, but, as one always finds in those situations, the naked truth can be a chilly, knobbly kind of companion too. Also, just as in New York and Chicago, it had gradually begun to seem absurd that one should spend one's time going about writing articles for *The Times*, so now in Berlin it rapidly began to seem even more absurd to sit observing events and trends, writing an occasional short story or articles for Leftist American newspapers, and news agencies. If one were not going to disintegrate under the pressure of events, the thing to do seemed to be to organize oneself into something coherent and effective.

Once again I might have dithered about for weeks or even months had not something jogged my elbow. This time it was Hitler. He came to power. I was high on the Nazi black list. I fled to Vienna.

There I sat down to consider seriously a notion which had been buzzing in my mind for some time. It had started buzzing when I worked – off the record – with a publicity expert in Washington who was conducting a one-man battle against what was known as the Radio Trust. I had noted at the time, and the note appears in the book which I wrote just before leaving Washington, that 'among the technical devices which as everyone knows are revolutionizing the workings of modern government, the humble mimeograph machine is seldom mentioned. Less spectacular than the other wonders of the age, as for instance the mass-production newspaper, the telephone, the radio and the talking picture, it exercises, in its cheap and incessant activity, an influence scarcely less than theirs, and seems to have reached the peak of its activity in Washington, D.C., at the present period. Washington is in many respects the ideal field for a mimeograph machine to work in. For this little device requires for its most effective functioning the smallest possible geographical area, containing the largest number of persons who are influential, either because of the position they hold, or the money they have, or because like newspapermen they are sitting at the feeding end of a pipe-line with millions of people at the other end of it. . . . It is commonly agreed that the Press, the radio and the moving picture are the most powerful forces in existence for moulding public opinion. To control any or all of them, or even to get the opportunity to use them as a medium, requires a great deal of money. The people who have enough money to control them are therefore sitting pretty in the democracy, but not nearly so pretty as they would be sitting were it not for the mimeograph machine. Naturally they have mimeographs too, but here for the first time their competitors find themselves on an equal footing. The police force can supply itself from larger sources with tanks and armoured cars and laboratories for the manufacture of tear gas. It is only in the possession of the automatic pistol that the enemy of the police finds himself on a level with his opponents. A mimeograph machine is one of the few remaining weapons which still gives small and comparatively poor organizations a sporting chance in a scrap with large and wealthy ones.'

The general idea which I had had then was revived in my

mind later in Berlin by, of all people, General Schleicher, who ran, in his own interests, a weekly mimeographed sheet of information and comment which circulated by mail and was not sold on bookstalls. The total circulation was very small, and of course it did not do General Schleicher very much good in the end, but from my viewpoint the important thing about it was that it exercised an influence out of all proportion to its circulation. That is to say, in terms of influence, one reader of Schleicher's sheet was, on an average, worth about five thousand readers of one of the daily newspapers. (It was, for example, 'must reading' for all foreign newspaper correspondents in Berlin, and for all the embassies and legations.)

This phenomenon had reminded me of another aspect of the situation which I had often discussed with Wilmott Lewis in Washington. The discussion had arisen over the late Hamilton Fyfe's *Life of Northcliffe*, in which he makes this central point:

When Northcliffe started the *Daily Mail* in the nineties, Fyfe suggests, he was not 'playing a hunch' but tapping a mathematical certainty. He argued: The Education Acts of the 1860s have changed the entire character and extent of the literate public. But in the years since the 1860s the newspapers have not changed at all. Therefore there must exist somewhere a new pool of potential readers not taken care of by the existing newspapers. And this pool, if correctly tapped, could provide a new multi-million readership.

There was not much doubt in my mind as to the sort of people who would constitute the 'pool'. Anyone in, for instance, London or New York or Berlin or Vienna who frequented any kind of club or other meeting-place where, say, diplomats, lawyers, bankers and newspapermen gathered together and talked, must have been deeply aware of the strange contrast between the colourful information and significant rumours – for rumours can often be as significant as facts – circulating in the clubs, and the awfully tight-lipped drabness of the newspapers being sold on the club doorstep.

I got most of the English daily newspapers in Vienna and was struck once again by the fact that what informed people were really saying – and equally importantly, the tone of voice they were saying it in – were scarcely reflected at all in the newspapers, and that these people themselves were more or less acutely aware of this lack in the newspapers.

A further conclusion followed. It was that such 'pools' could only be effectively tapped by a paper run 'on a shoestring'.

The moment any kind of big financial commitment came in question – even the investment that would be needed to launch a printed weekly paper – it would begin to be necessary to 'broaden the base', 'extend the appeal', in fact lower the Highest Common Factor. The advertisers alone would see to that.

What all this added up to was that I had better go to London and start a weekly paper of a new type. For the third time, extraneous circumstances precipitated a decision. I discovered with dismay that the money I had had from the American publisher was almost gone. It was evident that, if I waited any longer, I should scarcely have the fare from Vienna to London, let alone enough to support me during the two or three weeks which I felt sure would be needed for the organization of the paper.

It took in point of fact nearly six weeks, the result, I suppose, chiefly of the fact that since out of the past six years I had spent only a little over two months in England, and that had been three and a half years ago, I knew almost nobody, and I had forgotten how important people think it in England to know not only where you are going but where you have come from. Also when the news of where I had come from did get bruited it was not always an advantage – learning of my resignation from *The Times*, people on the Right thought that I must be a Red and shied off, and the Reds, since I was not a member of any known Left organization, were if possible more suspicious still.

The atmosphere was both depressing and exhilarating. Even the most detached citizen must find it occasionally depressing to find his country so reduced in circumstances that it had to have such a man as the late Ramsay MacDonald for its Prime Minister. It was, on the other hand, exhilarating because the smug smog in which the Press of that time enveloped the political realities of the moment was even thicker than I had anticipated, and thus offered even better conditions for the conduct of my experiment. The one or two old friends I had, and the people I presently got to know, were for the most part sympathetic but discouraging. And many of my few acquaintances who expressed a flattering and uplifting interest in the idea turned out to be firm believers in the axiom that one should never put off till tomorrow what one might possibly be able to do the month after next.

It is hard to imagine what justification the English suppose themselves to have when they sneer gently at the Spaniards for their alleged *mañana, mañana*. Probably the fact is that everyone is much lazier than he likes to admit, and, when he finds himself procrastinating wildly, comforts himself with the thought that someone across the seas is lazier still. I remember remarking bitterly at the time that if I wrote a book about England I should call it *What About Wednesday Week?* which is what English people say when they are making what they believe to be an urgent appointment.

I was constantly frustrated too by the habit people have got into of considering that nothing important can be done without going through the ritual of 'a conference' and for two pins they will set up a committee. In my experience all but the very rarest kind of committee meeting can be placed in one of two categories. There is the committee meeting at which everything has been decided in advance so that the whole meeting is unnecessary anyway, and the meeting at which nothing has been decided in advance, nothing is decided at the committee meeting, and when everyone is leaving the building two men get together in the corner of the lift and fix up what is to be done next. Several times during that six weeks I had to tuck my idea under my arm and run with it to prevent it being suffocated by some well-intentioned conference or by a committee.

Frustrating and even alarming though all this was, it was at the same time amusing, helped me to extend my 'contacts' and to pick up a smattering of information about the state of affairs in Britain. But after the first three weeks or so I realized clearly enough that until I actually produced my paper 'of a new type' I should never be able to explain to anyone what it was I had in mind – and I realized too that a lot of them would not like it if I did.

Everyone had been well-meaningly discouraging about the money. Some said that even the smallest weekly paper could not possibly cost less than £5,000; others said £10,000. It was agreed that such a sum could probably be raised, but I understood now that to raise it would involve introducing the very frets I was seeking to avoid. There would be advertisers and shareholders and even, it was hinted on several sides, some kind of editorial board, and what we should end up with would be just another weekly newspaper.

In any case I had not left *The Times* for the purpose of saddling myself with another editorial board and some more shareholders and advertisers. After thirty days of patient investigating I had grasped more firmly than ever the truth that what one must do was to ensure that this paper was all of a piece and all under one control. That it should express one viewpoint and one viewpoint only – my own. In other words, size must be sacrificed to coherence and to unity of style. Thus after four weeks of bumbling more or less agreeably about London I came to the conclusion that the thing to do was to cut the cackle and start the paper regardless of what anybody might say, warn or advise.

I went out to Berkshire and found an old Oxford friend – a novelist who had for some time been vegetating unwholesomely in that section of the home counties. By this time I personally had only five pounds left, and I had reckoned that we would need at least forty pounds to start the paper. I suggested to him that it would be good for both of us if he lent me forty pounds for the paper, in exchange for which he would have a job on it as a kind of manager. This was not merely an inducement to him to part with his forty pounds, but was based on a genuine feeling that it would do him good to come back into circulation in London, and also on the knowledge I had of his habits – he was an extraordinarily neat man and I thought that some neatness in our office would be desirable. He agreed.

Fortunately he had been quite out of touch with the sort of people I had been talking to in London, so that to him it seemed no more improbable than it did to me that one could start a weekly newspaper of importance for forty pounds. He agreed to return to London with me that evening and start to get things going. On the return journey I explained to him all over again my precise purpose.

G. K. Chesterton, I reminded him, had written of editors that they lived in the shadow of three fears – fear of misprints, fear of libel actions and fear of the sack. We would aim, I said, to disregard all considerations of that kind, more particularly the second, because what we had in mind was a revival of the uninhibited eighteenth-century English tradition of the News-letter. It was going to give the customers the sorts of facts – political, diplomatic, financial – which were freely discussed in embassies and clubs but considered to be too adult to be left about for newspaper readers to get at them.

In our Newsletter anything interesting could get a U certificate. The slogan was, '*Mais si, devant les enfants!*'

I pointed out to him that by the method we proposed to use – that of the mimeograph machine – we should kill two birds with one stone: we should on the one hand ensure that we were in total control of our own paper, and on the other that people who wanted to bring libel actions could of course do so, but probably would not, because most libel actions are brought for the purpose of getting money, and it would be evident to one and all that we had no money of any kind.

After that things moved at a fairly brisk rate. We found an attic in Victoria Street approached first by a shaky lift and later by a staircase which was rather more of a ladder than a stair. There was room in it for a kitchen table, four chairs and a smaller table on which we installed a duplicating machine bought on the hire-purchase system so that the libel-mongers would have even less to gain than they might have hoped. We found a brilliant and devoted secretary – again a person who had not been involved in the type of calculation which was so common in London, and at once saw the possibilities of the idea.

At that stage we had only two troubles. The first was a row between myself and my partner, who hoped that the sheet would look clean and dignified. I, on the other hand, thought that the important thing was that it should be noticeable. Given the price of paper and duplicating ink, there seemed no possibility that it could be both. In the end we made it notice-able. It was mimeographed in dark brown ink on buff-coloured foolscap. It was not merely noticeable, it was unquestionably the nastiest-looking bit of work that ever dropped on to a breakfast-table.

The other trouble we had was from people who had heard what we were about to do and wanted to help. There was a man from Vancouver who knew about business and insisted he could get a lot of advertising for the paper. I told him we did not want advertising, but it did not diminish his enthusiasm. He quite evidently regarded me as a kind of babe in the wood who must be protected from the wild animals that are loose. In view of this touching solicitude it was impossible to turn him out of the office, and he used to stand there for hours talking and explaining his general plan for making us more money than anybody could have dreamed of. He stayed with us, in fact, throughout the launching of the paper and for three weeks after it had begun to come out, but then he went out of his mind just outside the Army and Navy Stores where he knelt on the pavement one morning, addressing me as his Brother in the Sun. As I drove him to the nursing home I realized I had been right all along about advertising.

Lawyers volunteered to help too, but I had to point out to them that either they were good lawyers, in which case they would have to keep saying, 'You can't publish that, it's libellous,' or bad lawyers, ignorant of whether things were libellous or not. In either case what use would they be? It was sad having to fight off so many well-intentioned offers of assistance, but I had to keep firmly in mind that what we were running was a pirate craft and we could not burden ourselves with conventional navigators and mates, however skilled and knowledgeable.

I had decided early on that we would not attempt to sell the paper on the bookstalls and news-stands. To begin with I did not want to get involved in a distributive organization which would be beyond one's own personal control. Also under English law, so far as I understood it, the wholesale newsagent can be held responsible for damages awarded in a libel suit against a paper distributed by him. For this reason the wholesale distributors are forced or encouraged to exercise a kind of long-term censorship over the products they handle. (That was why some time later we had the ridiculous situation in which the people who handled the London circulation of *Time* magazine had to spend hours with scissors snipping out of the paper, when it arrived from New York, those stories which might be considered libellous in England; that was how it happened that when the British papers were keeping mum about the abdication crisis of 1936 and *Time* magazine was running constant stories about the King and Mrs Simpson, *Time* reached the British bookstalls full of holes where the most interesting stories ought to have been. Yet even then you could meet people who would declare that there is no Press censorship in England.)

It seemed to me that we could turn this circumstance to account and use it to deepen the 'confidential' atmosphere around our paper. For the same reason I preferred, although it cost three times as much to do so, to mail the paper to subscribers in closed envelopes.

All these questions of production and circulation, interesting as they were, took up a good deal of my time. My partner, as I have said, was a novelist and short-story writer who had a positive horror of business, and was totally ignorant of it. He scarcely knew where to buy a stamp. Also it had been part of our bargain that I should not bother him with anything of that kind – what he wanted to get in exchange for his forty pounds was, so to speak, a tiny airstrip in London from which he could take off for social and literary trips about the town.

The secretary was a young married woman, daughter of a backwoods baronet living somewhere in East Anglia, and until about this time her idea of a major event in Home Affairs had been the exclusion of some friend from the Royal Enclosure at Ascot, and when I once expressed regret that I did not have time to dash down to Rome to take a look at what was going on there, she looked at me with surprise and said that surely it was the wrong time of year to go to Rome. She was pretty, energetic, intelligent and loyal, but she could not type and most of the people who dashed in and out of the attic in Victoria Street were as alien to her as though they had escaped from the Zoo.

However, in addition to her other qualities she had a great

deal of commonsense, and the business of occasionally explaining to her what we thought we were up to helped to clarify one's mind. All the same, it was difficult in the circumstances to spend as much time as I should have liked on the organization of our news sources. By this time of course I had a lot of 'contacts' in London – particularly in the City. But we could hardly have come out when we did had it not been for the cooperation of a number of foreign correspondents in London, many of whom I had known in Berlin or Washington, chief among them Mr Negley Farson, then London Correspondent of the *Chicago Daily News*. I met him only a couple of weeks before *The Week* was due to come out, but he was immediately enthusiastic. He shared, so far as I know, none of my political ideas, but he liked the idea of *The Week* as such, and at that time was one of the very few people who at once grasped the possibility of something so small becoming, in its effects, big.

Zero hour was a Wednesday in the mid-spring of 1933. We had chosen Wednesday as 'press day', so that *The Week* would reach people ahead of the existing weekly newspapers. I had had a great deal of difficulty in getting hold of a mailing list. There was no money to hire one of the lists which were available, and instead I had borrowed one which contained names of the subscribers to the then temporarily defunct weekly paper *Foreign Affairs*.

It was a list of about 1,200 names. Myself, the manager, the secretary and the man from Vancouver had spent the previous night addressing foolscap envelopes, and in the very early morning, in order to make our deadline as late as possible, I wrote the entire issue covering three sheets of foolscap written on both sides, and then cut the stencils.

All the things that always happen on such occasions happened. None of us had ever used a duplicating machine before and stencils cracked like sails in a gale and the place was bespattered with sticky brown ink. The valuable Pekingese dog belonging to the secretary became disgusted and spitefully chewed up the reserve tubes of ink. The man from Vancouver was already showing signs of the mental unbalance from which he later suffered more spectacularly. Also the manager's highly developed sense of neatness was offended by the way in which we were folding the foolscap sheets and shoving them into the envelopes and he kept taking them out in order to refold them in a neater but rather delaying manner. By early evening we had the whole lot enveloped and mailed and staggered to the Café Royal to drink champagne.

To my companions and fellow-workers I pointed out that the whole thing was absolutely sure-fire. Here we had a list of 1,200 names. Our product, *The Week*, was sensational, brilliant, irresistible. However, let us be cautious and assume that some of the people on that list are ill – too ill to fill in a subscription form – or they are dead. Say 300 of them. Then assume that there are some fools among them – boneheads or embittered maniacs who will not be charmed by *The Week*. Say 100 of them. That leaves a residue of 800 people who by tomorrow evening will be sitting down to send off their twelve-shilling postal orders for the Annual Subscription.

Unfortunately no one had warned me that the *Foreign Affairs* list was years old. Forty per cent of the people on it were dead, indifferent, or had radically changed their attitude to world affairs. Also there had been a serious miscalculation regarding the mentality of the British public – its readiness to jump for something new or love the highest when the editor saw it.

The number of paying customers secured by that first circularization was seven. Just seven.

The news spread rapidly among friends and acquaintances that my big idea had misfired.

Personally, since I regarded the existence of the 'pool' as a mathematical certainty, I was not discouraged, although I could think of no convincing reason to offer anyone else as an explanation of my continued optimism.

And yet little less than two years later this small monstrosity, *The Week*, was one of the half-dozen British publications most often quoted in the Press of the entire world. It included among its subscribers the Foreign Ministers of eleven nations, all the Embassies and Legations in London, all diplomatic correspondents of the principal newspapers in three continents, the Foreign Correspondents of all the leading newspapers stationed in London, the leading banking and brokerage houses in

THE WEEK

June 17th. 1936.

28 VICTORIA STREET
LONDON, S.W.1

No. 166.

TELEPHONE:
VICTORIA 1956

NOTICE FROM ROME

The British Government has for some reason not yet seen fit to make public
the most influential factor in the Cabinet discussion which preceded the
now famous Chamberlain speech at the 1900 Club.

It was that from the Italian Ambassador in London the Government had
received a perfectly formal and definite notification that unless sanctions
are removed at the League meeting this month, Italy will move out of the
League.

That some "impression" had been hinted; Mr. Garvin, who
presumably knew the facts, asserted that that was what Italy would do if
sanctions continued, and one newspaper suggested Italy would declare war.

Nobody thought it nice to mention that th———
at the probable Italian attitude———
than a notifica———

THE CLIVEDEN SET

Behind a confusion in the press partly deliberate and partly accidental,
British Government policy moved this week nearer towards a crisis very
different in character from the simple, public, "sanctions" and "anti-
sanctions" row which has held the headlines long after -- so far as the
Government was concerned -- the thing was settled.

———isis of which the outcome will sooner or later -- and pro-
———ily affect all people.   In view of the attitude of
——— to report in some detail upon some decisions,
——— some reason or other scarcely get re-

Awe.

If everyone treated the policy of the Astors and of the "Times" with no
more than the deference due to this queer concatenation of social accidents
and psychological foibles, the matter would be unimportant.   When Mr. Ward
Price -- following the lines forecast a couple of weeks ago in The Week --
writes a piece in Lord Rothermere's "Daily Mail" this Tuesday urging an
Anglo-German-Italian lineup to defend the world against Bolshevism from
Moscow to Paris, the political results are minimal.

When the Astors and the "Times" pursue a similar policy on a similar
level of political and strategical thought and knowledge, that has results.

For one must recall the awe with which many politicians
the "Times", and also the fact that from the politician
what hope to be "rising young men" from the politici———
more important the——— dinne———

"The Times".

Into the centre of the present picture has moved the London "Times." The
influence of the London "Times" -- sometimes exaggerated, sometimes underestimated -- is one of the features of British politics most misunderstood
by foreign observers.

For it is necessary to understand that the direction, extent, and
general character of "Times" policy and influence depend on factors which
are never anything but tortuous in their workings, and, over and above
that, continually shift.

Half the statesmen in Europe pored anxiously this week over the
increasingly peculiar editorials of the "Times", culminating on Tuesday in
the plea for secret negotiations between Hitler and the London Government.
They studied, too, the strange story of the "Times" Parliamentary correspondent, who put himself unenviably on record with the profound thought
that the Chamberlain speech was to be "explained" by the fact that Mr. Chamberlain had not had time to think much about what he was going to say.

To understand what has happened -- and what has happened is important --
it is necessary to report upon certain apparently trivial and often pitiable
circumstances of the "Times" as it stands today.

London, Paris, Amsterdam and New York, a dozen members of the United States Senate, twenty or thirty members of the House of Representatives, about fifty members of the House of Commons and a hundred or so in the House of Lords, King Edward VIII, the secretaries of most of the leading trades unions, Charlie Chaplin and the Nizam of Hyderabad.

Blum read it and Goebbels read it, and a mysterious war-lord in China read it. Senator Borah quoted it repeatedly in the American Senate and Herr von Ribbentrop, Hitler's Ambassador in London, on two separate occasions demanded its suppression on the ground that it was the source of all anti-Nazi evil.

Admittedly none of this seemed at all probable at the end of that first week when the total circulation stood at seven. Apart from the moral shock – disclosure of low mental level all round, nation sunk in apathy – this lack of response left hardly any money to circularize anyone else and raised the whole question of how to go on living at all.

I was forced to live meagrely on the twelve-shilling postal orders which occasionally came in, spending much of my time at the Café Royal, then in its last phase as a gathering-place of just the kind of people who ought to be reading and talking about *The Week*.

It made – since a bottle of good wine cost three shillings – a fine, nearly free, place to do business in. People coming in for drinks who had vaguely heard of *The Week* would often pay over their subscription money in cash, though they probably would never have got around to sending in a subscription form and a postal order. The late Professor Joad brought in quite a freshet one night by shouting his congratulations on *The Week* all over the Café Royal and declaring that no man in the place could claim to have any idea upon what was going on unless he were a subscriber to *The Week*.

Even so, things remained extremely difficult for several weeks, until one day, with the circulation awfully steady at thirty-six, the Prime Minister intervened.

The World Economic Conference – some joker had housed it among the fossils in the Geological Museum – was a big thing in his life. Figuratively speaking, he had his name in lights all over it. Yet, the Premier excepted, almost everyone from

Leadenhall Street to the Afghan Legation knew that the Conference was dying on its feet. But it was thought not very good taste to point in public. 'Useful spadework' was what the newspapers said was going on.

The Week, in a special issue, reported extensively upon what was really being said *sotto voce* by informed observers. It remarked that the only spade at work on the Conference was the grave-digger's. Quoting Charles Dickens, it saw fit to liken the position of the Conference leadership to that of the Dover Mail, which 'was in its usual genial position that the guard suspected the passengers, the passengers suspected one another and the guard, they all suspected everybody else, and the coachman was sure of nothing but the horses; as to which cattle he could with a clear conscience have taken his oath on the two Testaments that they were not fit for the journey'.

On the day this appeared Mr MacDonald came down to the Conference looking, as someone remarked, as though he were on his way to Clarkson's to hire a crown of thorns. He convened a special off-the-record Press conference in the crypt. He said he had a private warning to utter. Foreign and diplomatic correspondents from all over the world jostled past mementoes of the Ice Age to hear him. For as a warning-utterer he was really tip-top. In his unique style, suggestive of soup being brewed on a foggy Sunday evening in the West Highlands, he said that what we saw on every hand was plotting and conspiracy, of this, that and the other kind, in the larger sense, and here in his hand was a case in point, tantamount to just that sort of thing.

Everyone pushed and stared, and what he had in his hand was that issue of *The Week*; and he went on to quote from it, and to warn one and all to pay no heed to the false prophets of disaster, activated by motives of this or that or the other thing. This was good strong stuff and stimulating to these people who hitherto had never heard of *The Week*, and, but for this, possibly never would have.

Regrettably I had to miss a good deal of it. I recalled that this was the hour when the manager would be sitting in a barber's shop in Curzon Street where he spent a rather large part of each morning, and that the secretary was away attending some society wedding. The office was deserted. I urgently desired to know what else Mr Macdonald had to say, but equally I urgently needed to dash back to Victoria Street so as to be there in time to answer the telephone which, as could easily be foreseen, would soon be vibrating with voices of the anxious *cognoscenti* of international affairs.

It was ringing all right. 'This is the diplomatic correspondent of *Le Matin*. I want . . .' 'Here is the diplomatic correspondent of *Frankfurter Zeitung*. I require immediately . . .' By tea-time the circulation was in the seventies, with Pertinax and Mme Tabouis, then in their heyday, well up there with the leaders.

And then to prove that it wasn't just raining manna, it was pouring it, another big shower of it fell.

While I was still scribbling down the names of the new subscribers, I heard afar off a muttering and puffing, and then upon the ladderlike stair leading to our attic I heard the thunder and crack of impetuous feet. In a split trice the place was heaving and bulging with enormously moustachioed men, and women with mauve veils, speaking excitedly of the Prophet Isaiah. What did they want? They wanted subscriptions to *The Week*. Why? Because at a neighbouring hall – Caxton or Central – there was in session a congress of citizens taking the view that the future may readily be foretold by measuring the Pyramids and that the British (even, stretching a point, the Americans) are the lost tribes of Israel. Someone had read aloud to this gathering a passage from an earlier issue of *The Week*, and it absolutely confirmed, apparently, something Isaiah had said. It could be that *The Week* was divinely inspired by the prophet. In any case they wanted forty subscriptions quick.

They were solid people with cash in their hands, and I could hardly refrain from taking time off to telephone the café manager at the Café Royal to tell him that in an hour or two it would be in order to wipe clean my terribly congested slate.

One of these enthusiasts, a secretary from the organization somewhere in the north, waited to talk with me. He had the air of maintaining an – how shall one say? – if possibly more normal relationship to reality than some of his co-believers. Trading on this, I ventured to ask him whether he was not a good deal pestered by the sort of person who really thought he only had to look up the length of some gallery in the Great

Pyramid to know what was going to happen in the middle of next year. That, he said, was quite frankly only too often the case.

'You get,' he said, 'a lot of these people who rush in expecting an answer to such a question right away. People cannot realize that to work out a thing like that accurately often takes several days.'

13
BLOODY FACTS

'IF you go on like this,' said Mr John Wheeler-Bennett, then head of the Royal Institute of International Affairs at Chatham House, 'you will soon, I should think, be either quite famous or in gaol.'

'Lots of people,' I said, 'have been both.'

'That,' he said, turning upon me his luminous smile, and beaming as though an awkward question had now been satisfactorily resolved, 'is so.'

A lot of people who, by constantly talking of The Week, complaining of it, denouncing it as a horrible liar, and even praising it, were helping to make this tiny sheet 'quite famous', were also of the opinion that something terrible must be going to happen to The Week pretty soon. Mr Kingsley Martin, editor of the New Statesman, who had been very kind to me personally and wished us well, was one of these. Once he wrote in his column in the New Statesman that he had been waiting for a fortnight for 'the heavens to fall' as a result of a particular disclosure in The Week – it was fairly clear from the context that what the heavens were going to fall upon was me. Another time he came briefly to my office to tell me that he had just read the current issue and wanted to warn me that to his mind the only doubt as to the result was whether I should get out with a heavy fine or suffer a sharp gaol sentence into the bargain.

The Criminal Libel Law and the Official Secrets Act, one or other of which we apparently infringed about twice a month, were the instruments which people imagined were going to send me to gaol. Since, as I have said, I had no lawyer to bother me about such things, and since nobody but myself could possibly be involved in whatever unpleasantness might arise, I was saved all the advance worry which nags at people on other types of paper when they are handling dynamite, and by being simply ignorant of whether I was infringing some law or not, saved myself from the temptation which otherwise I make no doubt would have often been irresistible – to omit or tone down reports of facts and reports of rumours merely on the ground that to publish them might land one in the Courts. We were of course repeatedly threatened with libel actions, but none of them was ever brought and none was ever settled out of Court. When deciding whether or not to write a story which was obviously, in the legal sense, libellous, but which I believed to be true and of some public interest, I used instead of a lawyer a simple criterion of my own.

In case he brings an action, I asked myself, which of us in the end will look more ridiculous? On the whole, this criterion worked fairly well. When the emissaries of the libelled came to see me with threats and menaces, they were immediately discouraged by the evident poverty of our organization. Their usual technique was then to demand an unqualified apology. This I invariably refused on principle, although always expressing readiness to write another story on the same subject giving any facts they might choose to supply tending to show that the earlier story had been baseless. It was at this point that one could usually detect from their expression that the thought passing through their minds was that which had passed through mine earlier – namely that if their client took the case to Court he would probably make more of a monkey out of himself than he was likely to make out of me.

How often we really infringed the Official Secrets Act, or were suspected by the authorities of espionage or improper relations with public servants for the purpose of extracting state secrets, I have no idea. For the first eighteen months or so, at any rate, we were highly suspect – naturally, and for the same reason I had been suspect in Berlin, namely that we had no easily recognizable fancy dress and the authorities were somewhat in the position of the drunken Dutchman in the musical comedy who gets by accident into the middle of a fancy-dress ball and runs frantically from person to person imploring them, 'Do please tell me once and for each what are you *as*?'

Obviously the authorities would much rather deal with people who are visibly members of some recognized political organization, and I had a lot of evidence that they were considerably worried by not knowing what I was 'as'.

Long ago Wilmott Lewis had drawn my attention to what he called 'the factual heresy' or 'the illusion of spot news'.

It would be tedious to examine the historical phenomena which had produced in the public mind a belief that the desirable thing to read in a newspaper is 'the inside news', and still more the illusion in the public mind that the newspaper, or rather the reporter, really has 'inside news'.

Wilmott Lewis, who was usually right about such matters, took the view that about ninety per cent of what the public conceived to be 'inside news' or 'spot news' is either something so trivial or obvious that it is not worth writing about, or else is not 'inside news' at all in the sense of being something secret and confidential, but is the kind of information which any highly informed and reasonably intelligent person could piece together from, say, a week's reading of all available newspapers and a week's conversation with all available sources. And even this, he used to insist, is not enough. News, he used to say, is in itself nothing. Presentation is almost everything. The entire question, he would insist, is a question of style.

I have seen people who, as he made these observations, came rapidly to the idiotic conclusion that the creative journalistic process is much simpler than it really is – you could see them beginning to imagine that all the man had to do was to sit about reading and talking and presently, having developed his 'style', present the matter in coruscating prose. This of course is untrue too, and the reason why Lewis, for example, leaned over backwards talking about style, and the reason why it is necessary to do so repeatedly, is that, although in the early days of journalism style was emphasized to the point where the role of the 'facts' was merely forgotten, nowadays the 'factual heresy' is a dangerous one.

To hear people talking about the facts you would think that they lay about like pieces of gold ore in the Yukon days waiting to be picked up – arduously, it is true, but still definitely and visibly – by strenuous prospectors whose subsequent problem was only to get them to market.

Such a view is evidently and dangerously naïve. There are no such facts. Or if there are, they are meaningless and entirely ineffective; they might, in fact, just as well not be lying about at all until the prospector – the journalist – puts them into relation with other facts: presents them, in other words. Then they become as much a part of a pattern created by him as if he were writing a novel. In that sense all stories are written backwards – they are supposed to begin with the facts and develop from there, but in reality they begin with a journalist's point of view, a conception, and it is the point of view from which the facts are subsequently organized. Journalistically speaking, 'in the beginning is the word'. All this is difficult and even rather unwholesome to explain to the layman, because he gets the impression that you are saying that truth does not matter and that you are publicly admitting what he long ago suspected, that journalism is a way of 'cooking' the facts. Really cunning journalists, realizing this, and anxious to raise the status of journalism in the esteem of the general public, positively encourage the layman in his mistaken views. They like him to have the picture of these nuggety facts lying about on maybe frozen ground, and a lot of noble and utterly unprejudiced journalists with no idea whatever of what they are looking for scrabbling in the iron-bound earth and presently bringing home the pure gold of Truth.

When I had to start explaining what *The Week* was trying to do, I did myself a good deal of harm by being rather too frank about this matter. To make matters worse, I went about saying that rumours were just as important, just as significant, just as – in the last analysis – 'valid' as 'facts'.

This shocked people horribly, although if you pressed them and asked whether it was not true that ninety per cent of 'information received' by such serious persons as Ambassadors and Chiefs of Police really consists in significant rumours which can be interpreted by the person who knows enough rumours, they were usually bound to admit that this is indeed the case. Contemporaries on the existing weekly newspapers used to complain that *The Week* published rumours which they themselves refused to publish until they were confirmed. One was reminded of the atheistic young man who told the believer that he would never believe anything that he did not understand, to which the believer replied, 'Young man, your beliefs are likely to be small.'

In the same way people who refused to print anything that was not a confirmed fact were likely to print very little of general interest. And I found that attitude arrogant, for, unless one imagines one is God, how on earth can one tell truth from rumour in less than perhaps fifty years? And fifty years is too long to wait if one is in the business of issuing a weekly newspaper.

So far as *The Week*'s news-gathering operations were concerned they were conducted for the most part on a barter basis with a group of what were then the best-informed and most lively-minded correspondents in London.

They included Mr Farson, correspondent of the *Chicago Daily News*; Mr Stefan Litauer, correspondent of the Polish News Agency; Mr Paul Scheffer, correspondent of the *Berliner Tageblatt*, and a varying group of French correspondents.

Two or three times a week we met around noon in Mr Farson's office at Bush House and pooled our information. And on the days we did not meet we pooled information over the telephone. To describe this pool as a 'group' would be to use too formal a word, but – owing, I think, to Mr Farson's guidance – we all of us came to realize that there was something to be said for regular exchanges even when there seemed to be no news at all. The mere fact of each in turn going through a kind of 'total recall' of what had been said by informants – diplomats, financiers and others – during the course of the past forty-eight hours was clarificatory and often produced a piece of the great jigsaw which otherwise could have been overlooked or forgotten. Usually of course there was plenty of news. There was news which – for example – Mr Farson could not handle for his paper but which was exactly suited to *The Week*. Everyone had something to contribute, everyone picked out of the bag what suited his own requirements. Apart from what *The Week* could directly contribute to the pool, it had a special role to play, a special utility. There were innumerable stories which, for example, Mr Farson or Mr Litauer could not venture to send directly to their papers or news agencies but which they could send if they had just appeared in *The Week* and could thus be quoted instead of being sent on the responsibility of the correspondents.

The French were particularly good at playing this game. And, as time went on, this group – every member of which had his own special contacts with news sources in London, his own confidential sources of news in his own country and a lively awareness of the difference between the apparently significant news and the news that really was significant in the light of knowledge of the basic trends – made up a pretty formidable information centre.

And then naturally the whole business 'snowballed'. When it was seen what kind of stories *The Week* uniquely would handle, all sorts of people – for motives sometimes noble and quite often vile – would approach *The Week* to draw its attention to the most extraordinary pieces of more or less confidential information. Sometimes it came from frustrated newspapermen who could not get what they considered vital news into their own papers. More often such confidences were the outcome of obscure financial or diplomatic duels. They would come, for instance, from the Councillor of an Embassy who was convinced of the wrong-headed policy of the Foreign Office and the Ambassador, and wished, without exposing himself, to put a spoke in their wheel.

The savage tensions of the 1930s naturally produced a situation favourable to this type of development. Under the frightful overhanging menace of Hitlerism, there roamed through the capitals of Western Europe people who were half saint and half bandit – the sort of people who would commit a murder for twenty pounds and suicide for a good idea.

For many months one of *The Week*'s principal informants in Berlin was a principal secretary of Herr von Papen. This man, who at times acted as von Papen's Chef de Cabinet, was an energetically devout Catholic and an astute anti-Nazi.

At that time it was still necessary for Hitler to treat von Papen with caution and a kind of respect, so that it was impossible to conceal from the von Papen bureau more than about thirty per cent of what the Nazis were really up to.

It was of course impossible for this secretary to send his information through the mails and I had, in fact, insisted that nothing must be written down at all. I had a messenger – a former sports writer of the Ullstein press – whom nobody suspected of being anything but a damn fool, travel to and from Berlin to talk with this secretary, memorize his information and bring it back to London.

Unfortunately the secretary was less careful than he should have been. He kept a file of *The Week* in order to check up on the way in which we were handling the information which he gave us. One day in June my messenger, who generally had very little interest in politics and was not particularly alert to what was going on, arrived in Berlin and went to see the secretary.

The copies of *The Week* were covered in blood – the man had been shot at close range by the S.S. assassins who had just invaded the house. Our liaison man escaped, by an estimated four minutes, before they returned to the lower floors after a search of the bedrooms to find someone else they might like to kill.

Probably this was one of the reasons – this event and its repercussions – why Herr von Ribbentrop, German Ambassador, thought that I and *The Week* were the centre of all anti-Nazi intrigue and propaganda in London.

The fact that he thought so – that he could be such a fool as to think so – helped to give me a measure of the Third Reich which could employ such an Ambassador. One is not much alarmed about people who are reasonably intelligent. What was terrifying about this man was that he was a damn fool – and could only have been employed by a régime of, basically, damn fools, who could blow up half the world out of sheer stupidity.

A satisfactory thing about Herr von Ribbentrop was that you did not have to waste time wondering whether there was some latent streak of goodness in him somewhere. He was all of a piece. He had me followed about London by enormous blondes. From the fact that *The Week* often spoke disobligingly of the Foreign Office, too, he of course deduced that it must be secretly run by the Foreign Office. The disobliging remarks were a clever blind, and there was Ambassador Ribbentrop seeing right through it. Vansittart foiled again.

Also, to help mould his ideas, I had arranged to have conveyed to him the information that my real name – now clumsily translated from the German – was Hahnbrandt, and that my father came from Czernowitz. Supposing that this piece of intelligence had been treacherously sold to one of his agents by a friend of mine, Ribbentrop was inclined to think it true. He never really believed any report honestly come by.

The blondes were sometimes female, sometimes male. One of the males had the job of getting a seat beside me on one of those plush-covered benches by the marble-topped tables in the old Café Royal, which at that time I used as an alternative to my office, on account of the superior amenities. Most of the full-time Nordic representatives one encountered were swarthy chaps about five and a half feet high, but this fellow was a true chip off the Herrenvolk. He would have made Lohengrin look quite a dago. Often he got so close that you could see the tiny yellow hairs quivering deep inside his ear.

Not wanting anyone's time to get wasted, I arranged for use on these occasions some informative little dialogues with whichever friend happened to be sitting with me.

Me: Say what you will, you cannot deny the Gentiles started the last war. Wormed themselves into key positions everywhere. Asquith, Bethmann-Hollweg, the Hohenzollerns, Poincaré – all Gentiles, old boy.

Friend: But look at the thing broadly – think of their contribution to literature, culture in general. Look at Shakespeare.

Me: Shakespeare I grant you – if he really was a Gentile. But if you want to talk about writers, what about Wells, and Shaw? Typically disruptive, *negative* Gentile mentalities. Mind you, I've many good Gentile friends myself. But taken in the *mass*. . . . Besides, I always think there's something queer about their eyes.

Ten minutes of this, and the horrified Wandervogel had had about all he could hold, and was off to the little door on the Duke of York's steps to report on the swelling arrogance of crypto-Jewish conspirators, and add another page or so to my dossier.

14

PUNDITS AND FRIENDS

IT was at about this time that Mr Pollitt, Secretary of the Communist Party of Great Britain, whom I had never met, was suddenly announced on the telephone – would I, he asked, take the next train, in twenty minutes or half an hour, and report a mine disaster at Gresford, North Wales. Why? Because he had a feeling that there was a lot more in it than met the eye. But why I in particular? Well, because, it seemed, Mr Pollitt – who was worrying at the time about what he believed to be a lack of 'reader appeal' in the *Daily Worker* – had been reading *The Week* and thought I might do a good job.

I like sudden decisions, and went, and I did a good job.

And a few days after it Mr Pollitt asked me to call on him and said to me, 'How much d'you make?' I told him I had never figured it out – I kept getting new jobs, like being newly appointed first London Correspondent of *Time* magazine, and then, as a result of complex journalistic fantasy, first London Correspondent of *Fortune* – magazine of American Big Business.

(The short list had got shortened to two names – so at least I was told by Mr Ralph McAllister Ingersoll, then Managing Editor of *Fortune*. There was myself, and there was Mr Randolph Churchill – who had the backing, it appeared, of Mr Brendan Bracken. We made the deal in the foyer of the Savoy Hotel and took off for Brussels in a specially chartered plane to see the head of the Belgian Radium Trust who, when we got to Brussels, turned out to be in the Savoy Hotel, London.)

Mr Pollit said, 'Well, anyway, do you make more than thirty pounds a week?' I said that, at least, I could certainly not deny.

To this Mr Pollitt replied, 'Well, how'd you like to work for about four pounds a week – and half the time you won't get even that? How'd you like to work for the *Daily Worker*?'

This suggestion would probably have been in any case irresistible – and it was the more so because of my experiences among the British Labour people and Liberals. I was as certain as I ever have been of anything that I could never possibly appreciate their viewpoint – not, that is to say, to the extent of becoming enthusiastic about it, writing honestly and creatively in favour of it. To put it in slang, the Labour people seemed to me to be about where I had come in in Germany years and years before. And if there were things to disagree with the Communists about, what I felt at the time was that they were a lot nearer being a creative force in British politics than any other that I could see.

Also they were a force that was small, poor and adventurous, and the distance between their thoughts and their actions appeared to me to be a lot shorter than it was when you came to the Labour people, the 'progressive intellectuals'.

Decisive in this situation was that I had, for a short time – some months before Mr Pollitt made his offer – worked for a weekly newspaper called the *Clarion*, run by Odhams Press, owners of the *Daily Herald*. I wrote a weekly page of paragraphs on foreign affairs. It was not a bad page, but it had something false and brittle about it, and I knew the reason – the things I really thought were happening could not be expressed directly in that Labour-organized newspaper, and once again I faced the same inhibitions and distortions of expression, of style, as I had faced at *The Times*.

Misled, probably, by sensational literature and the motion pictures, people said one thing was certain, and that was that it would be very, very different from *The Times*. They said they could hardly imagine a bigger change than going from *The Times* to work for the *Daily Worker*. Like most statements made without fear of successful contradiction, this one turned out to be full of error.

True, the plain-clothes detectives of the Special Branch of the C.I.D., bulging in the saloon bar just across the street, struck a note unusual in Printing House Square. So did the social viewpoint of the cartoons presented to the publican by a former artist of the paper in payment for services rendered.

Then I noticed the expression upon the face of the van-driver waiting to rush next day's paper to the stations, and became aware of something at once rare and familiar. I had seen it on the faces of *Times* drivers, but – until now – nowhere else.

It was an expression which said the edition was going to come off the press long behind schedule, and he was going to risk his neck tearing along the streets to Euston and Paddington, and if he caught the trains at all it was going to be a flaming miracle. And just why was the paper going to be late? Not, you could bet your life, because a big murder story broke at the last minute, or floods menaced thousands, or heiress's secret wedding exclusive, or any of that class of caper, but because the leader-writer – the flaming *leader-writer*, well, I ask you – was still batting out a pronouncement on something or other and they were holding the whole edition for him while he reached for the *mot* flaming *juste*.

A nice state of affairs in the middle of the twentieth century. Who did he think he was? Gladstone?

Within the building, at the entrance to the editorial offices, the sense of familiarity, of *déjà vu*, deepened. This was not entirely due to the fact that at that date the offices of both newspapers looked, in contrast to Fleet Street, like something Dickens had set out to describe, and then left to be continued by someone who was just starting to read up on this new-fangled steel construction you heard about. Functional they were not. They reminded me of Boston. But, more than this, it was an organizational detail which evoked a memory of Printing House Square.

Naturally, all newspapers have guardians whose business it is to prevent eager but irrelevant people bursting in and disturbing the editorial inmates at their tasks. At *The Times*, when I worked there, this protection had been considered particularly important. And I had been told that as for the *Daily Worker* I should find it guarded, they said, like a fortress.

Of course, the character of the most probable intruders differed, up to a point, in each case. *The Times*, I had always been given to understand, was protecting the editorial staff against the onset of people with plans to reorganize the Church of England, people who wanted it to publish a five-column letter demanding State subsidies for otter-hunting, and people who were going to beat up the racing correspondent because of the ruinously misleading thing he foreshadowed about the third race at Newmarket.

At the *Daily Worker* the job of the man on the door was rather to keep out people with plans to reorganize the Communist Party, people who wanted to get a five-column letter published demanding State subsidies for Esperanto, and people who were going to beat up the racing correspondent because of the ruinously misleading thing he foreshadowed about the fourth race at Wolverhampton.

First time I called at *The Times*, I got right to the editor's door without being questioned, and learned that the obvious reason for that must have been that the person who kept people out had had to slip away for a minute to make some tea. At the *Daily Worker* the arrangements were, in truth, more elaborate. There was a cubby-hole for the guardian to sit in, and a small *guichet* for him to peer out of, and a door which would open only when he was satisfied and pulled a string. On this occasion the door had been wedged open with a piece of wood, the cubbyhole was empty, and as one walked unchallenged up the stairs one caught, at the end of a passage, a glimpse of the guardian's back as he pored over a gas-ring, making some tea.

On the voyage to the interior, other well-remembered sights were witnessed. That man, half-crazed by worry and frustration, shouting about trains leaving and peering over his shoulder towards the leader-writer's room with the mixed rage and awe of one who is trying to get an archdeacon to step on the gas, must obviously be the manager. These chaps, eruditely discussing in a mood of high-minded levity the racial composition of the Saar and that business about the M.C.C., can be none other than the Foreign Editor and the Diplomatic Correspondent. And clearly the tense-looking man scribbling away at the end of the table is the world's greatest expert on something and, though ostensibly sub-editing a small item of late news, is really writing a definite article for a quarterly or monthly review.

After all this, the sight of the leader-writer himself, a Scotsman, it need hardly be said, or at any rate one of Nature's Scotsmen, came as no surprise at all. One had seen virtually the same man coolly holding up production of *The Times* while his sinewy pen wrestled mightily with Unrighteousness, a spiritual descendant of Covenanters and of the sort of preacher who held that if a full and proper exposition of The Word was going to cause the sermon to go on for five hours, then five hours was what the sermon was going to go on for. Feather-pates might babble of parishioners falling exhausted in the aisles, or trains leaving the termini without the paper. That was just too bad about the parishioners and the disappointed readers.

Occasionally, in those early days at the *Daily Worker*, the readers at the far end of the long-distance lines would get together in protest, claiming they would rather have a paper with a political howler in paragraph four of the leader than no paper at all. These explosions shook the building. Campaigns were initiated for more hustle, modernity and snappy popular journalism all round. People sat gazing sadly at the *Daily Express*, with a view to imitating it. Over the problem of how to get snappier there raged discussions comparable to those at *The Times* office when some ruthless modernist, shouting for the Common Touch and plenty of it, came in with that shockingly vulgar suggestion about sticking in a crossword puzzle.

In the midst of one of these periods of controversy, I came down to the office to find a big section of the library space occupied by a broodingly thoughtful Burman, the entire table before him covered with books, brochures and manuscript documents. It looked as though the article he was evidently going to write on the situation in Burma was going to cover the subject pretty comprehensively. Next day he was still there, writing down figures in long columns – statistics of rice production, I supposed. His books and papers now took up so much room that it was hard to move about the library at all. It seemed it must be going to be quite a series of articles. And about all this research there was something impressive and solemn, making one feel that any other article written for the paper was going to look trivial and superficial.

On the third day I took alarm and placed the whole question squarely before the editor.

I yielded, I said, to no one in my appreciation of the gravity and world importance of the situation in Burma. A couple of rousing pieces about it were, I did most profoundly realize, what the paper needed as badly as anything. But, so far as I could judge, our friend aimed at turning out a minimum of twenty such articles, and frankly, and without in any way seeking to minimize the vital urgency of getting the facts in front of the public, was this project entirely in line with decisions recently taken about developing more zing, zip and popular appeal? Would a series of twenty articles on Burma Today be the snappiest thing imaginable? As a circulation-getter, was it just what the *Daily Express* would do?

The editor, who personally would rather have enjoyed reading twenty longish articles subjecting the Burmese situation to an exhaustive analysis, listened with an air of melancholy. Painfully, as though revealing that in the rush for the Common Touch we had decided to go in for some kind of pornography, he explained the position. The Burman was not, in fact, writing an article about Burma. He was not an expert on that country. What he was an expert on was greyhound racing. And what he was doing with all those books and papers was working out greyhound form for the coming season. Thereafter a section of the paper was going to be devoted to greyhound tips and greyhound results.

So, indeed, it came to pass. People who were expecting a piece denouncing the Bank of England and found instead a bit tipping Blazing Killarney Boy for the White City were disgusted, and wrote letters saying this could never have happened in the Old Days and the Tolpuddle Martyrs were rolling in their graves. Others were delighted, for, however shaky he may have been on Burma, as a dog-tipster he was the tops. In the raw financial blizzard which blew continuously through the office for months on end, he was a big comfort to the staff. Perhaps if the Moscow Gold other people wrote about had really existed one would not have bothered so much about what was going to happen at the tracks. Things being as they were, Blazing Killarney Boy was worth a whole lot of imaginary roubles.

The financial blizzard affected me less seriously than others because – although I had had to abandon *Time* and *Fortune* simply because I had no working hours left after dealing with *The Week* and the *Daily Worker* – *The Week* was now climbing steadily, and even making a profit.

It was also exerting a certain – quite undefinable but still perceptible – influence.

About the time when Hitler was marching into the Rhineland, in the spring of 1936, I was somewhat diffidently approached by Mr John Strachey, with a mysterious, if trivial, proposal. He desired me to furnish him with a potted autobiography. It must be done at once. It must be impressive. And I must not ask for what purpose it was wanted.

Mr Strachey was at that time very far indeed from being a member of the Government. On the contrary, he wrote for the *Daily Worker*, was generally, though mistakenly, believed to be a Communist, and spoke harshly of the leaders of the Labour Party. He was in touch with some of the Churchillian group of the Conservatives who were already alive, like him, to the Nazi menace. Also, as it turned out, he knew a man who knew a man who knew the King.

'But what *is* it wanted for?' I said once, twice and three times, and the third time Mr Strachey agreed to tell all, but not where walls might have ears. We hurried out and walked round and round Primrose Hill. 'It's simply,' said Mr Strachey in a low murmur, 'that the King wants to know who you are.'

Mr Strachey, it seemed, was the friend of an intimate of Lord Louis Mountbatten, reputedly one of the closest and most influential advisers of King Edward VIII. And Lord Louis Mountbatten, said Mr Strachey, was a student of *The Week*.

Lord Louis was an early and, at that time, somewhat lonely anti-Nazi in high places. He was, Mr Strachey murmured to the discreet air of Primrose Hill, using *The Week* to convince King Edward that the real shape of things to come was very different from that foretold by Premier Baldwin and his colleagues. *The Week* had recently given a good deal of rather sensational advance information on Nazi moves which had proved correct. The King, it appeared, was impressed. 'But,' he had complained to Lord Louis with understandable petulance, 'you are asking me to prefer the information of an obscure political scandal-sheet, run by someone I never heard of, to that of all my Ministers.'

This was where the potted autobiography was to come in. It was to show His Majesty that the editor of the obscure scandal-sheet was one of the Right People, with ancestors, and an Oxford accent and a former connexion with *The Times*. In the interests of this high-powered and beneficent project, I reached for a halo and rapidly presented Mr Strachey with a glowing testimonial to myself in about four hundred words. Later I received messages saying that things were going well. I gathered that *The Week* had become required reading at Fort Belvedere. I hoped His Majesty would not leave it lying about where an archbishop might see it. I also hoped we might soon see some practical political results.

I waited for months, and what I saw in the end was Mr Strachey, more serious than ever, suggesting that we take another open-air walk, – this time, as I recall, in St James's Park.

We were in the middle of the Abdication Crisis. The news-papers were victims of a more than usually painful attack of discretional lock-jaw. They were determined to show respon-sibility, delicacy, restraint and the Best Possible Taste if it was the last thing they did before total paralysis gripped them. In the suffocating silence the trend was running strongly against the King.

In this situation, Mr Strachey murmured to a passing swan, Lord Louis Mountbatten had conceived the idea that if certain 'inside information' of a particularly sensational character could be suddenly forced into the open, the trend might, just possibly, be reversed in the King's favour. There were facts which it was thought the regular newspapers and weeklies would be most unlikely to print. On the other hand, it had been noted that on several occasions in the past *The Week* had suc-ceeded in securing wide publicity for matters thought 'not fit to print'. Things had, apparently, come to the paradoxical point where the 'obscure scandal-sheet' might be the most effective weapon available to save the King.

Lord Louis, I was informed, was of the opinion that if he could present the King with this concrete possibility, the King might agree to try it. The question therefore was: Would I, 'in principle', be prepared to publish certain facts if they reached me from Fort Belvedere? I was warned that they would immediately be denied by the Cabinet, that the resulting row would be certainly appalling and possibly catastrophic. His Majesty, I was told, as yet knew nothing of this project.

I was rather far from being a passionate champion of the monarchy, but the atmosphere of pompous discretion was almost unbreathable, and anyway it looked as though whatever happened we should have a lot of fun. Also, one got the impression that Lord Louis Mountbatten was a bonny fighter who ought to be encouraged. I accepted, of course.

Mr Strachey rushed to and fro with mysterious messages. I said that I would publish the story that was to save the King in a special edition of *The Week* – we could turn it off on the duplicator in a couple of hours. The police always showed a keen interest in the contents of *The Week*, and there was just a chance that it might be held up in the mails. I therefore arranged that there should be a score or so of my friends with cars and motor-cycles ready to rush a few hundred copies by hand to a selected list of influential subscribers in London and the home counties.

Late one Thursday afternoon I received word that the material would be in my hands within the next few hours, and should be published immediately. It would be brought by a dispatch rider to *The Week*'s office in the garret in Victoria Street.

I mobilized the necessary typists 'for special duty' and overhauled our rickety second-hand duplicator. The flying squad of distributors was alerted, and its members told to stand by their telephones.

At eight in the evening the main door of the office building was closed, and a sentry had to be posted there to meet the impending messenger and get the documents from him.

The two typists, the boy who turned the handle of the duplicator, the two friends who would stuff the finished product into the envelopes, and myself, sat eating sandwiches in the tiny office which would comfortably accommodate three people.

At eleven o'clock there was a telephone message to say that there had been a 'slight delay', but that the material would reach us before midnight.

By half an hour past midnight I was standing on a chair to lean out of the small, high window of the garret, listening to the profound silence of Victoria Street.

It was nearly one before I heard quite a long way off the loud noise of a big motor-cycle being ridden very fast.

I rushed down five flights of stairs and got to the street door at the same time as the dispatch rider, who had shot past and had to turn. He handed me a small unaddressed envelope, and I knew from the size of it that it was going to be no good. I called to him to wait, there might be an answer. He said no, he had been told there was no answer. Inside the envelope was a single sheet of plain paper with this typewritten line.

It read : 'The situation has developed too fast.'

15
LOST SIERRA

But for a good many months I could devote very little time to it. The Spanish war had broken out.

A complacent ass who was, temporarily, Propaganda Minister of Catalonia, said to me : 'This is the most photogenic war anyone ever has seen.'

Considering that people were dying all around us – many of them having come to meet death with extreme heroism because they believed this to be the final battleground where, as in children's stories, the Good get to grips with the Bad – his remark was offensive. Indeed it indicated to any clear-sighted observer that the man thought we were probably going to lose, and was making jokes until he could make up his mind which way his cat would, or could, jump.

All the same, there was a streak of truth in what he so ineptly said.

That terrible war was also 'photogenic' in the widest sense of the word. Not just the Press photographers turned up, everyone turned up who wanted to be in on the decisive thing of the century, the thing that was going to prove either that Democracy was going to stand up to the enemy there and then, or else that Democracy – it was the phrase people used at the time, and they believed in it – was going to take a terrible beating, and after that there would be a bigger and worse war.

The massacres and the battles and the subsequent massacres took place, too, in lovely surroundings.

I got there because I was a Red newspaper reporter and I had a job to do, but I do not share the sneers of those who, looking back, think disparagingly of a lot of people who really had no business to be in Spain at all, but who went there because – intellectually – the affair was so photogenic.

It is true that after the defeat – and it has often seemed to me that intellectuals somewhat tend to exaggerate both defeats and victories, as though taking it for granted that either of them might be final – a lot of European intellectuals left their souls dead on the soil of Spain and never again were able to face the continuing realities of life. (There were also some intellectuals who faced the Spanish realities with such sturdiness that they left their bodies on that soil too. These heroic men were the first proof to the nineteen-thirties that when some people talk about dying for a cause they mean it.)

But the others – although many of them never found out what it was all about, and, in their disillusionment ended up by being a nuisance – set a good example too. They proclaimed, however briefly, that a moment comes when your actions have to bear some kind of relation to your words.

That is what is called the Moment of Truth.

Naturally, the role of the intellectuals, the troubles and dissensions and heroisms of the intellectuals, were in reality matters of insignificance compared to the troubles, dissensions and heroisms of the men who mainly fought the war – and they ranged from peasants out of Almanza, who walked all the way to Madrid to fight, to a steel-worker from Budapest who travelled all night hanging on to the undercarriage of the Orient Express so as to get to Paris and be sent on to fight, to men from Glasgow and Liverpool and Brooklyn and San

Francisco who gave up everything they had to go out there and fight.

Nobody under the age of about thirty-five today has much notion of what the Spanish War meant to the people of that distant period in which it was fought, and nobody over that age will agree with any generalization anyone makes about it. I personally disagree with about half the generalizations I made about it at the time. Rather than tussle with all that, it is better perhaps – for the moment at least – to remember some pictures.

When I got there, the man everyone went to see, if they could, was General Mangada – the only army general who had not joined General Franco's revolt and instead had remained loyal to the Republic. He was, I believe, a Cuban, or half a Cuban, and he looked strangely like some sort of cross between Gandhi and Gandhi's goat.

The other man who drove out with me to see him at his headquarters in the Sierra was a young man described as a 'Mexican', who, in reality, was one of the first of the Russian technical advisers sent to Spain. (This was at the early period when the Russians, who were rather naturally anxious to avoid doing anything that would give the Western Governments an excuse to turn the Germans loose on them in a war which would be described as having been 'provoked' by 'Red intervention' in Spain, were leaning over backwards being discreet, while Mussolini's bombers were already hovering above the supply routes of the Republican armies.)

General Mangada, after we had drunk a glass or two of sherry with him, asked if we would care to visit the front. We said Yes. We walked for a mile or so across lovely, deserted country – partly a sort of parkland, partly mountain foothills, with outcrops of rock baking in the sun.

We passed small detachments of troops sitting in what shade they could get, and then – after another mile or so during which we had seen nobody – we saw, perhaps six or seven hundred yards away, a line of riflemen in open order, moving about on the low ground ahead of us.

'Those, I suppose,' said the 'Mexican', 'are your advance patrols?'

'Not at all,' said General Mangada, surprised, 'those must be the advance patrols of the enemy.'

For the 'Mexican' and myself it was an ugly little moment. There we stood in no-man's-land, and there seemed a high possibility that within about ten minutes Spain's only Loyal General was going to be captured by the enemy, I was going to be shot as a Red Agent, and the 'Mexican' – unless his gullet was wide enough to swallow a lot of documents very fast – was going to be Exhibit Number One in a nasty international incident.

Awfully slowly, as it seemed to me, the General – who had the air of a man walking around his estate in Somerset on a Sunday afternoon – turned from his dreamy contemplation of the enemy patrols and we strolled back to his headquarters.

The 'Mexican' – a conscientious young man – said that perhaps he might be privileged to meet the General's Staff. General Mangada shook his head in his gentle manner. 'No Staff,' he said. 'In war Staff means betrayal.'

The 'Mexican' – a conscientious young man – said that perable speed, and said, 'Well, I am afraid we do not have a great deal to offer, but we have made some remarkable progress recently in mapping, and it occurred to me that our experience in that department might possibly be of some assistance to . . .'

Mangada interrupted him. 'No,' he said, 'no maps.' He put his chocolate-coloured hand on his left breast and tapped it gently. 'In war,' he said, 'the heart must be the map.'

In the vast requisitioned convent in northern Madrid where was being organized at nearly breakneck speed the Fifth Regiment, which was to become the model and nucleus of the New Army of the Republic, I talked one night with the Commandant and organizer-in-chief. At that time I knew this husky, bull-necked man, who combined almost super-human driving power with an unbreakable gaiety, simply as Carlos, and all I knew of his past was that he had once been a steel-worker in Chicago. Later, he turned out to be an Italian called Videla, who was supposed to have organized the assassination, in Mexico, of Leon Trotsky.

He spoke of the problems of the New Army, and while he

was talking one of them blew up right outside the room. From the former chapel of the convent we heard first the sound of shooting – volley after volley – and within minutes the barrack square was a scene of the wildest riot and turmoil. We rushed out, Carlos carrying a pistol in each hand – and he needed them because what we ran into when we got outside was a mob of armed militiamen milling about in the moonlight, looking for the Commandant and threatening to lynch him. By an extra-ordinary effort of domination and the help of the pistols, Carlos held them at bay long enough to get them sufficiently calmed down so that they allowed the man who seemed to be their leader, or one of them, to start to explain what it was all about.

The men were recruits – very poor peasants from somewhere in the south, who had, of their own free will, marched half across Spain to join the New Army and fight for the Republic. They had reached Madrid and the convent late in the evening, and had been hastily bedded down for the night on the floor of the chapel. They had fallen into exhausted sleep, but a couple of hours later, when the moon rose, two or three of them had awakened, and what they saw was the moon shining upon the statues and images of saints which it had not occurred to any-one to remove. The men's reaction was one partly of terror, partly of rage – terror because these images could ill-wish them, could be far more dangerous warriors than the Franco troops they expected to meet on the battlefied, and rage because they believed that they had been lured into a trap; whoever was responsible for exposing them to these deadly powers must be an agent of the enemy.

The first men to wake up grabbed their old rifles or sporting guns and started firing at the images and statues, yelling to the others to wake up and help them fight their way out of this trap. Everyone started firing at the saints, and then rushed out to find the Commandant and kill him, too.

'You see,' Carlos said when things had quieted down under a powerful jet of oratory and exhortation from himself, 'our problems are not quite simple.'

They changed, but they got no simpler. When I, some weeks later, joined this same Fifth Army as a private and went to the Sierra Front with a company of barely trained peasants, the first time we went into action – our commander, a former captain in the Foreign Legion, soon deserted to the enemy, and in his capacity as military saboteur had ordered us to charge straight up a bare hillside against a fort full of Moorish machine-gunners – a lot of the men charged holding their rifles high above their heads with one hand and giving the clenched fist salute with the other.

It emerged that they had taken the highly stylized and symbolical posters designed by the Madrid intellectuals, showing a Soldier of the Republic in this posture, as illustrations of correct military practice.

When they saw me dodging along, bent half-double and taking whatever cover there was, they thought the posture unworthy, despicable. A lot of them were killed or wounded before they got converted to the idea that, as instructional diagrams, there was something wrong with those posters.

For people who, like myself, have a claustrophobic distaste for organization and discipline, this makeshift, ramshackle quality of the Spanish War, which could be terrifying because it kept reminding one of the odds against our sort of forces being victorious over the trained troops of the other side, was also a factor compensating the periods of terror and the periods of tedium which are, alternately, so large a part of any war.

Also the nature of my job kept me moving fairly briskly between Madrid, London, Paris, Geneva and Gibraltar – where I went to do a mixed job of propaganda and espionage, and escaped being assassinated only because a pro-Republican waiter in the hotel where I stayed warned me just in time to get out of town. I was afraid at the time I might be taking unnecessary precautions, but years later I met one of the organizers of the attempt who assured me the waiter's warning and my own fears had been perfectly well grounded.

I had been only a few weeks at the front, and had been promoted corporal after two of our sergeants followed the Foreign Legion captain across the lines to the enemy, when I was summoned abruptly to London to take a hand in the campaign to influence the policies of the Labour Party and Trades Union Congress against non-intervention. Despite my protests, I was billed as the star speaker at an enormous meeting in Shoreditch

Town Hall – a grave mistake, because I am one of the worst public speakers who ever bored and exasperated an audience. I always had the feeling that no member of the audience at any of these meetings would ever read my written reports with much confidence again.

I was thankful when I was summoned to the Communist Party Headquarters by Mr Pollitt and ordered to write a book about the Spanish War instead. 'We need it,' said Mr Pollitt, 'in a hurry.' 'How much of a hurry?' 'Before the end of the week,' said Mr Pollitt, and I was locked into a bed-sitting-room in a nursing home run by a friend of mine, and told not to come out until the book was done. A nurse was in attendance to give me shots in the arm in case I fell asleep or dropped dead from exhaustion.

When I returned to Spain the atmosphere was a great deal more harsh, the aspect of the whole war more grim than it had seemed in the summer, but – although Franco was literally at the gates of Madrid – hardly anyone, I believe, even imagined that we could be defeated.

The food had become scarce and abominable, and the shells from the batteries outside the city kept falling in the Gran Via and around the Telefonica building, where the Correspondents had to go to transmit their messages. At breakfast one day in his room at the Florida Hotel, which more or less overlooked the nearest part of the front, Mr Ernest Hemingway was very comforting about the shelling. He had a big map laid out on the table, and he explained to an audience of generals, politicians and correspondents that, for some ballistic reason, the shells could not hit the Florida. He could talk in a very military way and make it all sound very convincing. Everyone present was convinced and happy. Then a shell whooshed through the room above Mr Hemingway's – the first actually to hit the Florida – and the ceiling fell down on the breakfast-table. To any lesser man than Mr Hemingway the occurrence would have been humiliating. While we were all getting the plaster out of our hair, Mr Hemingway looked slowly round at us, one after the other. 'How do you like it now gentleman?' he said, and by some astonishing trick of manner conveyed the impression that this episode had actually, in an obscure way, confirmed instead of upsetting his theory – that his theory had been right when he expounded it and this only demonstrated that the time had come to have a new one.

Everyone was very happy to have Mr Hemingway there, partly because he was obviously a fine man to have around when there was war and trouble, and partly because to have so famous an author there, writing on behalf of the Republic, made people feel less alone in the world – in a sense, which was no fault of Mr Hemingway, it helped to foster the illusion that sooner or later the 'world conscience' would be aroused, 'the common people' in Britain and France would force their Governments to end non-intervention, and the war would be won.

The Russians, who lived in the Palace Hotel at the other end of the Gran Via, seemed to be the only people who could do without this illusion and still not become defeatist. Although they wrote as big words as anyone for publication, they could get along without them in private conversation. They had an attitude which could be called cynical or just tough. They were refreshing because there were so many people about at the time – particularly the Visiting Firemen, VIPs of one kind or another from the United States and Britain – who seemed to have an irresistible need to use phrases as though they were facts, and if anyone punctured their phrases they became distressed and frightened about the future.

I spent a great deal of my time in the company of Mikhail Koltzov, who then was Foreign Editor of *Pravda* and, more importantly still, was at that period – he disappeared later in Russia, presumed shot – the confidant and mouthpiece and direct agent of Stalin himself. He was a stocky little Jew – from Odessa, I think – with a huge head and one of the most expressive faces of any man I ever met. What his face principally expressed was a kind of enthusiastically gleeful amusement – and a lively hope that you and everyone else would, however depressing the circumstances, do your best to make things more amusing still.

He had a savagely satirical tongue – and an attitude of entire ruthlessness towards people he thought either incompetent or even just pompous.

People who did not know him well – particularly non-Russians – thought his conversation, his sharply pointed Jewish jokes, his derisive comments on all kinds of Sacred Cows, unbearably cynical. And others, who had known them both, said that he reminded them of Karl Radek (an ominous comparison).

To myself it never seemed that anyone who had such a powerful enthusiasm for life – for the humour of life, for all manifestations of vigorous life from a tank battle to Elizabethan literature to a good circus – could possibly be described properly as 'cynical'. Realistic is perhaps the word – but that is not quite correct either, because it implies, or might imply, a dry practicality which was quite lacking from his nature. At any rate so far as his personal life and fate were concerned he unquestionably and positively enjoyed the sense of danger, and sometimes – by his political indiscretions, for instance, or his still more wildly indiscreet love affairs – deliberately created dangers which need not have existed.

As the Spanish War ground its way to its gruesome conclusion, and all over Europe people who had supported the Republic became truly cynical, despairing, without faith or enthusiasm for anything, I found myself looking forward more and more eagerly to conversations with Koltzov, journeys in his company, estimates from him of the course of affairs. He was a man who could see the defeat for what it really was, could assume that half the big slogans were empty, and a lot of the big heroes stuffed, or charlatans, and yet not let that bother him at all, or sap his energy and enthusiasm.

For a good many months before the end of the Spanish War I had been working chiefly in London, Paris and Geneva, and occasionally in Prague. It was strenuous, stimulating work, because my function, as I saw it, was to develop on the one hand the 'circle' influenced by *The Week* – to mobilize, scare and prod into greater activity all those people who could be so prodded or assisted in what was now, evidently, a desperately critical phase. These 'friends of *The Week*' were, for the most part, very far from being Communists, and many of them were Conservatives, or their equivalents in the various capitals where *The Week* still circulated. To command even a little of their attention *The Week* needed the most sensational kind of 'inside news', but above all it needed to present the news in a particular style and pattern, so that even when there was really no available 'inside news' people felt that they were reading something new, getting a fresh and more exciting picture or story than they got from the newspapers, and getting it in, so to speak, a tone of voice such as they were accustomed to hear in their clubs. On the other hand, I regarded my work as Diplomatic Correspondent and reporter of the *Daily Worker* as equally – perhaps more – important in the business of bringing to bear against Nazism and the forces making for war such pressures as could be brought. But the effective style for the *Daily Worker* was entirely other than that required for *The Week*, so that it was necessary to develop, stylistically, a double personality. This, as I have said, is strenuous, because if you lose for a moment a vivid awareness of either of these two so different audiences, the story will fall to bits.

In Prague at the height of the Munich crisis, it seemed as though half the international figures one had known in Madrid had assembled there, and the sight of them seemed to be ominous. You felt that soon there would have to be shells cracking against the hotel to complete the picture. (It reminded one of the story of the famous Hearst reporter, specialist in political disasters, H. R. Knickerbocker, when he came to Vienna at some moment of crisis. 'Good God!' cried the hotel manager. 'You here, Herr Knickerbocker? Is it then already so bad?') It looked like the end of an act, and it was.

I spent a lot of time with Koltzov at the Russian Legation, for that was the place where, if anything decisive were to happen, it would happen. And I knew that Koltzov was at least as important a figure on the stage as the Russian Minister, and perhaps much more important because of his double position at *Pravda* and at the Kremlin.

From this place of vantage I saw at very close quarters what really was the last scene of the act – everything that happened after that was anticlimax.

It was the moment when there still seemed to be an outside chance that either the League of Nations, or at least Britain, France and the Soviet Union, would stand together on behalf of Czechoslovakia against Germany.

The Czechoslovak army was in position on the frontiers, and at the headquarters of the commander-in-chief in the field there was no doubt whatever that war was a matter of hours. In the same belief, the Soviet Union had dispatched to Prague a force of fighter planes and bombers – an advance force which was to be massively reinforced at the moment of war. For obvious reasons this advance Soviet force was not officially there at all, and there were a good many people in the Czechoslovak Government who did not care for its presence – they thought Hitler would use it as a provocation.

As the tension grew almost intolerably, a message from President Benes urgently summoned the Russian Minister to the Palace. The message said that the President wanted to put some urgent questions.

In the circumstances, it seemed likely that this meant that the forces in Czechoslovakia demanding resistance to Hitler (even if it meant that the Red Army would have to occupy Czechoslovakia in Czechoslovakia's defence), had won the day.

The Minister rushed off. When he got there, he told Koltzov afterwards, he found the President looking, as he said, 'like a photograph of himself'.

'If,' said Benes, 'the League of Nations declares for resistance to Hitler's demands upon us, even at the cost of war, what would be the Soviet attitude?'

The Soviet Union, said the Minister, would in those circumstances certainly fight. He could hardly keep the impatience out of his voice as he answered so otiose a question.

'If,' said Benes, 'the League does nothing, but Britain and France declare themselves ready to stand by us, even at the cost of war, what would then be the Soviet attitude?'

The Minister was impatient to get this question settled quickly, too. Of course, he said, the Soviet Union would fight.

He waited confidently for the next question – the third, the vital question. He wanted Benes to ask what would happen if neither the League nor France and Britain acted, and if, nevertheless, Czechoslovakia resisted Hitler's demands at the cost of war. For he was authorized to state that in that case, too, the Soviet Union would fight.

There was a long pause. Neither of them moved. At last the

Russian, disregarding diplomatic discretion, broke the silence. Was there not, he said, a third question which Benes would care to put? A third potential situation?

Benes sat absolutely still for several minutes.

'No,' he said wearily, at last, 'those are the only two questions I have to ask.'

Gloom and a sense of futility enveloped the Legation when the Minister returned with his report. It could only mean that after all there would be no resistance, because neither the League nor Britain and France would carry resistance to the point of war. Glumly orders were sent to the airfield to tell the Soviet flyers that their mission was over before it had begun. All they could do now was to go home. Even Koltzov at this moment seemed to have lost resilience. And then, it must have been a couple of hours later, came an abruptly urgent call from Benes.

Would the Minister secure immediately from Moscow an exact, up-to-the-minute verification and reassurance of previous estimates of the pace and volume at which Soviet air power could get into action from Czechoslovak air bases? The Minister said he could get the required facts within an hour, and would rush with them to the Palace.

The Legation was wild with excitement, Koltzov dancing and kissing people and hurling his big beret repeatedly into the air. Counter-orders were rushed to the flyers at the airport. Two or three of them had just taken off, and one officer was so excited at the change in the news that he actually loosed off an anti-aircraft gun at them as the most emphatic possible signal.

And then – things were moving so fast now that policies were being made and unmade almost by the half-hour – the plot twisted again; someone, some force somewhere, intervened. The Minister dashed off to the Palace once again with the required information. And when he got there he was not even admitted to Benes's presence.

'The Czechoslovak Government,' he was informed, 'is no longer interested in the reply to this request.'

With that, it was once again a certainty that Czechoslovakia would not act with Russia alone as her ally. The shape of the next act was certain. Hitler's next triumph was assured. It was the hour, too, in which the Russo-German Pact became inevitable.

Sadly, Koltzov reminded me of the story I had told him about M. Claudel in Washington.

'Once again,' he said, 'the only thing to say is that in the little moment that remains to us between the crisis and the catastrophe, we may as well drink a glass of champagne.'

16

CONDEMNED TIMES

THOSE were indeed, in Clarendon's bitter phrase 'reproached and condemned times'. In other places and periods, people might have felt that the only thing that could suitably occur next would be the end of the world. One did not, in the winter of '38–'39 have to be so fanciful. The war would do the trick. The gas-mask was the expression of people's faith in the accepted apocalypse. Chlorine would give the final quietus. The expectation of those stinking and lethal clouds rolling round the Ringstrasse, the Boulevard des Italiens, and Piccadilly Circus, was serviceable, too, as affording a satisfactory explanation of why it was so much harder for us than for the members of any previous generation in all history to do those things which ought to be done. It accounted, also, for cultural inertia, alcoholism, sexual muddle, and cold feet.

At some meeting about that time of statesmen – in Paris or Geneva – a French black-and-white artist said to me, 'I am by profession a caricaturist, but here photography suffices.' It struck me as poignantly true then, and has often so struck me since. Reality goes bounding past the satirist like a cheetah laughing as it lopes ahead of the greyhound.

It was a time when one experienced a sharp need for some kindly lights amid the encircling gloom – a gloom which somehow seemed worse in London (where a lot of people still thought you were a tedious maniac if you said there was certainly going to be war), than in Paris where most people thought you a bore, and raving at that, if you pretended to suppose anything else. For a while I had been more tethered to London than I cared to be because my friend Michael Koltzov, foreign editor of *Pravda*, had recently appointed me London correspondent of that newspaper.

In this situation there was, from the outset, an element of embarrassment, because people supposed that in such a position I must have special facilities for getting to understand Russian attitudes, 'inside' sources at the Russian Embassy and so on. People sought to pump me about Russian policies, and were suspicious and offended when I said I knew no more about it than anyone else with a reasonable amount of common sense and appreciation of the fantastic. No one in London (where you must always put your needle in a haystack if you want anyone to find it) would have believed the truthful statement I could have made about my stint with *Pravda*.

Soon after I had started writing daily dispatches for the paper, the administrative people at the Moscow office rang me up and instructed me to open an office in London. I said it was entirely unnecessary – the correspondence could be done from my own flat, or on a typewriter here and a typewriter there. The simple fact was that I do not like to have an office and secretary and all that implies. In an office of your own you either get through your work early, and then you feel guilty because you are not fully utilizing office and secretary, and so you start dictating letters which otherwise need never have been written; or else, particularly in London, you want to work through the night and then charwomen and caretakers come and peer at you with hatred and suspicion.

But the *Pravda* people were annoyed because, not understanding these phobias, they thought I was being a little insulting in a Western kind of way; suggesting, in effect, that they, with the largest circulation of any newspaper on the turning globe, could not afford to hire a smart piece of Fleet Street. What they wanted was something with prestige to it, a classy type of job, as for instance a half-floor in the Reuter building. If I had suggested negotiating for a penthouse above the *Daily Telegraph* they would have thought the better of me. Money, they made clear, was no object.

I still dragged my feet a little and was soon not sorry to have done so, because the next thing that happened was that various wives of Koltzov – he had wives in several Western capitals – started to telephone me to say that they had heard on the grapevine that Koltzov had been arrested and was due to be shot any day now. Many of Koltzov's wives were known to me – three of them had been in Spain. All of them were lovely, intelligent women, all in love with Koltzov. They hoped, because they were in love with him, that I would do something to save him. Because they were intelligent they understood at once that there was nothing whatever that I could effectively do.

It was true that I talked daily with *Pravda* when I telephoned my article or articles to Moscow, but I did not feel that a sudden plea from me: 'Do not shoot my boss and friend of my bosom, he is innocent' would carry a lot of pro-Koltzov weight in the Kremlin. It was well known that for several years he had been the personal mouthpiece and trouble-shooter for Stalin in Spain and other *partibus infidelium*, and in Moscow Stalin's intimate. One had but to remember the truth of the American saying to the effect that the bigger they come the harder they fall. He was shot.

A little later *Pravda* took my by-line off my articles and news stories, which now appeared anonymously. I was disproportionately upset by that, because I recalled the loving care Koltzov had taken to try to find the absolutely correct Russian transliteration of the name I then wrote under – Frank Pitcairn. It was a question of differentiating, in Russian, the sound of the 'a' in Frank from that of the 'ai' in Pitcairn. He was a lover of language, and he liked to think about such things and get them right.

The articles continued to appear daily for a while, and then stopped. For a while the salary cheques arrived as though nothing untoward had happened, and then they stopped, too.

I did not, of course, know at the time whether Koltzov had even been arrested, let alone shot. A lot of sapient people said the whole thing was a blind and he had been sent to China on a secret mission of the highest importance. Since he had told me in Prague at Munich time that he expected to go to China, I half-believed these tales. On the other hand, *Pravda*'s behaviour to his appointee in London seemed, to say the least, suspicious.

I had no means of knowing whether I was supposed to continue telephoning daily to Moscow, firing words into the void, and whether the stoppage of pay was supposed to mean something, or was merely the result of some technical hitch or muddle of a kind which would surprise nobody at all accustomed to the bumbling workings of the Comintern.

Besides, what about the office, for which I had just begun to negotiate?

I asked questions on the telephone. The man at the other end said he had no information about anything. I wrote to Moscow. There was no answer. I visited M. Maisky, then Soviet Ambassador in London, and asked his advice. He was sympathetic and at the same time sardonically amused at the spectacle of my encounter with Russian bureaucracy. He said if I would write once more to Pravda he would give me a covering letter, explaining my sense of bafflement. I wrote and he wrote, but no reply was ever received. (It occurs to me now that quite a lot of people were probably arrested and jailed or shot just for getting a lot of letters from me. It would have been Stalin's idea of being on the safe side.)

I remarked to Maisky that I was glad that at least I had not gone out on a limb with that glamorous office. He said he admired my instinctive sense of balance.

All this caused me to wonder sometimes how right or wrong people were when they asserted that I had special knowledge of Russian attitudes.

Oddly – or perhaps not so oddly, because I have always liked Americans, and the sort of man that likes Americans is liable to like Russians – a prominent light in my part of the gloom was my old friend Mr Vladimir Poliakoff, formerly diplomatic correspondent of *The Times*. (It was he who had first, perhaps inadvertently, provided the information which ultimately led to the discovery – or invention, as some said – by *The Week*, of the famous – or notorious, as some said – 'Cliveden Set'.)

With the head of a Slav generalissimo, and a get-up vaguely suggestive of Homburg about 1906, this Vladimir Poliakoff strode and occasionally tiptoed around and about the diplomatic world of the twenties and thirties like a panther, which duller creatures deem merely picturesque or bizarre until they note what a turn of speed he has. Among his other notable qualities was an infinite capacity for taking pains to do everyone, from ambassadors to train conductors, small but unforgettable favours. A colleague, who regarded the very existence of Poliakoff with jealous disapproval, declared that there was not a Foreign Secretary in Europe whose mistress's dog had not been smuggled across one or other frontier by Poliakoff.

I met him for the first time in 1929 when I was tenuously attached to *The Times* office in Paris. The atmosphere in the office on that day was sulphurous. The chief correspondent, on calling to see the Minister of Foreign Affairs, had been informed by the *chef de Cabinet* that 'Your chief has just been with the Minister for an hour.' The correspondent was at first merely amazed that the editor should have come over from London without informing the office. Later, to his disgust, he learned that the supposed 'chief' was the peripatetic Mr Poliakoff on a quick trip to Paris. By virtue of a certain manner he had, he was quite often taken by foreign statesmen to be the 'man behind' everything from Printing House Square to Whitehall, and his sincere denials merely confirmed their belief.

Furthermore, the assistant correspondent had been apprised by friends in London that Poliakoff was accustomed to refer to him slightingly as 'the office boy with the silk moustache'. As a result of all this, the chief correspondent shut himself up in his room, his assistant put on his hat and walked out, growling, and I, to my alarm, was left alone with the internationally distinguished Poliakoff. I saw him examining me with attention, and feared he would ask me high diplomatic questions which I should be unable to answer, and thus become discredited.

He said, 'What you have is the grippe. Your temperature – I am not accustomed to be wrong about such things – is a little over a hundred.' Astonished, I admitted that this was precisely the case. The tails of his grey morning coat flapping suddenly behind him, he bounded from the sofa.

'A-ha!' he shouted. 'I am the one to cure that. A special remedy. Ordinary ones are futile. I proceed at once to the chemist on the corner to give my instructions. Relax. I shall return.'

In ten minutes he was back and, seating himself beside me, took from his tail pocket a small clear-glass bottle from which he poured a few drops of liquid on to a huge silk handkerchief.

'Breathe deeply. Inhale the remedy of Poliakoff.'

He had his arm round my shoulder and held the handkerchief to my nose with the air of a field-marshal succouring a stricken private. The result was immediately beneficial. But I noticed, too, that the smell and general effect were exactly those produced by a well-known, widely advertised popular remedy, the name of which I have forgotten. I was sufficiently curious to inquire later from the corner chemist whether a certain gentleman – Poliakoff was easy to describe and unforgettable – had, a little earlier, bought a bottle of this well-known product and arranged for it to be specially decanted into a plain bottle. Such had, the chemist said, been the case.

I found this little manœuvre, this taking of so much trouble to please, both impressive and endearing, and years later, when I had left *The Times*, was delighted to renew acquaintance with Mr Poliakoff at some diplomatic reception in London or Paris. He had a house in a square in South Kensington and there I used to drink Russian tea or vodka with him, or walk round and round the gardens while he exercised his two small Afghan hounds and talked to me derisively, in his harsh Slavonic accents, of the international situation. Even when he later brought a libel action against me our walks and talks continued amicably.

Being a supporter of what was called 'the Vansittart line' – the notion that by a friendly policy towards Mussolini it might be possible to split the Axis and isolate Hitler – he was fervent in denunciation of those powerful personalities in England who, on the contrary, saw in Hitler a bulwark and potential crusader against Bolshevism and thought friendship with the Nazis both possible and desirable. The vigour of his campaigns and intrigues against such elements was naturally heightened by his knowledge that some of them lost no opportunity to convince everyone that he himself was a hired agent of Mussolini.

His sources of information from anti-Nazi factions in the British and French Foreign Offices were thus first-rate, and the stories that came from them had that particular zip and zing which you get from official sources only when a savage intramural departmental fight is going on.

I rushed about between London, Paris and Brussels, supplementing and checking such stories from other sources. Vigorous anti-Nazis in the City, too, and on the so-called Churchillian wing of the Conservative Party were also very ready with 'inside information'.

At length I thought I had enough and more than enough to write in *The Week* a longish 'think piece' about the nature and aims of those in high places who were working, sincerely perhaps, but as it seemed to me disastrously, for the 'appeasement' of Adolf Hitler. There were, of course, several references to gatherings at the Astors' Thames-side house at Cliveden. When I published the story, absolutely nothing happened. It made about as loud a bang as a crumpet falling on a carpet. A few weeks later, I ran the whole thing again, in slightly different words, and with similar result.

And then about a month later I did it a third time. There were only trivial additions to the facts already published but the tone was a little sharper. But it happened that this time it occurred to me to head the whole story 'The Cliveden Set' and to use this phrase several times in the text. The thing went off like a rocket.

I think it was *Reynolds News*, three days later, which first picked up the phrase from *The Week*, but within a couple of weeks it had been printed in dozens of newspapers, and within six had been used in almost every leading newspaper of the Western world. Up and down the British Isles, across and across the United States, anti-Nazi orators shouted it from hundreds of platforms. No anti-Fascist rally in Madison Square Garden or Trafalgar Square was complete without a denunciation of the Cliveden Set.

In those days, if you saw cameramen patrolling St James's Square at lunchtime or dusk, you could be nearly sure they were there to get a picture of the Cliveden Set going in or out of the Astors' London house. Geoffrey Dawson, then editor of *The Times*, and a prominent member of the 'Set', comments petulantly on this nuisance in his diary. If you talked to American special correspondents, what they wanted to know all about was the Cliveden Set. Senators made speeches about it, and in those London cabarets where libel didn't matter, songsters made songs about it. People who wanted to explain everything by something, and were ashamed to say 'sunspots', said 'Cliveden Set'.

And throughout it all the members of the Cliveden Set, furiously, wearily or derisively, maintained that they were not members because there simply was not any Cliveden Set to be a member of. It was a myth.

And the fact was that, however it started, it presently became a myth. Within a year or so, the Cliveden Set had ceased to represent, in anybody's mind, a particular group of individuals. It had become the symbol of a tendency, of a set of ideas, of a certain condition in, as it were, the State of Denmark. It had acquired a powerful and alarming significance for people who could hardly have named three of those who frequented Cliveden. The phrase went marching on because it first had dramatized, and now summarized, a whole vague body of suspicions and fears.

Occasionally, moderate-minded intermediaries who felt the story was stirring up dangerous thoughts urged me to tone it down in some way – curb the monster I had set loose. I had to reply that in the first place I thought the picture essentially a true one, doing more good than harm. In the second place, even supposing that, contrary to my own convictions, I were to get the B.B.C. to permit me to announce personally to the listening millions that the story had no foundation, that I had invented it, no one would pay the slightest attention. People would come to the conclusion that I had been nobbled by the Cliveden Set.

I was certainly taken aback by the wild improbabilities which some correspondents were writing about the Cliveden Set. It looked as though quite a lot of people were getting involved, were being branded as subtly scheming political intriguers, who would not have known a plot if you handed it to them on a skewer, and quite possibly had gone to Cliveden simply for a good dinner. But then, I reflected, if one is as ignorant of political goings-on as some of them claim to be, is it very wise, even for a very good dinner, to go at all? I am prepared to believe that a lot of the people I had cast as principal figures were really mere cat's-paws. But then a cat's-paw is a cat's-paw and must expect to be treated as part of the cat. Or, as the Chinese proverb puts it: 'Do not tie up your shoes in a melon field, or adjust your hat under a plum tree if you wish to avoid suspicion.'

What ultimately interested, and still interests, me about the entire affair were not the facts about the Cliveden Set but the journalistic detail – the way in which a phrase can 'trigger' to explosion a lot of facts which, for the most part, were already known to hundreds of people, but remained, as it were, inert.

'Newspaper writing,' said the great Thomas Barnes, mid nineteenth-century editor of *The Times*, and its true creator, 'is a thing *sui generis*; it is in literature what brandy is in beverages. John Bull, whose understanding is rather sluggish – I speak of the majority of readers – requires a strong stimulus. He consumes his beef, and cannot digest it without a dram; he dozes composedly over his prejudices which his conceit calls opinions; and you must fire ten-pounders at his densely compact intellect before you can make it comprehend your meaning or care one farthing for your efforts.' A newspaper story, he concluded, 'wanted a little devil in it'.

Poliakoff was a good man to help one put 'a little devil' into one's stories. Staid people naturally loathed him, as being an adventurer, a rapacious semi-oriental pirate upon the English seas. They had loathed in the same way the incomparable de Blowitz – and, indeed, one of the aspects of Poliakoff which gave me great pleasure was that his mind and personality, even his clothes, seemed in some way to connect the world of Henri de Blowitz, of the Second Empire, of Bismarck, and the Dreyfus case, with our own.

Probably this, too, was in part, at least, a courteous trick, a stage-show put on for my benefit, since he was always alert to note what people wanted, and then, if possible, give it to them.

'You,' he warned me several times, 'are a romantic. It is dangerous. On the other hand, it cannot be helped. Every man should be allowed to choose the brand of razor he cuts his throat with. A minimal human demand.'

As a result of this intense attention to other people, he learned, almost before I knew it myself, of an occurrence of great importance in my life. On a gusty morning in February, 1939, we were in his study, drinking a little vodka, and talking partly about the Government and partly about the unaccountable *malaise* of one of the Afghan hounds, when he said suddenly and angrily, 'Pointless to talk to you this morning. Of what use the wisdom and experience of Poliakoff? You are addled. You have fallen in love.'

And it was, oddly enough, the morning after the party at which I had for the first time met Patricia. I agreed that his diagnosis was correct.

'English?' Poliakoff asked. 'You would never understand an English woman.'

'Not at all. A glorious Irish girl who has just come out of jail in Uzhorod, Ruthenia.'

'Excellent,' said Poliakoff. 'I advise you to press forward. The omens seem favourable for your happiness.'

He was right. Happiness – which includes excitement, and an appalling extension of terrifying responsibility – stretched all the way from that encounter to the moment of writing.

But it needed so percipient an observer as Vladimir Poliakoff to see that the omens were favourable. To anyone else examining the entrails of the situation they would have appeared bad, even stinking.

We were on the eve of 'der Pakt'. It was the eve of the dark day when the tickers confirmed that Herr von Ribbentrop, tool of the Fascist hyenas and murderers had arrived in Moscow. In a soap-opera repetition of the first Rapallo he had shaken political, economic and perhaps spiritual hands with Molotov the Hammer. Hammer of what? Hammer of the world proletariat against the Fascist hyenas.

When that happened I thanked History for the Irish. For the fact, that is to say, that Patricia, being an Irish woman, had been brought up in an atmosphere in which the particular hypocrisies of Imperial Social-Democratic England, never prevailed. Neither she nor her family were ever so self-deceived as to suppose that what was good for the Anglo-Irish was good for the Irish peasantry. Nor that what was good for the Anglo-Irish was necessarily good for the British. Centuries before, that sort of people had been denounced as being 'more Hibernian than the Hibernians'. They were people with a singularly realistic view of politics. A gun, one might say, is a gun is a gun is a gun. But if you want to win, what you have to do is have a gun in the right place in the hands of the right man.

'Right man' in this case means someone who – like the rebels of 1916 – will fire his gun for ideological reasons long after it is apparent to the damnfool realists of the world that the cause was hopeless from the start, and is now visibly and irretrievably lost. Some years before he became Prime Minister of Ireland and President of the League of Nations Assembly, De Valera was about as gone a coon as you could find in international politics.

General de Gaulle in 1940 was another gone coon. He had no money, about thirty men, and an ideology which hardly anyone outside Carlton House Gardens and the Connaught Hotel understood. When they did understand it they were opposed to it – notably Roosevelt, and, in a more openly violent but less subtly corrosive way, Churchill. The silliest remark Stalin ever made – supposing that he made it – was his question, 'How many divisions does the Pope have?' If he ever did say so stupid a thing, it would indicate a strange lapse of memory on the subject of ideologies.

How many divisions did the Bolsheviks have at the London Conference of 1905? And as a theological student at Tiflis, Joseph Djugashvili must have encountered somewhere the news of another ideological movement which started with no divisions at all and in no very long time controlled the Army of the Roman Empire.

Friedrich Engels wrote a famous passage on the subject, and J. D. must surely have read that. It is an illusion to suppose that he was – Khrushchev at one time sought so to present him – a kind of boor. On the contrary, he was a great deal better educated, better read, too, than eighty per cent of his critics among Western statesmen. If one applies the standards supposed to be applied by the Western world to the Western world, it is laughable to consider – let us say – Dwight D. Eisenhower as a 'civilized' man.

It was the fact that she had been brought up right in the midst of the guns and the fertile – sometimes crazy, sometimes

183

sublime – ideologies of Ireland that enabled Patricia to view the world into which she now jumped in an exhilaratingly realistic manner.

Once, in a conscientious moment, I was trying to explain to her the probable dangers and difficulties of being married to a man of my convictions and activities. She said, 'You must remember that during most of my childhood I was never allowed in the streets because there was supposed to be a danger of my being kidnapped or shot by politically interested people. Also, during most of that period, the outer gates were locked from dusk until dawn, armed gardeners patrolled the grounds, and they had instructions to shoot at sight any person seen moving in the grounds.' 'I suppose,' I said, 'that they challenged them first.'

Patricia was quite indignant at my naïveté. 'Nonsense,' she said, 'that would have given away the position of the gardener.'

With further naïveté, I supposed that what the armed men were defending that old house against were Sinn Feiners, Irish Nationalists, anti-Raj types of every kind.

Not so. Patricia's grandmother had been a member of the organization of Irish nationalist women started by Parnell. Her mother had deep sympathy for De Valera. The house was all along in as grievous danger from the Black and Tans and the Auxiliaries as it ever was from the Sinn Feiners.

It was a house which, in its time, had taken a lot of defending. Sir Walter Raleigh, when he was Mayor of Youghal, and – temporarily – owner of most of Munster, lived in it. One of the things he did while he was there – apart from planting the potato and smoking tobacco under the aged yews which today people sit under arguing about cigarettes and lung cancer – was to invite the poet Spenser to stay with him and write.

As is known, Spenser had the devil of a long thing to write, and I have been told since that the climate of the Blackwater Valley is not a stimulus to writers. Soothing, soporific, are the words used about it.

But Spenser did at least get so far as to enable Raleigh to announce that some cantos of *The Faerie Queene* were written from 'my Oriel Window in Youghal'. I have sometimes sat at that Oriel window. It is perhaps sentimental, possibly even fatuous, to find a particular pleasure in reading a canto of the *Faerie Queene* while looking out of the window the man sat at when he wrote it. But perhaps it is legitimate to allow oneself from time to time the luxury of these sentimentalities, these fatuities.

What Raleigh esteemed about the house – not that it did him much good in the end – was that it had the town wall around it. This very same amenity appealed, a couple of centuries later, to Patricia's grandfather, Sir Henry Blake. He, lifting himself by sheer energy out of the backwoods of County Galway, had been Governor successively of the Bahamas, Newfoundland, Jamaica, Hongkong and ultimately Ceylon. When he finally retired, the situation in Ireland was such that it must have been obvious to a man of such experience that – whatever his own views might be – he could be ignorantly deemed a symbol of the Ascendancy and have his head shot off as he walked his fields.

The wall provided a partial and prudent answer to the question of how to have a big house and security too. It was also, in later days, a persistent reminder to his grand-daughter of the 'realities' of life. Statements about the 'realities of life', together with such allied phrases as 'politics is the art of the possible', are repeatedly mouthed by the mean-spirited to insinuate that the 'realistic' thing to do is simply to put up with what we have, to regard all theories of possible betterment with suspicion and deride them as dangerous 'messianism'.

The conclusion that Patricia drew from the 'facts of life' represented by the wall and the armed gardeners was different. If you find yourself in a position where, without them, you may get shot or burned out, then you must have them. But you tolerate that wall and those guns on the understanding that you are applying your best exertions to changing such an abominably uncivilized condition of life.

Politics may be 'the art of the possible'. But it is the business of serious political people – meaning all who concern themselves about the present and future of civilization – to extend the area of the possible beyond the limits bounded by a wall, and defended by armed men.

In the case of Myrtle Grove the physical defences were

supplemented by a spiritual one – the fact that her grandmother was supposed to have the power of the evil eye. When the old lady sat in the library, the garden boy used to creep past the window on hands and knees for fear of accidentally encountering that eye and being blasted. At the age of seventy or thereabouts she learned Hebrew, the better to study the Scriptures and compare them with other historical or mythical writings in which she was interested. As a child Patricia hunted half the day and in the evenings, supine on a board for reasons of deportment, lay drinking madeira wine and reading *The Golden Bough*.

If she complained from time to time that she had 'nothing to do', her grandmother was likely to ask her exactly how many petals there were on a rare flower in the garden. 'You don't know? Then go and count them. There's always something to do.'

Inspired by the energy and curiosity of this grandmother, and of her own mother too, before she was twenty she had ridden across the Rockies, lived for months in a hut in Tahiti, and walked right across Central Africa making a 'language map' for the Royal Geographical Society. She had also, as I have said, got herself jailed – as the traditional Beautiful Spy – in Ruthenia. It was a common love of that neck of the woods which brought us together at the party in London where we met.

For a person with that kind of background, the rocks and rapids of politics on the British Left in 1939 were less intimidating than they would have been to a properly brought up English girl – to, for instance, most of those who had been debutantes along with her at the time when debutantes still existed and were presented at Court with absurd formalities amid thickets of ostrich feathers.

Nevertheless, when the news of the Soviet-German Pact came in, I could not help wondering whether the rocks might prove more dangerous than any even she could have imagined.

17

SPIRITS OF THE AGE

SILENTLY released – if that is the word – by *Pravda*, I had resumed my habit of travelling at least once a fortnight to Paris, partly for the reason I have already indicated, partly because news of the kind I wanted to get was more 'available' in Paris than in London (where one would so often spend hours seeking to penetrate what one supposed was the discretion and 'English reticence' of some leading figure, only to discover that he knew nothing anyway) and more particularly to consult and exchange information with such old friends and fellow-workers as Otto Katz (then operating under the name of André Simone), and that revered genius, Egon Erwin Kisch.

Though he died abruptly at the end of a rope, pronouncing me responsible for his misfortune, historians ought not to forget Otto Katz. No portrait gallery – rogues' gallery, some would say – of the period would be quite complete without the putty-coloured visage of that most talented propagandist and intriguer.

Pretty soon every schoolboy will think he knows all about that time, certified as having been full of starry-eyed do-gooders with pink illusions which, when darkness came at noon, blew up in their faces and turned them a neutral grey or else deep blue. Not so much, probably, will be heard of the late Katz – a man, nevertheless, reeking of eighty-five per cent proof *Zeitgeist*, and producing some pervasive practical effects upon events. Manuals of journalism for schools should have a bit about him, too.

He had sidled into my life in the summer of 1932, when he was acting as a kind of assistant director of the great anti-war congress of that year at Amsterdam.

After the closing session, I found myself at midnight sweating horribly in an hotel bedroom where Mr John Strachey, Mr Gerald Hamilton, a vigorous Hungarian woman, and myself were translating the official German text of the congress manifesto into English which must be, all agreed, as jolly popular in style as the *Daily Mirror* and as rigidly exact as the Athanasian Creed. Just how I got into the act I cannot remember, and it certainly was exhausting.

The Hungarian woman knew German so much better than the rest of us that she concluded she must know English better, too, and made this clear. Mr Hamilton, whose natural prose style was Edwardian, became so discouraged that he took off his wig and sat silently nursing it on his knee, his head gleaming like a new-laid egg.

The presence of Gerald Hamilton introduced into the proceedings a peculiar flavour of somewhat sinister farce. In numerous subsequent encounters with him I came to recognize it in the way that one detects the presence of some curious ingredient in a curry. My feeling about him then, in Amsterdam, was expressed many many years later by the poet W. H. Auden at a convivial gathering in Brussels. Auden had written a rhymed toast to each of those present. His toast to Gerald concluded with the lines (I quote from memory):

> So it's you that I now raise my glass to,
> Though I haven't the faintest idea
> Of what in the hell you are up to
> Or why in God's name you are here.

In that hotel bedroom in Amsterdam, so naïve was I that it did not occur to me that one of our dedicated company might be already a double agent. Or at least marking time among the Communists while preparing to act as an agent of a French armament manufacturer, selling information about the Communist Party. I did not know that Gerald's real name was not even Hamilton. I had no notion that years and years later (in 1966) he was going – from a base in Madrid – to tell a British Sunday newspaper that he had been a lifelong foe of Communism and that his current hero was General Franco.

Gerald Hamilton has written many thousands of words explaining that he is not the original of Mr Norris in Christopher Isherwood's novel *Mr Norris Changes Trains*. And perhaps there are elements in Mr Norris which are not entirely Gerald Hamilton.

I do recall that in Paris once, he introduced me to a French armament manufacturer who looked like a carefully painted skull, and immediately offered me large sums of money to obtain military secrets for him in London. This same old man had a young mistress named Susie for whom he had a senti-mental-paternal affection so overpowering that it created an illusion of incest.

When the girl became pregnant, the armament man looked about for someone to marry Susie before she gave birth. It was necessary to find someone who, on account of his own sexual tastes, could be relied upon not to exercise, as the saying goes, his 'conjugal rights'. Gerald was chosen, and a fee agreed upon for his services. The engaged couple came over to London, where the marriage ceremony was to take place.

A more solicitous fiancé than Gerald was never seen. He would hardly let Susie cross Sloane Square for fear she might be bumped by some vehicle. As Christopher Isherwood, who was going to be a witness at the wedding, observed, 'Well, it's natural. There are several thousand quid for Gerald in that girl's belly.'

The wedding took place. A few weeks later Gerald tele-graphed from Paris, 'A bouncing boy. Father doing well.'

But that night in Amsterdam I saw him otherwise than as I later did. Particularly the removal of the wig struck me as evidence of a frank, candid personality. It has occurred to me since that possibly that was precisely the impression it was designed to make. It could have been the equivalent of the phrase, 'To tell you the honest truth, old boy,' which so often introduces a lie.

Every so often, a grave smile and a light sigh floated in from the corridor, both brought to us by a smallish, light-footed man with a big head and abnormally broad shoulders hunched in a way to suggest that his burdens were indeed heavy, but he could bear them, and yours, too, if you cared to confide them to him. His smile said that whatever might be the faults of others working for peace that night, our little group was the salt of the earth – so brilliant and devoted that we should certainly produce splendid results, dead on time, if it killed us.

He had the air of a stage manager going round the dressing-rooms of a troupe on the verge of hysteria.

When I asked who he was, they said, 'You don't know who Otto Katz is? Oh!'

After the sleepless night, he invited me at breakfast-time to drink brandy with him on the terrace, and we talked about the congress. I spoke with enthusiasm. He ascertained that I had been, until recently, a correspondent of *The Times* in the United States. Presently he went about his business, which, as it turned out, was to prepare and issue to the continental news agencies an interview with 'the distinguished former foreign director of *The Times*,' who heartily endorsed all objectives of the congress, and had some sharply disobliging things to say about the British Government.

I protested to Mr Katz, demanding corrections and denials of the story. People, I said, would think Wickham Steed had turned Red in the night. He said: 'But as a sincere supporter of our cause and an experienced journalist, you appreciate that any retraction could be damaging to the excellent effect already obtained. *The Times* will doubtless issue any denials necessary. It will all help to stimulate discussion.'

'But it's preposterous to describe me like that.'

'I felt the phrase made a clearer impact. In journalism,' he said, fluttering his hand in a stagy gesture, 'one should try for clarity of impact.'

His staginess had a basis in experience. He had worked in various capacities for provincial theatres in northern Bohemia. Almost the only way to anger him was to doubt his story that at some time during that period he had been married to Marlene Dietrich. You could abuse him with impunity, but, if you doubted those nuptials, he became passionate, challenging you to go to Teplice, or wherever it was, and examine the records.

Along some political or journalistic channel – it was certainly a career open to talent – he had moved into the tumultuous Berlin entourage of the late Willi Muenzenberg, whom many people took to be the main dynamo of the German Communist Party. Whatever may be the truth about all that, Muenzenberg – who claimed to be an illegitimate nephew of Kaiser Wilhelm II – had made a vital impact upon the political life of Europe.

He had snatched the journalism of the extreme Left from the hands of the pedants, insisted that a modern revolutionary newspaper could be as 'popular' in today's terms as an old-time revolutionary broadsheet, and that the technical tricks, skills, and 'appeal' of the stunting, pandering, sensation-mongering capitalist press were to be not despised, but learned. His success, particularly with the picture paper *AIZ*, which for a time was the largest-circulation weekly in central Europe, had important consequences in Italy, France and Latin America. Muenzenberg's offices in the Wilhelmstrasse, across the way from the Foreign Office, were also the centre of those numerous international organizations (the League Against Imperialism for example), which, while the Communists supplied the inspiration and driving force, did at moments of crisis rally many sorts and conditions of non-Communists and anti-Communists who wanted to get moving and found no other bus going their way.

In all this, Otto Katz was first the pupil, later the right-hand man and, ultimately, it was often asserted, the inspirer of Muenzenberg; he was certainly the chief engineer of the Muenzenberg machine. After Hitler moved in on both sides of the Wilhelmstrasse, Katz, who now called himself André Simone, operated from a series of headquarters in Paris. He padded about Paris, Geneva, London, New York and Chicago, exercising and developing an almost necromantic capacity for getting people who naturally loathed and suspected one another organized for joint action. The nature of the – so to speak – material he worked on seemed not to interest him greatly : he was as happy welding mutually hateful novelists and poets into a literary League for the defence of this or that, as he was when arranging for a couple of Tory Lords and someone from Transport House to turn up on a platform with the editor of *l'Humanité*. The more improbable the *combinaison*, the more it charmed him. Indeed, after a visit with him to the United States, the Roman Catholic Prince Loewenstein told me that, though prepared for anything, he had, after all, been startled when he saw Herr Simone-Katz 'genuflect three times and kiss the ring of a cardinal to whom he then presented a Marxist professor just out of jail in Rio de Janeiro.'

All this time Katz was busy, too, as a very sharp-shooting

press agent and public relations counsellor for the organizations in which he was interested. Almost weekly he brought off the tricky shot of planting a damaging anti-Fascist story in a pro-Fascist newspaper, and under his original impulse his stories ran about the world like snooker-balls. They certainly had 'impact'. He regarded journalism simply as a means to an end, a weapon. In this I found him sympathetic. Long before, in New York and Washington, I had come to the conclusion that the real humbug of the Press begins only when newspapers pretend to be neutral, impartial fact-purveyors, 'servants', so help me, 'of the public.'

Arriving in Paris from Spain unexpectedly one day during the Spanish War, I telephoned Katz at the office of the *Agence Espagne*, the news agency of the Republican Government which he organized and directed. As was usual when one telephoned any office run by Katz, an excited voice said, '*Si, si, mais, s'il vous plaît*, be so good speak *deutsch, bitte schoen, momentito*,' and then Katz came on the line shouting, 'Thank God you're here, come at once, urgent.' He plunged immediately into business. 'Have I ever told you that you are considered by many, myself included, the best journalist in the world?'

'Often, when you wanted to get something for nothing out of me.'

'Well, what I want now is a tip-top, smashing, eye-witness account of the great anti-Franco revolt which occurred yesterday at Tetuan, the news of it having been hitherto suppressed by censorship.'

I said I had never been in Tetuan and knew of no revolt there.

'Not the point at all,' he said impatiently. 'Nor have I heard of any such thing.' The point, he explained, was that a crucial moment had been reached in the supply of arms to the battling Spanish Republicans.

Occasionally, despite non-intervention, the government of Léon Blum, under pressure from the Left, agreed that all concerned should shut both eyes tight while military supplies were rushed across the Catalan frontier. At this moment a major battle was being mounted in Spain. On the frontier a big consignment of field guns was ready. The outcome of the battle might depend on its getting through. Next morning a strong deputation of Communist deputies and others was to call on Blum, asking for a little shut-eye. Blum, naturally, was always more malleable when anything happened to suggest that Franco might, after all, lose the war. It was thus essential, Katz pointed out, that a jolt of that kind should be administered now. Something with a clear psychological impact. What better for the purpose than news of a sudden revolt against Franco at the very origin and source of his first onslaught, Spanish Morocco? Why not, for instance, Tetuan? That, he said, would have impact.

There seemed to be just a chance, and we worked on that story at a high pitch of anxiety and excitement. Our chief anxiety was that, with nothing to go on but the plans in the guide-books, which were without contours, we might have Democrats and Fascists firing at one another from either end of an avenue which some travelled night-editor would know had a great hump in the middle. The fighting, accordingly, took place in very short streets and open squares. As we saw it, an important feature of the affair was that sections of the Moorish soldiery, sickened by losses in Spain, had joined with civilian victims of colonial oppression and Spanish anti-Fascists in united, if desperate, action. It meant that the same thing might happen in Spain itself. Katz was insistent we use a lot of names, of both heroes and villains, but express uncertainty over some of them – thus in the confusion of the struggle outside the barracks it had been impossible to ascertain whether the Captain Murillo who died so gallantly was the same Captain Murillo who, months ago in Madrid . . .

In the end it emerged as one of the most factual, inspiring and yet sober pieces of war reporting I ever saw, and the night editors loved it. When the deputation saw Blum in the morning he had been reading it in newspaper after newspaper and appreciating its significance. He was receptive to the deputation's suggestions. The guns got through all right, and the Republicans won that battle.

(I should say here that when, a little while ago, I published part of this story in New York, a defender of Blum wrote a furious denial that such could have been his attitude. He purported to know – I have no idea how – that no such motives could have actuated Blum. He may, of course, be right. Perhaps, for instance, Blum was interested because a revolt in Tetuan would shake the faith of betwixt-and-between Franco supporters in France, who thus would be less liable to make a scandal about the dispatch of arms to the Republicans. The defender I refer to wrote with such assurance that one is forced to suppose it at least possible that he really did have some knowledge not available to other people. The supposition is at least strong enough to make it seem only fair to put his view – which I still think quite mistaken – on record here.)

Many people to whom I have at one time and another told this little story of the Tetuan revolt have been themselves revolted, profoundly shocked. Or at least they said they were. When I first published it as part of an article in a weekly paper, Mr R. H. Crossman, Labour Member of Parliament, referred to it with disgust in a piece he wrote for the *News Chronicle*. Aware that Mr Crossman had himself played a considerable role in British wartime propaganda, I was in turn taken aback. Was it, then, possible that throughout the life-and-death struggle with Hitler our propagandists had all along taken the view that their paramount duty was to be gentlemen, and not to tell lies, however damagingly misleading these might be to the enemy? What about, I thought as I noted Mr Crossman's disdain for the Tetuan trick, the 'Man Who Never Was' and suchlike episodes?

Reading on, I was fascinated to find that what fretted Mr Crossman was not that the thing had been done, but that I seemed to be quite happy, retrospectively, to have had a hand in it. According to him, it was true that he and colleagues had done that sort of thing during the war, but they had done it with gentlemanly distaste. '"Black" propaganda,' wrote Mr Crossman, 'may be necessary to war, but most of us who practised it detested what we were doing.'

A comfortable ethical position, if you can stop laughing. To me, at least, there seems something risible in the spectacle of a man firing off his propaganda-lies as, one presumes, effectively as he knows how, but keeping his conscience clear by 'detesting' his own activities. After all, if he does not think the cause for which he is fighting is worth lying for, he does not have to lie at all, any more than the man who sincerely feels that killing is murder is forced to shoot at those enemy soldiers. He can become a conscientious objector, or run away. 'Paris vaut bien une messe,' and I do not recall that Henry of Navarre ever claimed that he had detested his own 'cynical' behaviour.

At any rate, Katz had none of these inhibitions and did his work con amore. He had, of course, his failures, most of them, so far as I could observe, resulting from a quality rather often found in people of his background, namely a tendency to get in a muddle about the English. I do not have that background, but I am conscious of being in a muddle about them too. He could simultaneously attribute to them almost super-human cunning and intelligence, and sub-human stupidity and credulity. He would thus sometimes spend time shooting, so to speak, at gun-emplacements which did not exist, and at others imagine that he had duped people by some manoeuvre which the simplest could see through.

He was very proud of having secured for whatever office it was he was finally running in Paris – I have forgotten what name it went under – the services of a young Czech who, Otto claimed, could pass anywhere as an absolutely typical young Englishman. I forget, too, just what benefits were supposed to accrue from this – perhaps the idea was that in this role he could better effect contact with voyaging V.I.P.s, make friends and influence people. A little difficulty was that, for reasons no doubt sufficient, the young man would have had trouble in getting a visa to go to England to get the 'tip-top' English clothes which Otto, by now quite intoxicated with his particular Pygmalion act, thought desirable. However, a Paris tailor was found who claimed to understand, more or less, what was considered correct for business or le sport by English chic (in both senses of the world) types. And they rigged that poor young Comintern-commando up in an outfit of which it could be said that anyone who did not immediately discern on seeing him coming that this must be some Czech dressed up in a Frenchman's idea of an Englishman would have needed his eyesight tested.

I said as much to Otto, who was offended and became moody. Then a fine idea cheered him.

'Are you so sure,' he said gently, 'that you yourself understand quite what is the correct thing in England? After all, my friend, you have lived so much of your life in central Europe, in the United States. And even in London, do you see a great deal of the right people, socialites and such? It is easy to lose touch with English Society. It is not,' he added kindly, 'your fault. All the same, in my view Tommy looks absolutely . . . what is the word? . . . pukkah.'

He laughed, repeating 'pukkah' with pleasure.

'Tommy?' I asked, incredulously.

'I want,' said Otto, 'us all to get used to calling him "Tommy". A good, non-committal name.'

Irked, I could only remark that the address of his new office was, in every sense, a good one – it was in the Rue de l'Ancienne Comédie.

I never knew just how Otto Katz got out of France a little while before the twist of events which produced in turn the Nazi-Soviet Pact and the suppression of the French Communist Party. He escaped the fate of those refugees who were first arrested by the French and then killed by the Germans. He spent the greater part of the war, I think, in Mexico, returning later, after the German defeat, to Prague, where he became a kind of foreign or diplomatic adviser to the official Communist newspaper *Rude Pravo*.

Some years later he was hanged by the Communists, and just before he went to the gallows made a confession saying that he would have done well enough had he not, at an early date, been misled and recruited by me as an agent of the British intelligence service.

Our friend, Egon Erwin Kisch, of whom I saw a good deal in that period before the war, had, so I believe, died before these events took place. At the time of his death or until just before it, he had been Mayor of Prague.

Polgar says somewhere of somebody that 'his dearest wish would have been to have been born in Czernowitz, and, since he is a darling of the Gods, even this has been granted him'. In the same way I dare say that Kisch, who loved Prague with a passion unsurpassed even by the passion of those who love Edinburgh or Dublin, would have considered that to be born in Prague and finally become Mayor of that city was about as final a consummation of dreams as any man could expect – except that he had, for most of his life, less than no reason to expect it, considering that as he grew up there he was spat on by all high authority as a loathsome little radical newspaperman, Jewish into the bargain, and later had to fly for his life, an exile who, were he to return after the Germans had taken over, would be not merely spat on but tortured and hanged.

Perhaps, if he had lived long enough, he might have ultimately joined Katz on the gallows, for in that panic 'purge' nobody was safe. However, Kisch was less vulnerable than Katz, being a sort of municipal, if not national, hero, his writings loved and admired by people who totally disagreed with him politically. Because his books were world-famous, the Prague people saw in him a world-wide advertisement for themselves.

Though little known in England, Kisch was an important phenomenon in the history of European journalism. For it was he who first introduced to central European journalism the Western, Anglo-American conception of reportage. Until his bustling, thickset figure, vehicle for gipsy-sharp eyes and an inquiring nose – he looked rather as a Scottish terrier would look if it were Jewish – first hustled into the back streets of Prague (streets which in the end were so long that they took him to Peking, Madrid, and Sydney), the term 'reporter' was not noble in Europe. Noble was rather to sit in an editorial office writing 'think pieces', or else – à la française – conduct huge-scale enquêtes into situations of various kinds, in which observed phenomena served as sparse pegs on which were hung a whole wardrobe of political speculation or general philosophy.

Within weeks of its first appearance Kisch's first book of articles – The Rushing Reporter – changed all that. It sold more than a million copies. To be a reporter became the fashion, and quite old men who hitherto had signed their articles as 'Doctor' this or 'Professor' that, proudly proclaimed themselves 'reporters' and claimed to be out for the facts.

As in the careers of all men who succeeded in doing what

they want to do and somewhat more, luck played in Kisch's career a notable role. He was, of course, lucky not to be assassinated in China or Mexico – lucky, indeed, as he said to me once 'being a central European Jew of the twentieth century to have lived a long time without being tortured even once'. Personally I have always been very interested in luck, and, to me, more impressive than these later instances was the luck he had in connexion with his first great journalistic coup in the strange and lurid affair of Colonel Redl.

Colonel Redl may well have been the greatest *agent double* of the twentieth century, so far as it has gone. Or else, perhaps he merely seems so because he was one of those who ultimately got caught. In such cases, as with murderers, it is only possible to assess the relative qualities of those who, in the long run, did not quite make the grade.

At any rate, he was good enough in that role to have achieved, a few years before the outbreak of World War I, the distinction of being simultaneously the chief of the counter-espionage system of the Austro-Hungarian Empire, and the chief of the Russian espionage system against the Austro-Hungarian Empire.

His start on the ladder to this eminence was commonplace enough – young officer of middle-class background trying to keep up with the aristocratic von Joneses, needs money, spotted by international spy-ring, gently lured, then trapped, then blackmailed. Homosexual too. The story so far is pure corn. However, what happened next was more unusual, and a tribute to Redl's personal qualities. He seems to have been one of those men who could make a virtue – if this is not a contradiction in terms – out of the most dire of necessities. He freed himself from the squalid international spy-bureau in Brussels by getting the people in St Petersburg to buy him out, promising them that, given enough money, he could get them their money's-worth many times over. From this point on, the ladder became a double ladder, like something in a circus act, and with astonishing aplomb Redl made each ladder cooperate with the other, all to the swifter advancement of Redl. Thus he pointed out to the Russians that it would be a great advantage from their viewpoint if he were to get on to the inside of the Austrian military counter-espionage organization. But to do so, and to get to any worthwhile position in it, he would need to render some services. Why not, for instance . . . ? The Russians saw the point immediately and gave Redl the names of a couple of their own spies in Austria-Hungary whom he then 'unmasked' – earning in Vienna the reputation of a smart man. The process continued until he was right at the top of both ladders. He would give little 'briefings' to Austrian spies going into Russia, telling them how patriotic and heroic they were. They were not to know that their jobs were even more risky than they supposed, since Redl had, when it suited him, tipped off St Petersburg to their identities, and they were shot almost before the Carpathians were out of sight behind them. Information and lives were swopped to the satisfaction of both intelligence services, both of which were able to prove – in St Petersburg as in Vienna – that they were getting results.

The result for Redl was that he became a member of the 'inner council' of the General Staff of the Austro-Hungarian Empire, and – *pari passu* – the most important Russian agent in the world. And in 1913 he sold to the Russians the whole of the Austro-Hungarian 'order of battle', laboriously worked out over many years, for the event of war on the eastern front.

One part of the climax came because of something which one may evaluate as one will – either as the spatulate bumbling of Russian bureaucracy, the casually criminal inefficiency of all intelligence services, or simply the fact that it is almost always fatal to pin any faith to the belief that the professionals in any line, from newspaper-proprietorship to the Field-Marshals, have much idea of what they are up to.

However that may be, the Russians sent off the preliminary payment for the big sell-out in an envelope addressed to 'Opera Ball Thirteen', Poste Restante, Central Post Office, Vienna. And Redl's own men, who naturally had no notion of their chief's double role, happened to intercept the document. The sum inside was so large that Redl was asked at a meeting of the 'inner council' whether he did not think that this must be the clue which would lead to the apprehension of whatever individual or group was responsible for numerous leakages which had recently occurred. He was forced, as a loyal member of the General Staff, to arrange for two detectives to be permanently on duty at the General Post Office, with a bell rigged up to inform them so soon as anyone came to claim that letter.

Naturally, Redl could not resist the suggestion. The detectives were placed in the back office with a bell. And Redl could have sat down to wait for ever, or until the heat went off, to collect his money, had it not been for his friend – a stable boy whom he had financed into an expensive cavalry regiment – who at this moment reminded him that he (the young lad) was madly in love with an actress, and that he proposed to see nothing further of Redl, unless Redl could see his way clear to buy one of the new-model Daimler cars and take him – the stable boy – on a glamorous motor trip through fashionable resorts in Switzerland and on the Riviera. Otherwise, true love would triumph, and it would be the actress. And the friendship-trip in the Daimler, if it was to come off at all, must come off now – at the most in a week.

Without the Russian payment Redl could not buy the Daimler. He took a chance. Just before the General Post Office in the Stefanstrasse closed, at five o'clock in the afternoon, he took a taxi thither, went in, asked for a letter addressed to 'Opera Ball Thirteen'. The clerk, as instructed, handed him the letter and at the same time rang the bell notifying the detectives that the big moment had come. But, as so often happens when the big moment comes, the detectives – already bored by their seemingly senseless vigil – were now reflecting that it was Saturday night, that the post office would be closed in a few minutes, that in an hour or so they would be escorting their girl-friends to the Prater. They had their trousers off and were ironing them to give the chic crease. It took them just that little while after the bell rang to leap into those trousers.

Nevertheless they did get into their trousers and out of the building just in time to espy the number of Redl's taxi; they had the good luck, a quarter of an hour later, to encounter that same taxi homeward-bound across the Stephan's Platz; they traced, point by point whither the fare had gone; and they found, as they cruised, down behind the back cushions of the taxi, a leather sheath – the sort of small leather sheath that would, in those days, be used for a paper-knife. He had needed it to cut open the Russian letter.

That was how they traced him to the Hotel Herrenhof, where they told the man at the reception desk they were looking for a spy, and he laughed, and they asked 'Why does that make you laugh?' and he said, 'Because this is the Vienna residence of our biggest spy-catcher – did you not know? – Colonel Redl.'

Nevertheless they asked the receptionist to show the little sheath to every guest who went in or out, and inquire whether he had lost it, and when Colonel Redl – in civilian clothes, and all ready for the trip to Switzerland and the Riviera – came down, perfunctorily showed it him, and he said, 'My God, yes, that's mine, now where did I . . . ?'

Then he saw the detectives, watching him. He walked about Vienna all evening, and by the time he returned to his hotel there was a military commission there to hand him a revolver. He waited until six in the morning and then shot himself. The military commission took off for Prague where Redl had his headquarters, and a communiqué was issued to the newspapers announcing that Colonel Redl had died suddenly of a heart attack. The Imperial Government was particularly anxious to keep secret facts which, if known, would provide propaganda ammunition to the Czechs, the Yugoslavs, the Socialists and all those others who proclaimed the régime rotten at the core.

This was where Kisch's luck came in. The day at whose dawn Redl shot himself at the Herrenhof in Vienna, was a Sunday. And for that day had been scheduled an Association Football match in Prague between a team from Dresden City and a team representing the Prague newspaper *Bohemia*. The advance betting was all on the *Bohemia* team, but they lost, because at the last moment their goalkeeper did not turn up and could not be found anywhere.

The Editor of *Bohemia* at the time – and if this did not make him a darling of the Gods nothing could – was Egon Erwin Kisch. Late that Sunday night, after the bitterness of the lost match, Kisch at length interviewed the missing goalkeeper – who excused himself by saying that he had had an urgent job to do. He was, by occupation, a locksmith.

'A job?' snarled Kisch. 'On a Sunday? Why not come right out with it and admit you were too drunk to get out of bed in time for the match?'

The locksmith told him things had not been like that at all. A military commission had been there – searching the personal headquarters of Colonel Redl, and they had needed the services of a skilled locksmith to force dozens of locks on Redl's private desks and drawers. Wide-eyed, the young locksmith told Kisch of the things discovered in those drawers – the autographed photographs of young men, the bundles of letters, the conversation about these matters that went on between the members of the commission.

By this time, Kisch had forgotten his displeasure at the defeat on the soccer field. He questioned and cross-questioned, and the next issue of *Bohemia* carried a *démenti* which ran to several columns length. Because of the censorship it had to be couched in a certain form. 'It is entirely untrue that Colonel Redl, who died a perfectly natural death of a heart attack on Sunday morning, was in fact . . .' The facts, all denied, then followed. And even at that more than half the issue of the paper was seized and burned by the police.

It was thus that Kisch, in his way, like – though in other ways so unlike – Poliakoff, for me linked past Europe with the present Europe and helped to make the present Europe more bearable, more intelligible. Whatever astounding and even dismaying things seemed to be happening, they were no more astounding or dismaying than a lot of things that had happened before.

We used, in that strange spring before der Pakt and the war which we all, erroneously, thought was going to be the end of everyone, to take, sometimes, the pleasant air of Touraine, in the company of a man whose real name I have never known nor asked – he was called simply Monsieur Bob. His parents were wine-growing peasants in Touraine, and he himself – I have been told, and I think it is true – was an officer of some French cavalry regiment which was attached (either as guard or demonstration) to the French Embassy in Russia at the time of the revolution.

Whether it was cavalry or not, the fact was that when the showdown came – when the French were supposed to rush at the revolting proletariat – this young officer refused to order them so to do. Indeed he ordered them, and they seem to have acted with vehemence, to assault the others – the Whites. At any rate, whatever it was he did was heinous, and he was sentenced to death in France, should he ever return to the jurisdiction. In the end there was an armistice on that sort of thing – I suppose as a result of the Franco-Soviet Pact (these things always seem of life-and-death importance at the time and afterwards you forget what on earth the sequence really was). So there he was in France, a gentle, dapper little man cocking a Touraine peasant's eye at the Comintern of which he was a principal agent.

I had met him a couple of years before in Spain where he had arrived suddenly on a tour of inspection. I had expected someone grim who, probably, would weigh me in the balance and find me much wanting. I took a terrible chance by recommending to him – a Tourangeois – a certain Catalan wine I had discovered, telling him that it was as good as a medium-grade French claret. Fortunately, for he was a fastidious little man, he thought so too, and we became friends over the first bottle.

Occasionally, when there was time, he would drive me and one or two other wine-lovers such as Kisch, down to his parents' vineyard. They were a gnarled old couple, looking as though they had been toiling in that vineyard since about the time of Voltaire. And although neither of them had ever been farther from home than Tours, they thought their son's sensational and even bizarre career quite a natural thing to happen in the world. On account of their almost rigorous hospitality, after a couple of hours at their farm-house one lived in a golden haze. They would open a bottle of their wine, give you a glass and ask what you thought of it.

You drank and commented admiringly – and it really was very good.

The old man would look at you as though he had found himself entertaining an escaped lunatic.

'Good? You think that good? But my dear sir, forgive me for asking, but where have you been all your life? Now permit me to draw your attention to *this* bottle. You will see the difference.'

You drank a glass or two of the next bottle, and you did see the difference and said so.

'Wonderful!'

'Wonderful? You can find that wonderful? Good, yes, I agree. But not wonderful. Now nearer to being wonderful is this.'

Bottle after bottle was opened on a deliciously ascending scale, until the peak of the sublime was reached. Once, ignorantly, I remarked of the last, the most sublime bottle of all, that it must fetch an enormous price in Paris. My host jumped as though at an indecent suggestion.

'Sell *that* to Paris? My dear sir. That is our best wine. We can't sell that. We drink it ourselves.'

It was during one of these golden interludes that Monsieur Bob first sought to convey to me, with infinite discretion, the possibility, theoretical as yet, of something in the nature of a German-Soviet Pact. To most of us at that time the notion was both outrageous and incredible. And if rumours were heard, we supposed them to have been put about by reactionary agents.

'But if,' said Monsieur Bob, sighing deeply and stroking the stem of his wine-glass, 'the British simply do not want to come to a serious agreement with Moscow?' (This must, I suppose, have been in late May or early June.) 'Suppose,' he said, 'that *le patron*' (it was the way Stalin was always referred to at that time) 'suppose *le patron* – on the basis, you understand, of in-information received – believes that secretly the British still hope to come to an agreement with Hitler themselves? An agreement which will send him eastwards instead of westwards? What do you think *le patron* would do? What could he do, except perhaps turn the tables on them and buy a little time for Russia by sending him westwards first, *en attendant* the real battle in the east?'

'But good God – an agreement with Hitler? With that aggressor and murderer, the leader and organizer, after all, my dear Bob, of anti-Communism everywhere?'

'Are all Scotsmen,' asked Monsieur Bob, oddly echoing Polia-koff, 'somewhat romantic? I would draw your attention to the fact that we are talking about serious international politics. But of course nothing of the kind may ever happen. Perhaps London will all at once come to its senses. I have great faith – perhaps it is I who am now being romantic – in English common sense. Perhaps' – and it was a phrase you heard over and

204

over again in Paris at the time – 'perhaps they will send for Churchill and put an end to all this fooling about.'

Perhaps it was the wine, perhaps it was the fact that Patricia was due to come over to Paris in a day or two – for whatever reason, I paid at the time too little attention to this conversation in which, as I saw later, my friend Bob was seeking to offer me, from his own inside position, a cautious, pre-view of the possible shape of things to come. So that when, a good many weeks later, the first unmistakable indications that 'der Pakt' was going to be a reality came, soon after midnight, over the ticker-tape at the Savoy Hotel in London, I was almost as startled as anyone else.

Nevertheless, when the earthquake occurred, I found that Bob's warning had subconsciously prepared me for it. Also his manner and personality were strong antidotes to panic. He was one of those who, at moments of exhaustion and darkness of mind, revive one's confidence in the human race. He had the virtues, such as courage, clarity of mind, and firm philosophy, which were to be found among the best Comintern agents, without the occupational vices of many of them, such as rigidity, pomposity, affectation, parrot-talk and the arrogance born of basic insecurity.

He was one of those men who really do love their fellow-men like brothers and are, literally, prepared to be martyred for their sakes. He accepted the most rigid discipline because he considered it necessary to victory. Some march in step because they find it easier than walking alone. Monsieur Bob was not one of those. He was one of those, however, who in shedding their illusions do not also shed their hopes.

18
POP GOES WEASEL

A MAN who claims to have been present at the time told me recently a poignant story of a discussion held in the Kildare Street Club, Dublin, in the last week of August 1939. I suppose if you amalgamated the London Carlton Club and the

Athenaeum and then stuffed the end product with moth-balls, you would get something resembling the Kildare Street Club. (It is, for instance, the place where two men quarrelled for life because, due to acoustics and confused mentality, while Mr A was making bitter comments on the coldness of the bath water, Mr B understood him to be aspersing, as frigid, Mr B's daughter.)

However, by the late August of that year the news that some kind of international conflict might well be brewing was already known at the Club. The late Earl of Wicklow, mulling over the situation with friends, said they could take it from him that the whole idea of war was nonsense.

'Austria-Hungary,' said he, 'has learned her lesson from the last war. If Hitler were to attack, Austria-Hungary would take him in the rear, and he knows it.'

With regret, his friends reminded him that Austria-Hungary, as such, no longer existed, and that its disparate portions were, directly or indirectly, under the control of Hitler himself.

The Earl reflected briefly and then said, 'Well, be that as it may, Hitler will still not dare to act. He has to reckon with the Serbs. The Serbs, and mark my words, the Serb is a good fighting man,' said he, 'hate the Boche. Serbia will take Hitler in the rear, and he knows it.'

Sadly they told him the situation regarding Serbia – how it had ceased to exist as a separate nation, been merged into Yugoslavia, and how, for various reasons, Yugoslavia was in no sort of shape to be conducting decisive attacks upon Hitler's rear.

'In that case,' said the Earl of Wicklow, 'the whole thing is reduced to an absolute farce.'

The idea that the whole thing had been reduced to an absolute farce was, with more or less justification, according to your viewpoint, the first reaction of millions of honest Britons to the news that 'hammer' Molotov and champagne merchant Ribbentrop were together in Moscow, arranging to be friends for evermore. Witty, encouraging and inaccurate to the last, the British Foreign Office spokesman said, 'All the Isms are Wasms.'

No one old enough to have been politically conscious at that time is likely to forget the bubble of passions, the frantic accusations and counter-accusations, the 'agonizing re-appraisals', the re-affirmations of faith, the hubbub of emotions, which thereupon broke out. And, of course, people too young to have been there must by now find a lot of the excitement irrelevant and incomprehensible. It was real enough that night.

After seeing the news on the ticker I went home and brooded much of the night, and in the morning took the telephone off the hook – it was sufficiently evident what the various people who would ring one up would, respectively, and in contradiction of one another, say. And indeed they have been saying it ever since.

In those days I had, perhaps, a rather more childlike confidence in the judgement of Stalin than – by pure hindsight – I have now. That is to say, I did not grasp to what extent he was the victim of excesses of occupational insanity. Even now, I cannot see that there was anything else he could have done in the matter of the Pact – and nobody on the British side has, so far as I know, ever produced a single official document to show that the British statesmen concerned were seriously interested in an Anglo-Soviet alliance, and were not more interested in an Anglo-German alliance. It is, of course, no crime on their part to have preferred the chance of one to the chance of the other. From their viewpoint and from that of many of their associates, they were justified. They would have gained a few years by launching Hitler eastwards, and, had he won, there would still have been a few years more before, with European and probably part of Asiatic Russia under his control, he would have swallowed up Britain and France.

Yet, despite these considerations, people became, at the time, quite frenzied with indignation. I recall a distinguished and sincere fellow-traveller of long standing, who, during those days, could not bear to leave the offices of the *Daily Worker*, where he daily beat his breast, except to visit the precincts of the Communist Party at King Street, where he beat it more. Choking with emotion, tears often on his cheeks, he totally neglected his own very lucrative business as he tottered bewilderedly up and down the stairs at both places with, it seemed, the general idea of telling everyone concerned – editors and functionaries of one kind and another – that something must be done. What he thought should be done never emerged, unless it was that the British Communists were suddenly to proclaim

207

that they were going to quit the Comintern as speedily as the European Socialists had retired to their national fastnesses when the earlier trouble broke out in 1914.

The memories of 1914 were, indeed, among the troubling factors. It would be interesting, if anyone had the time to do it, to make a study of events and dates which have reached out a long, paralysing hand to grip and twist future history. The French very notably, for a century and a half, surrendered themselves with apparent enthusiasm to this vicious mauling by the hand of history. It sufficed to suggest that somebody was acting like a 'man of the 18th Brumaire' or of the '11th of July' or whatever date it may be upon which some horrible thing was done, to set people against that somebody, or at least to lay on him the burden of proof that he was not up to something vile.

The English are victims (or beneficiaries, according as to whether you think this procedure by historical analogy a good thing or a bad thing), of the same tendency. For years and years the Labour Party was – perhaps to some extent still is – governed by the memory of how in the early 1930s Ramsay MacDonald split them and betrayed them to form the National Government. And, in 1939, the thinking of everyone on the Left was subtly or crudely influenced by the recollection of how, in 1914, the Second International, after its numerous gatherings in which its member parties from every nation had solemnly gone on record with the declaration that under no circumstances would they support their Governments should those Governments lead their countries into war, almost immediately went home and supported their respective Governments by voting, at the outbreak of World War I, for the war credits necessary to the financing of the conflict.

Anyone can argue – and every articulate person over the age of thirty has so argued – pro or con the Nazi-Soviet Pact. Suppose Stalin had thumbed his nose at Hitler, been attacked, collapsed, forced to surrender the rich spaces of Russia to the German, after which, with those resources behind him, Hitler had gone for the west? Suppose it – but you cannot know that it would have happened just like that. Or suppose Stalin had been just a little more trustful of Chamberlain and Daladier and Colonel Beck? And suppose that in that case they in turn had agreed that the Red Army could advance through the eastern border States – the point upon which, ostensibly at least, and, in view of what since has happened, intelligibly, the negotiations broke down. Hitler might, in that case, have been finally encircled and suffocated, and there would have been no World War II. One is certainly at liberty to suppose that.

But, to return to that harassing day in London in August, 1939, when history is moving along at a fast clip there is really no time to indulge in these speculations. Like Napoleon, when some ponderer asked him for a thoughtful statement about the *finesses* of military strategy, one can only say, disappointingly, 'Well, you join battle, and afterwards you see.'

Personally, if the matter is still of any interest, I thought that either the pact would scare the British and French Governments into revising their attitude to Moscow, or else they would have to face such consequences as are liable to ensue when you bet you can take on a continent and a half and lick it. (It would be incredible, were it not on record, that there were publications – the *Nineteenth Century* under the editorship of that defender of the English homeland, Mr Frederick Voigt, was one of them – which, while deploring the Russian attack upon Finland, found some comfort in it, on the ground that now we could go to war with Russia as well as Germany, thus tidying up the entire situation.)

It is the work of an instant now, of course, to attribute everything that went wrong to the wickedness, criminal lunacy and general mental debility of Joseph Stalin. I am bound to say that I did not think anything of this idea at the time, and admit I do not think much of it now. It is easy, then as now, to understand just why the British and French Governments were prepared to risk defeat by Hitler rather than do anything which could in any way favour the interests of Communism. But if you said, in those days, that the leaders in London and Paris believed that the struggle against international Communism was more important than the struggle for individual national survival – if you suggested, in fact, that we were moving out of the period of the 'nation state' which had dominated life and politics since the end of the Middle Ages – you were regarded as a foolish doctrinaire, and slanderer of the London Government.

On that morning of der Pakt I went down to the *Daily Worker* deliberately rather late – I had my own mind made up and I thought it would be tedious to have to watch a lot of other people making up theirs.

At that time, the *Daily Worker*, after being evicted from the Dickensian barn it originally inhabited in Tabernacle Street, where the electric light was constantly failing and much of the work had to be done by candle light, was housed in the City Road, and the public house we used, just across the road, was the original Eagle where the weasel went pop.

Naturally, being so situated, we had done a lot of research into the origins of the rhyme and what exactly the weasel was. Our consensus, for what it is worth, was that the 'weasel' was one of those big tailor's irons. A hundred and fifty years ago, the City Road was a road leading through fields and open countryside to pleasure gardens somewhere in the neighbourhood of what is now Camden Town – or perhaps still farther out. In any case, to go 'up and down the City Road' was a practice indicating dissipation and extravagance, and the expense was increased by the habit, fashionable it seems among the City apprentices and their masters, of breaking the journey by a halt for drink at the Eagle. And the outcome was that the out-of-pocket tailor had to pawn or 'pop' the principal tool of his trade, the weasel.

The public house was lavishly decorated with drawings by the *Daily Worker* cartoonist Rowney – formerly of the army in India and later killed in Spain. He had a strong, rough line, very suitable for harsh political cartooning and seen to great advantage on the walls of a profoundly cockney public house. There was a large one of a tailor actually popping his weasel which was particularly admired by the proprietor, who had rubbed Rowney's slate clean of heaven knows how many unpaid drinks when the drawing was delivered.

The place did good business in those days – partly because the *Daily Worker* staff and people from King Street who had come along to advise and supervise, and people from all over who had come to wheedle from the paper free publicity for their bazaar or protest march, all used it, and partly because, in consequence, there were rarely less than three plain-clothes men from the C.I.D., putting their whisky down to expenses inevitably incurred in the pursuit of important political secrets such as might be expected to drop from the lips of the subversive types regularly there assembled.

I remember remarking, as we sat that August morning in the gritty sunshine that came in from City Road, that it certainly looked like being a hard winter. For it was already evident that, however necessary the Pact may have been to the Russians, by signing it they had effectively dynamited everywhere all the Popular Fronts, the vague but comforting alliances between Reds and anti-Nazi Conservatives. We were out, from now on, in a very cold cold.

I was, it goes without saying, powerfully and instinctively moved to take that opportunity to break with the Communists there and then and brigade myself with the 'Churchillian Tories'. Personal considerations swayed me in that direction, not least among them the fact that Patricia had just run away with me and I felt that now, as a result of the latest turn of events, I was getting her to jump into a much deeper hole than she could have foreseen a few months before. On the other hand, quite apart from the high political rights and wrongs of the matter – and I was uncomfortably undecided as to who was right and who wrong – I was dominated by the feeling that I had, of my own free will, joined, so to speak, a regiment and that I had better soldier along with it, particularly at a moment when it was obviously going to come under pretty heavy fire.

It seemed to me that in those dead days of the Popular Front I had had a rather easy time being a Communist, and it would be, to say the least of it, shabby to quit now.

And, of course, there were other powerful reasons in favour of fighting things out on whatever line the Communists might finally determine to adopt. You cannot work closely with people for years without enmeshing yourself in a network of personal – sentimental, if you like – loyalties and affections.

Nevertheless, the fact that a person is swayed by his 'group' does not answer the question how and why – assuming that he had a choice in the matter – he got into the group in the first place. And in this matter I think that a good many people in England whose business it should be to understand why people become Communists are the prisoners of their own propaganda – always a dangerous situation and, in this case, useful only to the Communists themselves.

For years people have been going around and about saying that in Britain Communism is an alien thing, that it is repugnant to all but the physically starved or the mentally distorted or those who may imagine that they are going to float on a high tide of troubles.

Such an account of the situation is patently untrue, or at least miserably inadequate, and therefore, as I say, dangerous. The reality – and it is a serious matter – is that Communism can and does have deep affinities with British radicalism. Manchester and London did as much to shape Karl Marx and Marxism as did the Rhineland or the Paris Commune – perhaps more. And, paradoxical as it may seem, Communism has – or at least very often has – a particular appeal to people brought up in the British public schools and universities, especially people with a classical and Christian education. The Greek dramatists and both the Testaments smoulder with passages which, at any rate to a young man, are incitements to revolt against orthodox society, to throw in his lot with the 'have nots' against the 'haves'. And if you ask me what first – long before I experienced central Europe in the inflation time, or attended the American crash of 1929 – 'conditioned' me to be susceptible to the appeal of Communism, I should have to say that it was, for example, the Magnificat I listened to every Sunday at evensong in the village church, and Antigone's defiance of Creon in Sophocles' play.

To draw attention to the putting down of the mighty from their seats is by no means an innocuous proceeding – unless, of course, the congregation is asleep at the time and does not notice what is being said.

All the same, it was somewhat melancholy to sit there in the Eagle and reflect that at least half one's friends were soon going to stop speaking to one, perhaps for ever. I recalled a sentence written by my great-grandfather, then Lord Cockburn, who was a young Whig in the Edinburgh of the early nineteenth century, a time when, as he says in his memoirs, 'even in private society a Whig was viewed somewhat as a Papist was in the days of Titus Oates. Very dear friendships were in many instances broken, and although the parties may have survived till age and changed times made longer severance absurd, the reconcilement was always awkward and never true. This incompatibility of public difference with private cordiality is the most painful recollection that I have of those days, and the most striking evidence of their hardness.'

It occurred to me that world events were conspiring to make a lot more difficult even than it had looked at the outset any reconciliation between Patricia and her parents, of whom she was profoundly fond.

On the news that she was running away with me, her mother had said, 'Do you realize that, if your brothers were in the diplomatic service, a scandal of this kind would force them to resign?'

Patricia said, 'But in fact they are not in the diplomatic service.'

'That,' said Mrs Arbuthnot characteristically, hammering the floor with her stick, 'is not the point.'

Major Arbuthnot voiced a different objection. He had been proud, he said, of holding a certain record at the Carlton Club – he was the only member who had three sons and a son-in-law, all of whom were members too. Now, though Patricia's first husband would no doubt remain a member, he would cease to be the Major's son-in-law, and the record score would have to be wiped out.

Though endearing and nostalgic, these reactions seemed, at first, those of people imprisoned on the stage of a period piece. I soon found that the contrary was the case. Regretting the ruins of their Edwardian period – including the loss, first gradual, then sudden, of the greater part of their fortune – they yet managed a singularly lively and alert existence in the present. Like all honest and lively elders, their attitudes were annoyingly unpredictable to contemporaries suffering from arrested development. Major Arbuthnot, indeed, who could take pleasure in quite contradictory ideas at the same time, considered it his congenial duty to *épater* people of pompous or rigid mind wherever he found them. Mrs Arbuthnot, who superficially seemed the archetype of the Edwardian *grande dame*, was in profound sympathy with Irish nationalism, detested 'colonialism' and 'racialism', and first warmed to me when she learned that I had actually fought against Franco whom she despised as a disloyal officer and a puppet of the disgraceful Hitler. Both of them had that warmth and openness of heart which is the product of a deep inner self-assurance.

19

LONG COLD WINTER

THE situation which had become uncomfortable at the time of the Pact's signature became as painful as prickly heat when, after at first supporting the war, the *Daily Worker* received through the Comintern instructions to denounce it as an imperialist one.

Again, gripped by memories of 1914, I could not feel that the Comintern was necessarily wrong, although not to be encouraging one and all to go for Hitler seemed hopelessly wrong too. But then, I would reflect, sincere Socialists like Blatchford had felt, in 1914, that that war, too, was an exception to the rules he had been brought up on. It must, he thought, be wrong not to go for Hunnish Kaiser Bill.

Also there was at work in the minds of many people on the extreme Left at that time a general feeling that if, for example, Neville Chamberlain was on one side of a question and Georgi Dimitrov, hero of the Leipzig trial, was on the other, then the probability was that Dimitrov was right and Mr Chamberlain was leading one up the garden. Neville Chamberlain was saying that the war was necessary and just – that we were fighting 'the evil things'. Dimitrov was on record with a Comintern statement – he was secretary of the organization at the time –which concluded with the declaration that 'the working people of the world must put an end to this war after their own fashion, in their own interests, in the interests of all labouring mankind'.

As things turned out, and given the attitude of the working people of Germany and other lands, the statement – in so far as any practical international relevance was concerned – was mean-ingless. At the time, partly because I had a profound admiration for Dimitrov – he was one of those true heroes who really had been out in the wind and the rain, facing day after day the probability of torture and murder by Goering's young men – I considered it inspiring. But nobody under the age of fifty or so today can possibly have any notion of what Dimitrov was to us in the way of a symbol, a flame in darkness, a proof that, however bad things seem to be, the courageous, even the apparently foolhardy backers of a sixty-six to one chance may still win.

Reasonably enough, people used to ask me how I could bear to be pushed around and about by an international body like the Comintern. Today, when it is known that Stalin was not quite all that some people thought him to be – though I would not like to pretend, as some do, that all the virtues of Communists were their own, and all their faults Stalin's – and in the light of truly illuminating events in, for instance, Hungary, it is easier than it was then to regard 'subservience' to the Comintern as more crassly wrong-headed than it seemed at the time.

The way I looked at it was that if an international organiza-tion was needed at all – and it seemed to be – then the organ-ization had to have a place to meet (and Moscow was the most logical), and it had to have some power of discipline, of impos-ing its decisions on its members. What, otherwise, was the point of it? And the fact, which genuinely did bother a lot of English proletarian Communists, that the majority on the central com-mittee of this organization was composed of a pack of bloody foreigners, did not bother me at all. Put like that, of course, the statement that it did not worry me suggests that it was ridicu-lous and parochial for anyone to be worried by it. Such is not quite the case. We should have worried more, because of the certainty that the Russians, having shown how to win the game would always dictate rules of play. In the same way, it is reasonable for a sincere Roman Catholic to worry about the preponderance of Italian influence at the Vatican.

My own complaint about the Comintern was not that it operated with the 'ruthless and sinister efficiency' attributed to it by some propagandists, but that for so much of the time it wobbled along in a muddle which was frequently comical but, at the same time, depressing.

I had, certainly, been warned. When many sorts and conditions of friends first saw me moving, under pressure of many experiences, many hopes and aspirations, towards the Communist Party, they gave me from their sharply varying viewpoints their notions of why such behaviour was a mistake. They disagreed about almost everything except two points.

They were at one in declaring that the Communist Party was both ruthless and muddle-headed. Since I had spent years in newspaper offices, had closely observed many Foreign Offices and Embassies, and had been, for a while, an unofficial adviser and loose associate of an investment trust in New York, I found it difficult to see how these qualities could at all sharply differentiate the Communist organization from any other with which I had been connected.

The second point, of which at least the simpler-minded of my friends were sure, was that 'Moscow Gold' was pouring through the British Communist Party like water. Indeed, sitting almost penniless one day in the old Café Royal, I was accosted by an agreeable acquaintance – a Russian banker, refugee from the revolution – who said to me, 'I hear on incontrovertible authority that you are paid £2,350 per year by the Soviet Government for your services as Editor of The Week and diplomatic correspondent of the Daily Worker.'

In those days £2,350 a year was a more comfortable sum to try to live on than it would be now, and the mere idea of such a pay packet went to my head.

'Waiter,' I shouted with enthusiasm, 'bring this gentleman a large brandy and soda.'

When I came to pay for it with my last shillings it occurred to me with a sharp sense of deprivation that the exhilarating tale of this subsidy was a myth.

When I was at the Daily Worker the paper was more or less continuously on the verge of financial ruin – except during a short period at the very end of the war and in the first months of the peace, when, chiefly as a result of the battle of Stalingrad, Communists everywhere could enjoy some reflected sunshine.

Pay-day in the City Road was something like a game of hoop-la, with a lot of players and not enough prizes. Rarely indeed was there enough in the cash-box on Friday to enable everyone to get paid his full weekly wage – which was grimly meagre anyway. The total was shared out by the manager, a humorously tough type from the Elephant and Castle district who later was killed in Spain, on the basis of a kind of inverted means test. Staff members whose wives were about to give birth, or the ceilings of whose kitchens had caved in and had to be repaired at heavy expense, got a bit more than others.

Once, after that manager had been killed, I found a new, temporary manager sitting in his office on a Thursday morning apparently half dead of apprehension. He had looked at the available funds, and their low ebb had scared him. He felt it would be terrible to have to face the staff on the morrow with such more than usually bad news. And just as he was feeling like that, a man – sent he thought at the time by Providence, but by this morning he feared it might have been the Devil – had come in and given him a sure-fire tip on a 20–1 outsider running on Thursday at Haydock Park or wherever it was. And the temporary manager had taken half of all the money available for the wages and backed that horse with it.

'Should that animal fail,' he said, trembling – the tension was such that he felt he had to confess his rash act to someone – 'the lads'll about kill me.' However, the tipster had not been the Devil but Providence, and that week everyone got full pay and even some arrears.

In the whirl of events, editors succeeded one another in a hurried silence like that of a film in the days before sound. Right at the outbreak of war, Mr Pollitt moved down from King Street. Although in general I do not care for orators – perhaps I subconsciously see them as unfair competition to the writer – and Mr Pollitt is, or was, above all else an orator in the oldest English radical tradition, I liked him much; he was a slave-driver with a flattering tongue instead of a lash. His technique, well worth study by any executive, was to tell you he was about to make an outrageous demand of you, go right ahead and make it, and then remark that he would not have ventured to make such a demand of anyone else because no one else had the ability, courage, unselfish loyalty and heroic powers of endurance that you had.

He once persuaded me that I could get to Oviedo, Spain, live a fortnight there in the middle of a near-revolution masquerading as a mere tourist, and return to London all for the sum of £12. 'A pity if you couldn't,' he said, 'because that is all we have in the kitty.'

Much later, I did, at some party, say to him that I sometimes wondered whether anyone could really be as ultra-English and as forthright a down-to-earth human-hearted Englishman as he – even by the normally hostile newspapers – was so constantly reported to be. Was it not, I queried, all due to the happy circumstance of his having a strong Lancashire accent? His expression at that moment reminded one of George Robey blandly getting away with murder.

Mr Pollitt's editorship was enjoyable but short-lived, because soon the Comintern chiefs had their notable meeting, and the British delegate or representative – a cheerful ex-sailor with a head like a cannon-ball who once told me that in the course of a very tempestuous and danger-fraught life nothing had ever really upset him except piles – came back from Moscow with the news that the war had been assessed as an imperialist one. The reason was evident enough – it was supposed that the 'phoney' war was going to be permanently 'phoney'; that therefore, somewhere along the line, an agreement would be reached by which the Germans, with open or tacit British support, would attack Russia; and that therefore the main effort of the Communists must be to harass and, in the final event, totally hamstring or overthrow the Government concerned. In other words, it was the evident view of the Comintern that the declaration of war did not change the essentials of the situation existing during the period of 'peace'.

A few days later I met Mr Pollitt on the stairway landing and made some casual remark. He waved in a gesture half-clowning, half-serious. 'Farewell, my old companion in arms,' he said; and when I got into the office there was Mr Campbell, sourly, dourly humorous – one of those Scots who make you feel that real Scotsmen are more different from the English than the Chinese – peering at me from the editorial chair with a sardonic smile illuminating his gravity; an expression which, as was so often the case with Mr Campbell, said nothing and told everything.

One could not look at Mr Campbell without one's mind travelling back over a considerable, and considerably bumpy, stretch of recent history. He stood and walked, for instance, in a stiff, stumpy manner, and that was because his toes had been blown away in gallant action during the awful battle of the Somme, which – because of the gigantic manslaughter occurring on both sides, manslaughter on a scale the world, since the days of Genghis Khan, had not conceived as a present possibility – has been rated by many commentators as the true dividing line of our age : for, they say, it was the Somme which finally took the gilt off war's gingerbread, which awoke Britain, France and Germany to the realities of twentieth-century conflict, to the notion that it was not only a minority of fighting men that could be wiped out, but a whole generation, and that the bell tolled for them all. It was, they affirm, at the Somme that a big section of the European masses, as distinct from zealots and theorists, consciously or subconsciously took the turn into that angry despair of the present, that compensating, messianic hope of a violently realizable future, which for so many subsequent years dominated the mind of Europe.

Some of that may even be true. At any rate what Mr Campbell had following the Somme were a medal for courage, broken feet, and a new view of life.

Mr Campbell, this thoughtful, profoundly sceptical man – a man, that is to say, capable of devotion without loss of scepticism – had also been responsible, partly by direct action, partly by indirect consequence, for the downfall, in 1924, of the first Labour Government. At that time he had been editor of the *Workers' Weekly*, forerunner of the *Daily Worker*. He had written, or at least published, an appeal to soldiers not to shoot strikers. He was prosecuted for sedition. From Socialists throughout the country came a gale of protest, the fiercer because, although the Campbell case was important in itself, it was felt to be still more important as a symbol of the way the Labour leaders were going (an attitude to life and politics summed up a few weeks later by Mr Ramsay MacDonald in the assurance that Labour 'would serve the nation in Opposition as they had served it as a Government . . . It will still be a fight of gentle-men').

Prime Minister MacDonald dropped the charges against Campbell, was accused of so doing under political pressure, a blow at the very foundations of British justice, lost the support of the Liberals in the House of Commons, was defeated, re-signed, went to the country, and was defeated again – partly and perhaps mainly because of the timely forgery by the Intelligence Service of the 'Zinoviev letter' which, like all suc-cessful political forgeries, was effective because it expressed and dramatized an already existing idea and half-truth – the notion of the Comintern reaching out to control or manipulate levers of British public life.

Mr Campbell's editorship of the *Daily Worker* just after the outbreak of the Second World War was a strictly caretaking affair. Everyone was to mark time, or vamp till ready, until the battle between the supporters of the war and the supporters of the Comintern had been fought to a decisive conclusion. When that came to pass, with Mr Pollitt and Mr Campbell both in the wilderness, a new face, the skin of it seeming to be stretched as tight as a balloon by the bursting energy inside, hung like a rising red sun above the editorial desk. Mr William Rust had arrived. He was the most apparently supple, and yet capable of being the most rigid, of Communists I have ever known. Just so, he was the most cockney of cockneys, and yet – at least for a long period of his life – his thoughts, and still more his writing, were moulded almost completely by Moscow.

Later, particularly after a long stint with the International Brigade in Spain, his remarkable and at first contradictory qualities appeared quite suddenly to integrate.

I knew people who saw him as the typical party functionary – informed, energetic, and as cold as he was dry. Since that was the picture of him given to me before he moved into the *Daily Worker* office, I looked forward to his editorship with dull dismay. The apprehension was unjustified, and not for the first or last time I had a vivid appreciation of luck – a feeling, that is, that no one soldiering along through the Vale of Tears could possibly deserve to encounter so many good friends in so many places as I did. George Jean Nathan, the New York dramatic critic wrote – or else he told me, I forget which – a series of bitter animadversions on his many, many friends and acquaintances, explaining how this or that little trick or tic which they had made it impossible to stand them any longer, and he was forced to sever relations with them. In the end he had only four friends left. 'And I often wonder,' he mused, 'how in God's name those four stand me.'

I do not know how easily or otherwise Rust stood me – but he did it, and often defended my attitude and actions at a good deal of discomfort and (at least once) of danger, to himself. Whatever you might think of his opinions at a given moment, he was a man to go, as the saying is, tiger-shooting with. He never, for instance, abandoned you to fate and then explained that he had been forced to do so on principle and was very, very sorry. When he thought he was going, for his own reasons, to let you go out on a limb and leave you there, he told you so in advance. He had, besides a good head on his shoulders, a streak of the urchin and a bigger streak of the pirate. In other words, when, as sometimes happened, he was monstrously hypocritical, or lying horribly, he did these things with full consciousness, using these tricks as weapons. He had no 'lie in the soul', and, to my mind, one of the major differences in life is between those people who lie on purpose and those who do not even know whether they are lying or not.

Qualities such as those of the late William Rust were, of course, particularly exhilarating in an organization of an evangelical character, like the British Communist Party, where, inevitably but depressingly, there is always a lot of space occupied by characters similar – and similar for sound historical reasons – to the Evangelical clergyman, Mr Slope, in Trollope's *Barchester Towers*.

He is possessed of more than average abilities and is of good courage. Though he can stoop to fawn, and stoop low indeed, if need be, he has still within him the power to assume the tyrant; and with the power he has certainly the wish. His acquirements are not of the highest order, but such as they are they are completely under control, and he knows the use of them. He is gifted with a kind of pulpit eloquence . . . he deals greatly in denunciations, excites the minds of his weaker hearers with a not unpleasant terror, and leaves an impression on their minds that all mankind are in a perilous state, and all womankind too, except those who attend regularly to the evening lectures in Baker Street. His looks and tones are extremely severe, so much so that one cannot but fancy that he regards the greater part of the world as being infinitely too bad for his care. As he walks through the streets, his very face denotes his horror of the world's wickedness; and there is always an anathema lurking in the corner of his eye.

For a little while after Mr Pollitt and Campbell broke ranks, we had a situation best summed up, or so it seemed to me as we all argued and argued, in the words of the once world-famous Mr Dooley – the Irish-American philosopher dreamed into existence by the Chicago journalist Finley Peter Dunne.

'Whin ye see,' said Mr Dooley – whose observations on political life were first drawn to my attention by my father when I was eleven or twelve years old, and made a big impression upon me – 'whin ye see two men set in opposite corners while one mutters "thraiter" an' th' other hisses "miscreent", ye can bet they're two dimmycratic leaders tryin' to reunite th' party.'

Fairly soon the Government put an end to our more overt troubles by suppressing the *Daily Worker*. There came an afternoon in 1940 when one of those C.I.D. men who had so often and so attentively watched us playing the pin-tables at the Eagle came across the road and presented us with the notice of suppression. Noticing me among those present, he displayed a certain embarrassment, and presently revealed its cause.

He was a busy man. On that same afternoon he had another paper to suppress – namely my weekly newsletter, *The Week*. But it appeared that, under some British regulation attached to the Act which enabled them to suppress at all, there was also an obligation to serve the notice upon the owner or responsible publisher in person, and in that responsible person's own place of business. That, at least, was the policeman's interpretation of his duty, and so what were we to do? Here was I – also a busy man, and due to be busier still when we had to deal with the situation that would arise from the suppression – and we were in the City, and the offices of *The Week* were literally miles away in Victoria Street.

Asked, courteously enough, by the policeman whether I would engage myself to meet him a little later in Victoria Street for the sake of being put out of business a second time, I pointed out that I was likely to be working pretty hard in the next little while. It was an allusion which he perfectly understood, for it was obvious that the moment the *Daily Worker* was suppressed we should all be getting busy issuing illegal versions of it, which was going to be a dangerous and time-absorbing business.

Finally, the Inspector asked me whether I would care to have him drive me down in the police car, so that *The Week* could be suppressed with a minimal loss of valuable time. I thought for a moment that it could be considered unseemly for me to go cruising on such an errand at the expense of Scotland Yard. But, after a moment's reflection, I accepted the offer and we shot across the town in the police car, making excellent time between the suppressed *Daily Worker* and about-to-be-suppressed *Week*.

Within the hour, they had shut up *The Week*, and as they did so I had that peculiar sense of relief one sometimes has when they finally tell you you have to take to your bed, or go to hospital. You may be in pain, but the administrative side of things, the awkward decisions, are their pigeon now.

For a little while we did run an illegal *Daily Worker* – a tiresome business because one was aware that in fact the thing was a mere gesture, the publication reaching hardly anyone. And yet you could get five years hard labour if you were caught at it, just as though you had been pouring criminal incitements into the ears of millions.

I dare say the affair was almost as annoying for the Special Branch of the C.I.D. as it was for us – for in this strange charade they too had to pretend that whatever we were doing was of vital importance, and during that nasty butt-end of winter they had to follow us about in all weathers.

During that time of relative isolation you needed not only lights in the darkness (there were really quite a lot of them) but barometers to tap and thermometers to read, so that you could feel you knew rather more about the state of the weather than you could learn from the newspapers or the meetings of the faithful.

In this respect I found much pleasure, comfort and utilitarian advantage in the society of a Mr Harry, who kept, in our neighbourhood, a big public house which combined a rich Edwardian cockney flavour with a faint element of up-to-date garishness, according well enough with the big motor-cars of military men in his yard by day, and the aircraft overhead dropping incendiary bombs into the roadway by night.

Apart from keeping this public house Mr Harry was a member of a family vaguely connected with what might be called the down-to-earth side of cockney entertainment. Through a cousin he had an interest in a boxing establishment or prize-ring somewhere, and another cousin had a piece of a music-hall, and someone else of the clan was promoting some other little show in the provinces. In token of all this, Mr Harry himself wore spectacularly expensive suits, had a carnation regularly in his buttonhole and smoked – right through the worst of all the shortages so far as I can recall – big cigars.

He was a man who felt that the first business of an inn-keeper is to be tolerant to all who do not actually disrupt by their conduct the harmony and comfort of the inn – and in time of war, and savagely aroused political feeling, to maintain that kind of balance is a considerable achievement. Mr Harry liked to achieve it, so that without much danger of being suddenly assailed by a fellow-drinker as a Moscow-minion, a fifth-columnist and probable Jew-baiter in disguise, I could spend a couple of hours there taking the temperature and tapping the barometer of what people were really saying, sometimes in the saloon bar, sometimes in the public. It was understood that I was an eccentric who refused to be 'typed' as an unfailing *habitué* of one or the other.

Mr Harry himself liked to make people at home. But he was also a busy man, and often did not take time to find out whether some vague rumour he had heard about one of his clients was true or not. Thus, when I first took to going there, he had picked up from somewhere or other a report that I was a former diplomat currently doing hush-hush work of a military nature. He at once told me that, at an unspecified period of his early youth – at the time I speak he must have been in his late forties or early fifties – he had been in the Indian cavalry.

'Had my white charger, old boy,' he said, drawing luxuriously on the cigar, 'and rode all over India on it. Glorious. Never mind about the bombs – the old Empire will come through.'

Learning, a little later, that his earlier assumptions had been mistaken, and that I was something to do with 'the literary game', he told me, at a rather intense period of the blitz, that he himself had been, until very recently, a 'great reader'.

'Used,' he said, 'to like nothing better than settle down with something good.'

'What sort of thing did you read?'

'Well,' said Mr Harry, 'Thucydides, Dante – that type of thing. But d'you know,' he said mournfully, listening to the sirens, 'this thing's got on my nerves. I can't settle to that sort of thing nowadays. It's changed my reading habits altogether. Can you imagine what I read now?'

I tried to imagine what an enthusiast for Thucydides and Dante might be reduced to when his nerve broke.

'Dickens?' I guessed. 'Or some of the modern novelists?'

'Nao,' said Mr Harry, his cockney broadening in disgust at my naïveté, my underestimation of the nerve-shocks he had received. 'Nothing but the back numbers of *Men Only*.'

'The *back* numbers?'

'Yus. Just the back numbers. The up-to-date ones get on my nerves. Too much of all this around us. Too much war.'

When Mr Harry admitted to himself, as he must have known with one half of his mind almost from the outset, that I was in some way mixed up with the Communists, I knew that the political climate of Britain had considerably changed. It must have been a month or two after Hitler's attack on Russia that he mentioned to me that he had always been a close student of politics, and that he had always felt 'some sort of Socialism or Communism' to have a particular appeal.

'After all,' said he, 'you have to consider elementary human justice. Don't forget that, Claud, old boy.'

Because it was sometimes used by groups of fire-watchers the public house could on occasion, without interference by the police, stay open half the night. In an unusual upflare of common sense it was thought better that an incendiary bomb should be dealt with by a man who had been notably infringing the licensing laws than that it should be left to burn the neighbourhood. At one such moment Mr Harry and I were standing alone in the bar, very late, and he said to me, 'I can see it coming, Claud. The Communists are going to take over the country when this little lot's finished with. And I don't say they shouldn't. I don't say you haven't common human justice on your side, Claud. All I ask of you is just one thing.'

'What's that, Harry?'

'All I ask, Claud, when you and your pals take over and make that great revolution, that you'll just leave me my King, my constitution and my country.'

He had tears in his eyes, and it was hard not to be able to offer him a binding guarantee.

A year or more after the war was over, Mr Harry took a trip to the Channel Islands – the only bit of the British Isles actually occupied by the Germans during the conflict. He was enthusiastic. He described some huge beer cellar which the German military had remodelled and decorated in the Munich manner – a magnificent place, which, by its existence and the amenities it could offer to the English visitor, showed that out of evil some good could come.

I made some disobliging remark to the effect that I had read somewhere that a good many of the Channel Islanders had made quite a good thing out of the war – had collaborated with the invaders 100 per cent, given them lists of local Jews so that these could be deported, and so on. Mr Harry said he had heard similar reports in the islands, and judged them to be well-based.

'But you don't understand, Claud old boy,' he said, 'at the time they did that, those people thought the Germans were going to win.'

Within a couple of weeks of the German invasion of Russia, Mr Rust had begun to organize what turned out to be one of the most remarkable 'mass campaigns' in the history of the British Left – the campaign to lift the ban on the *Daily Worker* and, incidentally, *The Week*. With extraordinary skill he fused the enthusiasm for the Russian fighters, the general belief of millions of British working people that now a lot of real tough friends had come to their senses and were fighting shoulder to shoulder with them, with the immediate objective of getting the ban raised. I was told at the time that, from quite an early date, Mr Churchill had expressed himself as in favour – or at least not opposed – to such action. But, as a result of what could seem a paradoxical structure of British politics ever since approximately 1924, it was the leadership of the Labour Party which most strenuously resisted the move, and used all its influence and knowledge of Left politics to dissuade the rest of the Government from doing anything of the kind.

It was not until, to the visible and aghast astonishment of those on the platform, the Labour Party's own conference at Central Hall, Westminster, in the winter of 1942–3, voted against the ban by a small but respectable majority, that the final event became inevitable.

The Week was told it would be allowed out, too.

At this moment a curious episode occurred. Half casually, half intently, Mr Rust asked me whether I did, in fact, propose to restart *The Week*. I was astonished. We had been campaigning for the freeing of both papers for months. He then said that there were some people at King Street who felt, or might be expected to feel, that *The Week* constituted an anomalous phenomenon – one which could even be embarrassing. I inquired in what sense that could be so? He explained that what was anomalous was that on the one hand, as a result of recent events, *The Week*, which hitherto had, so far as a lot of its subscribers were concerned, been seen as merely radical, and even anarchistic, was now rated as an organ of the Communist Party. Yet, except in so far as its Editor was associated with the *Daily Worker*, the Communist Party had no real say-so about *The Week*, no editorial or financial control. He made it clear that this was a situation which gave many people at King Street nightmares. And I could see, in a way, why. It was made clear to me that nobody would take it amiss if I just failed to take advantage of the lifting of the ban and devoted myself in future exclusively to the *Daily Worker*.

In some ways the notion was attractive, for I could see that the situation, which was so entirely different from that which *The Week* had been founded to exploit, and of which it had so successfully taken advantage in the 1930s, no longer existed –

and had not, in fact, existed since, at the latest, the end of the 'phoney' war.

On the other hand, the cool suggestion now made irked me and caused me uneasiness. I had a feeling it might be better to keep my tiny boat in seaworthy condition. I could hardly express that thought very clearly to Mr Rust – who would have been quick to appreciate it – because it would evidently have confirmed whatever suspicions about my possible goings-on were harboured at Headquarters. It was desirable to emulate that Chinese General who, in the days before the Communists took over, was suspected by his Commander-in-Chief, Chiang Kai-shek, of moving over to the other side.

'Be not afraid,' cabled the General or War Lord from some fastness in West China. 'I have no thoughts of my own.'

I did, however, say to Mr Rust that I really could not put myself in the position of having stumped the country for months, demanding, in the name of British justice and the elementary freedoms of the Press, that my paper be released from the ban to carry out a task indispensable to the proper informing of public opinion and the health of the nation, and then, the ban being raised, walk away with a shrug saying that on second thoughts I deemed it a waste of time to take advantage of our arduously regained liberty.

William Rust, whose sense of humour you rarely appealed to in vain, accepted the argument as valid, and – or so I was told – put up a vigorous fight on my behalf against those who looked upon the existence of an 'independent' paper which also purported to be Communist as a gross, and even alarming, contradiction in terms.

20
L'HOMME QUI RIT

UNLESS you are in actual combat, or in some commanding position where you can play chess with it all, most of a war is apt to be horribly boring. It does not fill up your time interestingly, and yet it is too intrusive to let you get ahead with anything else. There are exceptional people who, under stress of war, seem almost literally to rise, as the phrase used to go, above it; people who can force themselves to turn the beastly necessities of war into virtues, and, in addition to combat, do whatever else they do – such as painting, or thinking, or designing engines – better in that atmosphere than in any other. They make, I believe, the finest fighting men and I suppose they are at the same time the people who in war-time really do 'save civilization'. Personally, I have encountered more of them among the British and French than anywhere else. There were several such – together, naturally with numerous scoundrels and poltroons – in the entourage of General de Gaulle, and, by a twist of the whirligig of time which now seems bizarre, there was at that time in London a working alliance between the Gaullists and the Communists.

Mutually they suspected that the British and American Governments were, even then, favouring collaborationists and appeasers in France, on the ground that they would, in the long, long run help London and Washington solve their grievous – genuinely grievous – problem of how to defeat Hitler without letting the Communists win.

As a consequence it could be surmised that they might be prepared to a certain degree to strangle or squeeze the windpipes of those sections of the resistance movement which could be proved to be, or strongly suspected to be, under Communist control. It would not have been an unreasonable behaviour on their part. Nobody can be amazed at people doing what they conceive to be in their own best interests. And if these people choose to place their bets that way – to gamble that they could afford to hobble some of the French resistance for the sake of other objectives on more distant horizons – it was their privilege to do so. As things turned out, they did bring about approximately the situation they were surmised to have in mind. The situation in France today cannot be fully understood without some reference to the policies prevailing and the struggles undertaken on one side and the other in the London and Washington of the early 1940s.

Nobody will ever know now how correct was that surmise, or what weight the people who held those views really pulled at the time. You could sift for months the official and unofficial records, the published and unpublished memoirs, and you still would find that your busy historical sieve had holes in it. Although the first Henry Ford was mistaken in thinking that history is simply 'the bunk', he was right in supposing that when people write history they have a temptation – conscious or subconscious, but seldom resisted – to put some bunk into it.

Any important and lively phenomenon of history is like the horse in Dickens's *Hard Times*.

'Girl number twenty unable to define a horse!' said Mr Gradgrind, for the general behoof of all the little pitchers. 'Girl number twenty possessed of no facts, in reference to one of the commonest of animals! Some boy's definition of a horse . . . Bitzer,' said Thomas Gradgrind, 'Your definition of a horse.'

'Quadruped. Graminivorous. Forty teeth, namely twenty-four grinders, four eye-teeth, and twelve incisive. Sheds coat in the spring; in marshy countries, sheds hoofs too. Hoofs hard, but requiring to be shod with iron. Age known by marks in mouth.'

'Now, girl number twenty,' said Mr Gradgrind, 'You know what a horse is.'

But those engaged – in both the English and French senses of the word – in any form of immediate activity are, as it were, riding the horse and can hardly hang about until it has been defined to the extent where it is known that in marshy countries it sheds its hoofs. At that time we were all riding horses, and nobody had time to bother much with defining the hoof-structure of Gaullism, or Communism either.

The '*mystique*' of Gaullism and de Gaulle was a word much in vogue at the time, and rightly so. It is strange that although the British have as much susceptibility to '*mystiques*' as do the French – though the British will commonly deny it, and slightly deride the French for that susceptibility – there is no word for it in our language. This lacuna – could it mean that a whole language can suffer from an inhibition? – is a problem for psycho-analytical semanticists, and they should get on with it.

The highlights of life and history are produced by the occasions and personalities which make two times two equal seven. This is a function of '*mystique*'.

It was in that sense that there was a *'mystique'* of the Spanish war, and with the emergence of General de Gaulle from the squalor and horror of the 'phoney' war and the subsequent French disaster, followed by a noise from Paris as of apes intriguing and disputing about coconuts while the extermination chambers trundled a little farther westwards, there sounded a pure and lyrical note which (though neither the Communists nor the Gaullists would admit it now), suggested to some people that Europe had not gone entirely tone-deaf at the moment when the Spanish Republican cause came to its dead end at Figueras.

The people who never can see how to make more than four out of two times two, and settle for that as the best that can be done with the arithmetic of life, had a jolt. France, like Evadne in *The Maid's Tragedy*, had brought many people near to

> . . . that dull calamity,
> To that strange misbelief of all the world,
> And all things that are in it.

General de Gaulle, and all that he implied, were an escape from dull calamity.

I have just said that there was a working alliance between the Gaullists and the Communists, and in the practical sense of the term – the sense that a cooperation of this kind existed and had effects – it is true. But both the Gaullists and the Communists may be right when, as they often do nowadays, they deny the existence of any such thing. Perhaps it was just an alliance between individuals who found one another sympathetic and thought that for the time being they were going the same way. So far as I was concerned my ally was that journalist and propagandist of genius André Laguerre (a very French Frenchman brought up in San Francisco, because his father was French consul there). After escaping from France and for a while tramping the pavement of Carlton Gardens with a rifle on his shoulder, on sentry-go for the Free French, he became – as a result of his energy and some unknown person's perspicacity – Public Relations Officer for the Gaullists.

At that time, the Gaullists were far from popular in London – partly because they were still less popular in Washington where

President Roosevelt took the view that, in terms of Rooseveltian philosophy, the relatively small de Gaulle bottle must be marked 'dangerous, to be taken only under American doctor's directions', like the much bigger bottle in which Roosevelt thought he smelled the inveterate imperialism and colonialism of Winston Churchill. The much over-simplified impression one had at the time was that Mr Churchill, who had his own troubles with Mr Roosevelt – not to mention the general and real undesirability of doing anything which might be difficult to explain to Mr Bernard Baruch – saw no good reason to compromise British policies by getting their name too closely linked with that of General de Gaulle.

Liberals and Socialists in France and England were suspicious of the General, too. Indeed, I suppose that if you made up a composite figure of every available element that would annoy, discompose, and arouse the suspicions of an orthodox English Labour Party leader, the General would have about filled the bill. He may have made, from time to time, some enthusiastic speech about democracy or the century of the common man, but, if so, I do not recall it. And the omission was a serious political mistake. It was one which M. Laguerre and myself did our best to repair.

Things would have been easier for us if it had been true, as was so widely asserted, that the General had no sense of humour. He was represented as an austerely unbending, rigid type of man who 'joked with deefficulty' – who could not, it was said, joke at all. To suppose so was to misjudge him seriously. In my estimation, at least, he could not resist a joke even when to play it was obviously against his best interests. Most of his jokes were about as harmless as a hand-grenade after the pin has been taken out. His amusement at seeing other people abruptly debunked or deflated often reminded me of my dog Zig. They were both, in this sense, highly astringent.

Cardinal de Retz, in his incomparable memoirs, records how he, after weeks of more or less successful intrigue in Rome at the time, 1655 or thereabouts, of the election of Pope Alexander VII, did himself grave harm because he could not resist making malicious jokes at the expense of M. de Lionne, French Ambassador Extraordinary, whom he should have been trying to conciliate. 'I observed on this occasion,' he notes sadly, 'though too late, what I have since observed on others, namely how extremely careful one ought to be, in great affairs still more than in others, to curb the pleasure one is inclined to take in telling funny stories.'

It is not apparent that de Retz ever subsequently acted in accordance with this sage axiom, and I dare say that even if Laguerre had, at my suggestion, presented General de Gaulle with a marked copy of the de Retz memoirs, having this passage underlined, it would have made no difference. Mirth is a habit-forming vice.

At one time, the Free French employed in London – much in the way that people employ hard-up peeresses to lead their daughters round the Season – a highly-connected but quite broke socialite to run a sort of *salon* for them. She gave lunch-parties and dinner-parties where loyal Free Frenchmen met English men and women of influence. (M. d'Astier de la Vigerie, who used to parachute, near-suicidally, in and out of France like a ping-pong ball, told me once of attending a dinner of this kind when an English Cabinet Minister and his wife were present. They were not unaware of the heroic doings of M. de la Vigerie. 'Are you,' the Minister's wife inquired, 'planning to return to France soon?' M. de la Vigerie, hardly able to believe his ears on hearing this fantastic indiscretion, replied to the general effect that that was as might be. Undiscouraged, the Ministress pursued her investigation. Would he, as and when he dropped from the skies into occupied France, be going anywhere near Bourges? Thinking, 'Good God, are these people having a war or not?' Vigerie replied that all things were possible. 'If,' said the Minister's wife, 'you happen to be in Bourges, I wish you would make a point of looking up two old servants of ours who returned there when we left France just before the invasion. I should like to let them know that my husband and myself are quite all right. You see, they may be anxious about us.')

After a while, it was decided for some reason or other that the *salon*-runner was not really earning her keep. I have forgotten whether the reason was that things were going so well for the Free French that she had become redundant, or were going so badly that even a good *salon* was not going to make much difference. It was decided to sack her. But de Gaulle's closest advisers were worried – she was a woman still of potential influence; the thing must be done with the utmost discretion. 'Discretion, General,' they said, and de Gaulle contrived to look as though discretion were his middle name.

They cooked up the idea of a little tea-party at Carlton Gardens where the General and one or two of the discreet advisers were discreetly to break the news that, great as this lady's services had been to the Cause, the Cause with the utmost regret was compelled, temporarily it was to be hoped, to relinquish them. The discreet, sighing with relief at the fact that things were going to go so smoothly, waited for her arrival. She was announced. De Gaulle, uncoiling suddenly from his chair like a long worm with a steel spring in it, strode beaming across the room to greet her.

'A-ha! Madame,' he said, 'the first thing I want to tell you is that you're sacked.'

Even months later he recalled with pleasure the expression on the faces of the discreet advisers at that moment. It was exactly the sort of thing that Zig would have done.

Our Gaullist campaign went so successfully that one day Mr Brendan Bracken, then Minister of Information, openly attacked and threatened me at one of those dreadful conferences of the Houses of Commons Lobby correspondents which used to be held several times a week. I liked Mr Bracken. He had a jaunty kind of acceptance of the facts of war which was refreshing. On the other hand I had been told (perhaps untruthfully, for I cannot think he was the sort of man seriously to resent such a remark) that he had been upset by my observation that a wartime Minister of Information was compelled, in the national interest, to such continuous acts of duplicity that even his natural hair must grow to resemble a wig.

And that same evening André Laguerre rang me up to tell me that President Roosevelt, at some press conference or interview in Washington, had, after sharp criticism of Gaullist policies, remarked in passing that a great deal of trouble and publicity was being caused by 'two small-time connivers in London'.

We founded on the spot the Small-Time Connivers' Club and

from time to time in the passing years, whenever conniving has seemed slack, we have sought to increase the membership. But as a result, no doubt, of laziness on the part of the foundation members, the membership remains steady at a total of two.

Naturally it was not without a great deal of trouble, and noble assistance from the National Union of Journalists, 90 per cent of whose members detested what I said but took a fine Voltairean attitude about my right to say it, that when (after the fighting men had driven the Germans and Italians out of North Africa), it was agreed that a party of diplomatic correspondents should be allowed to visit the scene, I was permitted to make one of their number. I have it on what I consider good authority that Mr Bracken – despite all – took a determined attitude about this, and insisted that to exclude me would be a picayune sort of politics. If it is true, I owe him a debt of gratitude. And, of course, if not, not.

However, when we got to Algiers – we had been there I think about twenty-four hours – two rather disconcerting things happened. The leadership of the pre-war Communist Party of France, a great parcel of ex-M.P.s who had just been let out of jail and seemed to have heard of nothing since August 1939 made it clear to me that in their view Communist policy in London towards de Gaulle had been grossly mistaken – the man was a menace, an anti-democrat, and an embryo dictator. They seemed, indeed, to be contemplating some kind of alliance – or perhaps they already had such an alliance – with the Giraudists. And I could not escape the discouraging impression that, because the assassin of Admiral Darlan had been a Royalist extremist of the Right, they disapproved even of that act.

The other upset to my schedule occurred when I was summoned to the relevant British authority – the Information people, I suppose, but I no longer recall who actually acted in the matter – and informed that I was expelled from North Africa and must take myself off within twenty-four hours. An aircraft would have a seat for me at Maison Blanche on the morrow.

It seemed a sad thing to have come all this way and have to return so soon. And I must confess that I was a good deal influenced by considerations other than those of political and journalistic achievement. The sun was wonderfully hot, and after the war years in London Algiers danced in the sun like a dream come true. I made up my mind that whatever happened I really could not quit the scene so soon.

Moreover, it was apparent to me that whereas the British had allowed me in, and were quite prepared for me to stay, the Americans were having an early attack of those security jitters which later developed into neuroses really harmful to those otherwise vigorous and healthy people, and had taken fright. They were in fact raising Cain with the British for having allowed me to become airborne Africa-wards in the first place. One more example, they were saying, of the sloppy British way of doing things. And the British were, at that moment, in no position – certainly at least in no mood – to make an issue of it, and find themselves quarrelling with their great and good friends over the case of a Communist diplomatic correspondent.

It seemed best not to be, for the moment, an issue; in fact, to disappear. I took refuge in the house of an elderly and heroic Jewish doctor – a man who before the Allied landings had risked his life over and over again in big and small (but continuous and relentless) actions against the collaborationists and the Germans and the Italians, and in whose house a part of the planning of the landings had actually been carried out. He was not only old but lame. When his big house was full of hidden conspirators he had been used to spending hours and hours, from dawn onward, limping wearily from market to market so as to buy food for a dozen young fighting men without attracting undue attention by the quantities he bought. I can think of no one I have ever known who, in his courage, physical endurance, skill and cunning in the face of enemy attack, and ability calmly to cultivate his cultural garden when he had a moment free from the threat of torture, was superior to that man.

It was in his house that the assassination of Darlan had been planned, and the assassin had been hidden there for some time before the act took place. There had been, as there always is in such affairs, some sort of muddle and, although I naturally did not ask questions about it, I gathered that somebody had, as the saying goes, jumped the gun – the thing had not been supposed to happen in exactly that way or exactly that time.

However, as I say, this is simply an impression I gained indirectly in the doctor's house.

It was a fine house to lie low in – several exits available and a favourable concierge. My notion was that, by keeping out of the way and not making myself into any sort of test case between the mutually embittered British and American authorities, I could probably avoid being physically thrown out of North Africa for at least a while, and at the same time – that house being the kind of house it was – could probably, in the ordinary course of conversation with the characters who stayed or visited there, find out more about what was really going on than I could have hoped to do in any other way.

I planned that after a time I would start making a test case in a slightly different way. The head of the Government was, after all, officially General de Gaulle. True, the British and American military were really in command, and true that in the event of any sort of serious physical showdown de Gaulle would be as powerless as a toothless dog. But nobody – not even the Americans – wanted that sort of showdown. And, at the same time, the General was very sensitive about his authority and rights. He would not, for instance, be much pleased at the intelligence that civilians were being expelled from his bailiwick by the British or Americans without so much as a by-your-leave to himself. It was my intention, at a suitable moment, to engage the General's interest on this point. But I had learned that André Laguerre, whom I had thought to find in Algiers, had been delayed, and I did not want to do anything decisive until he was there to advise and assist. When he did get there, I arranged to be invited to lunch with General de Gaulle at the nominal seat of Government.

Just in case the Americans might pick me up on the way, I had asked André to take steps to ensure that they were aware that if they did anything like that they were going to be offering a deliberate affront to General de Gaulle. In consequence, I was rushed up the hill to the Residency in an enormous car with tricolours streaming from the bonnet and even from the top, a sub-machine-gunner beside the driver, and a couple of motor-cycle police roaring ahead and behind.

Conceiving that this was the occasion for a jolly good joke, de Gaulle had told his entourage that, for political reasons, he was entertaining that day a notorious Red hatchet-man. The possibility of an assassination attempt must not be excluded. Vigilance was essential. Remember what happened to Trotsky. The joke was a big success. When I entered the hall, and while I waited for my arrival to be announced, I noticed that at two points of the pseudo-Moorish style gallery which ran round it at a height some few feet above my head, dedicated men were kneeling, evidently in concealment, with pistols in their hands ready to blaze away in case this O.G.P.U. desperado should get up to any tricks. And at lunch, in addition to de Gaulle and myself, there were two Colonels who could scarcely attend to their food because they had been instructed to remain on the qui vive, watching my every movement. The general disregarded them – indeed they were so rigid with anxiety that I doubt whether they could have taken much intelligent part in the conversation any way – so that our talk was an interesting form of the tête-à-tête : tête-à-tête with bodyguards.

It was not to be supposed that the General would see fit to disclose the inner secrets of his plans and policies – and, even had he gone mad and done that very thing, the information would have been of little value. For he was not in any position to impose his plans and policies upon anyone, and, being a man of great political flexibility (the flexibility you sometimes find in men like de Gaulle who live, as it were, *sub specie aeternitatis* and can thus afford to treat the day-to-day wangle of politics with the contempt it deserves), whatever he might today think he was going to do tomorrow could, by tomorrow, be forgotten.

I detest 'interviewing' people, and it was therefore with relief that I reflected that anything in the nature of an interview was pointless. I did, on the other hand, want to make a final formal little bow to him; to say, just for the sake of having it said, what I felt about the exhilarating effect of his actions, his personality and his *mystique* upon the mind of the Western world. He had, of course, heard the same thing over and over again, and I hesitated because I thought that a repetition from me might be tedious and spoil his lunch. However, one does not refrain from thanking one's host for the delightful party just because fifty other people have just said the same thing, so I said my piece. His courtesy – a virtue which always moves me and which I think is a part of that Charity that abides with Faith and Hope – was such that he pretended to be surprised and delighted by my tribute.

Once one is free of the confining and distorting requirements of the 'interview' – probably the most boring and useless discovery ever made by journalism, since the odds against any public man telling the truth for publication to a million readers can be calculated by anyone – one can get to the more serious business of finding out how the man's mind works, what is his basic attitude to this and that, what, in three words, makes him tick.

General de Gaulle, whom I had, of course, encountered in London, but always on strictly businesslike business, wanted, naturally, to have some talk about Communism. He asked me directly why I was – as I was at that time – a Communist. I told him, briefly, what I have already told in an earlier chapter of this book. Not much to my surprise – for I had a high regard for his intelligence, not to mention his inclination to prefer the disembodied theory to the sordid fact – he showed an immediate understanding of how I felt and why I felt it.

He added, thinking perhaps of all those out-dated Communist Deputies squabbling down the road, 'You don't think that your view is perhaps somewhat romantic?'

This seemed to be indeed the Devil rebuking sin. And I was in any case profoundly influenced by the fact that, so far as the resistance within France was concerned, the Communists were the toughest, supplest muscles of the movement.

There was no indication then of the post-war incapacity of the Communist Parties in Europe and outside Russia, to establish themselves prosperously even in territories where they had absolute power.

Yet to me it seems that the crime of the Communists in Hungary was not principally that they massacred people with tanks in the streets of Budapest. By the time it came to that, Russian control of Budapest could be considered as a matter dictated by the brutal necessities of world strategy.

The crime, monstrous in its fact and its implications, was that after nearly a decade of absolute Communist power, so many people were prepared to fight and risk ugly death rather than tolerate the régime. That rather than the military repression – there has been plenty of that on all sides at all times – is what gave the Hungarian events their jolting significance.

21

THE LONG TRAIN

GUIDED by hindsight, I should say that the attitude – mean, rigid and out-dated, as it seemed to me – of those quarrelsome and querulous Communist Deputies in Algiers may have effected in my subconscious mind a basic shift in my own attitude to Communism. It took a lot of the gilt off the gingerbread.

It is well enough to argue, as I have heard argued by people entirely opposed to the Communists, that from their own standpoint the Deputies in Algiers had a correct political appraisal of the situation. That is to say, they correctly anticipated that only de Gaulle could head off the victory of Communism in post-war France, so that their first task must be to undermine de Gaulle.

It sounds like a good point until you recall that, as of now, the French Communists have not got to many of the places they thought they were going to after Liberation.

The question is a little more than academic, because the basic situation is one which recurs, and probably will keep on recurring, at various times and in various lands. In other words, if the Gaullist *mystique* – which was a *mystique* of France a lot bigger than the personal one of General de Gaulle – had fused, so to speak, with the Communist *mystique*, it is possible, barely possible, that something would have emerged which would have been neither Communism, in the orthodox sense of the word, nor Gaullism in the orthodox sense of that word, but something new and vital, as an attitude to life and politics, of the kind which those in the Western world who reject defeatism and despair claim they are looking for.

At a time I had no very clear vision of this – simply a sense of disillusion and disappointment. I did report in London that in my view the Deputies, who had after all been arrested and deported at the end of 1939, were living a long way behind the times. William Rust saw the point, and for a while there was sharp divergence between the policy of the British Party journal and the official line of the French Communist Party. Later, of course, everything got straightened out – in strict conformity with the French Party.

Revolutionary organizations which are deemed, as a matter of course, to be living in the future, are often more inclined than others to live in the past. It is paradoxical, but not unnatural. In fact, on reflection and first-hand examination of their problems, it becomes evident that in the nature of things they are required, for their own maintenance, to emphasize the past – their own past – more heavily than are conservative groups of long standing. Every political and, indeed, religious organization requires a 'myth' – I use the word in the most strictly neutral sense without any connotation of truth or falsity – and for the creation of a myth are needed both a goal, a more or less messianic vision of the future, and a tradition, an iconic picture of the past. The newer the organization, the more sharply defined must be the tradition.

Heresy is a greater danger to a comparatively new and struggling organization, continuously threatened with disintegration from within or obliteration from without, than one long rooted in traditional soil. It is this fact which, within a revolutionary organization, inevitably weights the dice in favour of those who, like

> Hobbs, Nobbs, Nokes and Stokes combine
> To paint the future from the past,
> Put blue into their line.

To propound a new idea must always be to incur the possibility of a charge of heresy, of 'deviation'. The onus of proof is on the propounder of such an idea. Exceptionally courageous and energetic men can do it, realizing that they are thereby not only challenging the Scribes and Pharisees, but also stirring the genuine terrors of those who obscurely feel that the slightest deviation from the route-map sketched by the founding fathers may run them all disastrously into the bog. And, one should remember, often enough it does. And among such, those who can do it most effectively are men who – like Lenin – have themselves become myths in their own lifetime, so that opinions which in others would be heretical, are stamped as orthodox almost before they are uttered.

There are also the professional heretics – most common in my experience among Scotsmen and Jews – who, often rightly, are deemed mere cranks by their colleagues. I am still a little awed by the recollection of a man I once met in Edinburgh after making some speech there. He told me that he was a member of – if I remember correctly – the New Scottish Labour and Nationalist Revolutionary Party. Its membership was five, it having only recently been formed after the breakaway from the Scottish Labour and Nationalist Revolutionary Party, which up to the moment of the schism had had a membership of sixteen.

I inquired the reason for the break. It was, said he, a matter of principle. Those sixteen used to hold bi-weekly meetings, and these continued for two or three months, with unanimity expressed on all occasions.

'Then,' said my informant, 'a few of us began to realize that we were living in a fool's paradise. We couldn't just put our finger on what was wrong, but it stood to reason, man, there must be something utterly tainted and rotten about an organization where everyone just agreed with everyone else all the time, so we up and quit.'

But, by and large, the innovators and the natural heretics are a lot less numerous than those prudent 'revolutionaries' who would prefer never to do anything that has not been done before; to whom, in fact, the mere notion of any possible new 'synthesis' such as might, conceivably, have been achieved at Algiers, suggests dangerous treachery. You often read of revolutionary statesmen who are supposed to be having immense difficulty in 'restraining hotheads'. In my experience, most of them have to spend a lot of their time prodding the mass of their followers into keeping less than a mile or so behind current realities. A man who kept a bookshop told me once that on the day of the Invergordon mutiny in 1931, he was beset with demands by eager comrades for a history of the Black Sea Fleet mutiny of 1917.

It was impossible, after Algiers, not to recall – and it seems to me always important to keep in mind – the observation of Sainte-Beuve on the subject of people who do not adjust themselves to the times.

What a number of watches stopped, during the revolution, on this or that day of violent shock! Let us then try, even though we may take no pleasure in the present time, to wind our watches every evening and keep them right; it is an excellent mental habit.

A delicious example of what one may call the revolutionary-traditionalist, was a Polish-Jewish tailor, an enthusiastic and indefatigable attendant at meetings of the Communist Party in north-west London. He rarely failed to intervene in debate. His interventions and proposals rarely won general approval.

When shouts of 'No, no', and 'Nonsense' rose in volume, he would pause and raise a commanding hand. Silence secured, he would look round the room with a smile in which self-confidence and pity were mingled.

'Comrades,' he would say, 'have you forgotten, do perhaps some of you not even know, that once, in 1918, I carried a message for Lenin from Minsk to Moscow?'

He sincerely believed that this achievement, which was a fact, entitled him to a sort of plural vote in any gathering of the faithful. I only once saw him put out of countenance, when some irreverent new recruit asked whether the message had, in fact, ever been successfully delivered.

In that latter part of the war, Communists were suddenly so popular that it nearly hurt. Every district organizer seemed to carry the Sword of Stalingrad in his brief-case. And I think it can hardly be denied that the Communists, by their whole-hearted – one could almost say reckless – devotion to 'the war effort' during that period, really did constitute themselves a factor of serious importance in the maintenance and increase of production, in the elimination of industrial conflict or friction, and in the combat against 'war weariness' and apathy. They were, after all, the most highly-organized and efficient body of 'militants' in the country. To put it no higher, the fact that they were now prepared to pursue any course at all which would, in their estimation, increase productivity for war, even though it might involve the abandonment of all sorts of demands which a couple of years earlier had been fostered and pressed by the Communists themselves, meant that those in the factories and mines who, war or no war, were intent on pushing forward this or that 'just claim' of the working people, were left without any leadership at all.

It was a curious experience to shift so suddenly from membership of a hated sect, to a position on a quite high-powered bandwagon. It was fascinating to observe the varying types of people who calculated that this band-wagon was for them.

Apart, however, from the wave of cheerful opportunism, and although the development which now occurred was neither decisive nor permanent, it did have a peculiar significance as representing a novel, perhaps an unprecedented, fusion between nationalistic and communistic impulses in the British working class. On a tiny scale, it suggested the sort of situation that would have existed, if, by some no doubt impossible freak of history, Tsar Alexander I had seen England as a menace no less than France and chosen to fight both; if, as a result, Bonaparte and post-revolutionary France had been forced into alliance with the England not only of Pitt but of all those open or secret political societies and clubs which, only a few years before, had expressed the vastness of English sympathy for the Revolution.

Although, politically, I naturally welcomed the turn of events and the end of the nerve-racking period between the signature of the Nazi-Soviet Pact and the outbreak of the Nazi-Soviet war, from a strictly personal viewpoint the new situation, as it developed during the following couple of years, left me feeling increasingly at a loose end. Things were suddenly so cosy that one had the sensation that nothing one might write was really necessary – everyone was rushing in the right direction anyway.

It was naturally irksome to keep writing so much, so encouragingly, about the war effort without oneself getting into battle. We applied over and over again to get me credentials as a war correspondent. But Labour leaders opposed that, on the ground that having a war correspondent would increase the prestige of the *Daily Worker* – and anything was better than that. And the War Office objected, too – on the ground that a Communist war correspondent would be either a Russian spy or an agitator, fomenting grievances among the troops.

Aware of this last objection, I suggested to Mr Brendan Bracken, Minister of Information – whom I had often occasion to attack, but always esteemed – that the difficulty might be circumvented. I could be a correspondent with the bomber squadrons over Germany, held, if necessary incommunicado on the base between missions. And the risk of my subverting a bomber crew must, I thought, be regarded as nugatory compared to the havoc I might wreak amid the infantry. Mr Bracken was sympathetic, and I believe supported my request with vigour. But nothing came of it.

In addition to these frustrations, our charming little house in St John's Wood was blown inside-out by a fly-bomb. The only living creature in it at the moment was a cat of which I was very fond. It had been very fond of me too, and an agreeable companion. But the explosion drove it mad. It held me responsible and thereafter shunned and hated me.

I was almost exaggeratedly elated when, early in 1945, I found myself on a ship packed with diplomats; with hundreds of expectant mothers, brides of Canadian soldiery now being suddenly removed, by some War Office whim, to their new homes; with scores of journalists of numerous nationalities; with a sprinkle of expert intellectual mechanics from the garages where Anglo-American relations go for repairs; and with the customary number of professional spies – some masquerading as diplomats, others as journalists. The world being what it is, I dare say some of the expectant mothers were doing part-time espionage in order to defray the high cost of childbirth.

The journalists, the diplomats, the experts and the spies were all bound for the foundation meeting of the United Nations at San Francisco.

Much of what might truthfully be said about the gathering at which the United Nations was founded turns out to have been said, about ninety years before the delegates assembled at the Golden Gate, by Dean Stanley in his exhilarating description of the Council of Nicaea which met in the year 325. Indeed I used sometimes to enhance a reputation, in orthodox Communist circles, for frivolity by asserting – truthfully I think – that for anyone needing to know how assemblies, congresses, committees and the like really work, the only absolutely required reading should consist of these chapters by Dean Stanley, together with Cardinal de Retz's analysis of the papal consistory of 1655, concluding with the election of Cardinal Chigi as Pope Alexander VII.

William Sargant, in *Battle for the Mind*, emphasizes as a principal thesis that the methods and physiology of brain-washing and religious conversion may proceed in a similar or even identical manner, quite irrespective of whether the object in view is to bring people to Wesley or Mao Tse-tung. Just so, the behaviour-patterns of assemblies and committees show similarities and repetitions which are traceable alike in the Kremlin, in seventeenth-century Rome, and the hall where the Urban District Council meets.

Dean Stanley quotes the wholesome remarks of the former Vicar of Kensington, John Jortin, who, after a long, cool, mid eighteenth-century look at the way such things really happen, listed some of the motives by which assemblies – he was writing of Church assemblies, but he might have said much the same of a Congress of the Communist Party or the Republican Presidential Convention – may be influenced.

They may be influenced [said Jortin in 1750 or thereabouts] by reverence to the Emperor or to his councillors and favourites, or the fear of offending some great prelate . . . who had it in his power to insult, vex and plague all the bishops within and without his jurisdiction; by the dread of passing for heretics and of being calumniated, reviled, hated, anathematized, excommunicated, imprisoned, banished, fined, beggared, starved if they refused to submit; by the love of peace and quiet; by compliance with an active body and imperious spirit; by a deference to the majority; by a love of dictating and domineering, of applause and respect; by vanity and ambition; by a total ignorance of the question in debate, or a total indifference about it; by private friendships; by enmity and resentment; by old prejudices; by hopes of gain; by an indolent disposition; by good nature and the fatigue of attending; by the desire to be at home.

It might be healthy if anyone who ever goes to a conference of some kind and votes for something or other were to picture himself about the 1750s in the vicarage at Kensington, explaining to the incumbent why he personally was not seriously influenced by any of these considerations.

Partly because so many important delegates and officials came from 'austerity' areas – the mountains of China, the starved underground of France, not to mention the dreary subsistence levels of England – the San Francisco Conference put into practice on the largest scale the belief, the most cherished article of faith among diplomats, negotiators and promoters through the ages from the Homeric heroes to Krupp, that without free wine and women you either get nowhere, or get somewhere more slowly than otherwise.

Sometimes it was nearly eerie to watch Chinese and Saudi Arabians watching the San Francisco of 1945 – for many of them their first contact with America or, indeed, any part of the Western world. It was exhilarating, too, like being swung aloft by a crane and enabled to view the turmoil of the place and time from a fresh angle. Such a crane hooked itself into my belt one late afternoon in that roof bar, called the 'Top of the Mark', which, glowing like a jewel with fine carpets and woods and metals and a rainbow of liquor bottles, commands one of the most dramatic prospects in the world from the pinnacle of the Mark Hopkins Hotel.

I sat down to appreciate it, and found myself beside a Chinese of about my own age, appreciating too. He wore a beautifully-tailored suit of what seemed to be some fine silk. His hair and shoes shone smoothly in the Pacific sunset. He looked as smooth, as untouched by hardness or hardship, as if he had lived for years and years in places like the Mark Hopkins. Nevertheless, he was appreciating, and had a light in the eye. We fell into conversation. At the end of a quarter of an hour, it appeared that a topic which particularly interested him was the civil war in Spain.

'When I lived for some years,' he said, 'in a cave in Szechuan, as a guerrilla fighter you know, I read a book about it – it had been translated into Chinese from the Russian edition. But it was by an Englishman, a reporter who had also fought in the Spanish Republican Army for a while.'

'You recall the author's name?'

'I don't know how you'd pronounce it in English. It seemed like. . . .' He gave a fair rendering of the name Pitcairn.

'That,' I said, not even pretending to be calm at this coincidence and at the thought of my book, which I did not even know had been translated into Chinese, being thumbed by those legendary guerrillas of Szechuan, 'is my *nom-de-plume*, I wrote it.'

Nor did he try to live up to any myth of oriental impassivity. On the contrary, he shouted with an enthusiasm which made an explosive noise even amid the roar and buzz of the Top of the Mark at cocktail time.

We cut all other appointments and talked for hours, while the melancholy outlines of Alcatraz blurred into the ocean. As soon appeared, he, so far from having lived in the Mark Hopkins half his life, had spent many of his years fighting in West China, living in the caves for months on end or, with ragged columns of poorly armed men, struggling over terrible tracks on barely credible route marches – forays and agonizing retreats and evasions.

No Communist, he was in the fullest sense of the word a fellow-traveller, on foot and in philosophy. He had been, ever since his late student days, fighting first in the seemingly hopeless battle against Chiang Kai-shek, later against the Japanese, after the temporary alliance between Chiang and the Communists to which Chiang himself was later to attribute his downfall.

To talk on this and many subsequent occasions with this man was to experience that delicious stirring of the brain which comes only from converse with someone whose experience has almost nothing in common with one's own, but yet has been looking intently at the same scene, so that the events you have both been observing from such distant points form the link between you. Few things are more refreshing than to discuss a given situation with someone whose basic assumptions are not yours. He startles you every minute, and you him. Each of you has to take another look at what had seemed so obvious, so shopworn. It is the kind of conversation in which there is no such phrase as 'of course'.

It is stimulating in the way Greek and Latin – and, I have no doubt, Arabic and Hindi – prod and stir you in a way no modern language (whose basic assumptions are the same as those of your own language) can do. The first time you, as a schoolboy, discover first that the Latin word *honor* is not a translation of the English word 'honour', and secondly that the Romans did not have any single word meaning just what 'honour' (except in the Birthday or New Year sense) means in English, you are up there on that over-publicized but still exciting peak in Darien.

Adding oddity to our meeting was the discovery that we had been born within a mile or two and year or two of one another in Peking – I, as he joyously pointed out, in the British Legation, headquarters of the rapacious, imperialist foreign devils. And here we were talking in San Francisco, because he, fighting along with the Reds in the West China mountains, had read a book of mine about fighting along with the Reds in the Spanish Sierra.

The last time I saw him was the night of farce and nervous ulcer when we had both been invited to make – with a couple of others – a radio broadcast of reminiscence, comment and view-exchange – a meeting of minds for the public benefit. Anyone is at liberty to state that in their opinion the notion of a Chinese fellow-traveller and the correspondent of a British Communist newspaper being invited to get on the American air and chat is too fantastic to be given credence. The person who finds it so is unaccustomed to the abrupt changes that can occur in American political weather.

However, the event did not come to pass, because by that time both of us had come to take the technical and mechanical efficiency of the United States for granted. That is an arrogant mistake. One should enjoy it, but not lean on it too heavily.

Leaving the Top of the Mark in plenty of time to drive to the studio, we found that the lift had gone out of action. Few things are more daunting than to prepare for a mile-a-minute vertical ride so silent that a Senator's polite hiccup is disturbing, and find that what you are going to have to do is to undertake a leg-killing trek down the stairs. On the faces of many whom we passed, or even, occasionally, met sweating up that Matter-horn of stairs, there was the look people have in films about the breakdown of civilization or the shape of things to come.

Late, we rushed to the hotel car-park where my friend's car was parked under ideal conditions of security and freedom. The hotel gave bona-fide guests some gadget which they fitted into the ignition (or thereabouts) and this raised, for a sufficient number of seconds, an invisible electric ray which barred the exit to car-thieves and anyone else without the proper gadget-accreditation.

The place was, in a word, burglar and car-thief proof. Nowa-days it is called automation.

On this particular evening it chanced that the ray itself had somehow become stuck – you worked the correct gadget, but it still loyally, though mistakenly, turned off the ignition every time you got to the exit. We had to climb out and get the whole ray turned off – a serious business, because it meant the quick mobilization of humans to take on its functions as theft-preventers.

Then we shot out into the streets of San Francisco and almost immediately something went wrong with the traffic lights, half a mile ahead. Traffic jammed and halted. I swore that I had actually seen a couple of men get out of their car and set out for their destination on foot. My Chinese friend said that I must be dreaming, no such thing could happen in America. We sat there in the stench and uproar of idling motors, half-deaf and being slowly poisoned.

'Let me tell you,' said my Chinese friend, 'in a cave in Szechuan this couldn't happen.'

Since all hope of reaching the studio in time was now lost, I told him the story I had just heard from a friend of Thomas Mann, with which world figure he was flying from New York to New Orleans, where renowned thinker and novelist Mann was to give a lecture.

At that time, any American officer above the rank of, I think,

Captain, who wanted to hop a plane to go somewhere had the right to claim the seat of any civilian. At Asheville, Buncombe County, North Carolina, the plane made an intermediate stop. An American General and his aide fussed across the tarmac and said they had to get to New Orleans in a hurry. There was an impression that the Japanese could be landing any minute at Miami Beach. Thomas Mann and friend quit their seats and were left behind in Buncombe County.

Only when the General reached New Orleans was it discovered that the purpose of this intellectual soldier's dash to the city was to hear Thomas Mann lecture.

'Delicious,' said my Chinese friend. It made him happy because he was visibly thinking that in a cave in Szechuan that kind of thing couldn't happen either.

22

COLD WAR

IN the newspaper business it often seems that they wait until you have just got the hang of something and then ask you to go off to get the hang of something else. Essentially, it is the same complaint you hear from Foreign Service people who learn Turkish and get posted to Uruguay.

Perhaps, so far as the newspapers are concerned, this practice represents an attempt to carry out the advice proffered to journalists by the late Lord Northcliffe – 'never lose your sense of superficiality'. I certainly was beginning to feel somewhat profound about the true stresses and strains of the United Nations, to be aware of where the bodies were really buried which, when ultimately dug up, were going to cause trouble. And then came the news that a General Election impended in Britain, and on the heels of it a cable from William Rust bidding me hurry home, prepared to transform myself immediately from diplomatic correspondent to political correspondent of the *Daily Worker*.

I thought there must be some mistake. I had always felt more at home in the United States than in England, whose political climate I have never more than dimly appreciated. Someone – almost anyone – else, it seemed to me, could cover that British election for them. Perhaps by reason of being a Scotsman, perhaps because of other circumstances of my life, my ear has never been properly attuned to the way things are played in England; the drama of English life subtly eludes me – so completely indeed that I am often tempted to the error of supposing it is not there at all. Thus, compared with the big bout at San Francisco, whatever was going to happen over in England looked to me like pretty small beer, tepid at that. I wrote a careful cable to Rust explaining that it would in every sense be better were I to remain where I was. I inferred that his original instruction must have been the result of an impetuous aberration.

He replied: 'Return at once repeat at once.' I cabled again at length, and profoundly, touching on the world situation. He replied: 'Kiss the girls good-bye and take first available plane.'

A notion nagged at my mind, and I spent twenty-four hours or so in a state of indecision both exciting and painful. I was wondering whether the best plan might not be to remain in San Francisco so long as my American permit allowed, make arrangements – not by any means impossible – for the trans-atlantic transport of Patricia and our son Alexander, and then remove to Mexico where, during my stay in San Francisco, I had formed some useful connexions. Clearly in my ear I could hear the voice of Cacambo, giving his advice to Candide:

We have travelled enough on foot. By the river-side I see an empty canoe. Let us fill it with coconuts, embark, and follow the stream. A river always leads to some place. And if we find nothing pleasant, at least we shall find something new.

I dare say there are people who can recall truthfully just exactly what were the operative factors in some vital decision made in the past. Indeed it is something of a misfortune not to be able to do so. Years later people ask why one did this rather than the other, and expect a serious, well-informed answer. Not getting it, they suspect one of concealing something, and the word they will be using next is 'disingenuous'. It is not only troublesome, but makes one look either foolish or sly, but I have to admit that once the decision is made, the reasons for it – even the exact nature of the decision – tend to slide from my mind out of sight.

In determining not to go to Mexico instead of London I was certainly much influenced by the fact that, whereas at an earlier period of life the innumerable unknown facts would affect only myself, now they must be fateful also for Patricia and for a boy only four years old. Patricia, I gathered later, would probably have welcomed the idea. She would have been dismayed, if at all, not by the difficulties of getting to Mexico, but by the nuisance of having to learn Spanish when she got there.

As for Alexander – but there was the rub. On so important a matter for his future, he had, as of then, no vote.

So without enthusiasm I chose London. Flying over the Rocky Mountains and the prairies, I sank deeply into gloom. It was a state of mind to which I was but little accustomed. I hoped at first that it might be a hangover, something strictly physical, and fixed my mind on the thought that when Boswell believed himself suffering from moral despair or general *Weltschmerz*, his complaint was often nothing worse than alcoholic poisoning. But on making a tally of the drinks taken the night before, I could not feel such a conclusion justified. Something else must be making me feel unhappy. And watching the United States go by down below, I got an unpleasantly clear idea of what it was. I had begun to wonder whether I was not mistaken about the political shape of the world.

Years before, when I had first lived with and fallen in love with the United States, I had been vividly aware of what has so often been called 'the American dream' – and 'a faith' (to quote an earlier chapter of this autobiography) 'that there was still room on earth for the kingdom of Heaven'. And when I had returned to Europe and jumped into the Communist Party I had been considerably affected by the idea – this was in the days of the great slump – that ultimately it would be Communism which would lead America to the next attempted realization of that repeatedly frustrated dream. It was perhaps less paradoxical than it sounds that I should have been more influenced on this score by the United States than by the U.S.S.R.

But now, fresh from daily contacts with innumerable American Communists, I became oppressed with a sense of futility. I do not speak of, or suggest, individual futility, though naturally there are as many fools and stumblebums in the Communist Party as anywhere else. A lot of those people were able, a lot of them brave, and many were both. But that, it seemed to me, as we came in to land for the stopover at Cheyenne, Wyoming, made the problem more serious. For if the individuals concerned were no more faulty than is to be expected, why were they demonstrably getting nowhere?

In London I felt even more disorientated than, in San Francisco, I had expected to be. And, despite the excitement and activity of the General Election, I was almost continuously aware of that shadow of futility, drifting back and forth across my mind, which had pursued me in the transcontinental plane. And I was in constant danger of becoming infected by that disease of which the principal symptom is an awareness of having said or written all this over and over again, without, so far as can be seen, having had the slightest effect upon anything.

I have sometimes wondered since whether I really believed more than about 25 per cent of the tens of thousands of words I wrote at that time. In fact – partly because the good propagandist for the most part really does believe what he is writing at the moment – I did so. Among the many wise sayings of Lord Northcliffe was that 'you can never successfully put on the table of Demos what you would not put upon your own'. In other words, if you try to talk down to Demos, or to write with your tongue in your cheek, Demos will find you out.

True, I have argued with people who say that in approving of this Northcliffe saying and in approving, too, of what is called 'black' propaganda, I contradict myself. I think not. Well naturally I think not, since nobody goes quietly along with a charge of self-contradiction. But, to put it reasonably, what I feel about it is that what matters is not whether the weapon is good but whether the cause is.

At this point somebody mutters something about doing evil that good may come, or the end justifying the means.

This obscurantist formula has clouded thought for a long time.

Nobody should, I would suppose, willingly do evil that good may come; and if the end justifies the means, then the means are good.

I can conceive of a person saying that those people who organized the big lie about 'The Man Who Never Was' – that corpse on the coast of Spain which deceived Hitler's General Staff – were doing evil, because they were (as one used to be told in childhood) 'acting a lie'. To believe that is to take up the position that telling lies – in the simple sense of deceiving other people – is worse than anything else you can do. Worse, for instance, than deliberately permitting Hitler to gain some advantage because you cannot bring yourself to tell him a lie.

It is not only a possible viewpoint, but a perfectly respectable one. I regard it as abominable, but respectable. But it is only respectable if you really hold it and stick to it. Assume then that you reject it. How can it be both good and bad to lie to Hitler? How, in other words, is the lie bad and yet its effects are good? And how then is this doing evil that good may come?

To which the reply is made: 'But if you declare that, your cause being good, your means of defending it are good too, then you are setting yourself up as the arbiter of good and evil. How do you know your cause is that good?'

And to that anyone seriously engaged in the mêlée can answer no more than that either you believe in your cause to that extent, or you should go away and lie down in the shade – which, evidently, is a decision too. And should it turn out that you had underestimated the excellence of the cause, you would be committing an evil act by deserting it.

Simple thoughts of this kind – 'simple' some would say in the Irish sense of the word, meaning vacuous – occurred to me repeatedly during that 1945 election.

Specifically what bothered me was the necessity for a whole-hearted, full-blooded support of the Labour Party.

One of the elements which make a General Election both farcical and excruciating is precisely this necessity for being wholehearted about everything and everyone. It is a pretty widely accepted fact that you cannot go into a campaign saying, 'In my view, Mr X, though at heart on the side of the angels, somewhat stinks at the edges, so that while advising you to vote for him because his opponent stinks worse, I also advise you not to believe more than a very small proportion of what the man says.' That is not the way to gain friends for your candidate and influence people on his behalf. For the purposes of electioneering, the man is not only on the side of the angels, he personally is one.

The situation was, therefore, that because the Communist Party was so small – and why was it so small? was the question often and inevitably in mind – and had no hope of achieving power itself, the whole potential of the apparatus (not a small potential, because the apparatus was constructed of trained and dedicated people, people who would stay out longer in the rain than anyone else), was to be jerked into action on behalf of the Labour Party. Which, in turn, meant that one had to pretend to believe about 80 per cent of what the Labour leaders said. And that, when you came down to cases, meant believing in 80 per cent of what Ernest Bevin said. I had known Ernest Bevin, in a strictly professional capacity, for a number of years, and in my reckoning 80 per cent was a whole lot too much to believe.

I had watched Bevin at numerous conferences and congresses, watched for the moment when the sly, alert eyes of this John Bull in plastic would judge the moment ripe to switch from the sternly practical to the sob. Reporting any such event you could write, far down the page, 'Bevin lifts arms in Christlike gesture and declares "I am being crucified". Weeps.' You would rarely be wrong. He was a real John Bull, a professional Englishman, with the capacity of the professional Englishman – perfected through long years of colonialism – to have the tears gush from his eyes because nobody understood that it was only for the other boy's good that he was kicking him, or else it was in self-defence, because the wizened 'little boy' was a lot more dangerous, in reality, than he might look to those who did not know the facts. I have seen J. H. Thomas cry repeatedly, and muster votes by it. But Bevin's crucifixion was a better act – and pulled more votes.

I knew – and certainly it was no secret needing special sources of information to ascertain – that Bevin looked upon Communists and Communism in just the way that an old-time

Methodist looked upon the Devil. Some of the time you are genuinely frightened of the Devil, and believe he may do you a mischief. Indeed, that fear is at the back of the mind all the time, and the dread powers of the Evil One justify anything whatever you may choose to do in opposition to him. Other times, you believe in the Devil but consider him merely a smart operator who has overreached himself. He has failed to realize that God is just a little bit smarter. And at other times again you are not worrying about whether there really is a Devil or not, but you see how essential it is that people who might be wavering in their support of you should believe frenziedly in that sinister old Satan who, unless they rush to your aid, is going to jump on your back and sear you with his filthy fire, carry you off – unless everyone will please rally round – to his loathsome pit. This is where the Devil becomes an almost lovable object – at least, an indispensable accessory. For people who might otherwise criticize you sharply, or even desert you altogether, have – if they have any decent human feelings at all – second thoughts when they get the news that you are at this very moment engaged in a crucial life and death struggle with sin, and that a vote against you is a vote for Mephistopheles.

All politicians, from Moscow to London or Washington, have to have an active Devil on the string. Perhaps, indeed, if there had been no Sparta, we should never have heard of Pericles.

In this election of 1945, Mr Bevin had a new and ingenious idea about his relations with the Devil. He put about the alluring notion that, after all the bother and fuss there had been about the fellow, he and his associates would very soon fix things so that the Devil, previously irked by social coldness, would be mellowed by a series of understanding chats.

'Left understands Left', said Mr Bevin, conveying to the voters who remembered Stalingrad that whereas the Tories would doubtless involve us in some kind of war, hot or cold, with the Soviet Union, the Labour Party would soon eliminate all that type of rancorous nonsense and achieve what a huge majority of the voting customers wanted, namely an enduring prolongation of the wartime friendship between Britain and the U.S.S.R.

The bitterest pill to swallow, so far as I was concerned, was to lend support to this gross – as it seemed to me – deception of the public. And yet, what else could be done? The Communist Party by itself could do nothing. And, though its vote in the country was tiny, it remained true that its influence in 'the Labour Movement' was powerful to a degree out of all mathematical proportion to the vote. So that if, for example, the Communist Party and the *Daily Worker* started to slur the Labour Party there was a possibility – at least it looked that way at the time, since no one knew just how big the landslide was going to turn out to be – that this small, but highly organized interior opposition might tip the scales. By hindsight it can probably be reckoned that nothing the Communist Party could have done would have tipped the scales. The Labour vote probably was in the bag. But that was not the way it could be seen then. We thought it was nip and tuck. And so we had to throw whatever weight we had to such men as Bevin who, I was convinced, would, so soon as they had attained office, use their special position in 'the Labour Movement' of the world to upset the possibilities of sane relationship between Britain and Russia.

'Left understands Left' was a good slogan – and like most good slogans was something between a vague aspiration and a downright lie. The 'Left' does not understand the 'Left' – and the whole history of the relations between the various branches of the 'Labour Movement' in Britain and on the continent during the first decades of the twentieth century proves it. Or, put in another way, the one sort of 'Left' understands the other sort of 'Left' so well that it fires from the hip on seeing just what sort of manoeuvre other comrades are up to.

That is to say that either the 'understanding' is the understanding which exists between one hardened tactician and another, or it is simply not there at all. And Mr Bevin, far more experienced than I in that kind of business, understood it; must have understood it, perfectly. He cannot at any moment have thought that to move Transport House into Downing Street would improve the relations of Downing Street with the Kremlin.

On the contrary, as Mr Bevin demonstrated within a few months of the Labour victory at the election, he realized fully that one of the main functions of Labour in the immediate post-war situation was to carry out – as only Labour could – the essential British policy of driving a wedge between the U.S.A. and the U.S.S.R.

There was a moment when the cold war could, just possibly, have been averted. That was at Church House, Westminster, in the very early spring of 1946. Senator Byrnes was Secretary of State, and as a man of the Roosevelt era he was for friendly relations with Russia. To the United Nations Council meeting in London was sent Senator Vandenberg – a Republican Senator who, when even partially sober, was among the most intelligent statesmen of the Western world. He was there to demonstrate the bi-partisan nature of American policy.

Mr Bevin at once understood that here and now was the moment to use the leverage of simply being Labour. A Tory Foreign Secretary might have sought to inaugurate the cold war without making much impact on the Washington Democrats. But if a Labour Foreign Secretary started to attack the Russians, what on earth was an American Secretary of State to do? Could he appear redder than the British Labour Party, which the Americans – as Bevin so well knew – assumed to be at least pink? He could not. Senator Vandenberg and Mr Bevin played the game perfectly. Here were a Republican and a British Labour leader, both agreed. And both agreed to lambast the Russians – the Devil, in fact. Secretary of State Byrnes, newly established President Truman – none of them had a leg to stand on. The cold war had begun.

All this was only dimly apparent to me during that 1945 election campaign. Nevertheless, every time I found myself suggesting to the customers that they should trust Bevin and his associates to 'cement' the Anglo-Russian alliance, to move, in fact, a little closer to Russia and no closer than was quite necessary to the United States, I felt embarrassed, the way anyone feels when he is not quite sure that he has the wrong bottle of medicine, but is very far indeed from being sure that he has the right one.

So in 1945 we watched that well-known (and for Labour calculators dangerously seductive) figure 'The Middle Class Vote' being wooed and cosseted. What troubled me was that we had aided and abetted that process. We were accessories before the fact. I had a sufficiently clear notion of what the fact was going to be to heave a sigh of relief when the Editor suggested a trip to the Balkans.

Blue, grey or red I love the Danube valley, and the Balkans are among my dearest homes-from-home.

Patricia and I spent a wonderfully stimulating three months in Yugoslavia, Bulgaria and Rumania. In those countries at that time you could meet a genuine hero in every valley, on almost any street corner. Naturally a lot of fake heroes were there too.

Everywhere the theory and practice of Stalinism were dominant. By hindsight one could say that they were both noxious and unnecessary. But very few of the genuine heroes – inside or outside the *apparat* – thought so at the time. And they were intelligent and courageous men. They believed these to be the only theories and practices which could save and build their countries.

I believed them. But at the same time the experience of that exhilarating trip sharpened – perhaps paradoxically – my uncertainties about the role of the Communist Party in Britain, and about, more specifically, my own role in the affair.

23
EMERGENCY EXIT

NUMBERS of the new Labour M.P.s used to come to our house at that time, and they increased my sense of isolation, of being, somehow, in the wrong place and needing to move on to somewhere else. These, being for the most part members of the Left wing of the Labour Party, were people whom the *Daily Worker* and the Communist Party had, in degrees varying from the very small to the decisive, helped to elect. Talking, and sometimes working, with them, I was aware of a lack of sympathy on my own part which positively startled me.

It was easy enough, of course, to find reasons superficially satisfying to oneself; as, for instance, that some were grossly on the make, others insufferably conceited, and others more pusillanimous than anyone has a right to be.

I recall a remarkable occasion, and one which was sufficiently typical, when one of the innumerable 'revolts' in the Parliamentary Labour Party was in progress. These 'revolts', usually against some phase or other of Bevin's foreign policy, occurred about once every couple of months, and followed a scarcely varying pattern from the moment when the optimists declared that this time it was serious, and Bevin would have to mend his ways, to the later moment when the whole thing faded away, leaving Bevin and his policy unshaken and unchanged.

On the occasion I speak of, no less than fifty – I think it was more like eighty – Labour M.P.s had put their names to a resolution, highly critical of Bevin, which was to be debated at the regular 'secret' weekly meeting of the Party.

Since, this time, they had not merely gone about the lobbies talking of mutiny, but actually signed something in black and white, even my hard-learned scepticism softened. This time something really was going to happen. I hung about, waiting for the meeting to be over and the story of it to 'leak' – which it normally did about fifteen minutes after the secret session was over.

To my naïve astonishment, it transpired that not eighty, not fifty, not twenty or ten of the bold 'rebels' had voted against Bevin in favour of their own resolution. The number of such voters had been three.

I tackled a number of the un-rebellious rebels in the lobby and asked them how come? Their answers were singularly revealing of the way such matters are really conducted. One of them said that in the course of the long discussion his feet had got hot and swelled. He had been in pain, and had left the room to remove his shoes for a few minutes and let his feet simmer down. 'And would you believe it,' he said, 'when I got back in there, the vote had just been taken?'

Two of them said that, after all, the voting on a resolution was unimportant – the debate itself, they said, was the important thing, and they assured me that Bevin had been 'visibly impressed'.

Another had a more ingenious explanation of his failure to vote. 'It was obvious,' said he, 'that even if a large number of us voted for the resolution we should still be in a minority. And that would be an encouragement to Bevin. But if nobody voted for the resolution, or even abstained, in fact if we all voted for it, Bevin would have no clue to the true size of the rebellion, and that would frighten him.'

Rendered somewhat dizzy by this line of reasoning, I tried to envisage the consequences of its application to political struggles in general.

It was the kind of episode which constantly occurred, and to watch such events and write about them was naturally frustrating. But gradually I began to have to admit to myself that my lack of sympathy with the Labour men was not so straightforwardly political as I had pretended to myself. In any case, evidently, it was foolish to object to Labour legislators on the ground that they did not act like Communists. But I began to realize that what I found increasingly unsympathetic was not merely Labour but the atmosphere of English life in general – and that, as I came more slowly to understand, included the 'climate' of the British Communist Party and the *Daily Worker*.

People have asked me repeatedly – and the questions are natural in a period when the fact of Communism and everyone's relation to it are the central features of the world's political, social and intellectual life – how precisely I came to move into the Communist Party and how precisely I came to move out of it. Numbers of friendly reviewers dealing with the first volume of this autobiography mildly complained that it did not answer the first part of the question. That surprised me, because I had supposed that the whole book, all the way from nursery to the Spanish war, was, in fact, an answer.

A difficulty is that, with many examples before them, people are accustomed to expect something abrupt, sensational and Pauline in the way of a conversion – some explosion on the road to Damascus capable of explaining so drastic a decision. Things do, certainly, quite often happen that way. I can only say that in my case nothing of that sort occurred, and it would be misleading even to suggest that it did. And I am forced to give the same sort of answer, highly unsatisfactory to many people, and to some both offensive and suspect, to the second half of the question too. I dare say if I had been at the *Daily Worker* at the time of the Russian attack on Hungary that kind of 'explosion' would have occurred, and I should have quit in a blaze of disgust. It would be agreeable, but also dishonest, to state categorically that such would have been the case. It would be a respectable thing to assert. But no one can with honesty assert just what they would have done in circumstances which never arose. I can imagine, as a theoretical possibility, that – just as, at the time of the Communist change of line at the beginning of the war, a principal factor influencing my decision to stay with the paper was a perhaps overdeveloped sense of loyalty, and distaste for leaving the outfit when it is under fire – so, even under the pressure of events in Hungary, I might have taken the same kind of decision. I think not, but there is no way of knowing.

As things were in reality, there was no more of an explosion on the way out than on the way in. It was a gradual process, involving countless factors which were by no means all 'political' in the strict sense of the word.

It would, again, be respectable to pretend now that I was already alert to and horrified by the proceedings of the Stalin régime in Russia. There would be an element of truth in that, but not the whole truth. The fact was that like innumerable non-Russian Communists – and it is an important fact to keep in mind – I was sheathed, so to speak, against indignation and disgust regarding many atrocious events in Russia, by two suits of protective clothing. The first was the fact that during a great part of my life I had listened to anti-Communists telling the wildest lies about Communism and Communists, and on occasion had even seen the lies being manufactured. The result was that even when they told the truth one almost instinctively rejected it – certainly one treated it with a scepticism tougher than one would bring into play on other issues.

Almost exactly the same thing happened, during the early years of the Nazi régime in Germany, to people who had been pacifists during or soon after the First World War. From books and pamphlets by leading Socialist publicists like Arthur Ponsonby, they had learned a lot about the seamy side of wartime propaganda. They had discovered that a good many of the most hair-raising 'atrocities' supposed to have been committed by the German troops in their advance through Belgium had never happened. They discovered that the story of the Germans boiling down the corpses of soldiers to make soap or other fats – a story beautifully calculated to horrify British people, always easily disgusted by the picture of the ruthless scientist outraging decent humanity – had, in point of fact, been invented for the purpose of horrifying the Chinese and arousing their anti-German sentiments.

The people most affected by such revelations were, naturally, those who during the war itself had taken such propaganda at its face value and now felt that they had for years been the victims of a confidence trick. The result was that, having once believed too much, they now believed too little. They thought the stories of Nazi atrocities were inventions, too.

The other protective suit was of a different material and texture. It was woven principally of two beliefs. One was the belief that after all, on balance, the Soviet régime was, so to speak, on the side of the angels – that is to say that despite many deviations and shortcomings its mere existence was an asset to the oppressed of the earth, a challenge and a threat to the oppressors. In my view, and in the view, obviously, of millions of people from India to South Africa to the Southern States of the U.S.A., there was a most obvious truth in that. But out of that belief grew a second article of faith which was more dangerous – the conviction that, in such circumstances, actions which would be violently condemned if performed by any other régime must be quite differently assessed when performed by the Government of the U.S.S.R.

Anyone can see and say that that is a dangerous attitude. But to recognize it as such does not solve the dilemma of – in particular – the Western intellectual looking for peace, progress and the fall of the Bastille. For, the moment he accuses the Russian Communists of some hideous malpractice, he finds himself to his horror in the approving company of half the leading ruffians of the Western world, people of whom he feels certain that, given half a chance, they would behave in the same way themselves. It is like advocating the abolition of capital punishment and being patted enthusiastically on the back by the bloody hand of a man who has just murdered a child.

The dilemma is real. It is part of the more general one described by Jean-Paul Sartre: 'If the Communists are right, I am the loneliest madman alive. If they are wrong, there is no hope for the world.' Certainly that is not a comprehensive account of the true situation – nor, I suppose, did Sartre mean it to be. But it is a true account of a common and not discreditable state of mind.

So far as my strictly political 'doubts' about the Communists were concerned, they were concentrated less upon whatever evil the Communists might be performing than upon the good which they seemed, at so many points, unable to perform.

At that time, certainly, one could attribute this lack of performance to the aftermath of war. Nevertheless, after viewing the chaos of Rumania, the comparative stagnation of Bulgaria, and, above all, the arid desert of East Germany, the doubts nagged at me. Very well, so it was true that these conditions were the direct result of war and revolution. But I, after innumerable conversations with a wide diversity of people in all those territories, found myself afflicted with a painful uncertainty as to whether the classic Communist formulae for ultimately solving the difficulties were really calculated to bring home, as they say, the bacon.

Viewing the British scene, I found my doubts more obtrusive. It is always disconcerting, after long immersion in a particular kind of activity, to come up for air one morning and wonder whether you and your fellow-workers are getting anywhere at all. We ran faster and faster, and seemed to remain almost exactly in the same place. If Marx was right in noting that the crucial thing is not simply to understand the world but to change it, we seemed to be changing very little.

For example, to descend from the general to the particular, the circulation of the *Daily Worker* at about this period was not merely not rising, but falling. Well, of course, that was very easily explained – it was due to the war ending and the consequent change of political atmosphere. It was an explanation, all right, like another. But was it an excuse?

The size of Communist representation in Parliament, fluctuating at that time, so far as I recollect, between one and two, could also be fully explained: the voters almost everywhere were certain the Communist candidate could not win the seat, so to avoid wasting their suffrages they gave them to the Labour candidate instead. A very truthful account of the position. But just what *made* the voters so certain that the most sensational victory the Communist was likely to achieve was the saving of his deposit? Worse still, what made the voters' prognostications ninety-eight per cent right?

Newspaper propaganda designed to reach 'the masses' is a strident affair, and in political propaganda of that kind you have to keep telling people that you are winning. They may not, after a look at the form book, believe it, but at least they are supposed to believe that you believe it. But it becomes irksome to be endlessly proclaiming the imminence of victories which do not, in fact, occur. You find yourself annoyingly reminded of the old Sam Goldwynism – the one about the time, during the depression, when some banker in New York rang him up in Hollywood and asked, 'How's business?' 'It's wonderful,' shouted Sam, 'it's tremendous, it's impressive, it's colossal – but it's picking up.'

It would have taken a powerful microscope to detect just where our business was picking up, and powerful microscopes of that kind were in demand among many of the leadership and rank and file alike. Others preferred the telescope through which you could see Chiang Kai-shek being routed, and the Chinese Communists sweeping that mighty country. To some this brought immediate solace. But when you took your eye from the telescope and looked, say, at the results of a County Council election in Britain, the change in the view could give you a painful headache.

A more personal feature of this depressing scene was my growing conviction that, although some British Communists were doubtless proving immensely effective somewhere, my own effectiveness was sinking towards zero. Often I experienced that nightmare of the publicist in which he finds himself condemned to shout exhortations, warnings, funny jokes, and alarming disclosures down a telephone line with nobody at the other end of it. They have put down their receivers and gone to the pictures or a meeting of the Labour Party.

It was clear to me that if the circulation of the paper was

falling, or at least was failing to rise, the fault must be to a quite large extent mine. I was the most experienced writer there, I often wrote more of the paper than anyone else, and both before and during the war my writing had admittedly been effective, had had an impact – occasionally a major impact. I had a fairly clear idea of the nature of the fault. Just the same qualities, it seemed to me, which had made me an enthusiastic and effective commentator during, say, the period of hunger marches and anti-Fascist brawls and riots in London, Paris and Marseilles; the period of the Spanish war; the electrically sultry period of Hitler's advance from Munich to the war; the period of the war itself – these qualities and dispositions appeared in some way to unfit me for what were called 'the tasks of reconstruction'. For the first time in my life I realized what people mean when they use the term 'maladjustment'. Hitherto I had supposed it was something that only happened to other people.

It is all very well to recognize a fault, but it is not really much use when you recognize at the same time that it is a fault which it is now far too late to correct. I used to reflect that had I, for example, in years gone by, taken more trouble to study and steep myself in the history and essential character of the British Labour movement, had I exerted myself more vigorously to comprehend the British character, I should be better adjusted to the situation. But there was no time to start doing all that now.

I was thus in the unpleasing position of a man who has volunteered to help drive a car over rough roads and now finds that he has forgotten how to change gear and rather suspects that the car has taken a wrong turning anyway.

More personal reasons, too, played a role in bringing me – some time about the late summer of 1946 – to the point of, for the first time, seriously considering a move.

Patricia – it was a few months before our second son was born – was even more aware of, and oppressed by, a sense of futility and boredom than I was. She had always been more clear-headed than I about many aspects of the situation. She did not, to the full extent, share my propensity – often useful – for treating action as an end in itself; for acting, in fact, without asking ultimate questions; for taking hasty decisions and then

267

behaving as though the decision to follow this course or that had been the product of the most careful weighing of pros and cons. She was therefore more irked than I by the unanswered questions with which my political path was littered. And she resented more than I did all kinds of evasion and double-talk – every occasion upon which, after some impending possibility had been denounced as disastrous for weeks before it happened, it was suddenly 'proved' to be a boon-laden victory after it had occurred.

I had been in Paris attending some conference or other of Foreign Ministers, and she had gone for a short holiday at her parents' house in Ireland. On the evening of our mutual return to London I told her suddenly – I had never even hinted at it before – that I was thinking about the possibility of dropping everything and starting an entirely new life. I had expected her to be startled. Instead she coolly remarked that she had noticed for months that for me the savour had gone out of things, and that as for her she had reached the same conclusion, but had not liked to mention it.

'The only thing is,' she remarked, 'what exactly would we use for money?'

It was undoubtedly a ticklish problem. The pay at the *Daily Worker* was still small, though, in contrast to the sort of thing that had happened in my early days there, it came regularly week by week. But it was possible to supplement it considerably by writing for Communist newspapers abroad – notably in Poland and the Balkans. Also I could, very occasionally and under a plethora of pseudonyms, sell an article or short story to a non-political magazine, though my American outlets, which had been very profitable in the pre-war years when a known Communist could still sell to non-Communist publications in the U.S.A., had clogged up at the beginning of the war and never reopened. Patricia had a small allowance from her father. I have forgotten what precisely our average income, including my earnings and Patricia's allowance, amounted to at the time – I suppose about £600 or £700 a year, which would be reduced to somewhere between £200 and £300 if I quitted the paper and left London.

Furthermore, after years of more or less strenuous and somewhat specialized political journalism, I knew that it would take some time to develop, as it were, new muscles.

We had, naturally, almost nobody with whom we could discuss the position. Of course the people at the paper would have felt, quite sincerely, that the only proper course was for me immediately to go to them with my doubts and problems, so that a 'full and frank discussion' might be held. It would have been the correct Communist way of doing things. Equally sincerely, I felt that it would achieve nothing useful whatever, and must inevitably produce exasperation and suspicion on all sides. I could not see myself successfully explaining the nuances of my attitude in acceptable terms. The nuances, so important to myself, would, like certain wines, 'travel badly' into strict Marxist territory. The fact that I did feel that way was incidentally a proof that, despite all those years at the paper, I had not, after all, become a very good Communist. I thought that the more I kept my ideas and purposes to myself, the more I should be likely to save both myself and them a terrible lot of trouble. It was therefore impossible to take counsel with more than one or two intimate and truly reliable friends.

Nearly a year had passed, and my second son, Andrew, was four or five months old, before Patricia and I made up our minds that, if we postponed the move until we had carpentered together some assurance of future financial security, we should perish of economic paralysis in London. We decided to sell the balance of the lease of our flat, which brought in a few hundred pounds, and take off for Ireland at the earliest practicable moment.

There remained a vital tactical problem to be solved. I was naturally anxious not to do harm to my old friends and associates at the *Daily Worker* by making any kind of spectacular exit. It would, I thought, be unbearable to become the centrepiece of a press furore in which I should inevitably be treated as a kind of Kravchenko, dashing out from the Iron Curtain to write *I Chose Freedom*. Maybe I really was 'choosing freedom', but, in my case, that seemed no good reason for biting the old comrades.

(I remarked once, a long time later, to Mr Osbert Lancaster, that it would be nice if he could help to persuade some of the

Fleet Street chiefs that I was tired of having people expect that at any moment an *I Chose Freedom* was coming from me. Twirling his moustache and rolling his eyes in his fascinating manner, he said, 'But you might, you know, write an interesting little book called *I Chose the Galway Blazers.*')

I have nothing much to hold against the people who spend twenty years or so in the Communist Party, and presently dash out, tearing hair and beating breasts, to tell the waiting world what a murderous brothel they have been living and working in all that time. They are entitled to do that. But as a man in Youghal, County Cork, said to me one day, when Douglas Hyde or some other refugee from the salt-mines came to address the populace, 'Jesus, Mr Cockburn, he was warning us all against Communism which none of us ever thought of. And him, to hear him tell it, a member of that same organization for fifteen or twenty years or whatever the devil it was. Wouldn't you think now, Mr Cockburn, he'd do better tell the story down in Prague or some place like that?'

I see no sense, from anyone's viewpoint, in these – however sincerely felt – confessions. The brain-washed Westerner who talks to the Chinese and Russians cuts very little ice among people intelligent enough to pull any political weight. And the same is presumably true of people turning the other way round. If a man was fool enough to be fooled by a lot of fools whom he now declares to be fools, and furthermore was fooled for years on end, should any intelligent person pay much attention to his testimony?

In considering that kind of people, one is constantly reminded of the girl in Norfolk, Virginia, who was suing a man for alleged rape. The Judge said to her, 'When did this rape occur?'

'When did it occur, Judge?' said she. 'Why, hell, it was rape, rape, rape all summer long.'

The easiest way of avoiding that undesirably spectacular exit seemed to be to fall gravely ill of a diplomatic illness. When you are in reasonably good health, there is a certain charm in the process of selecting which illness you are going, diplomatically speaking, to have. In earlier days the whole business was, I imagine, easy. If the worst came to the worst you could say you had brain fever – that undefined disease which so often

270

hurried mysteriously to save the plots of so many Victorian novels. With the advance of modern medical science the thing becomes more difficult. In my experience, modern medical specialists do not worry unduly if you die, but they feel uneasy if they cannot record in some detail what you died of.

The more I studied possible diseases, the more difficult it became to find one which would really fill the bill. For, the moment I made public the news of my ailment, a posse of high-powered Communist Party doctors would be rushed to my assistance. I might even be offered a trip to a rest-home in the Crimea. And even if they failed to discover that there was nothing seriously wrong, in the end I should have to be cured, and perhaps offered some months of unexacting employment – in charge, perhaps, of the *Daily Worker* library, with permission to write one article a week about Fascist Tito, or Beria, watch-dog of the Russian people.

At this point a miracle occurred. I had (a strange thing for me) been sleeping badly, and used to take sleeping pills occasionally. One day I asked a friend of mine who, although not a doctor, was a distinguished chemist, whether he could recommend a pill which would induce sleep but would not, at the same time, give me an agonizing stomach-ache at the moment of wakening.

He inquired about the pills I had been using, inquired about the stomach-aches and said, 'I will get you some pills, but what you have to do is to get in front of an X-ray. What you have is a pretty severe stomach ulcer. The symptoms are unmistakable.'

He explained about some ingredient in my pills which, if you happened to have a stomach ulcer, touched it up and made you writhe.

It seemed too good to be true, but my friend fixed up an emergency X-ray for me in some laboratory, and when we got the pictures there it was – a genuine, entirely undiplomatic ulcer.

Just in case anyone thought this was a put-up job – which was of course exactly what everyone was going to think – I went to one of the big London hospitals and had another X-ray done there. The result was the same, and, this time, as it were, official. The doctor who told me the news was quite surprised. Possibly he had never before had the experience of telling a man he had a bad ulcer and seeing the man beam with pleasure and thank him warmly for the information.

In face of that neutral evidence, everyone agreed that a long rest was essential. I pointed out that as luck would have it I knew of a place which was ideal for the purpose.

In point of fact, Patricia, Alexander, and Andrew in his basket, had already flown to Ireland. The removals men had made preliminary arrangements for shifting as much of our furniture as had not been blown to bits in the house we had had before. And a few days later I was on the Fishguard–Cork boat, *en route* for the ancient town of Youghal, a town standing – like the poet Cavafy in E. M. Forster's description – 'at a slight angle to the universe'.

24

SEVEN-LEAGUE BOOTS

JUST once in a longish while you find you can write yourself an order for a pair of seven-league boots, and you travel inhumanly far in next to no time. It is only eight hours or thereabouts from Fishguard to Cork, but on the quay there in Cork I knew at once what kind of boots I had on. For whatever a person feels about Ireland – likes it, loathes it, or it merely blurs on him – it is a long way from England in all directions. Here and there it is a little nearer to America, but is a long way from there, too.

In the car to Youghal that day I re-lived the sensations of being seventeen and travelling for the first time across Central Europe. Not, evidently, that there is the slightest resemblance, physically or otherwise, between Ireland and Central Europe. It is simply the 'other-ness', the difference between this or that new sort of life and whatever rut you have somehow jerked yourself out of, which brightens the eye of the beholder. And you can be in a dull rut at seventeen as easily as at forty-five.

There are people who deny that there is an essential difference between being in one place and being in another. They are sincere. They use their seven-league boots without reference to geography. They, perhaps, need only to take their 'first look into Chapman's Homer' to travel far and fast. Myself, I have always found that geography helps.

We came into Youghal, running along beside the ocean where the thrust of the Blackwater's current fights the Atlantic tide. Here on the left, we had two neat new textile factories, claimed to be the most up-to-date boxes of machinery in the entire island, supervised technically by imported experts from Lancashire. A few hundred yards up the road behind them are a wishing-well and a magic tree where, surreptitiously, some people still hang rags torn from their clothes as they did before the Christians superseded the Druids. Some few hundred yards farther up the same road is the site where, in Ireland's last war with England, three men of the Irish Republican Army let off a land mine under the first truck of a British column. They had information that the truck was full of ammunition, but at the last moment there had been a switch and some boys belonging to the band were blown up instead.

At this end of town were the hotels, some with spacious names like 'Pacific' and 'Marine', and one called, with scrupulous honesty, 'Railway View'. It recalled a time when you could any day see an ocean, and a big river full of salmon and bass, and distant mountains, but to look straight out of the bedroom or dining-room and see a railway station was a worthwhile experience.

After that, the road narrowed to where the real Youghal lay, longitudinally squeezed, between the river and the hill; a beautiful, gnarled town where history smells as strong as blood.

It took us six weeks to find a house for ourselves, and more than two months to have it made habitable. For, as is natural in a country which has lived in a state of colonialism for centuries, there is a shortage of small country houses; everything seems either too big, with hundreds of acres of land, or too small. And for equally historical reasons many, many houses are derelict. People got poorer and poorer, or emigrated, leaving the house to very poor relations, who could not afford to do otherwise than let the roof cave in above them.

The house we found, on a hillside a mile and a half from the town, had once been the summer residence of the Mayors of Youghal. Why, with so small a town around them, they needed a summer residence at all is not exactly known. It is supposed that in hot summers the open sewers and gutters stank and were deemed unhealthy. At other seasons, the house and its courtyard were used for the collection of tribute from the country. The tributary cattle were brought in and penned in the yard behind a gate with powerful stone pillars. A little above the house there was a square watch-tower. When I say 'was', it is still there, like the house, but in those days – the early sixteenth or late fifteenth century – when the house and tower were built, the tower was a look-out place for the soldiery who from there could give early notice of any move by the natives to attack the place and possibly recover their cattle by force of arms.

At right angles to this ancient house, which had thick, rough stone walls and small windows and a general air of sturdy preparedness for the worst, they built, in about 1740, another house, on the spacious and elegant Georgian pattern, with wide windows twelve feet high in all the ground floor rooms. Through doors on the ground floor or landing you step through a couple of centuries from the old part of the house to the new.

For more than 130 years, the house was owned by some rich Anglo-Irish named Drew. Then, one time in the latter half of the nineteenth century, they began to smell something burning, politically. Peasant revolt, or at least an outbreak here or there, seemed imminent, and if it occurred here rather than there, what was going to be the position about those huge windows? Were they at all defensible against a determined attack by the neighbours? It was judged that they were not. Thereupon the Drews doggedly set to work to build something more adapted to modern conditions of living. About half a mile away they constructed a replica of a small medieval castle, with turrets for observation of the enemy, very small windows, and slits to shoot through or even, if it came to that, pour boiling oil through. It took them over a year to build, and at the end of that time they moved into it, abandoning their large rooms full of light and air, and settling down in a posture of defence. They had decided, in fact, that it was safer to live permanently in, as it were, the air-raid shelter.

I said to Patricia that it seemed odd to take all that trouble. Why, for instance, instead of building this other house, and living – at least in their own estimation – in serious danger while the building was going on, did they not go somewhere else; to England, for example? Patricia was surprised. 'Well,' she said, 'for one thing, if they'd gone to England they wouldn't have known any of the neighbours.'

When we found it, the house, or rather a corner of it, was occupied by an aged man in a rusty black cutaway coat and a stetson-type hat who gave the impression that he had worked in some capacity on the Mississippi river in the nineties. And he had, as a matter of fact, been a travelling salesman in Cincinatti. He was an energetic old man of great goodwill, but he was in no position to prop up the house. He lived, for the most part, in one room, where the ceiling was still intact, seated under an enormous crucifix, studying sacred books in Latin. The lower part of the house was invaded, not by neighbours now, but by fowl of many kinds, and sometimes by cows.

Very soon after we had taken the house, he died, and for a while it was hard to get anyone to work late around the place on account of his ghost. I never saw it myself, although I do not, in principle, disbelieve in ghosts. But I have never been able to understand why it is still so very generally supposed that ghosts are malign and therefore alarming. If the person who has now become a ghost was benign in life, why should he be sinister on his *post mortem* appearance? I used to argue thus with one or two of the workmen who seemed distressed at the thought of the old man possibly wandering about the passages. I convinced no one, and I think they probably supposed I was making up all this stuff about benign ghosts for the purpose of getting them to work overtime. There are, of course, explanations for this alarmed attitude towards the dead, to be found in many mythologies. What is odd is only that this fear should almost universally triumph over any other feeling about ghosts. Some ghosts are naturally terrifying. At Lep Castle in Ireland there is a ghost of a headless sheep which stinks horribly. A dog, confined for the night in the room haunted by the sheep, went out of its mind and jumped through the window to its death.

We were just settling into the house when an unpleasant thing happened. The U.S. Senate Committee on Un-American activities, or some cognate body, issued its list of the two or three hundred most dangerous Reds in the world, and included my name. It seemed an uncomfortable thing to have happen to one in the heart of Catholic, passionately anti-Communist, Ireland.

There was, obviously, a way to appease everyone – namely by taking this American attack as a peg from which to hang a violent renunciation and denunciation of the Communists and all their works. But this, as I have said earlier, was a thing which I felt it would be both dishonest and undignified to do. I did not think that anything would justify anyone saying things that would be quoted with approval by, say, Senator McCarthy, and I am happy to say that nobody I knew even suggested that I should, though an action of that sort on my part would have made life rather easier for my Irish friends and acquaintances as well as for myself.

To make any worthwhile statement or generalization about just how 'tolerant' or 'intolerant' is the 'climate of opinion' in the Irish Republic, you would need to spend years and years getting the evidence – and at that you would probably find at the end of it all that you had done grave injustice to some man who felt himself spiritually or economically hounded and persecuted, or else to some nobly fair-minded Roman Catholic priest.

It is, however, factual, I should suppose, to state that if I had been living in a village in Bohemia at the time when, a year or more later, the Czechoslovak Government denounced me as a sinister organizer of the Western Intelligence Services and arrested several score people in Prague for the crime of having once met and talked with me, I should have been subjected to a lot more inconvenience than I was in Youghal after that Senatorial denunciation.

Indeed in Youghal I was subjected to no more inconvenience than a dubious look here and there, and eager looks from those who felt that a certain amount of drama had been injected into the situation. The way I like garlic, the Irish like drama. It is no use telling me that too much garlic spoils some food; I dare say they are right, but I have never been able to get too much garlic, and mostly not enough. The Irish seem to feel that it is hard to get enough drama. Presence of a dangerous Red provides drama, regardless of what you feel about this subversive fellow personally. I am sure there are many people who would rather have a murderer in town, to observe and talk about, than a person who provided no food for thought and conversation.

One or two little informers had an unusually good time. They would sit in the secret 'snug' which almost all Irish bars have, taking note of my conversation with these and those in the public bar. It gave them a justification, one might say, for their existence.

With no harm done to me, the plot and conspiracy of which I might be the centre kept going for months – even for a couple of years. It was the Freemasons who formed the hitherto missing link. Personally, I have never been sure whether there are any Freemasons in Youghal at all. But, as I have remarked before, every politician and every political or religious organization needs a Devil. In a country where there is only the tiniest minority of Protestant opposition to the Roman Catholic Church, a Devil is more necessary than usual. It must be that, though the Protestants are few in numbers, and outwardly weak, yet they have a power of secret organization, through the Freemasons, which renders them nevertheless a menace. There were said to be four of these menacing Freemasons in Youghal. At one period of my life in that town, it was noted by alert people in search of drama that sometimes a certain well-known Protestant would meet me in the street, draw me discreetly aside, and press into my hand a document or documents. It was fairly evident what was happening. This Protestant, clearly, must be an agent of the Freemasons. The Freemasons, of course, were using the whole Protestant Church as a front organization. But who was using the Freemasons as a front organization? Unquestionably the Kremlin. And here was Mr Cockburn, attested Kremlin agent, getting from this go-between reports from the Freemasons on how the evil work was progressing.

I could almost have wished it had been so. For, as I pointed out when I heard the story, the 'go-between' – though he certainly was the sexton of the Protestant Church – was also the local process-server. He handed out the writs to people who were being sued and were supposed to appear in court. Those were the documents which, as a result of high expenses and low earnings during our first year or two in Ireland, he all too often had to press, as discreetly as possible, into my hand.

Being true, and susceptible of demonstration, this explanation of mine was annoying to many. It knocked a piece of drama right out of the middle of the situation.

Despite signs of continued interest at Scotland Yard, it was happily nearly a year before I heard the voice of London demanding a public statement of what I was up to. It interrupted a conversation I was having with my father-in-law about Sir Roger Casement.

Across a couple of pages of a recent biography of Sir Roger Casement fleets the figure of 'a certain Major Arbuthnot', offering as he does so a glimpse of what emerges as one of the few humane characters on stage during the savage last act of that terrifying melodrama.

He was my wife's father and it was in his house in Youghal, where Raleigh used to live and Spenser wrote part of *The Faerie Queene*, that we had previously stayed for some months while we looked for a house of our own. And as I came to know the Major well, I had come to feel that luck, which had played so many dirty tricks on Casement, had, at the very last moment, at least tried to proffer Casement a consolation prize by arranging for this civilized man to appear.

The biography tells how, when the friends and relatives of Casement are being driven from pillar to post, unable to force from the wooden-faced bureaucrats, some stupid, some sadistic, some ignorant, even where the prisoner is being kept, this 'certain Major' suddenly comes on to the scene, tells them where Casement is – namely in the Tower – and tells them, as a matter of urgency, that before they think of politics or the legal position or anything else, they must get him new clothes. Casement in the Tower was wearing the same clothes in which he had set out in the submarine from Germany, and the Major had that kind of simple human intuition which reminds you that there are times when a changes of clothes can be more important to a man than patriotic fervour or the prospect of death.

As a Major of the Scots Guards, doing a turn of duty at the Tower, Major Arbuthnot was in personal charge of Casement. He was the genuine kind of High Tory who believes that orders and regulations and forms in triplicate are probably all very well for keeping the machine running, and preventing other people from getting out of hand, but should be ignored by people like himself if they happen to interfere in any way with what seems to him good to do at the time.

There were strict orders from on high that no one, not even of his closest relatives, was to be allowed to interview Casement without the presence of the officer on duty. Political plotting was feared. But Major Arbuthnot was, so to speak, socially conditioned against paying much attention to those 'on high' – particularly if they happened to be, in his far from humble opinion, a lot of incompetent and probably corrupt politicians on the make. His chief interest in them was to wonder how on earth they had got there, and since his view of politics was that of an eighteenth-century landowner, the answer came to him in one word – jobbery.

Thus, when the relatives of Casement begged for a little time alone with him, the Major broke all regulations and granted the request.

Some of Casement's last hours after his condemnation and before his execution were occupied in conversation with this same Major who, partly because to do so was, for him, artistically irresistible, and partly to ease the loathsome relationship of prisoner and warder, spent the time making a portrait of the doomed Casement, and discussing it with him in a manner to suggest that after all there are more interesting things in life for civilized men to think about than the circumstance of one of them getting hanged for alleged treason.

It seemed to me when Major Arbuthnot told me about it – I had noticed the Casement portrait on the wall of the library at Myrtle Grove where we were sitting – one of the few alleviating episodes in an otherwise wholly horrible series of events. But despite the interest of the story, I have to admit that my attention was a little distracted by the fact that all the time on a table beside us was lying a telephone receiver through which a distant voice at intervals clacked, screeched and seemed to implore.

I suppressed my curiosity about the disregarded telephone receiver until the end of the Casement story, but at length asked the Major whether he noticed that the receiver was off the cradle and that someone seemed wishful to talk with him?

'Oh, that,' he said comfortably, 'that's the *Daily Express* office in London. They rang up an hour or so ago wanting me to tell them whether you had joined the Roman Catholic Church. They thought, too, I might supply them with some comments on my son-in-law, the formerly notorious Red. Awfully intrusive.'

Although he could affect, at a moment's notice, the attitude of the aloof aristocrat who hardly knows what a newspaper is, and in any case deplores the existence of 'the popular Press', Major Arbuthnot had, in point of fact, once worked on a part-time basis for the *Daily Express*. At that time, shortly before the death of a relative who later left him a quarter of a million, but was taking some time about it, he found himself rather pressed for money. He was a friend of Mr Blumenfeld, the Managing Editor of the *Express*, and, from discussion between them and (I suppose) many others, emerged the notion of the original *Beachcomber* column. The Major was, I think, the first *Beachcomber* – at any rate he edited and to a large extent wrote the column at an early period, when it had the character of a humorous column of satire and gossip.

Unlike most people today, he believed in the reality of unearned income as something to be relied upon, but felt uneasy about earnings. He thought that once you were in the position of earning money – except of course in the Army or Navy – 'they' would somehow contrive to do you out of your pay. He therefore made an arrangement with Mr Blumenfeld that his money was to be paid in cash as soon as each *Beachcomber* column was completed. He would finish the column, collect the money from the cashier, and get a taxi to Paddington where, on the days when he was working in Fleet Street, he had a special train awaiting him so that he could be sure to reach Windsor in time to go on guard duty at the Castle.

He had also, since 1912, been a regular contributor to the *Morning Post*, so that his pretended astonishment at the 'intrusiveness' of journalists was not very convincing.

He was, however, genuinely anxious to save me from annoyance. And as one who knew something of the newspaper business it pleased him to think of the face of the man at the other end of the telephone. When they had first rung him up he had expressed enthusiasm – asked them just to hang on while he went and fetched his 'notes', speaking of these non-existent notes in a manner which suggested that for months past, ever since my arrival, he had been assembling some very juicy comments on me. Then he had simply laid down the receiver, pottered about the garden, and finally returned to talk with me about Casement.

The Dublin correspondent of the *Express* had, as a matter of fact, already rung me up – also wishing to know whether I had been received into the Roman Catholic faith or was aiming to be so received. News editors have an occupational tendency to believe that anything that has recently happened is due to happen again, and since two prominent Communist journalists, one in New York and the other in London, had walked out of Communism into Roman Catholicism, they thought I must be going to do the same thing. Also, no doubt, they were victims of the widespread popular fallacy that there is some mysterious affinity between the Roman Catholic Church and the Communist Party. Just what this affinity is supposed to be I have never been able to ascertain, unless it be the existence, in both organizations, of a certain discipline – a fact apparently so alarming and sensational to some that it overshadows everything else.

I had been on the, so to speak, intrusive end of the telephone often enough to know that if you give a good newspaperman an inch he is capable of giving you half a column of hell, so I told the Dublin correspondent 'No comment, no story'. Nevertheless, he insisted that he should drive the 150 miles or so from Dublin to see me. I urged him, as one newspaperman to another, to consider whether he would be able to justify the expense account, and he said the London office was crazy about the story and he thought he had better come on down.

The Major finally put the receiver on its cradle and we went and sat in the pond garden, confident that if they rang again and the eloquent Irish butler answered it the resulting confusion would be enough to baffle even the skilled men of the *Daily Express*.

But in the town that afternoon I was suddenly cornered by the Dublin correspondent with two cars – the second of them a Dublin taxicab filled with a photographer and his apparatus. The correspondent proved to be a very nice man indeed and when, after some drinks off the record, he said it was a pity that I still kept saying 'No comment, no story', I began to feel badly about his expense sheet.

I cautiously amplified my remarks, and in exchange for my mild cooperation he agreed to let me off the photographer. Unfortunately this photographer was tremendously keen and energetic, and possibly had had a slight overdose of American newspaper films and seemed to think that he was being done out of his big moment. He pretended to agree to the 'no pictures' arrangements, but lurked. And when the correspondent went off to Dublin the photographer pursued me up hill and down dale.

I ducked him, and reached my house by a secret route, but a half-hour later heard imprecations and general uproar. Rushing to an upper window I saw that a girl who at that time worked with us had suddenly espied the keen young man squatting in semi-concealment just inside the back gate, his camera trained on the house. With a vague idea that he must be up to no good – invasion of landed privacy by vulgar Anglo-Saxon press, perhaps – she had snatched up a pitchfork which chanced to be resting against the stable wall, and charged.

I was alarmed, partly because I thought it might be disadvantageous for me if the *Express* got a picture of my landed privacy being defended with a pitchfork, and partly for the more altruistic reason that I knew, as the photographer did not, that she was a powerful athlete and if she got anywhere near him with that pitchfork he was done for.

I yelled so loud that he retreated just in time. He continued, however, to lurk in the roadway until moved on by a local Garda who knew nothing of newspapers and cared less, and supposed him to be loitering with intent.

I was happy to see later that the Dublin correspondent had got enough material to sweeten his expense account. It filled the William Hickey column, and made me sound fairly mysterious, without being embarrassing.

It made my house sound rather bigger than it really was, my whole establishment more imposing. And I much admired whoever wrote the column for being, I should say, the first man who ever made a bicycle sound a shade sinister. 'For transport to Youghal,' he wrote, 'Mr Cockburn rides a bicycle.' In the context, the reader might well wonder what sort of a blind this was. Perhaps behind those mysterious walls lurked an armoured Mercedes, not to be used 'for transport to Youghal' but for some less avowable purpose.

In a fable of R. L. Stevenson, the old man says to the young man, 'Why are you weeping?' 'I am weeping for my sins,' says the young man. Months later, they meet again, and the young man is still weeping, 'Why are you weeping now?' asks the old man. 'I am weeping because I have nothing to eat.' 'I thought it would come to that,' says the old man.

The first task, not easy, was to prevent it coming to that. We had reached the island and 'the natives', as explorers say, 'were friendly'. But from where we sat, it looked as though it would be a hard climb to reach the essential coconuts. During my long years as a 'red' political journalist, all other connexions with the journalistic and literary world had slowly but inevitably broken down. And it was not difficult to surmise that if I now appeared waving some kind of new leaf and asking to be paid to write on it, there would be considerable askance-looking by many. Every agent, publisher and Editor will truthfully tell you how important it is to build up a name. But the two names I had built up reeked of politics and subversion. It was necessary to act as though one were twenty-one years old, just down from

Oxford, and trying to break into, as the saying goes, the writing game.

(The only alternative was to write the familiar 50,000 words entitled 'My fifteen years in a Snakepit' which would certainly shake the coconut trees but would be otherwise undesirable. '*Nec propter vitam vivendi perdere causas*,' my father used to quote from Juvenal when the possibility from time to time arose of doing something lucrative but distasteful. It had been, as I recall, a somewhat alarming principle for his dependants – we thought that once in a while we would not mind seeing him taking a chance on losing the 'reasons for living' and just live.)

Salvation came in the shape of Mr Richard Bennett, at that time editor of the monthly magazine *Lilliput*. He liked my writing, and had no political inhibitions. At the same time, he and I believer – we may, of course, have been wrong – that some backward individual on the business side of *Lilliput*, might not like to have a person of my background writing for their paper. I became Kenneth Drew. The necessity for writing pseudonymously became still more apparent after I had made some financial calculations and reckoned that, at the rate *Lilliput* paid in those days, I would need to get at least two pieces into the magazine every month, and sometimes more. Without cast-iron pseudonyms that was going to raise a lot of eyebrows.

So I was not only Kenneth Drew but James Helvick and a man called Patrick Cork and, I seem to remember, Hector Hamish or somebody of similar name, and a couple of others as well. Coconuts thudded down, sparsely but just adequately. Later, Hulton Press launched a new weekly called *Leader*, which was understood to be going to revolutionize British weekly journalism, and Drew – I think it was he – wrote a long series of articles for it. It was a good paper, and I dare say it would have revolutionized British journalism if given the chance.

But one of the curses of contemporary British journalism is the increasing power and influence of a lot of people who know nothing about journalism, but have persuaded numerous proprietors and shareholders that they are in possession of

284

statistical gadgets and Geiger counters which, properly read, reel off the news of what the public wants. They conduct polls. They make surveys of 'representative groups'. They dip their thermometers into the water as assiduously as attendants at a thermal bath. Then they go to the proprietors or the advertising managers and report that three per cent of men earning more than £1,800 annually are allergic to science fiction, or crazy to read more about yachting or love. Naturally they get the right answer some of the time, though no more often than people using common sense and intuition instead of statistics and polls. But since everyone has an eerie awareness that he does not really know what the public wants, anyone who appears with a definitive and didactic statement on the subject is reassuring.

The result, all too often, is a kind of paralysis of the editorial will. An editor has no business to be worrying himself sick about what the public wants. He should be thinking about perfecting and producing what he wants and then making the public want it, too. The contrary principle can produce a situation like that existing at the kind of 'progressive' school where nobody tells the boys and girls what they ought to be at, and these pupils live in a confusing and, ultimately, mind-destroying vacuum – no orders, no order, no standards, no compulsive framework, no guidance, but instead a lot of pestering questions from teachers, designed to ascertain whether the pupils would like more cinematography in the ·curriculum, or would prefer that more time be given to Physics, Old English or Advanced Salesmanship.

Somebody proved that *Leader* was appealing to the wrong income groups, so that despite the energy and ability of its Editor, Sydney Jacobson, who fought hard to save the paper from needless extinction, and to give it at least a fighting chance, I learned in Ireland that there were not going to be any next six months – they were folding it up immediately.

In Fleet Street today this kind of thing is going on all the time – not necessarily in the extreme form of closing an entire paper on the strength of the statistical men's thermometer readings – but in terms of intrusion by these figure-stuffed bath attendants upon editorial responsibility. They tend to unnerve the editor as he tries to get on with the real job of giving the public the courage of his convictions.

A guest at my house wrote, at this time, in the visitors' book, a description of what he called the Literary Colony at Youghal. He claimed to have met Frank Pitcairn, ex-correspondent of the *Daily Worker* – a grouchy, disillusioned type secretly itching to dash out and describe a barricade. There was Claud Cockburn, founder and editor of *The Week*, talkative, boastful of past achievements, and apt, at the drop of a hat, to tell, at length, the inside story of some forgotten diplomatic crisis of the 1930s. Patrick Cork would look in – a brash little number, and something of a professional Irishman, seeking, no doubt to live up to his name. James Helvick lived in and on the establishment, claiming that he needed quiet together with plenty of good food and drink to enable him to finish a play and a novel which soon would bring enough money to repay all costs. In the background, despised by the others as a mere commercial hack, Kenneth Drew hammered away at the articles which supplied the necessities of the colony's life.

Helvick wrote a play which kept being accepted by Managements and then shelved for reasons good, bad and all inscrutable.

I thought that while awaiting further developments on the theatrical front, and keeping Kenneth Drew's nose to the grindstone, I might get somewhere by taking one theme from the play and turning it into a novel, *Beat The Devil*, by, of course, James Helvick. By the time the novel was written and published in Britain and the United States, it could certainly be said that things were definitely not going so well.

Our house in Ireland began to look more and more as though it had been invented by Somerville and Ross. Since we had not yet finished paying for the earlier structural repairs we could scarcely get the contractor to embark on a new series. Odd job men did their best, but the task was too great to be handled on a 'do-it-yourself' basis, and rain poured through the roof and ceilings.

The sexton-process-server, supposed link between Cominform and Freemasonry, was out to see me repeatedly. And the men wandering about the grounds were not guests or employees, but sheriff's officers, mentally pricing the horses and threatening to drive them off and sell them.

By great good luck, we decided that since there appeared to be nothing we could immediately do about this situation, the sensible thing to do was to let the process-server and the Sheriff's men carry on as best they could, and accept an invitation to stay, for the Dublin Horse Show week, with Lady Oranmore at her house in the Wicklow mountains. It was a big house party, and my pleasure was particularly great when I heard that my old friend Mr John Huston, film director, was coming.

He arrived in Dublin very late one night, and joined our party at a Hunt Ball there. At about four o'clock or five o'clock in the morning, around the time people start stripping to the waist and jumping off the balconies blowing hunting horns, I started to talk to Mr Huston about my novel. At such a time, I was well aware, Mr Huston would prefer to talk, for instance, about horses in their many aspects: things to hunt foxes on, things to put your money on.

However, he is a volatile man and I was afraid he might suddenly get a telephone call from Beverly Hills and fly off to Hollywood before anyone was awake after the ball.

Something of the kind nearly did happen a day or two later, because after he had promised to read it I found I had forgotten to bring a copy with me. At the last moment I found, and rudely snatched back, a copy which I had recently inscribed, in terms of the sincerest admiration and affection, to our hostess. She said it seemed rather sad to have been in possession of a tribute like that for such an unexpectedly short time, but surrendered the book for the good of the cause. Then I seemed to remember that Mr Huston – when travelling without benefit of secretary – might very likely lose just one copy. Just as he was leaving for the airport, I found that there was another copy in the house – warmly inscribed to Mr Terence Kilmartin. He, too, acted for the good of the cause, and I threw the two copies into Mr Huston's car as it started up the driveway.

Mr Huston is a good friend and proved it when he started to read the book the moment he got to London. Two days later I had a guarded message from his secretary to say that he was so absorbed in it that he had had a fall as a result of reading it while walking downstairs.

A week later he was back in Dublin. Mr Huston is one of those blessed men who, if they like your work, say so clearly and repeatedly. Such men know that, like Wilde, an author can stand any amount of flattery provided it is gross enough. Nor was his praise inhibited by any niggling fear that he was putting the price up. His own affairs were, as I understood it, in a considerable financial tangle at the time – it was, I think, just before the enormous gamble he had taken on *African Queen* paid off. He and Humphrey Bogart had a company called Santana which could buy the film rights of the book and arrange major financing for it afterwards. He said there was an ideal part for Bogart in *Beat The Devil*.

Thinking of my experiences with the theatrical managers, I imagined that about now there would be a long pause during which, for weeks on end, nothing would happen of a character satisfactory to creditors and Sheriffs. Our enthusiastic conversation took place at breakfast in Dublin. While I was talking to his wife, he was scribbling something. It was, I found a little later, a long cable to Mr Bogart in Hollywood, speaking in glowing terms of the book, advising him to buy the American edition instantly, and assuring him that in Huston's opinion they should buy the rights immediately too.

Partly for the purpose of talking about the possibilities of the screen play, partly because he wanted to ride in new country, we arranged that the Hustons should come down to Youghal at once and stay with us for a couple of weeks. From Mr Huston's hotel room, I rang up our home. The number was unobtainable. I became flustered. Mr Huston sat on the bed, watching me with sardonic sympathy.

'It's happened to all of us before,' he said softly.

He was the kind of man who knew from experience how easy it can be to run into a situation where the authorities cut off your telephone on account of the payments being long overdue.

At Youghal we had to keep our hats on part of the time as we talked about the screenplay, because of the leaks in the roof. Meantime, the local post office was handling some of the longest telegrams seen in those parts since the Easter Rising – cables between there and Beverly Hills. Finally a firm offer came – for a larger sum of money than I had seen for a very long time indeed, if ever.

'Look,' Huston said, 'this is a firm offer, but in Hollywood terms it isn't so damn big. Not so damn big at all. If you hang on, and especially if the book goes well in America, you can get three or four times that figure.'

I said, thinking of many phases of his career and of my own, 'Listen, we've both of us known times when ten dollars, cash on the barrelhead, now, is worth a whale of a lot more than a hundred the week after next.'

'If it's like that,' said Mr Huston – and considering the drip, drip from the roof it was not very difficult to note that it was just like that – 'what are we waiting for?'

If the hunters and ponies had known what was happening they would have danced in their stalls.

Mr Huston's purchase provided a breathing-space, a space for contemplation of the world at hand, and for experimental writing and, so to speak, writing drill, or practice, having the same purpose as that of a person learning the piano and playing scales on it. For me, after that long spell of polemical propaganda and high-pitched reporting, this type of practice was particularly necessary for the purpose of loosening the joints, strengthening muscles grown flabby from disuse, and improving the ear.

Apart from the lulling climate of the lovely Blackwater valley, there are other factors which sometimes seem to make writing in the country more arduous, more of a strain on the brain and emotions than in the city. What it amounts to is that part of the time the writer in the country is subjected to a series of interruptions – like alarms of foot-and-mouth disease, fences falling down, or a catastrophic drop in the market price of turkeys – which in the city do not impinge. From these, it is true, I was to a very large extent protected by Patricia who, in addition to being an expert with horses and turning a wilderness of scutch grass into a garden a whole family could live on, took other farm problems, of which she had no previous knowledge, in her stride.

But when you have shaken off those problems of life in the country, or rather have handed them to someone else, you are sitting there thinking, and your skin creeps slightly with the sensation that there is absolutely nothing between you and eternity – not some eternity in the future, but all round and behind you. You have the feeling you had as a child when nobody would tell you what there was beyond the place where outer space ended. A simple sensation, but eerie, too.

In our part of Ireland the sensation was heightened for me by the awareness one continuously had there of what may be called the presence of the past. There are, of course, innumerable places where what are called 'antiquities' are as numerous as here. But even in, say, Rome the past seems to me to be keeping its distance, and allowing itself to be judged and studied with a certain detachment. Here in the country it is not so. In the stony circle of the Druid wood at Blarney – a place which perhaps was sacred even before the Druids adopted it – you are tumbled, almost as though you had been physically pushed, head over heels into pre-history. The trees there, forming the grove in which is situated the ring of sacred stones, have been demonstrated by arboreal experts to be older than any other trees in the world, with the exception of the Californian redwoods. The grove, and the stones – the fact that this was a sacred place thousands of years ago – are, one can hardly doubt, the true explanation of the legend of the Blarney stone. Every century has had a different account of the origin of the belief in the stone's magical powers – explanations which are mystical, religious or matter-of-factly political according to the prevailing climate of thought. But there would have been no legend about the stone's powers if it were not associated with a holy place, though nobody knows what first made it holy nor how distant, primitive and furry were the first worshippers.

Across one of our fields runs the outline of a rath – a line of underground dwellings built, probably, as a fortification and defence against early Scandinavian invaders. They, too, had to abandon airier ways of living and take to the underground shelters, and they seem very close.

This lurking and sometimes intrusive presence of the past might perhaps be supposed to weaken or dull the impact of the present. The contrary is the case. This crowding in of history serves instead to intensify a consciousness of the pressures and contradictions of life and society in the present.

Perhaps that is why people are so repeatedly moved to discuss over and over again the 'Irish character', or the 'pattern of Irish life', as if there were a uniform character or pattern. It is hard to say whether such speculations are more tedious when undertaken by Irishmen or by eager foreigners. But they do have the value of being an acknowledgement of the fact of a peculiar obtrusiveness in Ireland of basic problems of life and thought which elsewhere can be muffled, or forgotten, in a brisk jog-trot down well-rutted roads.

The only pattern of Irish life that I can discern is the pattern made by a series of diversities and the sharpest contradictions. There is no statement that can be made without it soon becoming apparent that its opposite is true too. Not that one statement is a lie and the other true – both are true. It could be said that this is the case everywhere, and to pretend otherwise is absurdly to exaggerate the peculiar quality and position in the world of that island – not its peculiar place in past history, its peculiar place now.

Certainly such contradictions are part of the dialectic of life everywhere. The point is not that they exist uniquely in Ireland, but that – perhaps because of the physical smallness of the area and population – they are muffled by nothing. In other words, you are forced daily on to your mental toes. You are forced to take note that nothing about human life, thought or activity can be taken safely for granted.

In such a situation, all sensibilities are heightened. For example, when I remarked to someone that – viewing the development of Communism and the Communist Parties, and in particular the agonizing development of events in Hungary – from Ireland, I reacted to them more violently than I probably would have from any other watch-tower, he immediately assumed that I was alluding to some obscure influence upon me of the circumambient Roman Catholic air.

I meant nothing of the kind – and, indeed, that particular atmosphere might possibly have had an opposite effect. I meant simply that the 'other-ness' and the vivid contradictions of life

291

seen in the Irish microcosm must increase one's awareness, and prod one almost brutally from any kind of mental slumber in which one might ignore the shifting realities of the world.

You can doze off in that way in England – sometimes in a kind of resignation to a situation which at so many vital points appears to be out of control by any influence you might help to exert. In the United States and the U.S.S.R., the habit of the mental doze is more dangerously widespread, though the fact that millions of people are taking a siesta from original social or political thinking is greatly obscured by brilliant technical achievements. But, as Professor Blackett, President of the British Association for the Advancement of Science, said recently at its meeting in Dublin, technology and science cannot take over the functions of politics in the widest sense of the word. There comes a point where social and political thinking, social and political action, have to deal with the human situation, however advanced or backward its technological position may be.

Ireland, good and bad and dubious, can be a cure for the siesta-habit, a stimulant stronger than any tranquillizer a person might be tempted to take. One looks at the world and thinks again of Cacambo's remark to Candide, urging him to take a chance on getting into the canoe and going somewhere. 'For if we find nothing pleasant, at least we shall find something new.' A man said to me in some agitation, 'But suppose the world exerts itself to find something new, and then it is horribly, abominably unpleasant?'

I said that in my view nothing could possibly be more unpleasant than what the world would get if it failed to find something new.

25

GLASS HOUSE

WHEN the first two friends came to visit me – dying, it was reported – in the hospital in Ireland, they themselves escaped death narrowly, the main highway in our town caving in just behind them. A hole opened in it, and a big girl dropped twenty feet on to the rubble of the ocean shore. A dog dropped through with her. Retaining its senses while she lay stunned, it made its way to the hole at sea level through which the sea had been for years sucking away ton after ton of the road's foundation. It was the dog's emergence on the beach which alerted everyone to the nature of the damage. An investigation disclosed that by now there was nothing left of the highway along that stretch except just its fine-looking macadam surface with the buses and lorries rolling along it. All beneath had been eroded, and – from below – the basic four foot or so of the telegraph poles could be seen sticking through, founded in nothing.

By this incident, when these two friends told me about it in the hospital, I was disgusted. For this purely adventitious episode which might just as well have occurred in Columbus, Ohio – whereupon it would have had a different significance – by occurring precisely in Ireland had given them a mistaken view of a particular situation – one which, it is true, does not fit exactly into the accepted slots of the Western world, but which would be of value to both Western and Eastern worlds if it could be understood.

It happened that just at that time, under the influence of the streptomycin and other drugs taken by victims of tuberculosis, I was particularly bothered by the effort to sort the hallucinations from the realities. In a more normal existence the distinction between the two is not so important – you have no time to worry about whether that light is a false one or true, you believe that the essential is simply to make up your mind what you want to do with and in the world, and keep steaming. For purposes of navigation – particularly in politics or philosophy – a false light can be useful as a true one in apprising you of where you are.

In a hospital bed, however, having all around one those intimations of mortality which a man in his health keeps in the pending tray or frankly sweeps under the sofa, a person can become actually perturbed by such considerations. Hallucinated myself by the effects of streptomycin – we soon all got very matey with this potent drug and called it strep – I had become painfully troubled about the existence and nature of all kinds of illusions, political, social and even religious.

And now, by way of a tiny teaser, came this crack-up of the Cork highway, which was going to cause – had already caused – my two dear friends to form erroneous views regarding the Western country they were in. Just to add to the misleading course of events, they had hardly reached my home the previous night when the electric power failed throughout the district, goats broke in somewhere, and rats had eaten the candle reserve. They were by no means amazed. And this was what to me in the hospital – a magnificent installation where even the crucifixes in our cubicles were provided by the Irish Sweep – seemed particularly sinister.

They were going to say 'Isn't that just typically Irish?'

I was not much worried about whether they went away from there with some foolish notions about Ireland or not. God knows there are enough of such, but I conceive the Irish are well enough able to take care of them without the resident stranger dashing officiously to the rescue. Not but what there are times when the impulse so to dash becomes nearly overpowering. What, just for instance, is a person to do when some brisk boy from the Labour back benches comes over and remarks that Ireland is beautiful and quaint, but stagnant? So you push into his hands the latest report of the International Housing Commission of the United Nations. It puts on record the fact that this winsome, wambling landful of priests and leprechauns has the highest achievement in rural and urban housebuilding of any country of the Western world – not excluding New York State, or those exemplary people in Bonn who, after designing Buchenwald and Auschwitz, still retain the necessary *élan* to lay out, in the Ruhr and scenic Rhineland, so many workers' settlements, youth hostels and other amenities.

I, not being much interested in Irishism *an sich*, but interested in Ireland as a unique phenomenon in the Western world, was inevitably horrified by the notion of this uniqueness being squeezed into yet another scruffy pigeon-hole. For it is this type of squeeze which causes civilization to stagnate. A capacity to accept, appreciate and utilize what is strange, horrifyingly novel, or even apparently miraculous and in contradiction to the laws of nature, is an indispensable quality of civilization.

Also, with the streptomycin vigorously at work, and one of

my visitors adumbrating a plan for getting into the shrine-and-hotel business in a big way by establishing a grotto on the beach in celebration of the wondrous escape of the fat girl who fell through the road and saved the lives of countless lorry drivers and commercial travellers, buzzing carefree along the ever-so-thin macadam, a still more disturbing thought came to jolt me. These people, I thought, have been led to suppose that the caving in of a highway is significant of a general situation appertaining to this section of the world. They are wrong. Well, then, suppose everything that happens, every phenomenon and notion which one supposes to be significant of something, is really without any significance beyond itself, or is significant of something quite other than one imagines?

Catching myself at this point, I realized that I really must be very ill – degenerating, perhaps, into some kind of second adolescence.

It was always a pleasure to listen to this man who visited me. He is one of those not very common people who can amuse and interest children. This is a sign of goodness. Many good men cannot do it very well. But no bad men can do it at all.

Forgetting philosophical speculations, I was irked only by a fear lest his voice, suggesting that an instrument for grinding up iron filings had been introduced into the orchestra, might penetrate the glass walls of my cubicle and his fantasies give offence to bed-ridden Catholics. However, I reflected that my immediate neighbour could, and with any encouragement would, come up with some contrary flight of the imagination more or less subtly distressing and subversive to the views of Jews, Protestants and infidels, and would have his opportunities for many weeks and months to come.

For what purpose this ward we were in had originally been built, nobody seemed certain; probably as an observation ward for children. The building was single-storeyed, the windows opening on to a field pleasant to the eye but a vexatious affair for the farmer who had leased it from the hospital. Rock cropped out extensively in the middle of it, and indirectly exercised a therapeutic effect upon farmers and agricultural labourers among the patients. Sick, they yet had the compensatory pleasure of lying in bed and watching the struggles and frustrations of the healthy, toil-worn farmer and his lads when the tractor hit those rocks. Occasionally, the farmer worked late into the night, and while some of the sick cursed the whirr and rattle of the unseen machinery outside, one of my fellow inmates, who had done back-breaking work in the fields all his life, told me that it was a real pleasure to him every time he heard the machine grinding and smashing on to the outcrop, and its owner cursing out there in the dark.

The interior of the ward was divided into cubicles with walls of glass. From your bed you could see clear through to all the other cubicles from one end of the wing to the other. But these glass walls were semi-soundproof; unless people raised their voices loudly in dispute or song, you heard at most a susurration. So that the visible world of the ward was a continuous pantomime, a film of the period before the invention of the sound-track.

This glazed pantomime was no doubt rendered the more lively by the incidence of the various drugs employed. One of these has effects which, according to a notice from the manufacturers which once came accidentally into my hands – a notice evidently designed for the attention of doctors rather than the ultimate consumer – range from manic euphoria to epileptic collapse. In general, whether by their individual properties or in combination, the drugs, so far as I could make observation of myself and others, tend to produce irregularly alternating states of abnormal quiescence and abnormally heightened awareness. Also it seemed that the drugs – or, possibly, simply the inevitably peculiar circumstances of hospital life – had the effect of temporarily developing everyone's qualities or characteristics to slightly larger than normal lifesize. A man who was in the ward for a couple of months who in life outside, I was told, was in no way remarkable, let alone sexually off-beat, showed feminine tendencies so strong that one would not have been surprised to see him have a change of sex on the spot. He would trip delicately about the corridors, pirouetting and wagging his hips in invitation, and his eyes, accustomed in the outer world to ogle the girls of the village, would droop and swivel under flickering eyelashes like the eyes of a Turkish courtesan in a primitive Hollywood movie.

There is a line beyond which the heightened awareness of reality becomes a mental derangement. The possibility of such derangements made a good many people nervous. For the organizers of the sanatorium, in general finely equipped, had made no provision for the housing of anyone becoming mentally deranged. There was thus, in the minds of several inmates, a fear of being sent off to what was called 'the mental'.

The prospect was justifiably daunting. I am not sure how things are now, but a couple of years ago the mental hospitals in this part of Ireland were cruelly overcrowded. To find oneself tubercular, mentally deranged, and sleeping on a floor-mattress in a ward jam-packed with similar sufferers would be to reach a very low degree of the human condition. (Not so low, certainly, as would be experienced in a German concentration camp. Among the historically criminal effects of those camps is the fact that they set a standard of horror such that it enabled brutes everywhere, and the brutal instincts in everyone, to claim, openly or subconsciously, that some horror being perpetrated today is thereby mitigated, lessened by comparison. A friend of mine who passed a part of World War I in prison told me that when the prisoners complained of nearly intolerable conditions they were regularly told by the warders – and the warders were terrifyingly sincere about it – that anyway they were 'better off than the poor lads in the trenches'. They probably were, at that. But what ghastly view of life's necessities and possibilities is that intended to prove? And what does the existence of such a state of affairs prove in fact?)

Naturally there were nurses who, exasperated by the notorious cussedness of tuberculosis victims, did not resist the convenience of hinting that another rude word or act of indiscipline could easily be interpreted as a sign of mental aberration, a slippery step towards 'the mental'. The cool figures in white, as anyone who has ever been in a hospital anywhere knows, are not as a rule much cooler than the generality of people – particularly when a man, by his inordinate demands for care, by his sudden fear that he will have a screaming nightmare unless he can get a sleeping pill, or simply the fear that he has taken a sharp turn for the worse and is dying unless he can get extra attention, may involve the nurse in missing her bus to the city and with it her last chance of seeing the movie everyone is talking about.

A man who had made a nuisance of himself in this way seemed to be unalterably headed for 'the mental' when he rang his bell for the nurse – delaying her on her dash for the city bus – and told her that what was bothering him now was that a horse kept coming up to his window and peering in at him. He wanted something done about the horse. No such bizarre complaint had ever been made before and the man's prospects appeared dark indeed until, by a fortunate chance, as I lay in bed that very night, I too saw silhouetted against a not quite black sky the head and shoulders of a horse. I rang for the night nurse and rushed to the window. By the time the nurse could get to my cubicle the horse itself had malignly disappeared. But I begged the nurse – a woman of goodwill – to stand absolutely silent, listening. Sure enough, though one could have sworn the beast was trying to walk tiptoe so as to maintain its reputation as a figment of diseased imagination, we heard it soft-hoofing away across the field. The outcrop of rock betrayed it, and the nurse was able to testify that the creature was real.

The disclosure did the man who had first seen the horse no permanent good. A little later he saw an entire fête and gala going on in the field outside. There were clergymen and dowagers and numerous lovely girls dancing with young officers amid stalls heaped high with glorious flowers and set on a wonderfully manicured greensward. Whether at some distant period he had actually witnessed or participated in such a scene, or whether he had read stories about such things (supposed to have been going on in the days before World War I), and thus was having an illusion about an illusion, was never revealed. I suggested, not hopefully, that perhaps what he had seen was an archdeacon of the Church of Ireland who used to visit the Protestant patients. I said it was perfectly natural that the sight of an archdeacon should set off a train of thought leading to visions of a brilliant church fête and gala.

The archdeacon was in every respect all that an archdeacon should be, very suggestive of gentle and genteel amenities. He told me once that his great sorrow was that, although always intending to be a writer, the weeks and years had somehow kept gliding by without his actually becoming one. When he saw an advertisement of one of my own books in *The Times Literary Supplement* he asked 'How long did it take you to write that book?' I told him, 'About three months.' 'Ah, there you are,' he said. '*I* never get that much free time.' I was impelled to remark huffily that if I had had a little more free time in my life I would not have been just an archdeacon, I would have been a bishop.

Despite the aura of the archdeacon, it was not thought that his existence explained that church fête, or put it on as rational a basis as the horse. The authorities felt that they could no longer be responsible for a man who saw things like that. Fortunately, although removed from the sanatorium, he had some private resources which saved him from 'the mental'. He had been an irascible, occasionally arrogant, and not popular figure during his stay in the ward. But on his departure everyone spoke of him as 'good old X' and told stories redounding to his credit. There was a school of thought which insisted he had been as sane as anyone else, but driven mad by the nurses.

The nurses received all such accusations with a calm only occasionally broken by outbursts of honest fury in which the drop of hatred which almost all nurses must, of course, feel towards almost all patients came finely to the boil. The English training manuals counsel nurses to preserve at all times an impersonal attitude towards TB patients. Probably this is sage advice. But it can evidently be exploited to justify an attitude of frozen indifference to the patient. Since the notion of a lot of Irish women maintaining an impersonal attitude to anything or anyone is laughable, the effects of such training were much mitigated – sometimes by laughter and endearments, sometimes by howls of abuse, curses hardly less agreeably warming to the bored victim of the disease.

The consolations of psycho-analysis – as administered by some young woman half-remembering a few words of a lecture on the subject delivered years before in London or Birmingham – were a good deal more annoying. A nurse complained to me of the conduct of a man in the ward – a cattle-drover by profession. He was always asking, she said, for sedatives. 'The trouble with that man,' she said, 'is that he's got an anxiety complex. What we call *Angst*, d'you follow me now?'

The cattle-drover had acute TB, a sick wife, two dependent children and a son whom he had been trying to teach the business but had now had to leave to sink or swim by himself; his prospects on leaving the sanatorium were perfectly clear to his mind: he was either going to rot on the dole, or else return to cattle driving through all the weather, suffer a relapse and perish.

'What d'you mean "*Angst*"?' I impatiently asked that nurse. 'That man doesn't have *Angst*, he just has some goddamned awful worries.' I told her the story of the man on the railway station in Tulsa City, Oklahoma, to whom some breezy type remarked, censoriously, that he looked depressed. 'Stranger,' said the sad-looking man, 'my wife is in yonder waiting-room, being seduced by a comparative stranger. My son has been arrested on a drug-peddling rap in San Francisco. My daughter is a whore in Kansas City and writes to say life's fine. Stranger, would *you* be depressed?'

Indeed there were times when, surveying my own state of physical collapse, my enforced isolation, too, from the ordinary activities of life on this earth round which the sputniks were beginning to twirl in so stimulating a fashion, I felt somewhat depressed myself.

26

UNFINISHED BUSINESS

DARKENING further this mood of gloom came an X-ray which seemed to say that I had, in addition to TB raging in both lungs, what medical men, in their anxiety not to startle, call a 'little tumour', and other people call cancer. It is, I conceive, always disconcerting when the X-ray says 'cancer'. Cancer can sometimes be cut out. But in this case there was an obtrusively obvious complication. Since I had TB so badly, any chest operation was out of the question. I understood that a whiff or so of the anaesthetic alone would put an end to that enterprise. It followed that one would have to let the cancer alone to get on with what it was doing. And as and when the TB had been reduced to the point where an operation for cancer was practicable, the operation itself would have lost its objective; the cancer would be flourishing and the patient dead.

Later, some people told me with indignation that the doctor 'had no right to tell you that thing about cancer'. This appears to me in any context an astounding viewpoint. It is as though one should say that the lawyer must not reveal to his client how bad his case really is for fear, it is presumed, that the client will have a heart attack in the dock. Or your platoon commander is desired to fool you into thinking the chances of holding this ill-sited, out-gunned position are fine, simply fine, kid. Naturally a grown person with a little experience makes his own assessment of what the doctors and the lawyers, the Captains and the Kings, tell him about what they estimate to be the situation.

Sometimes in the sanatorium my wife, in her deep anxiety and fear lest I act impetuously, used to ask me, 'But don't you trust the doctors?' It was only a passing fear, and disappeared when I explained to her that I trust doctors in the same way I have from time to time trusted Generals and Circulation Managers and pollsters and famous solicitors and other experts on a given line of activity. It is their business to give you their assessment of what, by virtue of the long hours they have presumably put in studying the subject, they suppose the situation to be. It is your business to make up your mind whether they are right or wrong, or how much right and how much wrong there is in that expert assessment. And it is still your business, and not theirs, to decide what course of action to take once the assessment is in.

The doctor at the sanatorium who – with careful qualifications – told me what he told me, was a man having, on top of his great expert knowledge, a swift intelligence, an acute sensitivity to other people's problems, and a toughly-rooted understanding of what life may reasonably be considered to be about. He saved my life three times – twice by simply telling me the truth about my condition, and once by making the generous and perhaps even risky effort to deal, a long way beyond what the Americans call 'the line of duty', with a situation which could not have been otherwise than alien to him. He further paid me the compliment of believing that I was telling the truth when I explained to him that I needed to know, at all relevant times, what the situation of my health really was. I had responsibilities and priorities which could not be figured out on a quicksand of misinformation.

When he told me what the X-ray showed, I asked him about how long he thought I had – given the 'inoperable' circumstances. No doctor – and here, I believe they are right – will take upon himself to answer that question. One need only think of the number of people who were supposed to have so-and-so many weeks to live and, for good or ill, are among us yet. Some of them we wish had died at the time the doctors appointed for them, and thus done less harm in their day. Others we are happy to see confuting the doctors and, despite hell and high water, good for years to come.

Seeking to pin him down to a practical estimate I said that I had a commission for a novel and was at the same time trying to get a short story off the ground for the *Saturday Evening Post*. 'Given,' I said, 'that in the event of my death my family will need every penny that can be made available, which of these tasks would you recommend me to undertake?' He was amused by this attempt to trap him into a definite time estimate, and after he had talked gently around the subject for a while I started work on the short story.

Philip Jordan told me that he once asked Compton Mackenzie, at the time of the latter's sixty-fifth birthday, whether there was any one particular thing which he felt he had learned with increasing age. Mackenzie, according to Jordan, replied that what he had learned was that 'most of the copy-book maxims are true'. Everyone has heard quoted *ad nauseam* Dr Johnson's 'copy-book' comment on the unfortunate Dr Dodd, executed for forging a bond in the name of Lord Chesterfield, whose last sermon, *The Convict's Address to his Unhappy Brethren*, Johnson had 'ghost-written' for him. When someone doubted whether the Reverend Dodd could have been capable of writing such a sermon himself, Johnson, to preserve Dodd's posthumous credit, offered the explanation that, 'When a man knows he is to be hanged in a fortnight, it concentrates his mind wonderfully.' It came to me at this time, that this was one of those copy-book maxims or quotations which might be actually true; or, if not, so to speak, automatically true, might yet be made to be so.

I had often noted that on the few occasions when I and millions of others had been in immediate danger of death in battle or bombing, a most vexatious feature of the position was precisely that no time was offered one in which to concentrate the mind. I recalled how, when briefly fighting in the ranks of the Spanish Republican Army on the Sierra north-west of Madrid, the first bombers had flown low over our exposed ridge-top position and I had caught myself muttering over and over again just before they let go with the bombs, 'Now just a minute, just a minute.'

Now there was at least time for the act of concentration. Johnson's remark might have been intended to suggest to the snooper who suspected him of 'ghosting' that sermon that the knowledge of impending death could somehow automatically have pulled together the evidently ramshackle faculties of the unhappy Dodd – a man, I noted with sympathy, who had 'unhappily contracted expensive habits of living, partly occasioned by licentiousness of manners'. But in, as the easy phrase goes, reality, Dodd would have had to make a positive effort of concentration.

The person [Boswell records] whose name Dodd thus rashly and criminally presumed to falsify, was the Earl of Chesterfield, to whom he had been tutor, and who, he perhaps, in the warmth of his feelings, flattered himself would have generously paid the money in case of an alarm being taken, rather than suffer him to fall a victim to the dreadful consequences of violating the law against forgery, the most dangerous crime in a commercial country; but the unfortunate divine had the mortification to find that he was mistaken. His noble pupil appeared against him, and he was capitally convicted.

In all dealings it is indeed desirable that a person should avoid 'the mortification of finding that he was mistaken'.

Dodd had some sensible views on life. When some of his 'pious friends were trying to console him by saying that he was going to leave a "wretched world"', Boswell reports, 'he had honesty enough not to join in the cant. "No, no," he said, "it has been a very agreeable world to me."' To which Johnson added, 'I respect Dodd for thus speaking the truth; for to be sure he had for several years enjoyed a life of great voluptuousness.'

I certainly could not pretend to myself that I was leaving – if I was due to leave it – a 'wretched world'. In what possible sense could a world in which there co-existed the Einstein equation, the Dogma of the Assumption and the Sputniks be considered 'wretched'? A part – only a part, but a considerable one – of the sadness with which I prepared to bow out, was the realization that one was being forced to quit a world, a century, compared to which all others could seem dull. A few more years of the twentieth century – and I dare say people in Europe felt the same in the seventeenth – and what tremendous, even horrifying, but still uplifting mental jolts one may experience. Now, now I kept thinking to myself, is the time. What a time to have to drop off and die in. Just a minute now, I could catch myself saying to the tractor whirring out there in the field, just a minute while I ring someone and fix this. But there is no one to ring, and none other than myself who can fix it.

To everyone who supposes himself at, as the saying goes, death's door, this maddening knowledge of 'unfinished business' must, I imagine, be a major factor in consciousness. With the relatively comforting awareness that this was what everyone who thinks he is dying must be doing, I thought that the best thing to do would be to sort out the 'unfinished business' into its separate compartments, and then see what could best be done about the material thus sorted.

Through the kindness of the chief doctor, I was permitted to establish a small dictating machine on the little closet beside my bed. For I was not at the time strong enough to use a typewriter, and it was apparent to everyone who could count that to write by hand would take too long. (In any case to push, literally, a pen is to me so laborious that the work of manipulating the primitive instrument is itself partially inhibitive of all other thought.) I made up my mind that in the circumstances the only thing that could make the little while worth anything was a large output of short stories for the American magazines.

The other aspect of 'unfinished business' was more complex. No doubt everyone similarly placed finds it so. Essentially, the problem seemed to be to rid one's mind of all those concepts and evaluations which in any way derive from the notion of life lived, so to speak, horizontally – those dependent, that is, on the length of time available for living. It is desirable to develop instead a sense of life in depth – depth with the meaning attached to it by the American philosopher Tillich. In such a context, the wearisomely commonplace notion of the 'crowded hour of glorious life' – which in practice customarily means painting the town red before the fatal battle – has to be extended. Whisky and the loved one do, it is a fact, act beneficially in such circumstances. But in a hospital bed these assistances are not available. And even were they available would they, in the altered circumstances, contribute effectively to the intensification of life in depth?

A further consideration then arose. To contemplate life exclusively in depth would be, surely, to deny the value of that 'horizontal' life which one had hitherto led. Yet it would be wrong thus to indicate that the minutes added to the minutes and the years to the years – years, indeed, in which one had grown to love and know people and have a family – were without value. So that one had to be careful of falling into the heresy of such a denial. And these considerations resulted in a position rather tricky to evaluate.

However, the fact ineluctably remained that if one had only a brief, immediately measurable time to live one felt one ought to take some particular advantage of the hours remaining. One could and, of course, did reflect that logically speaking everyone has only a brief, immediately measurable time to live, and that there ought to be no difference between, say, a month and seventy years. To the liver or dier there is all the difference in the world. It is only in the West that people suppose they may have seventy years or more to live through. Until recently the expectation of life in India was, I think, twenty-four years. To what extent then, I used to ask myself at that time, is our entire view of life and its activities determined by what is told us by the Men from the Pru? Are we, and our ideologies, really the sport of the insurance companies?

There is a good deal of support for this idea in the news which comes out of the United States and Britain in this age. There were several years during which an American doctor simply dared not physic a man half dead on his doorstep for fear that he, the good physician, was somehow not properly insured against some complaint of ill-treatment that the patient might afterwards make about him. And whenever there is a public transport strike in Britain, the native good Samaritans – pulsing with human eagerness to help their fellow-man – will not pick up anyone in their motor-cars until the relevant Ministry of Government has issued a blanket guarantee that they are covered, insurance-wise, for any mishap that may occur to the footsore pedestrian, while taking advantage of this most Christian offer of assistance.

The true heroism of the original good Samaritan on the Jericho road was that he risked major trouble with the police and the health authorities. Supposing the wounded man had been there as some kind of a plant? Did the Samaritan, before putting him into an hotel – foisting him on the hotelier, who himself seems to have been lax – inquire about the exact circumstances of the alleged attack? Did anyone find out whether the fellow could actually *prove* that he had been 'going down from Jerusalem to Jericho'? What diseases did he, or might he, have had, anterior to the attack complained of? He may have been a foreigner. Someone should at least have asked to see his passport. At the best it is certain that had anything, as the saying goes, 'happened', the Samaritan's insurance company would not have paid up. The consensus in the bars of Jericho was probably that the Samaritan was damn lucky to get away with it, and may have been queer at that.

It seemed important to get away from what one may call the actuarial way of life – that sort of living in which today can only be justified by the assumption of a tomorrow; in which a person considers that what he does between 10 a.m. and 5 p.m. will have been valueless if the 5.30 from Waterloo piles up and leaves him mangled on the wrong side of the North Downs. It is true enough that, as things stand statistically just now, not a great many more people have been killed in trains, aeroplanes and motor-cars than were killed in a few days by old-fashioned, strictly experimental A-bombs at Hiroshima and Nagasaki. And to hear people talk you could suppose that the fear of death by H-bomb is more important as a factor in the life of Western man than fear of death by any other means – except, perhaps, cancer. The fear is justified. The horror of the H-bomb is justified. The only unjustifiable and depressing part of this situation is the discovery that a considerable number of people truly feel that if the world does take such a bad turn that the barbarians wherever they are – including the barbarian in everyone – really do loose off that bomb, then life up to then will somehow not have been worth living.

It is that which, to date, has been the most deleterious effect of the H-bomb.

In such circumstances there turns out to be a nearly alarming number of important subjects to which one has never paid fully concentrated attention. It was necessary to prune the list, because I planned to devote between one and two hours daily to thought about one or other of the subjects chosen. (People who have never been in a hospital or sanatorium naturally imagine that the patient has at his disposal deliciously long hours of uninterrupted leisure. This is untrue. The mechanics of institutional living (the Army, any army, is a horrid example), quite inevitably operate so as to reduce the individual's spare time to a minimum. A man on his own can eat an excellent lunch in fifteen minutes or rather less. In an army or hospital the operation, from the time, say, that you have to put away your books and papers because they want to lay the knives and forks on your tray, to the time when they ultimately remove the débris of the pudding, can be easily an hour.)

I thought it just worth while to devote a small part of the day to a do-it-yourself faith healing experiment. All very sick people are naturally attracted to the psychosomatic aspect of disease. It seems, at least to the imagination of the sick man, only logical to suppose that if, as is generally agreed, many cases of illness are psychosomatic in origin; if, that is to say, a physical deterioration can be mentally induced, then the opposite must also be true. The process should be capable of reversal. If one can psychosomatically become ill, one should be able to psychosomatically return one's body to a state of health.

Many doctors have taken the view that so far as TB is concerned a majority of patients have surrendered to the attacks of the ever-present but normally lurking bacillus as an escape from other pressures which have become intolerable. Certainly my own observations in the sanatorium, limited and scientifically sketchy as they were, tended to confirm this opinion. That is to say, every one of the fifteen or twenty men whom I got to know well enough to discuss their intimate affairs certainly had succumbed to TB at a moment when those affairs – financial, domestic, and even religious – had produced a stress so extreme that a subconscious act of escape, the escape to TB, could have been suspected.

Thinking along these lines was notably encouraged by a story in, I think, *Time* magazine, about a woman diabetic who experienced a false, or psychosomatic pregnancy. It is a fact that in a genuine pregnancy, a diabetic does not require insulin – the relevant organs do, during the period of pregnancy, the work which otherwise the insulin would have to do. In the case I am referring to, the same thing happened. The woman's organs worked normally, and insulin was not required. Yet the pregnancy was a false one. So that, by simply supposing herself to be pregnant she had produced a profound physical effect upon the organs involved. It seemed to me that if the mind could jolt the pancreas into action, there was at least an outside chance that it could also arrest, and perhaps eliminate, a tumour on the lung. I concentrated my attention to this purpose, seeking to produce a condition in which the subconscious would get, so to speak, on the job and stay with it night and day.

All this made for a full and busy day, and the worst moments were those in which visits of my wife or sons would poignantly remind me of all the happiness and excitement I might perhaps be going to leave. Though I looked forward passionately to these visits I was at the same time in a state of alarm lest I somehow betray to my visitors, who naturally knew nothing of that menacing X-ray, the actual state of affairs.

27

ANIMAL KINGDOM

THE cancer scare slid away as suddenly and stealthily as it had appeared. The sinister formation on the X-ray film, apparent even to my lay eye, had all at once reduced itself to nothing. The doctors expressed themselves delighted and – so far as doctors will ever admit to such a thing – even a little surprised. They went on as a precautionary measure taking blood tests and so on but there were no horrible reactions. The expectation of life elongated itself in a manner that was almost disconcerting. The future became, once more, a reality to be pondered and dealt with.

Before Alexander the Great set out for Asia he divided his kingdom up among his friends. 'My Lord,' said Perdiccas, 'what have you left for yourself?' 'Hope,' replied Alexander.

In this statement Alexander disclosed how profound was the gulf between the conquerors from Macedon and the defeated men of ancient Greece. It may even be that the true division between the ancient Greek view of the world and the modern view began to make itself visible just then. Schoolmasters and dons anxious to 'soft sell' ancient Greek culture to the modern world constantly yield to the temptation of telling the modern world that the ancient Greeks were 'very much like ourselves'. It would probably be more valuable if they indicated the differences. Their attitude to hope – Elpis – was one of them. To Alexander hope was one of those things which kept you going, ultimately saved your life. To the earlier Greeks, it was the final disaster. However badly things might be going there was still a chance that a man might fight his way out of his difficulties until, quite brightly and insidiously, Elpis appeared. To have hope was to succumb to illusion, and catastrophe followed.

It would be desirable for a scholar to trace this idea through the ages. A person could make a thesis of it.

One day we learned that as a result of the closing down of a sanatorium in another part of the area, five or six patients from there were to be transferred to our ward. The effect of this information was stimulating. The two principal card players in the ward, bored by the ineptitude of the patients with whom they had been playing every night for months, found reason to hope and believe – the information had been supplied by all sorts of reliable nurses, ambulance drivers and other functionaries – that the majority of the newcomers were skilled and passionate card players. Others, who liked to drink illicitly in the evenings, but whose spirits had been damped by the tea and milk addictions of their neighbours, were convinced that these fellows were going to prove hearty drinkers – the type of men with whom you could sit behind a locked door on a lavatory seat, keeping your feet well out of the sputum and little rivulets of urine on the floor and share a half-bottle of whisky in a spirit of conviviality. This, too, was news well supported on the grapevine. People with less specific demands on the new arrivals were hopeful – always, of course, on the basis of information received – that they would prove to be cousins or friends of friends, men capable of bringing the very latest gossip from the home-town and thus bringing a fresher breath of real life into the monastic atmosphere of the ward. One day when the ambulance from the closed sanatorium arrived at our ward all those among us who still retained hope were aligned in the corridor to watch them debouch. All were discouraged – even the drinkers. For although these additions to our number were certainly drunk they were less than convivial. Two of them crawled through the rain from the steps of the ambulance to the steps of the ward. Still on hands and knees, and afraid of hostility on the part of the authorities, they swore muttered oaths against the use of liquor and bound themselves never to touch the stuff again. One of them, who apparently had been told that should he present himself drunk at a TB sanatorium he was liable to be flung out to die in a ditch, was quite simply obsessed by the fear that if he were to lie down on his bed he would roll off and thus expose himself as drunk. As a result, resisting the efforts of the nurses, he insisted on placing himself for his night's rest on the floor under the bed – thus, he thought, averting any possibility of suspicion.

None of them, it turned out, was much good at cards and the

one on whom the highest hopes had been placed, an officer of the army from the west country, divided his time between lying in bed swearing mournfully in Irish and – a thing he did with absolute regularity – making apple-pie beds for his acquaintances. It was almost the only thing that seemed to rouse him from melancholy lethargy. Familiar footsteps moving down the corridor on the way to the lavatory would bring brightness to his eyes and energy to his body. He would jump out of bed, peer out of his cubicle door, ascertain that it was indeed one of his friends who had passed and in a trice was in the friend's cubicle wrecking the bed in a fashion liable to cause the friend a maximum of astonishment and dismay.

Tubercular patients hope and believe, wherever they are, that somewhere else a wonder drug – a practically instant cure for the disease – has been discovered and is in regular use. They think that as of now, no one in Vienna, Milan, or Detroit spends more than about three weeks in a TB hospital. The doctors in those centres are clever and kind. They use this new drug. And, this being so, it logically follows that there must be some very sinister reason for the failure of this particular sanatorium where we are – wherever it is – to employ these beneficent drugs. A doctor in the sanatorium where I was, told me that in the years immediately after World War II it was an almost universal belief among the patients that a drug was available in Chicago which would cure TB in a matter of three months. It was further believed that malign influences must be at work preventing the distribution of such drugs to patients in Ireland. Opinions were divided as to whether these malign influences were exercised by the British, in a last vengeful campaign against Irish freedom, or by the Irish Government itself – seen, by those who chose to see it so, as an incompetent set of rogues making a packet, don't you see now, out of their vested interest in the outmoded drugs foisted upon the Irish hospitals. In so far as these almost had any substance at all they were based upon irresponsible articles in local newspapers reporting various experiments conducted in Chicago with drugs some of which years later were more or less perfected and were put into use in the Irish hospitals, one of them was found to be certainly deadly to the tubercular bacillus but also productive of acute kidney disease, cirrhosis, and raving lunacy. Despite these disclosures hope and belief continued to parade over the hospital hand in hand. What we had here in an acute form was a parallel with the psychosis which sometimes affects nations and social classes when their fortunes go awry. They believe that somehow, somewhere, there must be a quick solution for their difficulties. Everyone else is doing well, so why are we not? The answer must again be 'malign influences'. What malign influences? Here one may take one's choice. It could be the Jews. It could be Communist agitators. Whoever they are they must be treated as pitiless enemies since they are evidently withholding from us something which it is our proper right to have at our disposal.

Political thought is based on notions of this kind and a sanatorium where, as I have said, everyone's awareness is somewhat over-sensitized, is an excellent place from which to observe these reactions. I mean to observe them not simply in others which teaches one very little but to observe them in oneself – to observe in oneself the obscure workings of rumour, of fear, of frustration and suspicion.

I, too, found myself believing that somewhere, possibly in New York, possibly in Moscow or London, the cure for TB had been notably speeded up, and from that thought it was but a step to the construction of a whole theory demonstrating the abominable mismanagement of the modern world in general and Ireland in particular.

It has to be said – and it surprises nobody, although perhaps it should surprise them – that almost everyone in a hospital believes that the authorities are conspiring to evil ends rather than good ones. And once the notion of some type of ill-intentioned conspiracy is accepted there is hardly any limit to what the supposed victim of it will believe. Everyone knows this to be a fact, labels it 'persecution mania' and has it swept under the rug in a minute. This is unfortunate. For there are real persecutions and real victims. And the sane bear the burden of the insane's illusions. This is evident wherever an individual or a group is in constant conflict with the authorities or the police.

> The toad beneath the harrow knows
> where each tooth of that harrow goes.
> The butterfly upon the road
> preaches contentment to the toad.

Everyone on top of anything accuses everyone else of persecution mania. When I ran my news sheet *The Week* in England in the 1930s and would happen to mention that my telephone was tapped, my mail regularly interfered with and my friends irregularly beaten up by the police I could see the words 'delusions of persecution' forming close behind the eyes of the listeners. Among encouraging facts in an occasionally discouraging world is the evidence coming constantly to hand that in England today people are somewhat less sceptical, less complacent about such matters. They seem less inclined to believe that whereas possibly all other police are men equipped with dangerous powers and susceptible to all the temptations which such powers give, their police are wonderful. Very few people in England would now assert – except, of course, for public consumption – that their police are incorruptible, still less that they are impartial. It is an advance in public realism. Newspapers and people who make pronouncements deplore what they term the deterioration of the relations between public and police. Yet it is better that relations should deteriorate than that good relations should persist on the basis of illusion and hocus-pocus. The reasons for this improvement in the public vision are probably not far to seek. It developed during the Second World War and realistic visibility was further increased during the immediate post-war period when the Labour Government not only came to power but looked to many people as though they were going to stay in power indefinitely.

Paradoxically it was the upper and upper middle class which were really responsible for the new and notably cold look at the police then and subsequently taken by the public. The upper and upper middle class had hitherto collectively taken it for granted that any little maladjustments in the policeman's sense of absolute impartiality and justice would in general work to the benefit of the upper and upper middle classes. And, taking things by and large, this is still generally true. But the upper classes with their customary tendency to hysteria and panic and – in England – their proneness to the belief that the mildest shift in social balance is either a revolution in itself or the precursor of revolution, were startled into a new appraisal of the forces of the law. Their sudden doubts and scepticisms filtering down from the clubs to the saloon bars were largely responsible for the public admission of what previously had been merely 'bad thoughts' in the minds of the poor or the politically subversive who had more or less direct personal experience of where the teeth of the harrow went.

The physical confinement and inactivity of a hospital, together with the break-up of the ordinary patterns of life, are the compensations it offers for its frustrating and sordid disadvantages. Immediately the ruts of life begin to show up in high relief, like real ruts on real roads when the sun goes down. The patient realizes sharply how much of his time he has been spending in simply getting from here to there, in talking civilly to people whose company is as distasteful as their opinions are valueless, or in simply waiting for the occurrence of something which is supposed to be going to happen. In hospital only routine happens, there is nowhere to go but the bathroom, and the sort of person who wastes your time in outside life will not waste his own by coming to see you. In these circumstances the mind is liberated for the active consideration of all sorts of problems for which previously it had 'no time'.

A passage in *Aids to Tuberculosis Nursing, a Complete Textbook for the Nurse*, published by Baillière, Tindall and Cox, states that 'the mycobacterium tuberculosis is an obligatory parasite, that is to say it is unable to live an independent life, reproduce, or establish any kind of comfortable or permanent existence, unless it finds a home in a human or animal body'.

A first reaction, naturally, was to consider the remarkable applicability of this description to many friends and acquaintances. Somebody – Philip Jordan, I expect – pointed out to me the distinction that ought to be, but often is not, made between adventurers, spongers, and passers of false cheques on the one hand, and on the other the true eighteenth-century-type parasite. The former, after intriguing to get invited to stay in somebody's house in Ibiza for a month and being then offered, say,

£150 to support him somewhere else in lieu of board and lodging, is delighted – he likes the cash money and the freedom of manœuvre. He can put £50 of it on a winning outsider at twenty to one. The parasite is not pleased. For him the cash is not everything. He needs a cocoon, a home from home, familiar faces around the dinner-table. He needs, in fact, in every sense a host. And without it he, like the mycobacterium tuberculosis, is 'unable to reproduce, or establish any kind of comfortable or permanent existence'.

In comparison, however, with the pressing realities of the mycobacterium tuberculosis these anthropomorphic analogies must appear frivolous. Not so, however, the further implications of the passage quoted from the book. For in the mind of any sincere person it raises, in the sharpest and most challenging possible manner, the entire question of our relationship and attitude to the rest of the living creation. Admittedly the problems of the mycobacterium tuberculosis are painted in this passage in perhaps unusually pathetic colours. It would be a ludicrous affectation to pretend that when this mycobacterium is swarming in one's lungs one hesitates for even a fraction of a second to encourage the doctor to slaughter the little creature in multi-millions – or rather not to slaughter it outright, but to cause it to be immured in walls of flesh tissue behind which it dies a lingering death. It is easy to regard this sharply oppositional attitude of the human patient to the mycobacterium tuberculosis as not merely obvious, but a final statement on the subject. Yet final is exactly what it cannot be, unless we accept the extreme position that a man's relationship to the rest of creation is to be guided by his own interests to an extent which would be impermissible in his relations with his fellow-men.

In point of fact at the very time when I was brooding on the mycobacterium tuberculosis a case occurred in south-western Ireland of alleged cruelty to a donkey. The guards had arrested some boys who were riding races on ageing donkeys. A couple of the boys had armed themselves with sharpened nails which, bound to the end of sticks, they drove into the flanks of the donkeys. The guards finding the donkeys lacerated and suffering, supposed they had a watertight case. The magistrate, however, a devout Roman Catholic, took another view. He give it as his general opinion that it was absurd to assess 'cruelty' to an animal as though the word had the same connotation as in the case of 'cruelty' to a human being. And this opinion he based on the ground that human beings have souls and donkeys do not. In this it is true he ran counter to the opinion expressed by the late Pope Pius XII who (persuaded thereto I believe by the then Duchess of Bedford) made a statement in favour of humane treatment being accorded to animals. Still the magistrate's opinion, though disgusting, could not be said to be totally illogical.

Mr Vincent Sheean, a sincere disciple of the Mahatma Gandhi, used at one time to irk visitors to his home in Vermont by his Hindu-religious attitude to mosquitoes. When a few of these little creatures would penetrate the defences of the house or the veranda the guests would seek to kill them. Vincent shouting 'My brother the gnat!' would seek merely to drive them forth. His attitude was supposed to be ridiculous; but whether it was really so, or whether the guests were displaying a low, flesh-bound, and unphilosophic state of mind I have never been able to decide. Certainly nobody but a fool would suppose the question to be a simple one. Moreover, the very same people who were happy to kill or wound and incapacitate the mosquitoes, would very likely break out in assured protest at the sight of a Spanish peasant torturing his overworked mule with hunger and blows. In Monsieur Romain Gary's novel *The Roots of Heaven* – a book which I happened to be reading in the hospital at the time – the suggestion is repeatedly made that the brutality of human beings towards (in this case) the elephants must be disastrous not only for the elephants but for the human beings themselves, since it can only serve to perpetuate that human sadism or human indifference to suffering which if perpetuated and intensified will destroy the human race itself.

Macaulay, as everyone knows, derided the Puritans for their attempts to suppress bear-baiting with the suggestion that they did so 'not because it gave pain to the bear, but because it gave pleasure to the spectators'. In the personal and social circumstances he enjoyed, Macaulay was perhaps less uncomfortably aware of what that particular type of 'pleasure' might lead to in terms of human action than either the Puritans or ourselves. Yet the problem was one which came vividly enough to the fore in the early part of the nineteenth century when the Acts intended to reduce cruelty to animals were being painfully smuggled on to the Statute Books – smuggled in the sense that the reformers did not dare to pretend that they were seriously interested in the welfare of the beasts but rather in obviating ill-effects upon the human beings.

The introduction of legislation for the protection of children, lunatics and animals [wrote T. A. Ingram], is a proof of the growing humanitarianism of the age. There was at one time a tendency among jurists to question whether, for instance, the prevention of cruelty to animals was not a recognition of a certain quasi-right in animals, or whether it was merely that such exhibitions at bull- and bear-baiting, cock fights, etc., were demoralizing to the public generally. The true fact seems to be that the first introduction of such legislation was undoubtedly due to a desire for the promotion of humanity, but that the principle for the recognition of which the time was not yet right had to be excused in the eyes of the public by the plea that cruelty had a demoralizing effect upon the spectators.

In the collective consciousness – if one may use the phrase without being struck at by some over-heated Freudian partisan – of the early nineteenth century, the problem of cruelty to animals was inseparably interlaced with that of the problem of cruelty to children. Pit boys and pit ponies were to suffer or be liberated together. Evidently there were those who, having linked children and animals together, reached the conclusion that both of them must continue to suffer extreme cruelties since only by means of such sufferings could 'the community' prosper. Without coal what would happen to Britain? But by a pretty and indeed encouraging, dialectical process in the mind of that generation this notion was first stood on its head and then developed into something new – the conception of cruelty as such, regardless of its object or victim. A vital point it would seem in this development is that the animals helped the children as much as the children helped the animals. The records show that because the animals – whether pit ponies or bears – were more obviously helpless and, of course, somewhat less useful than the children, many people found it easier to speak up on behalf of legislation against cruelty to animals than to demand restrictions on cruelties to children. In this mysterious way the pit ponies and the bears and cocks became – like Monsieur Gary's elephants – a sort of symbol through the naïve simplicity of which the mind was enabled to appreciate deeper and more complex realities involving, ultimately, that conflict between the *raison d'état* and human rights which in our own day plays a role so urgent and enormous. One sees that the Puritans may have been at least as right as Macaulay.

In the rocky field beyond the windows of the ward a company of hares performed extensive ritual movements of a nature and purpose incomprehensible to the onlookers. The performance had the air of a dance and perhaps really was one. Since the patients were immobilized by one mycobacterium tuberculosis the hares had acquired a great sense of security and conducted their dance without haste. This was their downfall; for later in the year they were set upon by eager beaglers and several of them torn to pieces by the dogs. These small massacres were condemned by the generality of patients on two grounds: first, that the hares had after all been doing no harm to man or other beast, secondly, that it was utterly disgusting that a pack of strangers should in the course of their hunt burst into the grounds of the hospital, and dash shouting and hallooing across this field in front of a lot of men who were in no position to do anything of the kind.

The rabbits had disappeared long before. Here the consensus was that the deliberate spreading of myxomatosis had been a good thing. It was a pity that the rabbits had been condemned to die in agony, and the sight of those swollen pop-eyed heads on writhing or torpid bodies, when suddenly encountered on path or roadway, had given many people quite a turn. However, it had made the farmers a bit of money, can you deny that now? The men working in the field were called upon to testify to the fact.

Not only was this no lie, but (as I pointed out at the time) it was no lie either that Hitler at least expected to make a bit of money out of exterminating the Jews in the gas chambers.

I remembered how in myxomatosis year I had published with

interesting results an article in *Punch* reporting how two West Indian scientists had found a means of inflicting a pair of English with the germs of an incurable disease which caused the whole breed of English to swell up, turn purple and die in acute pain. The consequences had been in almost every way desirable. Naturally, it had been unpleasant for Indians and Americans passing through, say, Cairo to find the lobbies of good hotels temporarily littered with English, dying in a manner obnoxious to the sensitive, and liable perhaps to cause some trauma to Indian or American children. This was, however, a purely temporary phenomenon. On the credit side of the balance sheet there was the self-evident fact that in a world where population pressures were building up, the disappearance of the English would immediately provide at least some extra space. And more importantly it could be demonstrated that with the English out of the way the wealth which they had previously controlled must accrue to somebody else. You could not ask a Russian or American who was making a big profit out of Anglo-elimination to wax sentimental about the disappearance of the breed. The question of how much money was made or saved must, as in the case of rabbit myxomatosis, be the decisive factor.

The reaction of *Punch* readers to this report was passionate indeed. To judge by their letters some seemed to be actually whirling mentally round and round like mad dervishes in their rage and confusion of mind. The shock of learning that there was someone actually capable of thinking of human beings (particularly English human beings), and animals (particularly rabbits) in – so to speak – the same mental breath, seemed virtually to have unseated the reason of many. Others seemed to be choking in the foam from their own mouths as they tried to explain that while they favoured the use of germ warfare against rabbits, were they to see anyone raise his hand in cruelty against a horse or dog they would shoot the scoundrel down like – well, like a dog. The most agreeable of these letters came from two quite separate individuals both of whom, however, had the same theme. They could see from my name that I was a Scotsman. They noted from the article that the word used for the 'breed' was 'English' and not 'British'. 'So at length it is blazoned to the world,' one of them wrote, 'what has been plain to some of us for a long time – namely that the Scot in his heart not only hates the English but longs for nothing better than to see them exterminated by germ warfare. As a life-long student of Anglo-Scottish relations from the earliest times to the present day I have myself for years been convinced of this fact and have done my best by writing and by word of mouth to warn my fellow-Englishmen of their peril. You, Sir, have at least rendered some service by blurting out in this fashion the true plans of your race.' He concluding by noting as a fact that in this anti-English conspiracy the Scots were, of course, allied with the Jews. He did me the favour of enclosing a small pamphlet in the same vein which he had had privately printed a few years previously, and a copy of the *Protocols of the Elders of Zion*.

To one or two of the saner-seeming of my correspondents I wrote that since I did not suppose myself to be God, and, therefore, lacked any lowdown on the purpose, if any, of the universe, I really could have no idea as to whether myxomatosis was a good thing 'in the long run' – a phrase all these correspondents had used as though it had some meaning, at least for themselves. I could only state that in the short run – meaning here and now – I was sorry for farmers who lost money as a result of the depredations of rabbits, and was sorry for the rabbits. I was, however, sorriest of all I explained for anyone who, whatever their final judgement, took it for granted that in such a case no problem was involved and thus no judgement necessary. For that was the kind of person who by this brutally pound-counting actuarial sort of thinking was helping to land himself with an overdose of radio-activity and a couple of two-headed children. I suggested that if the problem were really one of deciding between torturing rabbits to death and ensuring the human food supply, then serious and humane people – people that is with the interests of humanity itself at heart – would insist on refusing to accept this as a true dilemma. For it is ludicrous to suppose that the society which has produced (chiefly it is true under pressure of war or preparation for war) the technological advances of the last twenty years could not find quite other and superior means of solving this problem. Naturally, so long as people regard it as permissible and possible

to solve a problem by torturing rabbits they will torture rabbits.
And so long as they think it both permissible and possible to
solve their problems by massacring Jews rather than by re-
organizing their economic system, the Jews – or any other
group that gets in the way – will be victims. To accept gross
cruelty as 'the only way out' is in fact stultifying to science
and technology; for the bad money of laziness will drive out
the good money of thought and energy, and continue to do so
until a catastrophe occurs.

Not much to my surprise, these reasoned arguments so far
from interesting, let alone appeasing, my correspondents,
seemed to enrage them even further. To say something exasperating is one thing; to argue that one had an excellent reason
for saying it is another, and a much worse one in the eyes of
whoever has been exasperated. (All that occurred, of course, in
the days of Malcolm Muggeridge's *Punch* when there were real
opportunities for exasperating people of that kind.)

A jolly good laugh, of course, but a little frightening all the
same – this sudden realization, which comes to all people who
receive letters from 'the public', that somewhere, beneath the
visible part of the iceberg which everyone thinks about, writes
about, evaluates and assumes to be steering the berg, is some
mass, its volume unascertained, of which the motives and
objectives appear in the eyes of those sitting in the Arctic sun-
light atop the glacial structure, insane.

28

THE ROLE PLAYERS

'IT's perfectly useless for me to know,' wrote Paul Valéry in
his notebooks, 'that which I am unable to change.' It is,
evidently, one of those quick-change artists among remarks –
almost in the blink of an eye it can appear as a tarnished im-
becility or a gravely profound observation. As is often the case
with such aphorisms you remain uncertain as to whether the
man is talking through his hat or taking a really valuable rabbit
out of it. However that may be, it is certain that a sojourn in

hospital is a healthy injection against the creeping disease of the faculties which causes a person – particularly perhaps a normally very active person – to read this, and ascertain that, and discuss the other thing, all on the assumption that by doing so he will be enabled to change the matter under discussion. Eighty per cent of the time this activity, in so far as it is actually supposed to change something and not to be a mere exercise or end in itself, is absolutely futile. This makes no difference to the fact that to fail to recognize that other twenty per cent of occasions when your knowledge, your thought and your action really could shift the course of events a fraction this way or that is an unpardonable sin of omission. Perhaps active people can only keep themselves awake and in trim for the brief period of effective action by maintaining their illusions about the vastly longer periods when to suppose that they can change what is going on is ludicrous.

I have known many sufferers from this 'activist's' disease and have suffered from it myself. In acute cases the victim not only believes that he is going to have, or is having, an effect upon events, but afterwards, when it is clearly apparent to everyone else that for all the effect he has had he might as well have stayed in bed with his hat on, he still mystically believes that, contrary to all the evidence, his activity – which in reality had no consequences whatever – did have some sort of result. When I worked in *The Times* office in Washington with Sir Wilmott Lewis, who collected and savoured absurdities of this kind, he told me as a cautionary tale of a conversation he had had with Wickham Steed, that great and powerful publicist, after the Washington Disarmament Conference of 1924. 'Before the French delegation left Paris,' Steed recounted, 'I learned that it was their intention to go to the Conference with all their cards up their sleeves, to finesse at every point, and in general to outsmart the Americans. I knew it was a disastrous policy. I rushed over to Paris, I saw Poincaré, I saw Briand, I saw them all. I argued with them right through the night. I begged them on the contrary to lay their cards frankly on the table, to abandon all ideas of finesse, of trickery and of "playing it smart". And just as dawn was breaking over the Place de la Concorde I convinced them.'

'But surely,' Lewis said in bewilderment, '"playing it smart" was just what they did do throughout the Conference. They were as tricky as hell. They played the Conference like a crooked poker game.'

'I know,' said Steed, quite unperturbed, 'it must have been on the boat going over that they changed their minds.'

For days at a time it seemed to me futile even to read the newspapers or to read anything more than the headlines. Instead I let the news come trickling in to me through the ear-phones, which in themselves provided a comfortable limitation of horizons and possibilities by being incapable of listening to anything but Radio Eireann and the Light Programme of the B.B.C. The resulting sense that one had almost no valid information of any kind, or that at best one was being fed with about one-tenth of the possible interpretations of events was not – as it might have been in the outside world – irritating or frustrating, because of the enforced non-participation; a situation which made Valéry's remark seem true in its application to a limited and particular state of affairs. No doubt all these sensations would have been produced by any hospital, but in one where all the staff and 98 per cent of the patients are members of a particular and dogmatic faith – in this case the Roman Catholic – the adjustment of one's attitude to history in the making was more than customarily stimulating. Such an adjustment is inevitable when you find yourself in circumstances where you are well aware that almost no one with whom you are in contact is having reactions to events in the least similar to your own. It is an excellent way of avoiding mental clichés. Nobody on the staff bothered her head about General de Gaulle or the Algerian parachutists. And nobody was in the least interested by the British and American landings in Jordan and the Lebanon. Nobody was at all badly scared by Mr Khrushchev or Mr Dulles. In that community the event of the year was the death of Pope Pius XII. And the only shock anyone experienced was produced by the disclosures regarding the behaviour of Galeazzo-Lisi, the Pope's apparently almost all-powerful physician, who was discovered to be trying to sell candid camera shots with descriptions of His Holiness's final days on earth. At least a year before in London I had been given by devout, but well informed (and, therefore, scandalized or apprehensive) Roman Catholic friends, who knew Rome well, a sufficiently lurid account of the state of affairs then existing in the Vatican. They made it clear to what an extent the situation in the Vatican expressed and mirrored the almost farcically luxuriant corruption of Italian political life at large. At the time I had even discounted some of these stories for I have often noticed that very devout Communists, for example, would sometimes take what must appear a perverse pleasure in telling startling stories about goings-on in the Kremlin. I have always supposed that this tendency is due partly to a natural human desire to shock and startle, but is strengthened by another element – that is to say, the devotee who tells such stories is in reality demonstrating the pure strength of his own absolute faith. 'If *you* witnessed such incompetence, corruption and general wickedness,' they seem to be saying, '*you*, being a feeble and faithless intellectual, would lose such shreds of faith as you might have previously had. *I* on the other hand know these things to be true but my faith is unshaken.' And a good deal of experience among Roman Catholics suggests to me that they sometimes are motivated by the same impulse. However, since I did believe at least half of what I have been told I had to be particularly cautious not to offend the Roman Catholics around me in the hospital by seeming to take the behaviour of such persons as Galeazzo-Lisi too much for granted. I had to go through the motions of shock and amazement mingled with incredulity. But in dealings with the faithful such delicacies are often quite unnecessary. I was speaking rather gingerly to one of the nurses about this physician. She said immediately that the man was evidently a Communist. I said I had not seen any reference to such affiliations in any newspaper nor had it been proclaimed on the radio. She replied that she had no need of such sources for she had studied the photograph of Galeazzo-Lisi in the paper and had seen at once that he had a Communist face.

Did it not, I asked her, seem strange that the Pope with his high personal intelligence and also with the vast sources of information at the disposal of the Vatican should not have detected something of the kind – either by simply looking at the man's face, as she had done, or by investigating his record.

'But of course, the Pope knew that he was a Communist,' she said.

'He *knew*?' I said in the greatest astonishment. 'Then why did he do nothing about it? Why did he pass so much power into the hands of this agent of anti-Christ?'

'Because,' she said 'the Holy Father possesses infinite qualities of understanding and sympathy. He knew exactly what this man was like but forgave him.'

I became indignant. 'All very well to forgive him,' I replied, 'but what about the consequences of this man's presence in the very heart of the Vatican? And I don't mean just his medical consequences either although it would seem that they were sufficiently disastrous. What you are saying is that the Pope harboured an evil influence right in the headquarters of your Church.'

'Nothing the Pope did,' said the nurse equably and with a smile of the purest assurance, 'could possibly be harmful to the Church. The very fact that it might look so to the ordinary person is a demonstration of the superiority and uniqueness of His Holiness.'

I, so far as I know, only once committed a serious offence against the susceptibilities of the Roman Catholics in my ward who tended and befriended me, and this on an occasion where it had not occurred to me that offence could be given. I tipped the winner of the Papal Stakes. I said that if anyone were prepared to bet, and naturally a large number of people were, then I was prepared to bet that the chances of John of Venice winning the race were eight to one. When John of Venice came in the winner the effect so far as I was concerned was a little dismaying. Anyone who had both considered other political situations and to some extent played the horses could have made a successful bet on approximately the same basic assumption. A fortnight or more before the winner was announced there was, as you may remember, a good deal of interest in the French and the Armenian contestants. They had, I concluded, the sort of appeal which would seem compelling to outsiders – outsiders in the sense of non-Italians, Protestants, and hopeful intellectual thinkers who wishfully thought that the Mother Church would proceed upon lines deemed desirable, helpful, and progressive by themselves. Scanning the reports I considered that there was not the slightest chance that this type of outsider would make any showing on the hard ground of the Vatican. What looks to a 'sympathetic' intellectual like a splendid chance for the Catholic Church does not often look to the Catholic Church like a splendid chance. The same intellectuals are constantly explaining what the Kremlin ought to do, but the Kremlin so far as can be seen pays very little attention to them. Which is not to say that the intellectuals do not have a remarkable long-term influence upon both the Kremlin and the Vatican. It is only to say that you cannot consider this influence as important in placing a short-term bet.

I decided right at the outset to eliminate all non-Italian contestants.

After that it was a question of judging first some perfectly concrete factors like the age of the Cardinal candidates. It was sufficiently obvious that the Cardinals were not going to elect a man so old that he would join God the Father and his Papal predecessor before he had had time even to begin to tidy up the sometimes distressing mess left by the distinguished predecessor himself. On the other hand none of them were going to be so rash as to elect a man so young that he might in fact maintain himself in office until the year 1980 or even later. For this would be to expose such a man to just those pressures of long enduring autocracy to which his predecessor had partially succumbed. By these perfectly concrete factors a good many contestants were in my mind eliminated. After that there were a number of necessarily vague considerations any one of which might have some bearing on the result – such as alleged 'diplomatic' ability and 'political' tendencies. Of these, of course, one received only the most fragmentary indications in such newspapers as were delivered to the hospital. And in any case it is always exceedingly dangerous for non-Roman Catholics to seek to interpret the political or social tendencies of the Roman Church. A reporter who is not a Roman Catholic but attempts to evaluate the political considerations in the mind of the Vatican is in very much the same position as a reporter who is not a Communist attempting to evaluate the considerations in the mind of the Kremlin. Both are at sea because both are trying to estimate the actions of men who are in fact acting in accordance with doctrinal principles understood fully by themselves but not always fully understood by the reporter. In the past I have frequently read reports from or about the alleged policies of the Kremlin which patently were based on a total incomprehension of how either the Communist organization or the particular organization of the Kremlin hierarchy works. And although I know almost nothing except what I am told about the similar workings of the Vatican one can often detect in such reports a similar ignorance – a similar attempt to equate the workings of that type of organization with, say, the workings of the Town Council of Market Harborough. However, after making some effort to evaluate these factors I came to the conclusion that John of Venice should rate odds of about eight to one. Naturally, in considering a contest of this kind one has to compare it with a very open race, with a large field, in which there are, on form, no genuine favourites. There were no favourites in this case. Therefore, eight to one was a reasonable bet and it seemed to me that there was no other runner in sight who rated better than approximately one hundred to eight.

When my candidate came through I noted that members of the staff and others, though congratulating me in their civil Irish way on my perspicacity, were in effect looking at me askance. I was distressed and, of course, disappointed, because I had expected everyone to congratulate me on my fine tip. The truth was disclosed to me by my friend Mr Michael Inchegeelagh (as I prefer to call him). Sardonic and delighted he pointed out to me the truth of the situation. This was that in Ireland, as everyone ought to know, the successful gambler is an object of a certain reverence. And the reverence is increased if he is successful in betting the horses rather than winning at roulette. Secondly, said Mr Inchegeelagh, in the popular conscious mind and in the sub-conscious minds of perhaps everyone, the gambler is invested with a certain aura of power, of magic, of super-humanism. He knows something. And if he knows something he must be someone. This is as illogical, he admitted, as throwing salt over one's shoulder or touching wood but it is a fact. There is a universal human myth about gamblers. On the other hand the deliberations of the Cardinals who are seeking to elect a pope are directly presided over by God Almighty. It is He who inspires them to vote this way or that. And their decision is God's decision. Therefore, for a gambler – even a Roman Catholic gambler – to bet upon the result of the Papal election involves one of two suppositions on the part of the gambler : – either he is denying the existence of the Almighty's inspiration to the Cardinals and is treating the matter as though it were a general election or a horse race, or else he is claiming to have advance knowledge of the Mind of God, and the next thing you know he will be bragging that he had a stable tip from the Archangel Gabriel. Both of these are monstrous presumptions on the part of the gambler. But in the event that he is a Catholic they might in some way be explained and forgiven. But supposing the gambler is a Protestant? In this case the situation becomes really offensive and one which a decent-minded person would not care to contemplate – not, that is, to contemplate its implications. Above all one would not contemplate the implications of a non-Roman Catholic who does this thing and actually turns out to be correct in his bet.

Naturally, Mr Inchegeelagh pointed out to me, nobody actually argues this thing out in his mind in these words but that, he said, is the reason for the apprehensive if not actually dirty looks which you are at this moment getting from one quarter and another.

Mr Inchegeelagh was one of the people who helped to save my life in that hospital. In fact with the exception of my own family he did more to that end, I suppose, than anyone else. He had left the hospital before I myself arrived but had returned on a visit to a friend and after some conversation at the friend's bedside had later made it a practice to visit me regularly. He came from Cork where he lived and worked. He was a man of approximately forty, with the head of Ezra Pound on a six foot six high body. He could have been considered as a manifestation of the spirit of the City of Cork. That is a confusing city, of which Irishmen everywhere who do not come from Cork profess to be afraid. And it is a fact that while it reclines there between the arms of the River Lee, looking beautiful and a little raffish and a little tired, as though it had too many things to remember, it is also a volcano of energy spouting out people

328

who go out and take over great tracts of government and industry in Dublin, Pittsburgh and Sydney.

He was by no means such a one as to be astonished or scandalized by news of political, moral or other forms of corruption in the Vatican. If the stories were, to his own knowledge, ludicrous, and evidently contradictory of what any good Roman Catholic would know about the technical organization of his own Church, he pointed out the fact. I recalled how in parallel circumstances I had occasionally drawn the attention of literary friends – I recall a particular conversation with a best-seller – to what seemed to me sheer impossibilities in their plot-patterns in so far as they related to the Communist Party and its organization. It is well enough for a novelist to claim that for 'the purposes of his plot' he chose to assume that the Communist Party or the Roman Catholic Church functioned in this way or that. But it seems to me that in both cases the novelist should pay some attention to the realities and seek to adapt his plot to them.

But, by and large, Mr Inchegeelagh was quite prepared to admit that the lurid tales current at that time in the newspapers, and those which I relayed to him from my Roman Catholic friends in London, might well be true. He would have found it, however, ludicrous to suggest that the Roman Catholic faith, the dogma and the doctrine stand or fall by the human behaviour of the Ministers of the Church. To suppose that the Nature of God is affected by the question of whether a given Pope did or did not sleep with his niece, or even with his uncle, is to betray a crassness indicating an incomprehension of the nature of religion itself. If there were a God, and if He were to set up a doctrine and series of dogmas, it would be strange that He should permit the whole thing to depend upon the peccadilloes of priests. Any member of any properly organized religion would feel the same. It was in this respect that Mr Inchegeelagh felt that the Protestants had no leg to stand on. On the other hand he was fully prepared to admit that an atheist, a total non-believer like myself, could maintain on this issue a logical position.

He had in fact the absolute assurance of a man who has absolute faith. And his absolute faith gave to him, as it should to all faithful of whatever creed, but as it so infrequently does, the ability to regard himself, the opinions of others, and the general situation with candour, with courtesy, and even with humour.

He was thus prepared to discuss with candour and humour the social, political and moral situation of the priesthood in Ireland and not only of the priesthood but of Irish Catholicism in general. For he recognized that Irish Catholicism, like most other manifestations of Irish life, is unique. And he was a man who understood the peculiar value of its uniqueness, and at the same time the points at which it could be considered particularly vulnerable to the criticism of the rational, the humane and perhaps even of the sane.

In the course once of some discussion of the behaviour of the Irish priests during the war – I think it was on the point that they used to secure special petrol rations to attend race meetings – I remarked that while I had met a few saintly and very many good priests – good I mean in a sense surpassing the ordinary goodness of the people one meets – I sometimes had the impression in conversation with my friends and neighbours that the priests, for good or ill, really occupied a position in the community not very different from that of secretaries of the Communist Party in small communities in countries beyond the Iron Curtain. He agreed that this was indeed the case and that it was apparent that these two organizations – there are probably many others of a similar kind, but these may be mentioned as being the ones which have the greatest impact upon the Western world – are in a given period under the necessity of organizing themselves and society in this particular way. And just as I felt when I was a Communist that the misdeeds, defalcations, arrogances, and stupidities of this or that Communist were irrelevant to the total meaning of Communism, so he felt that if a priest were found drunk in the street, or looting the parishioners for the purpose of erecting a new house for himself, or indulging his sadistic instincts by beating the hell out of boys in the nominal interests of the Faith, these matters were basically irrelevant to the Faith itself. Or if they were relevant at all they merely proved that the Faith was so strong that it could carry on despite the feebleness of its individual human ministers. (This, of course, was a view more generally, and – if one may use the term – automatically accepted in the Orthodox Russian Church. The Orthodox Church carried the argument a little further – suggesting that the Church flourished not only despite its Rasputins but, in a sense, with their assistance since the Church required the membership of men who were at the point where the extremes of mortal sin and knowledge of God meet. It can seem that it is more logical to assume that God – were He to exist – would be more interested in the observance of various rituals and in the occasional mystical contemplation of Himself than in following the sexual or alcoholic capers of His followers here on earth.)

In the course of my conversations with Mr Inchegeelagh I was reminded of an impression I had had when I first many years before had come to live in Ireland. It had seemed to me that I smelled something in the air. And what I smelled was a resemblance between the atmosphere here and the atmosphere in Catalonia as I had known it before the Spanish Civil War. The analogy is always – as is the analogy between modern Ireland and Catalonia of 1934 or 35 – grossly inaccurate. But it is equally an over-simplification to suppose that grossly inaccurate analogies are always grossly misleading. Frequently they give a hint which points in the direction of truth. Every traveller has had the experience of this smell in the air on a day when he first arrives at some city or in some country which he has never visited before. He smells it during those few days, and then gradually, as his knowledge and experience of the locality deepen, the smell fades away and for a time he believes it was never there. Then something happens which recalls to him that first scent, and he realizes that although it did not tell him the truth, it was not in itself meaningless, it was perhaps a warning or perhaps a promise of things to come. The particular scent which hung in the air, it seemed to me when I first came to Ireland, was the scent of two flowers of the modern European mind luxuriating together – the flower of Roman Catholicism and the flower of anti-clericalism. The scents are, of course, antithetical but form a continual synthesis. And it is only in predominantly Roman Catholic countries that you find them both blooming together. In Catalonia, in the very early days of the Spanish Civil War, it was possible in the villages to find men whose only hesitation in shooting the priest – regarded as an oppressor of the people, a bloodsucker and an agent of the Bank of Bilbao – was his fear lest absolution for such an act be unobtainable. In other words the hatred of the priest, and even of the priesthood as such, in no way obliterated in this Christian Catholic's mind the belief in the institution and function of absolution. And I suppose it is no blame to the human mind to state that it is capable of holding two apparently contradictory ideas in itself at the same time.

As stated, close analogy between old Catalonia and new Ireland could be horribly misleading. Nobody – or hardly anybody – in Ireland much wants to shoot a priest. And if he did, there would be agreement among the sane that the occasions of offence and friction offered now and again by the clergy are insufficient to justify anyone harbouring even the thought of such an action.

But there really are such occasions, and there is a continuous – perhaps a wholesome – friction, to overlook which is to misunderstand not only modern Ireland, but also the place of the Roman Catholic Church in the modern world. The friction was at its most cruel when everything else was at its most passionate and cruel, too. There was a man in the ward who was conscious, as only Irishmen can be, that his future was already in his past. As a very young lad he had carried a gun for the I.R.A., had seen himself as privileged to jump without a gap from battling with imaginary Redskins to battle with real British soldiers. He saw, now, his whole subsequent life as a descent – not unpleasant but not glorious either – from that peak. And when he thought of those days, most vivid in his memory was the agony of mind he was put into by the action of the then Bishop of Cork. For the Bishop, representative, it seems, of one major element in the Vatican strategy – a strategy as complex as the situation itself – had instructed the clergy of his diocese to refuse absolution to any of those gunmen of Irish freedom who might confess to the killing of British soldiers, auxiliaries, Black and Tans or other allies or assistants of the occupying Power. This open gesture of disapproval by the Church was in itself sufficiently distressing and disconcerting to young men

332

who, for the most part, believed that it was for the Roman faith as well as for Irish freedom that they were killing, and risking their lives.

But the distress did not remain on the spiritual plane.

For there was a way of getting absolution. To do so you had to travel a road and cross a bridge to another diocese, where there was another bishop with another attitude to the matter.

Whatever the Bishop of Cork may have thought or pretended to think, the British were under no illusion as to the fact that they were fighting a war. Although they made, in England, propaganda out of the phrase – attributed to the Irish – 'killing no murder', they were not foolish enough to take their own propaganda seriously They killed when they wanted to, and deemed it no murder. And they had the other apparatus of war, too – such as an active spy service. So that it was no great difficulty to estimate the spiritual situation of the young Roman Catholic gunmen; to assess their need for absolution after the deed, and then to organize a particularly careful watch on such roads and bridges as a young man on the run from the military and hell fire would be apt to cross. The Cork gunmen thus encountered mortal hazards of a kind not usual in modern warfare.

No such tensions as existed then have existed in Ireland since. But it would be a mistake to suppose they are not there. Paradoxically, it is a mistake which, when made and accepted by foreigners, harms both the Irish and their Church. For one of the ignorant charges brought against both is that the Church – or 'the hierarchy' as it is commonly termed in this connexion – runs Ireland, and that the Irish citizenry, besotted and priest-ridden, are as supine as old-time moujiks in its grip.

It is necessary to be in Ireland at the moment when some lightning-like event illuminates the scene to observe how little this easily contemptuous notion corresponds to the truth. When Honor Tracy wrote some articles in the *Sunday Times* which were deemed pejorative and libellous by certain of the Irish clergy, the *Sunday Times*, in its apologetic attitude to the priests concerned, published statements which Miss Tracy considered, in their turn, pejorative and libellous of herself. She sued the *Sunday Times* – and won her action. The case was followed, in

Ireland, with a degree of passionate interest such as I have never seen evoked by anything but the all-Ireland Hurling Final at Croke Park. Every trend of opinion and deep sentiment was abruptly disclosed. There must, of course, have been a large majority who – on nationalist as much as on religious grounds – resented the whole business as being an intrusion into Irish affairs of the notoriously materialistic if not, in this case, down-right devil-worshipping British press. Also the notion of a woman actually poking her nose into the strictly male business of the priesthood was, to many, in itself revolting. All that was what anyone could see, and what most people did not bother even to look at because they took it for granted.

But to the eye of the person on the spot something else was apparent – namely a deep, almost vicious excitement at the spectacle of the familiar behaviour of the clergy, the accepted *convenances* of the priesthood in its relation to the populace, being suddenly held up to hostile examination, discussed in the harsh light of a court of law, and, by implication at least, con-demned. It was on that occasion that I heard, for the first time, the clergy referred to – with glee at their seeming discomfiture – as 'the men in black'. And in the excitement the phrase was used in my own presence – the presence of an unbeliever. When the damages – amounting to several thousand pounds – were announced, a group of fishermen and others in my own town, who had been mulling over the news with pleasure, went on to wonder just how the 'men in black' would raise the money. They hoped it would be a nasty jar for them. When I explained to them that the damages were not awarded against the priest but against the *Sunday Times* their faces fell. The savour had gone out of the case.

The type of people who doubted whether that sort of thing means anything, had a jolt of a different, perhaps more signi-ficantly characteristic kind a little later. We had come a long way since the gunmen sought absolution on the borders of Cork, and the illuminating flash in this case was provided by a football match; an event, one might say, as modern as a jazz festival or a motor-scooter picnic.

Some time in the spring or summer of 1955, the chiefs of the Football Association of Ireland invited to a match in Dublin, the

A team of Yugoslavia. The match was scheduled for October 19. President O'Kelly himself, and a couple of other members of the Government, announced their intention to be present at Dalymount Park on this international occasion, showing good-will and a feeling for peace through sport. The Number 1 Army Band was also to be on hand, and a score of the Yugoslav National Anthem was flown to Dublin in order that the Army band could practise it before playing it in the arena. The Irish National Railways arranged cheap excursions to Dalymount from all over the country. It was going to be a big, though by no means a gigantic, occasion. People who were interested in association football were interested, and nobody else paid much attention.

On the evening of October 14, Father O'Regan, Chancellor of Dr McQuaid, Archbishop of Dublin, telephoned to the Secretary of the Football Association of Ireland, a Mr Wickham, and told him that the Archbishop had 'heard with regret that the match had been arranged'. The reasons for his regret hardly needed emphasis. The Yugoslavs were godless and – whatever their differences with the Russians – Communistic; they actually boasted of their Marxist materialism. And on top of all that, as the Archbishop's Chancellor pointed out, the Yugoslav régime was at that moment holding in durance Cardinal Stepinac, leading Prince of the Church of Yugoslavia.

The news of the Archbishop's intervention was no sooner known than all those whose dull habit it is automatically to assume that when 'the hierarchy' says 'turn' everyone in Ireland turns, shrugged their shoulders and stated that, of course, the match would now be called off. Indeed a lot of non-Catholics and anti-Catholics were quite pleased at the prospect – it would confirm everything they had been parroting for years. The Catholic 'activist' organizations – with the Supreme Secretary of the Knights of Columbanus in the van – rushed into battle. The heat, as the saying goes, was on, and the prospects of any football getting played at Dalymount Park on October 19 seemed dim indeed.

So discreetly as to appear almost reluctant, President O'Kelly 'let it be known' that he would not be attending the match after all. The Army Band's playing orders were cancelled.

Sidestepping a demand that the entry permits issued to the Yugoslav team be cancelled too the Department of Justice issued a strange statement to the effect that it had secured from the F.A.I. a guarantee that the Association would pay – apparently in perpetuity – the living expenses of any member of the team who might remain in Ireland for a longer period than was allowed by the terms of his entry permit.

This, which may possibly have been pleasing to the Knights of Columbanus, was, on the contrary, shocking to the League of the Kingship of Christ. For the League, taking an optimistic view of the potentialities of the situation, and evincing faith in the attractions of the Western way of life, thought it not improbable that at least some members of the Yugoslav team would, on contact with the soil of Holy Ireland, opt to quit Tito and stay where they were. 'We must distinguish,' wrote the League in a published statement, 'between the State-controlled Yugoslav soccer team, which represents a tyrannous régime of persecution, and the human persons who are members of that team. These latter, even if they are not also our brothers in the Mystical Body of Christ – and a number of them quite possibly may be such – are certainly our brothers in another sense.' Yet as a result of the Department of Justice demand for the aforesaid guarantee, serious and unnecessary difficulties would now be put in the way of any such brother who might want to overstay his permitted sojourn in Ireland. The implication, no doubt a valid one, was that the degree of Christian brotherhood existing in the F.A.I. might not be strong enough to get a payment of life expenses for such brother past the accountants.

The North was, of course, immediately heard from. The Minister of Education [sic] in the North of Ireland Government was unfeignedly delighted. He spoke a triumphant piece pointing with alarm and disgust to the impertinent interference of the Hierarchy with the soccer match, and in just a skip and a jump was citing the affair of Dalymount Park as proof that to oppose the partition of Ireland was to favour the subjection of one and all to the oppressive rule of the Vatican as now exercised over the servile population of the South.

In London, Dr Velebit, Yugoslav Ambassador, issued the kind

of statement which Embassies keep in, as it were, stereotype for use on such occasions. He was, it seemed, absolutely amazed that a Roman Catholic Archbishop should see fit to interest himself in the matter at all, or that a Government of Roman Catholics should pay the slightest attention to him if he did. Governments, he implied, ought not to be influenced by ideological considerations. The Yugoslav Government, just for example, was interested simply in good sportsmanship, together with peace and goodwill. Evidently something fishy was going on in Dublin – dark manœuvres of a kind both shocking and almost unintelligible to the candid eye of Marshal Tito's Ambassador.

In this atmosphere the chiefs of the Football Association of Ireland met on the night of October 15. As they gathered, the betting among the experts was that within an hour or so they would emerge with the news that they felt certain it was going to freeze so hard on Tuesday and Wednesday that Dalymount Park would be reduced to the consistency of permafrost, so that it would be best to cancel the match now. What in fact happened was that with one single dissentient vote – that of the official representative of the Army Athletic Association, who explained that as a serving Army officer he must oppose – the Association voted that the match go on. One eminent speaker gained nearly unanimous applause for the statement – audacious and original considering the countries concerned – that this was a 'match between two sporting nations who are members of the European Football Federation and are not interested in religion or politics'.

Cocking a firm snook at the Archbishop and the Department of Justice, Mr Leo Clery, the representative from Leinster, said it would be 'a sorry day for Ireland when visiting players and officials are asked their politics or religion'.

The general public heard of the Archbishop's protest and the Football Association's decision more or less simultaneously. And the effect was nearly as palpable as an electric shock; not just in Dublin but all over the country. I could feel it in Youghal and the City of Cork, and people who were scattered about the country at the time have told me, even two or three years later, that this same stimulating shock was experienced wherever they were. In a few hours the match had been transformed from a game of soccer into a kind of demonstration, a small declaration of independence. Newspaper reporters and numerous others who went to Dalymount Park that Wednesday have described to me the odd exhilaration of the event. The score of the Yugoslav National Anthem had been quietly bootlegged from the Army Band to a small group of entertainers in Dublin who, after some hectic eleventh-hour rehearsal, had made a recording of it which was played over the public address system at the Park. The Yugoslav team received a roaring ovation, more sustained than the welcome normally given to a visiting team. But the loudest cheers of all came at a moment when normally there is no cheering – the moment, that is to say, when Mr Oscar Traynor, T.D., President of the Football Association of Ireland, appeared in the stadium. That was an unscheduled and spontaneous outburst. Nobody present had any doubt of its significance. Outside the ground a man carrying a Papal flag walked up and down in solitary protest. And inside, the match – which the Yugoslavs won 4–1 – was watched by a crowd which included several thousand people who had never seen a soccer match in their lives and probably will never see another; unless, of course, someone, perhaps an Archbishop, tries to get it stopped.

Mr Inchegeelagh, who had taken one of the excursion trains from Cork to view an event which he rightly judged to have a certain historic importance, described it to me with pride and enthusiasm. For this conversation took place at the moment of another uproar centring on Archbishop McQuaid, with the Archbishop this time emerging the winner against the ill-organized and often mutually warring cultural forces of Dublin in a noisy brawl which resulted in the ignominious last-minute cancellation of Dublin's internationally publicized Theatre Festival. To hear some people tell it – and they were honest people who truly thought that the Archbishop, perhaps in revenge for Dalymount Park, had deliberately struck Irish culture and Irish prestige a shattering blow behind the ear – the Hierarchy had on this occasion justified everything that a man like the Education Minister in Belfast was apt to say about it. The facts, Mr Inchegeelagh pointed out, supported no such allegation. All they proved was that some of the Festival organizers were damn fools, and some of them cowards. And it looked much as though there might have been some *provocateurs* at work somewhere. For what had actually happened was that, as the star attractions for the Festival, these organizers had chosen the Joyce adaptation *Bloomsday*, and Sean O'Casey's *Cock-a-doodle Dandy*. And then, at some meeting just before the opening of the Festival, some person or persons had suggested that it would be a nice thing indeed if Archbishop McQuaid were to lay on a Votive Mass as a kick-off for the entire enterprise.

Perhaps whoever was originally responsible for this suggestion was a mere damn fool, or perhaps he had some other ploy in mind. For the result was predictable, and more discreditable to the Festival Committee than to the Archbishop. Until asked to arrange this Votive Mass the Archbishop may possibly have had his 'regrets' about the way culture was moving, but had swallowed them in silence. Whether he welcomed the opportunity for breaking this silence which was afforded by the request for the Votive Mass is not known. But the opportunity was offered and seized. Naturally, the Archbishop explained that he did not feel able to offer this degree of Hierarchial support and approval to a Festival containing works such as those of Joyce and O'Casey. And having said that much, he had an excellent chance to make clear just what was his own opinion of the character of the Festival as planned.

In the ensuing uproar the organizers – who were now in grave trouble with everyone from the Knights of Columbanus to the *Irish Times* and Sean O'Casey himself – clapped their hands over their ears and ran away in all directions, babbling and finally declaring the whole undertaking cancelled.

Why anyone should have supposed that the Archbishop would accede to the request regarding the Votive Mass is mysterious. Would anyone expect the Secretary, say, of the Moscow District of the Communist Party to organize a solemn meeting to usher in a Theatre Festival in Moscow of which the highlights were to be plays by prominent opponents or deriders of the Communist Party? And over and above that question, since a good many British critics and drama-lovers joined loudly

in the contemptuous outcry against the censored state of the
Irish theatre, just how far would you get with a London Theatre
Festival featuring, for example, a pantomime designed to take
the mickey out of the Queen and the Duke of Edinburgh? The
smugness with which some of the British – notably on the Left
– treat Ireland does little enough harm to the Irish, but fatally
rusts and corrodes the judgement of those critics themselves.

29

THE DEVIL BUSINESS

IN the passive detachment of the hospital, the skeleton, as it
were, of propaganda is apt to show up as though X-rayed. And,
like the human skeleton seen on an X-ray photograph, it shows
up as a depressingly primitive, ill-fashioned bit of work; unless
it be that the most primitive, nearly idiotic, type of propaganda
is really the best. I have, for instance, always been interested in
what one may call the Devil-need, the Devil-shortage, and the
Devil-supply. Every cause needs a Devil who will bring ruin to
that Cause unless everyone drops whatever he is doing and
rallies unsparingly to the support of the leaders of the Cause.
Ideally, the Devil has to be immensely big and strong – a real
Goliath. And only if all the little Davids put in some real home-
work on their sling-throwing can we hope to defeat him. If the
Devil is visibly only about three feet high and puny, then there
are only two things to be said: either he is not actually the top-
devil but only an agent and catspaw, or else he is very, very
cunning – devilish cunning. Even so, during that tubercular
summer, I have to admit I was fascinated to note that the British
press and radio, with the guidance, naturally, of 'official spokes-
men' was actually making a sporting effort to get the customers
to view Iceland as an acceptable Devil and not laugh when the
Icelandic Government was trundled on to the stage of the
melodrama in this guise.

Iceland was the most remarkable of all Devils which performed on the earphones that year, and there were quite a lot
of them. Iceland, it suddenly became apparent, was menacing

poor little old England in a truly devilish manner which called for truly heroic, neo-Elizabethan action by the British Navy against the Armada of Icelandic trawlers. To the student of Devil-manufacture, the case was particularly rich in interest because Iceland turned out to have both the qualities essential in the Devil who is no Goliath, to the eye of the uninstructed. It was a catspaw-Devil, with Big Devil Russia pulling its strings. It was also an independent little Devil, but so wickedly cunning that – unless we could act with sufficient speed and ruthlessness – it could walk up and down in the earth rousing the 'opinion of small nations' against us.

One must judge the Devils this or that factory produces not solely by their ultimate effect but by their quality, their workmanship, indicating the degree of true craftsmanship that went into the making of them. Any ham-fisted tinker can fashion a Devil out of Russia or the United States. But Iceland, now; there's artistry. Among other Devils of the Year we had Archbishop Makarios, who had quite a long run in the part until he had to quit the role in order to appear, at the next performance, as the Moderate, or Shrewd Conciliator and true spokesman of the Cypriot people. Colonel Nasser played the Devil even longer, and was the more execrated inasmuch as when we abruptly attacked his country with bomb, shell and bayonet, he neither fought nor fled, but simply waited for something untoward to befall us, which it certainly did.

A few months after I had come out into the world beyond the hospital, the Devil-situation in the Middle East had become uncomfortably confused. There were times when there seemed to be either too many Devils or too few. This was brought sharply home to me one night when I was dining in London with a former M.P. and the Foreign Editor of one of our great national newspapers. It was the night of the Mosul revolt against the new Government of Iraq under Colonel Kassem. The Foreign Editor arrived very late for dinner, but fully justified himself by bringing us this bit of news. What, we eagerly asked, did it all mean? How did the correspondents on the spot assess the situation? The Foreign Editor was agreeably candid. 'The trouble,' he said, 'is that at this moment our man in Baghdad is in Beirut.'

He had requested, from the man currently, and so unfortunately, in Beirut, a 'profile' of the Colonel who was understood to be leading the revolt. Disappointingly, the man in Beirut had to report that nothing, but absolutely nothing, was known of this Colonel beyond his name. Nobody even knew what he looked like – let alone what he had ever done, or on behalf of whom or what he had done it. In the circumstances it was evidently going to be necessary to paint whatever word-picture of the Colonel seemed desirable and necessary in London. To make bricks without straw at such moments of crisis is part of the craft and the duty of the journalist who does not wish to let the public down. But in this case there was a serious difficulty. Was this Colonel a little Devil, sinister instrument of heaven knows what Big Devils in the background, or was he, perhaps, not a Devil at all, but at least an amateur angel? It was a question essential to decide before so much as a sentence could be written about him. After a good deal of careful thought I suggested, and the Foreign Editor agreed, that the best that could be done was to prepare at least two sets of phrases descriptive of the fellow, and then hope that something would come through from Beirut or Baghdad enabling the paper to plump for one or the other. Evidently the type of adjective properly used in the description of a Devil is quite different from that suitable to an angel – and only the correct adjective will automatically tip off the reader's heavily conditioned subconscious as to which the man really is.

It was our consensus that there must be one version of the story which stated something to the effect that 'tough, swarthy, fast-moving Colonel So-and-So' was the man in charge of the operation. No reader could doubt that such a man was, if not actually an angel, at least on the side of the angels – our side in fact. Tough, swarthy and fast-moving are all essentially good things to be, and we are happy to have such a man standing up for our interests. Alternatively, one must be ready, at the flash of a news agency dispatch, to describe this trouble-maker as 'ruthless, sallow, trigger-happy Colonel So-and-So'.

Hours after dinner, long after the Foreign Editor had returned to his office and we judged he had had sufficient time to find out where this equivocal Colonel stood in relation to Devil Kremlin and Devil Cairo, we rang up and asked whether the man turned out to be tough or ruthless, swarthy or sallow, fast-moving or trigger-happy. The news was depressing. No one knew, even now, at half past one in the morning, whose side the man was on. However, there was a brighter side to the situation – whatever he was up to, one certain thing about him was that he was now dead. He had ceased to need any adjectives at all.

For the connoisseur of Devil-manufacture, the Russian product lacks interest. The tendency is to turn out and test a prototype and, on this proving satisfactory, to proceed with and continue the output of a small range of reliable Devils of simple design over a longer period of time than would be thought desirable in the West, where the public demands a much greater variety in design, and is avid for new models.

Is the cosy significance of all this, then, that there are no real Devils about? Not so. The trouble is that while people are ooh-ing and coo-ering at the synthetic ones, the real ones are uninterruptedly busy with the pitchforks and brimstone. Just as the faithful were rejoicing at the downfall of Yellow Devil Japan in 1945, the news began to leak that the real Devil that people had to be frightened of was the one that jumped out of a plane over Hiroshima a couple of weeks earlier.

Dominant among the strident noises of the world that seeped, muted, into the hospital that summer was the noise of people everywhere awakening to the realities of the H-bomb. That was a great day indeed when the Archbishop of Canterbury felt impelled by this same noise to utter his word on the subject. It was a sage word, too, for the chief of the established Church which, in wars and preparations for wars, is expected to provide the State with a full orchestra of tom-toms. On the other hand, there is the poxy business of simultaneously filling the church pews, which could involve some appeal to people who like to think there might be some difference between the attitude of Jesus of Nazareth and that of the P.R.O. at No. 10 Downing Street. As the poet Lowell put it:

> We was getting on famously down in our village
> With good old ideas of what's right and what ain't.
> We kinda thought Christ was agin war and pillage,

343

And that epaulettes warn't the best mark of a Saint.
But John P
Robinson he
Says all that kind of thing's an exploded idee.

The Archbishop of Canterbury met the problem with a more radical and far-reaching proposition. He suggested that perhaps the destruction of the human race by the H-bomb or some even more efficient agency of the kind was 'part of God's plan for the world'. He had other words of comfort too (and, listening to them, I found the sense of attending some bizarre burlesque show, or mad pantomime, almost overpowering). He pointed out that there is a lot of horror and suffering in the world anyway, and implied that to worry over much about the consequences of the H-bomb was in some way unfair to the victims of other forms of human suffering. He seemed of the opinion that there is only a limited supply of human energy available for the alleviation or prevention of suffering, and that anyone who draws more than his ration of energy to avert the H-bomb catastrophe is committing an injustice towards those starving on the streets of Calcutta or mutilated in a motor smash on the Portsmouth road.

Naturally, a prelate in the Archbishop's position can, within very wide limits, write his own ticket as to what is in the mind of God. It is permissible, theologically, for him to assert that God may be scheming to have the human race blow itself up. Less clear, and perhaps a mite worrying to the faithful, is the question whether, in these circumstances, the proper role of Christ's Ministers is to lend a hand in pushing God's plan along wherever they see a chance, by word or deed, to speed up the outbreak of atomic war, or whether they are justified in sitting quiet and just letting God do it. Brooding in my glassy cubicle on the character and policy of Dr Fisher's God, I recalled a more sympathetic interpretation of the Deity which had enchanted me many years before when it was advanced by the young son of my late friend Geoffrey Pike, that sad genius who zig-zagged across the 1930s like forked lightning and became, almost at last, one of the great Backroom Boys of World War II.

Many years before all that, after some unusually sharp financial vicissitude involving the loss, in stock market speculation, of a considerable, though very temporary, fortune, this literally restless man was living with his son, aged about twelve, in a hut or caravan at the bottom of the Devil's Punchbowl. On the son displaying what are vaguely called 'literary leanings', Pike, taking the view that if you want to write books you ought to know how to print them, provided the boy with a hand printing press. The boy got to work, and after some time wrote and personally set up in print a small book. What was the book about? It was about, he said, God. Pike, who was the son of some Edwardian Cabinet Minister and highly connected in all directions, took occasion to write to a number of selected Bishops, announcing his son's achievement. In these days when young people were showing such a lamentable indifference to religion, was it not indeed heartening that a representative of what might be called the Youngest Generation, should have applied himself to such a task? It was the boy's intention to strike off a number of copies for private circulation. What better than that the little work should be prefaced by a few words of interest and commendation by one or more Bishops of the Church? One or two – I forget exactly how many – Bishops responded to this appeal with enthusiasm, and their expressions of approbation for the project were set up by way of preface.

Their enthusiasm was doused when they received their copies of the work. The twelve-year-old had brooded long on the problem of God's personality and behaviour. After a great deal of painful cogitation – for he determinedly believed that there certainly was a God – he had come up with an explanation. He had been brought up in an academic, Oxonian and Civil Service atmosphere, and it was in all the talk about Oxford and the Indian Civil Service which he had at one time and another overheard, that he found his clue.

His thesis, as expounded in his little volume, was that the gods who have charge of the various worlds, including our own, are appointed roughly according to the degree of their success in the Final Honours examinations at some University – attendance at which is a *sine qua non* for aspirants to god-status. Some of them came through with First Class Honours. Others received only the equivalent of a Second in Greats. And there were those with Thirds and Fourths, too. Naturally, the plums, the best worlds, went to those with the highest Honours. And these brilliant gods, eggheads yet with highly disciplined minds, were naturally capable of giving the worlds in their charge a really competent administrative service. After a long cool look around, the twelve-year-old concluded that what we had was a God who had scraped by with a Fourth – and lucky to get anything better than a Pass at that. Naturally, he could not be expected to be very bright. Naturally, under his bumbling supervision, things were constantly going awry, and the bemused fellow was left scratching his head in bewilderment as his Province repeatedly erupted into wars in which millions died. It was pitiable, opined the boy author, to think of the scenes in Heaven when our God was 'called home for consultation' and there hauled over the coals for his failure to deal adequately with a complex human situation which he was in no way equipped to understand. The lad's attitude was throughout benign, and his final appraisal of the situation may have given comfort to any of the Bishops who were interested in a Christian approach to the matter. For he pleaded for a better understanding of our poorly-equipped God, for less carping criticism of One who, though the consequences of His ineptitude might be malignant, was not Himself malign. While recognizing, as we could hardly avoid doing, the faults and weaknesses of the Divine Ruler, we should cooperate with Him and with one another in an effort to mitigate our situation as inhabitants of a third-rate world, worthy only of a third-rate God.

The sad little sack of a God postulated by the twelve-year-old, seemed at the worst a more endearing figment of the imagination – and the product of a pleasanter imagination – than the Planner of general doom conjured up by the Archbishop. However, it was reassuring to learn that the alarmed outcries of the flock had at least been sharp enough to elicit from him this piece of theological speculation. It probably came as news to quite a number that on this occasion God, such a help in ages past, might have cast His sheep in the role of the Gadarene swine.

I have to admit that a good many of my visitors from England brought into the hospital a complicated way of thinking about the H-bomb and all that it implied which was quite foreign to the general atmosphere of the place. It was tempting to draw some moral from the contrast between the straightforward, invulnerable attitude of a score or so of manual labourers in the ward, with the tortuosities and hesitations of some of these political men from England. Indeed, it is always tempting to suppose that the relatively simple are of more worth in the world than the relatively complex. Unfortunately, it is in general true that the simple, capable of viewing the issue with absolute candour and clarity, are in general too simple to be capable of taking any action whatever. The activists at least act. But lacking simplicity they are in ever-present danger of imitating the sage in the rhyme – 'the philosopher Hegel pursued Truth like a beagle, but he ran so much faster that he sprinted right past her.'

Still, after years in Ireland and months in this Irish hospital, it was truly astonishing to be visited by men very active in Labour politics in England, still wondering whether 'unilateral nuclear disarmament' were 'possible'. Mr Inchegeelagh, who, like perhaps too many Irishmen, enjoyed seeing people pontificating out of the backs of their necks, used to enjoy these encounters richly. For the most part he enjoyed himself in silence, but from time to time, when his liver was acting up, he would be moved to address my friends.

'Not blabbing any secrets,' he would say, 'let me just tell you that you don't need to worry any more about whether unilateral disarmament by one country alone is possible. It's happened. It's happened here. The Irish Republic, sir, has voluntarily re-nounced the manufacture of the H-bomb, and it is a pleasure to inform you that on the day I learn that the Irish Government proposes to spend one penny of the money I pay in taxes on the production of that weapon, I shall see the inside of a jail before they see any more of my money.'

At this point, the visitor would as often as not goggle and slightly giggle and seek to pass on to some point which could possibly complicate the affair out of all recognition in the way that politicians do when you ask them to take their minds out of the pigeon-hole and dust them off.

But you cannot so easily escape a fact, even when it is a small

347

fact, like Ireland. There are many other examples in the world of successful neutralism – Mexico is a notable one among them. But, if the British Left is looking for an example near home, then Ireland is the nearest and the least easy to look away from. Ireland does not have an H-bomb, does not want an H-bomb, and would not build an H-bomb if the World Bank offered her a billion dollars to do so.

Yet this, according to a huge and heterogeneous collection of opinions solemnly enunciated elsewhere – and notably in London – is a situation which simply cannot exist. Or, if the hypothetical possibility of its existence be admitted, then the consequences of such a situation – a situation of effectively total disarmament – must be fatal for the nation which permits itself to fall into so helpless a posture. For a start, it will lose all influence in the counsels of the nations – it will be incapable of imposing its will on others. It will go naked into the conference chamber. And to go on with, it will be the powerless prey of invaders from other nations who have been prudent enough to devote a really noble proportion of their national income to the maintenance and extension of their armaments.

If Ireland were on the other side of the moon, or even on the other side of the world, such arguments in the mouths of English thinkers of the Left might be just barely intelligible. But Ireland is here next door. A really grave myopia or astigmatism is required to overlook it. And to anyone looking at it, and the other positively neutral countries on the one hand and Britain on the other, some facts are apparent which could soothe the agitations and fears of those who think themselves on the road to collapse unless they spend the better part of their income on armaments which will never be big enough to be effective and which they are unlikely ever to get a chance to use, except in very minor games of cops and robbers.

This stuff about the 'nation's voice in the world's counsels' is clearly discernible from Ireland as the purest guff. If it means that nobody at, say, the United Nations pays attention to the opinions and proposals of a small, unarmed nation such as Ireland, then it is demonstrably untrue. On at least three occasions during the past couple of years, the attitude of the Irish delegation – notably in the matter of the discussion of the admission of China to the U.N. and in the question of Tibet – has, admittedly, and of record, crystallized the opinions and rallied the support of a wide range of delegates.

If the fact of Ireland taking a leading part in the demand that the admission of China be discussed was without weight or importance, then it is curious that there should have been such a hubbub about it, and such excitement amid the members of the 'China Lobby' of Chiang Kai-shek. Things got so that Cardinal Spellman himself was approached and urged – with no reluctance, it may be supposed on his part – to tell the Irish where they got off. For the China Lobby, too, was under the impression that the Irish Government is run by the Hierarchy, so that a light word from the senior Prince of the richest section of the Roman Catholic Church in the world would no doubt bring the erring Irish to their senses. Cardinal Spellman promised to do what he could, and, as luck and the calendar of Saints would have it, was able to fly to the Lourdes Anniversary on the same day that Mr de Valera appeared at the solemn opening ceremony of that festival. In this most Catholic atmosphere the Cardinal reasoned with the then Premier of Ireland. I have been told that the Cardinal was more than a little amazed to find that that light word he had been commissioned to speak was not going to be enough. Huffed, he continued to press upon Mr de Valera the notion of how scandalous it was for Holy Ireland to be publicly urging at the U.N. a policy which could end in the advancement of the interests of Red China. Mr de Valera explained the basis of Irish policy on this issue, and then, perhaps detecting on the face of the Cardinal an expression of outraged authoritarianism, remarked casually enough, 'Of course, you'll recall that I've already been excommunicated once in my life.'

If on the other hand someone wants to state that Britain, on account of its armament expenditure, can impose its will on other nations in respect of any matter regarded by the United States or Russia as of vital interest or importance, then it is also untrue. And paradoxically Ireland, this small, unarmed, physically helpless nation, enjoys in many respects a greater freedom of action and manoeuvre than Britain does.

Or perhaps it is not truly paradoxical, for the basis of this situation is logical enough and it helps to explain some of

349

Britain's current neuroses and *malaises*. You listen to a British statesman, Conservative or Labour – it makes no difference – trying to say something about almost anything, and you immediately experience the kind of sensation you get watching some senescent entertainer in the juggling or conjuring line, who was once proficient but knows now that the act has really got beyond his powers, but he has to keep on with it because he has to pay the rent and this is the only thing he knows how to do. His jaunty smile does not quite conceal the fact that he knows that tonight, or tomorrow night or some night soon he is going to bean himself, amid general ridicule, with one of those Indian clubs, or there will be a weasel in the hat instead of a rabbit, or he will, by accident, really saw the young lady in half and the police will come for him. And just because the awareness of these potential calamities makes him nervous, the cards really do fall out of his sleeves before he is ready. The British statesman finds it's nearly impossible to make a simple statement – even a simple lie – about anything because if he says that, obvious though it may be, it might annoy Tom, embarrass Dick or raise merry hell with Harry. He is worrying so much about what he calls the repercussions that he can scarcely give you the time of day without wondering what effect such a disclosure might have in Kenya, or Malaya, or Kansas City, or Bonn. There is, or rather there appears to him to be, absolutely nothing he can straightforwardly say which might not inadvertently pull the plug on himself and flush him and his whole box of tricks round the bend and down the drain. And it is precisely his nervous awareness of this, and his determination to say nothing which could possibly have such an effect which, in his own eyes, makes him a statesman and distinguishes him from the terrible horde of the 'irresponsible'.

In the brief historical interlude during which Britain not only had an Empire, but the material means to maintain it, and to impose the will of the British ruling class upon subordinates and rivals, statesmanship did not chiefly consist of this nice perception of Browning's 'vista of horrible eventualities past calculation to the end of time'. A person could speak his mind, call a spade a spade. And no doubt, in the unsteady jog-trot of history a point will be reached when British statesmen – having cut themselves and their ideas down to size – will be able to do it again as Irish statesmen can today, without fear of tipping some crazy pyramid of apples from the cart into the gutter.

For one pathetic aspect of our decrepit performer is that nearly half the time his fear of repercussions is groundless, for the sufficient reason that a good many members of the audience have stopped eyeing his antics with any keen kind of interest, and certainly are not hanging on his words the way they used to do. In considerable areas of the world what the British have is not so much power as nuisance value. (A nuisance value which, if recognized for what it really is and not confused with power, can be applied to very good and fruitful ends.) The people of those areas know it, and many millions of British people know it; but too many statesmen continue to talk as though they still exercised controls which really are no longer within their grasp, and meditate on decisions which are no longer theirs to make. They maunder on about the pros and cons of 'quitting Egypt' or 'standing pat in Cyprus' just as though the final choice lay with them, whereas it is regularly demonstrated that if the locals eventually decide to kick them out, kicked out is what they will be.

Sainte-Beuve, in his wonderful essay *Les Regrets* – a warning to those who fail to 'wind their watches every day and keep them at the right time' – remarks that it is difficult for people to 'get over not having any longer to govern the world'. It is particularly difficult for the British, since their power-position has not been blown sky-high by any single cathartic eruption, but rather has been undermined and eroded in a process continuing over four decades. In consequence they still keep believing they have responsibilities and potentialities which they really do not have and could not exercise or exploit if they had them.

The country has grown too small for its boots.

Nobody can be truly happy if his boots are the wrong size, and this is true of classes, communities and nations no less than of individuals, sometimes jammed into overtight footwear, sometimes incommoded by boots as cripplingly huge as those of the old cabman whose slithering hobble along Kennington Road originally inspired Charlie Chaplin's choice of outfit. It is these boots, relics of a wardrobe fitting for what was really a different society in a different era, which so often give a clownish air to British policy. Ireland, and – to judge by the printed record of what goes on – Mexico, are countries whose boots are approximately of the right size.

Apart from the self-evident political and moral considerations involved, the real anguish, bitterness, and fury aroused in Britain by the Suez affair was caused just by the realization that wherever we were trying to go, we certainly had the wrong boots.

I used to hear a Jewish story in New York about a man who is in a barber shop getting shaved when another man dashes into the place yelling 'Schulz! Schulz! Rush! Hurry! Your place is on fire! Your wife! Your poor miserable children! Ai-ai-ai! But hurry!' The man in the chair leaps up with a shriek, gashing his cheek against the razor, and dashes into the street with the blood flowing from him and the towel still round his neck. He pounds along to the tenement where he lives, pounds up the four flights of stair to his own door. Just as he reaches it he stops, panting. 'Hell,' he says, 'my name ain't Schulz.' It is hard for a country like Britain, after so many recent changes in its world status, to remember at all times just what its name is, as of the present time. It hears the cry 'Schulz! Schulz! You need an H-bomb!' and goes pelting down the road without stopping to reflect that maybe its name ain't Schulz.

Lenin, as everyone knows, said that 'freedom is the recognition of necessity' – the recognition, that is, of those realities within which it is necessary to exist and operate. It is in this sense that Ireland – and other countries which do not try to live, as the saying used to go, 'above their station', or keep up with the Joneses, are more free, more independent, than Britain.

Disgusted by this view of the situation, which they chose to consider perverse, my English visitors would switch to the other aspect of the 'impossible' Irish situation. What did it feel like to be helpless? Physically and materially helpless, that is? What would happen if the Russians invaded – or, for example, the Americans decided to take you over as an indispensable rocket base or something of the kind? What could you here in Ireland hope to do about that? The answer, of course, is 'absolutely nothing'. But then the answer is exactly the same if these hair-raising questions are applied to Britain. The only difference is that in the case of Britain one part of the question is not at all hypothetical. The country is already used by the Americans as a base. A majority of British people are certainly uneasy about the situation, and a considerable minority actively opposed to its continuance. But just as soon as the matter is seriously raised, the ugly flood-lighting has to be flicked on for a moment in order to illuminate for one and all the degree of freedom of manoeuvre and independence we actually have. The repercussions, it seems, of a request to the Americans to go away and do their stuff somewhere else would be shocking, absolutely shocking. The mere suggestion sets the mind of the statesman-like statesmen quivering like a jelly, and the political conjurer starts pulling the flags of the N.A.T.O. nations out of the seat of his pants as a distraction. High on the peeling façade of our floodlit monstrosity we discern, briefly, a sharply-carved list of Our Commitments – which, on inspection, proves to be a list of the IOU's we have been compelled to issue in order to maintain our standard of life among the international Joneses. Default on one of those, and the Joneses will never speak to us again.

This frightened gibberish is not only humiliating but misleading as to facts and consequences. General de Gaulle made a gesture of independence in this sphere, abruptly telling the Americans that France was France and intended to control its own bases. The predictable result was that the Americans immediately became more deferential and wary of him. In the international circumstances, it is richly laughable to watch the British – of all people – pointing with sorrow or derision to the supposed *folie de grandeur* of General de Gaulle. It would seem from the record of the Free French in the outcast days in London, and the record of the General's policy towards Algeria – that here is a man who, whether his policies are proved in the long run successful or not, at least has a perfect understanding of what size he and France, take in boots. He has given repeated proof of his capacity to 'recognize necessity' – an act which some people imagine to be in some sense passive. The contrary is true. If freedom is to result from that recognition, then the recognition must involve activity, the active operation, and maximum exploitation, of the real possibilities.

Do we want the City of Cork blown up by a Russian rocket? No indeed. Shall we view with equanimity the descent of twenty thousand Red Army parachutists on the race course at the Curragh? Certainly not. But by now there is a fair extent of agreement among the *cognoscenti* – including such impeccable non-Comms as the Military Correspondent of *The Times* – that all the money and effort Britain spends on armaments, atomic and otherwise, all the sacrifices of independence which she makes to the United States, do not, in fact, render Edinburgh or Epsom Downs any more secure than are the cities and wide open spaces of Ireland. Britain just spends more to achieve the same degree of total insecurity. And in totting up the cost, one might find that the loss of independence is a more truly damaging item than the waste of cash, time, and manpower. For what this means is that the emergence of a Britain suitably shod for the time of era, a Britain with some kind of coherent and integrated personality is hereby delayed. Delayed, I mean, not only by that dependence on America which is 'necessary' only on the assumption that we want to cut an international dash on a scale beyond our means. I mean that Britain's true independence and chance to develop a new personality – there have, after all, been several absolutely distinct British personalities even since Dr Arbuthnot invented John Bull – is hampered and strangled by all those who would rather play costume charades than learn how to act in the real international theatre. And only some sourly anti-British character, or one deceived by the superficialities of current British politics or bewildered by the temporary national schizophrenia could doubt either that the emergence of such a personality is possible, or that if tiny, unarmed, but philosophic and purposeful Ireland can carry some weight in the world's counsels, Britain, discarding its Chaplin boots, could carry a lot more.

Ezra Pound, in one of the Cantos, says 'Wars? Men start them that couldn't build a good henhouse.' Anyone reading historical memoirs, ancient and modern, can see the large element of truth in that. Personal experience has often forced me to the same conclusion about many enterprises other than war. Once in New York I was temporarily called in to act as an 'adviser' on certain European affairs to an outfit – an investment trust – having at its disposal literally tens of millions of dollars with which it proposed to gamble on the ups and downs of the then sharply fluctuating European exchanges. Expensive experts were sent expensively to Paris, Amsterdam, Berlin, Warsaw and points south. To protect itself against the villainy of rivals – one would not put bribery of telegraph officials beyond them – the experts were provided with a code in which to transmit their so valuable information. The code was in terms of vegetables – 'leeks', for example, meaning gulden, or 'cabbage' the Polish zloty. The first cable arrived. It said the cabbage crop was in poor shape. That seemed to mean that the Trust should sell zloty short. But then it appeared that these men of genius had lost – somewhere up on the 66th floor of the Manhattan Bank building – their own copy of the code. Nobody could recall whether 'cabbage' meant zloty or Austrian krone or what. Such, however, is the resilience of our financial system that the Trust made a packet of money just guessing that 'spinach' meant 'dinars' and so on. They would buy for a rise, or sell short, in millions. This operation was so 'secret' that half Wall Street knew of it within a few hours. Other firms followed suit, with the result that the sheer weight of buying or selling from New York made the hoped-for change come true.

I was constantly reminded of the ramshackle way in which quite considerable enterprises are conducted, when round about the early fifties, I twice spent some time in London working – very profitably for myself – on newspapers which did not fold or fail for the reason that they never appeared at all. For a time I was co-editor with Maurice Richardson of a mighty new weekly called *Seven Days*. Even the advertisement manager approved the final 'dummy' when he saw it, and the circulation experts said they could sell three million a week of a product like that. Then, according to the Manager, the proprietor's wife vetoed the project on the ground that its 'tone' (acerbic to scurrilous) could injure her advance up the slopes of the upper classes and prevent her becoming a friend of Princess Margaret. Later, I was Diplomatic Editor of a costly affair called the *Sunday Star*. There was a large staff, headed by that journalist of genius the gay yet very serious Reverend Marcus Morris, creator of *Eagle*. We produced a 'dummy' every week for many weeks, and were very well paid for it. Then it emerged that the proprietors had forgotten to get an agreement about the distribution of the new paper. The retail newsagents wanted an increase in their commission on the amount they were getting from existing Sunday newspapers. The Newspaper Proprietors' Association stated it would expel the proprietors from its midst, and ruin the paper from the start by refusing it admission to the newspaper trains, if it gave in to the retailers. All this could have been ascertained before a penny was spent. As it was, the undertaking had to be quietly abandoned, and I returned to Youghal with a big increase in my bank balance, and no loss of scepticism about the wisdom of those on high in our society.

30

DU CÔTÉ DE CHEZ BOUVERIE

A FEW months later, I got a letter which surprised me not a little – an invitation to write an article for *Punch*, which I had not even dreamed of reading for years. Not only that, but it was signed by my friend Anthony Powell who, it astonishingly appeared, had become *Punch*'s literary editor. A pleasure of living in Ireland is that you can, so to speak, turn England on or off as desired, and at that time I had no knowledge of the volcanic disturbance which started to shake Bouverie Street with the appointment of Malcolm Muggeridge as editor of that publication. Furthermore, had I heard this bit of news it would certainly not have occurred to me that it boded me any particular good. True, I had no intention of writing for *Punch*, but if I had, the appointment of Mr Muggeridge would have seemed to me to rule out any possibility of successfully so doing. For although we had never actually met I had hated him for years. Those were, of course, principally my Communist years when Malcolm Muggeridge had great prominence in our Rogues'

Gallery of men who, for example, had gone to Moscow to bless and stayed to curse; of hardened, obstinate and vicious enemies of Truth and Progress; of particularly able, and, therefore, particularly detestable and dangerous journalistic and literary swordsmen in the ranks of wickedness and reaction. Nor was conflict with Muggeridge in those days restricted to the battle of the typewriters. For he was often deadly active in the affairs of the National Union of Journalists – his activity always directed towards frustrating or defeating some vital activity of our own.

At that time the National Union of Journalists was as a running sore to the anti-Communists of the T.U.C. For the London Branch, being by far the largest in the Union, was at most times able to play a preponderant part in framing the policies of the Union as a whole, and the London Branch, in its turn, was for long periods at a time, dominated by the Communists for the sufficient reasons, first, that the Communists were united in pursuit of various objectives whereas the anti-Communists were in general united only in their anti-Communism, and secondly, that the Communists were the only people who held it as a holy though often irksome duty to attend the Branch meetings. (These were usually held on Saturday afternoons at the St Bride's Institute, in one of the lanes just south of Fleet Street. There are not many drearier meeting halls in that part of London, which is saying a good deal, and in any case Fleet Street on any Saturday afternoon is one of the dreariest places anywhere. Add to this that I personally detest meetings and speeches, and all the business of resolutions and points of order. Naturally, I am entirely aware that all this is of the absolutely indispensable essence of democracy, and that when you attend such meetings you are seeing and taking part in the true life and work of democracy. All the same, I wished profoundly that it were possible for me personally not to have to do that thing.) More than once it had happened to me that my reason for asking to be excused attendance at St Bride's on a given Saturday afternoon had been accepted as valid by the Communist Party leaders, and then, just as I was rejoicing over such a release, the word would come that Malcolm Muggeridge was going to attend that particular meeting, was going to launch some major attack; in consequence all 'leave' was cancelled, no excuses for non-attendance were any longer to be deemed valid. On such Saturdays I looked upon that man with more than ordinary political hostility. I humanly loathed him. In a paradoxical manner he represented all those disciplines of Communism and democracy which I had always found excessively irksome. He embodied for the moment everything that could make life vexatious, particularly on a Saturday afternoon in the desert parts of London.

Knowing nothing of his appointment to the editorship, I was still bewildered by the presence in the literary chair of Anthony Powell whom I had known since Oxford and whose novels, with their exquisite sinuosities and profound risibility had enchanted me for years. What, I had to ask myself, in God's name was *he* doing in that *galère*? And what, admitting that he personally was aboard the sluggish old hulk, on earth made him suppose that *my* presence would be welcome? Just making the matter more mysterious was a note in his letter – he was asking for an article about Ireland – saying that he would like the piece to be 'somewhat astringent'. If he were simply trying to do me a good turn by arranging for me to get a small piece of money out of *Punch*, surely, knowing my general line of literary brew, he would instead have put in some cautionary note urging me to draw it mild?

After a few weeks of writing astringently, Tony mentioned in a letter that if I chanced to be in London in the near future he would be particularly glad to have me call upon him at the *Punch* office. I had arranged a small 'bandit raid' on another quarter of the city, which made it convenient for me to go over almost immediately. I visited the *Punch* office, and spent an agreeable half-hour in the office of the distinguished literary editor. The *Punch* offices have a peculiarly solid, Edwardian air about them which is agreeable enough to the detached observer, but made me a little nervous. I was a great deal more nervous when Tony, who supposed I knew all about it already, incidentally disclosed that the enterprise was now under the guidance of Malcolm Muggeridge. To my further discomfiture, he made the suggestion that we now take a walk down the corridor and visit Mr Muggeridge in person. I positively babbled. I tried, in a few hurried words, to explain the relationship existing between this Muggeridge and myself. I tried to make clear that while it was already incomprehensible to me that Muggeridge should be publishing articles from me – it seemed to me that he must be imagining that I was a different, perhaps an Irish, Cockburn – it was certain that a personal meeting should at all costs be avoided. 'I have every reason to suppose,' I said, 'that he detests me as deeply as I detest him. Let us keep this whole thing as far as possible in the old boy net – let me deal exclusively with yourself. A meeting with Muggeridge can end only in bitterness and disaster.'

Pooh-poohing and laughing – idiotically, I thought – Tony insisted; in fact he actually held me by the arm and steered me down the passage and into the bugbear's den. Of that first conversation I remember very little, except that it was from the start tumultuous and at the end – hours later – hilarious. Neither of us, I imagine, was much inclined to revise or regret the opinions we had had of one another in the past. For neither of us, I think, enjoys wasting time wondering whether this or that thought or act perpetrated in the past was or was not mistaken. But it is a natural corollary of this attitude – the attitude I mean of a belief that one's past actions were not mistaken but correct – to acknowledge freely that life and situations are fluid, and that a position which it was correct to maintain then may be ludicrously erroneous now. There are, of course, people who believe that to accept this rich fluidity of life is to abandon principles. Many such people are sincere, although I have noticed that a good many who talk most rigorously of 'principle' are in reality too lazy, too nervous or too cold-hearted to recognize the moment when what they think of as their 'principles' have transformed themselves from vehicles of healthy, and even perhaps beneficent, action, into notions about as useful to them or anyone else as a ball and chain round the leg. Certainly, as I remarked earlier, 'the copy-book maxims are true'; and there are times when the thing to do is maintain with the utmost rigour not merely the principle, but the outer – even the verbal – formulation of it. But it is also true, as everyone with any knowledge of religions and creeds well knows, that too often the formulation remains, an unburied corpse, a long time after the spirit, so to say, of the principle has left it and taken up its habitation somewhere else. In my own experience it has always proved a lot easier to stick to a principle than to know when to change it.

Within an hour of meeting Malcolm Muggeridge I was aware that there was the sort of man who, if he caught himself feeling comfortably convinced of anything for a longish period of time, would start ringing alarm bells in his own head and heart; a man who felt immediate guilt on discovering that he was taking anything for granted; that in fact to take anything for granted – even the truth if it were the truth – was more heinous than to spring up with a restless effort and, quite possibly, bound straight into an abyss of error. He was, in fact, an enemy of mental and spiritual placidity, one compared to whom many who believe themselves to have alert, inquiring minds, appear on the contrary sunk in comfortable complacency. Particularly during that early period of his editorship of *Punch* – coinciding with his advance to prominence on TV – he was continuously attacked either for being inconsistent and contradictory in his opinions, or else having no genuine opinions at all. It is, I should think, true to say that he regarded all opinions as being necessarily in a state of more or less violent evolution; and I suspect, too, that he was a good deal less afraid of involving himself in truly frantic contradictions than of getting, as it were, bogged down in some sticky morass of opinion which real life had already left behind. It is this quality which puts him among the relatively few people – though I have been happy in meeting quite a number of them – with whom a genuine conversation can be conducted. For, taking this evolutionary view of the nature of opinions, he positively hopes and desires that the conversation or argument may change his opinions, and has the same hopes and desires about whatever opinions you may start out by expressing.

The quality, almost immediately apparent, took me agreeably by surprise. Dealing with editors and executives and such, I cannot help starting with an assumption that one is not going to be able actually to communicate with them at all. We shall both, I think, boom and babble away, sending streams of words past one another's ears, but it will all be quite irrelevant to what one is really going to do, or write. This has led me into some difficulties. A conversation of that kind must, for the sake of propriety, go on for a certain length of time, for if you sit with such a man for only five minutes and then quit, he feels you have wasted five minutes of his time and resents it. But if you can keep things humming along for a half-hour or so, he is inclined to think that something worth while must have been achieved. It can thus occur that, just for the sake of making a nice atmosphere, you say whatever comes into your head, you speak with seeming enthusiasm about some notion that entered your mind just that minute and will leave it again two minutes later, and next day you get a telephone call from the man saying that he has been thinking deeply about that thing you said and he would like you to get to work on it right away and develop it. If you ask him at that stage what on earth it was you were talking about he is chilled and disappointed.

Malcolm started, after a while, to speak of Jesus Christ. It is of interest that the figure of Christ can still act as a kind of catalytic agent or, so to speak, as a form of introduction between people who are of west European and Anglo-American background but are otherwise strangers or, as in this case, old enemies. A person's reaction to Christ, or the idea of Christ, can still often enough offer a convenient shorthand *précis* of his more general attitude to life and its phenomena. Christians are sometimes even vexed by the fact that this should be so among non-Christians or possibly anti-Christians. But in reality this fact simply emphasizes that the creation and elaboration of the Christ-myth (I use 'myth' in its exact and neutral sense), was a necessity for the Mediterranean, and subsequently European, mind, and was one of its most profoundly characteristic achievements, only equalled – perhaps not even equalled – much later in its formative power by that of Marxism-Leninism. A person who was simply unaware of Marxism-Leninism – not just someone who had never read a line of Marx or Lenin, but one whose consciousness had been somehow sterilized in this respect – would have a difficult time making himself understood or understanding anyone else in the Western world now. This is self-evident. But it is a fact, too, that a similar unawareness of the Christ-myth would in reality though not so apparently inhibit communication. This is not always self-evident to non-Christians, who – sometimes thoughtlessly, sometimes as a result of anti-clerical wishful thinking – under-estimate the role of the Christ-myth in the consciousness of the Western world. (Equally wishful-thinking anti-Marxists, for their part, can make the same kind of mistake.)

Yet the co-existence of these myths in the Western consciousness is a fact of basic importance. For it is this which offers at least a possible prerequisite for the creation by the Western mind of a new myth, higher in the spiral of human aspiration. To overlook or deny this restless co-existence is to suggest that the Western mind has come to a dead end.

Despite my general nervousness, despite, too, the parquet flooring of the *Punch* office with carpets on it, all so very gentlemanly, and the thought that if they tired of the newspaper business the owners could sell this bit of Bouverie Street from right under our eager feet for millions of pounds, I began to have the feeling that with this fiercely gentle, chivalrously ungentlemanly man on the far side of the grandiose editorial desk, jerking and flashing his eyes and from time to time cackling out a cacophony of furiously raucous expressions like a sailor's parrot loose in the Mission Hall, something new and special in the way of clowning and satire might yet be made of this ancient publication, once so rowdy, later so often muffled nearly to the eyes in old school scarves. The room at large was as dead as a whited sepulchre, but you could feel some life crackling behind the desk, as though someone, for a joke, had thrown a fire-cracker into the mausoleum. There were some portraits on the walls, including some horrifying depictions of Edwardian and neo-Georgian *Punch* pundits, sell-outs, some of them, of the type who would suppress a joke or blunt a satire rather than be black-balled at this Club or thrown with contumely out of that one. But, as Malcolm pointed out with pleasure, by just twisting in his chair he could look down into the street half blocked a lot of the time by the great lorries bringing ton after ton of newsprint to the door of the *News of the World*.

The sight of that mammoth across the road was always relevant to our conversation in the *Punch* office because, even in its sedate modern incarnation, the *News of the World* recalls the best scurrilous traditions of the British popular Press, and is in the direct tradition of the first popular newspapers of the mid nineteenth century, born after the abolition of the stamp duty. They, too, were denounced as unseemly, in the worst possible taste, by people who, though they pretended that they were merely interested in raising the moral and political tone of the reading matter offered to the lower orders, were in reality horrified at the notion of the lower orders being able to afford any newspaper reading matter at all. This physical confrontation across Bouverie Street of *Punch* and the *News of the World* was comical, since *Punch* had come to epitomize the aspects and trends in English life most aloofly alien to the tradition of the *News of the World*. Paradoxically – since a newspaper or magazine is about the most public thing you can have – there is almost always a difference between the actual contents of a given publication and the 'image' of it in the public mind. It would really have been out of the question for the numerous brilliant men working on *Punch* long before Malcolm Muggeridge took over to have produced so entirely arthritic a magazine as *Punch* was widely considered to be. On the other hand, it required something in the way of a violent explosion to enable them to break out of the traditions which by then encrusted the paper. It is a great deal to the credit of the owners and particularly of Mr Peter Agnew that they – by their appointment of Muggeridge to the editorship – recognized this fact. Whether they grasped, at that time, just how much dynamite was going to be necessary, or who and what would get blasted in the essential detonation is uncertain. For what we had here was a trouble or dilemma a lot deeper and sharper than the trouble or dilemma of a mere magazine. *Punch* had fallen into its existing condition because of the condition into which the British middle class – or upper middle class, if the phrase is more meaningful – had fallen. Anyone reading the *Punch* of the immediate pre-Muggeridge period can see that the staff-men of that time were repeatedly making efforts to alter that condition. For they – the writers and Mr Agnew – were certainly not at all the type of men who had much sympathy with that other type of man commonly thought of as the 'average *Punch* reader'. Yet, given the situation which had developed over the years, to whom else were they supposed to appeal? Admitting, or merely assuming, that this typical *Punch* addict was a man in retreat from the tide of modern life, halting now and then in his nervous scramble up the beach to throw a bitter pebble at the waves, and cackling with imbecile glee when these waves seemed to be momentarily arrested and deflected by some rotting breakwater, was there any more desirable figure in sight to whom *Punch* might address itself?

What Malcolm had in mind at that time was the possibility – the bare, outside possibility – that the supposed 'revolution' in Britain (a supposition necessary to justify the existence of the Labour Party) really had produced some new ways of thinking, and with them some new hankerings for adult satire. A triviality? A 'marginal' demand perhaps? Perhaps. It was one of the things that had to be found out. There is no law that says people have to laugh. And there were times, sitting there in Bouverie Street, when it looked as though maybe someone had brought in a law telling people not to. Caution, good taste, helpfulness and discretion were all hall-marked on the bottom of the State as it was presented to Britain a few years after the Russians and Americans at last met on the Elbe. And yet, on the other hand, this could not be – it could not be that the British as a whole had gone down the drain with the British upper middle classes. Indeed no, for there they were, bowling up and down Fleet Street between the City and Mayfair in their big cars, richer and happier than ever – the great NEP-men of the 1950s, men to whom if you said 'Right' or said 'Left' it was to them the same thing, which was nothing. And you had to remember that at that period there was a notable tendency among the intellectuals, too, to adopt this 'anti-ideological' position. (And, as is known, by the summer of 1959, the ideology of anti-ideology had become a near-creed of the Western intellectuals. They took whole suites of a German hotel to meet in and discuss it.)

Personally I thought that the trick could be turned, that there were enough people extant to make a living for a rawly satirical paper – a paper which (on the principle I have always held) would write the way people really talk. And if the customers were there at all, then there was no doubt the people at *Punch* given the green light, were entirely capable of meeting the demand.

I think that for about the first two years of his editorship, Malcolm believed this to be a correct estimate of the possibilities. Believing that, he saw too that the prerequisite for success was to make a loud, nasty noise of the kind nobody associated with *Punch*. If the potential customers for a new kind of magazine were lurking anywhere, such a noise would alert them and they would come running.

Inevitably there was some heavy thinking – even among those who favoured the attempt to seek out this potentially existing new public – on the question of whether it was going to be possible to flush enough of the new customers before too many of the old ones cancelled their subscriptions. A good deal was said about the 'retired Colonels in Cheltenham' who, traditionally, were supposed to be the *corps d'élite* of *Punch* readers, and on whose defection the entire position would crumple up in ruin. I argued that, first, there are no retired Colonels in Cheltenham because this great British revolution we understand we have had has changed all that and, secondly, if there are they are lovers of Picasso, members of the Labour Party, and, in many instances, pansies. I was told that the circulation department actually sent a man down to those parts to find out whether this was or was not the case. It may – given the way things are in Fleet Street – have actually happened. I was pestering the Old Guard with my attacks on the Cheltenham syndrome, and since carrying out some kind of poll is the only answer they know to any argument perhaps some man did actually go knocking on doors in Cheltenham and interviewing retired Colonels as to their artistic and sexual tastes. I should have liked to have been there – and it would have made a good article for the new *Punch*.

I cannot recall – because I was back in Youghal at the time – just when Malcolm emitted his first Bronx cheer, his rallying-call to the frustrated lurkers in the underbrush who were going to emerge and say, 'this is what we've been waiting for'. Probably it took a little time to do that, while waiting for the heavy thinking to end. And quite probably, too, that delay was fatal to the really existent possibilities of success. (I am not saying that *Punch* is not a success today – indeed I believe that the circulation is rising from the level at which Malcolm, in his final and furious mood, left it. I am only saying that what we have there now is not the paper that was at that moment envisaged.) I do recall a day when he came to visit me in Ireland and, as he sprang from the train at Limerick Junction, remarked with profound satisfaction, that the issue of the magazine he had just sent to the press was 'likely to get us all into a lot more hot water'. This piece of intelligence encouraged me a good deal as we bowled across the plains of south Tipperary and into the astringencies of County Cork where, unless you want to be made a common fool of, you are on parade and on your toes all day and half the night too. Kitty Muggeridge, Malcolm's wife, received the news with less enthusiasm but with experienced calm. She was a niece of Mrs Sydney Webb, and had, in youth, had a close-up of Fabian politics and then of almost every other sort of politics. She and Malcolm had been together present, for instance, at that summer school in Surrey where H. G. Wells seduced the wife of a fellow-Fabian, who – the husband, I mean – forgave him, in a spirit of freedom and no-prejudice. It was assumed – it was part of the Fabian bargain – that as a result of this forgiveness Wells would see the error of his seductive ways and concentrate more on the lecture showing where Henry George was so wrong. What Wells actually did was to lure the girl-wife into the rhododendron bushes growing very lush in that part of Surrey, and seduce her all over again. A motion was brought in that evening at the meeting of the Society stating that 'in the opinion of this House Mr Wells is a cad'. Naturally it was passed. In the Fabian book a lot of people were cads.

Mrs Webb, Lady Passfield, I conceive to have been one of the most disagreeable women produced by the British race. Malcolm told me once that when he went to stay there – in the pursuit of love, I suppose – she used to order Sydney Webb to go for a walk before lunch because it would be good for his physique. (It was during that period when people still believed that exercise is good for other people. Just now the doctors say it can be nearly fatal.) The great economist and ex-Cabinet Minister used to set off, with Malcolm, at a quick jog, while Mrs Sydney Webb watched from the front door. Then Webb would dodge behind a barn, seize Malcolm by the arm, indicate a nice bundle of hay where reclining could be done, and the two of them would spend the next hour there, talking of Communism and the future of the world. The only disagreeable feature of these expeditions was that the return to the house – a distance of a couple of hundred yards – had to be accomplished at the double, because when Sydney returned Mrs Webb was apt to assure herself that he was genuinely in a sweat – a sweat, she thought, poor woman, such as could only be worked up by the five-mile walk she supposed they had been taking while she was writing her assessment of something or other.

I met her once when I was very young. She and Sydney Webb had just returned from the Soviet Union. On their way back they had visited Trotsky, then in exile on the island of Prinkipo. The Webbs talked Fabianism to the exile. He for his part told them they were talking nonsense. There was no such thing as gradualism in revolution. He declared that Britain would be no exception to the general rule. There, too, the streets would run with blood and the exploiters would be hanged from lamp-posts. And what, someone asked, had the Webbs replied to these assertions? 'We told him *no*,' said Mrs Webb.

As I recall, the cartoon that was expected to heat the water for us that time was a singularly disobliging study of the ageing Winston Churchill, apparently sunk in senile reverie while the affairs of the country went to pot. It had, immediately, the desired effect. Leading Conservative publicists and politicians howled with rage, helping their din to notify one and all that Britain had something a little new in the way of magazines. Inevitably a cartoon of this kind – a kind that, in relation to the Grand Old Man, had been taboo for years – produced a little friction and head-shaking even inside the office. (Equally inevitably we heard from a number of people in Fleet Street and Westminster that this act of bad taste, this stab in the back of the great Leader, had been suggested and promoted by ex-Red Cockburn. It was untrue – I had been hundreds of miles away at the time, and in any case had absolutely no influence on the choice of cartoons. But this rumour, too, was useful – it gave people something to talk about, and increased the amount of verbiage they issued on the subject of *Punch*.)

In the newspaper business compromise is always dangerous. And it was in the nature of the situation at *Punch* that Malcolm was frequently forced to make compromises between his own ideas of what was effective and permissible and the ideas other people had. His own notions often enough appeared outrageous even to some of the members of the staff. I remember a discussion at the office about the cartoon that was to be done on the occasion of the first grave illness of President Eisenhower. The way it finally came out in the paper was as a picture of the sick President, in the role of Moses, having his hands held up by the Republican Party bosses. The way Malcolm had suggested it, the scene was to have been Eisenhower in a hospital bed, with the Republican bosses shown as the clips that are used in hospitals to keep the patient's lips open. It would have made a lot of talk. And it might even have wrung some protest from the American Embassy. But there had to be this compromise – this one and a lot of others. For people always think that by trying to get the best of both worlds they are playing it safe. Excite, they think, new possible readers, but do not unduly offend the old customers. In reality this is about the most dangerous thing you can do. You do not utter a shriek piercing enough to reach the inattentive ears of the new, and yet you give the old the impression that you are not quite as nice as they used to think you.

Despite compromise, the 'new', yellowish *Punch* did make a certain impact – the circulation rose sharply enough in its first few months to seem, in my view, to justify the gamble on the existence of some new kind of public. More oddly, the magazine began to get prestige, snob-value in – of all places – New York. Numerous travellers returned to report that for the first time in magazine history men and women of Manhattan were considering it smart to display *Punch* rather than the *New Yorker* on their drawing-room tables.

Malcolm felt, for a few months anyway, that he had in his hands some sort of sacred flame, something both searing and illuminating. When he thought the glim was being doused by the old, the sour, and the truly bad, how could he – and it is necessary to remember that he was raised a Christian, and had the marks of the Fabian-educated Christian-Socialist, was a child, that is to say, with sunset clouds of hope trailing all about him – how would such a one not be dismayed almost beyond reason by the awful badness of the world?

It is said, and it may even be true, that this atmosphere of hope – the hope of some general improvements in the human condition – is to be regarded as peculiar to certain more or less easily definable periods. The mid-Victorians were supposed to have had it. The socialists of the years shortly before World War I were, too. And people who think of the 1930s as a 'period' accuse the people of the said period of the same general tendency. It may, as I say, be true. Equally it may be true that this attitude to life and history exists in every period among enormous numbers of people, but that it does not always find organized expression – as, for instance, in some political party or movement – or formulation in any kind of philosophy or doctrine. Myself I have the deepest sympathy with the hopeful, although I have never fully shared this kind of hopefulness. But it seems to be a fact that unfounded hopes can generate equally baseless or exaggerated disillusions and despairs.

I am about the same age as Malcolm Muggeridge, and we have often got a lot of pleasure and amusement from contrasting the 'atmospheres' or 'climates of belief' in which we severally grew up. I was raised by and among people who thought there was soon going to be a war; that such a war would be a disaster for civilization; but that, since to win it would be a lesser disaster than to lose it, a main activity of the time must be to prepare vigorously for the conflict.

In childhood I never (to my knowledge) met anyone who thought that the current international rivalries would, or could, be solved by any means short of war. On the other hand I cannot recall anyone in our house suggesting that the coming war was going to be one 'to end war' – still less that it was going to 'save civilization'. On the contrary, it was taken for granted by people like my father and his friends that it would do civilization irreparable mischief. And their general attitude to the situation was that on the one hand one can hope for very little improvement, but that on the other only a sustained and

strenuous effort can prevent a gross and perhaps fatal deterioration. When I became a Communist, it never crossed my mind
that Communism was going to solve all the problems of
humanity. I did not think, even, that it would do more than a
little good here and there. I did think that without it the crack-
up of civilization everyone spoke of was going to occur sooner
rather than later. I saw Communism, that is to say, as essentially
a conservative force – a means of conserving civilized human
values. Nor do I now regard that assumption, or gamble, as
having been merely ludicrous. I still quite often meet people
who tell me, quite sincerely, that they 'simply cannot understand' why or how I should ever have become a Communist.
Their incomprehension can suggest that perhaps they have
never looked closely at their own political faces in the mirror of
our times.

Whatever judgement anyone may make on all that, it is certain that the climate of my childhood – powerfully affected by
a strictly old-fashioned 'classical' education – was one which
was inimical alike to exhilarating hopes and to resignation, not
to speak of cynicism. Very early – and for this both Thucydides
and Cicero were in part responsible – I had assimilated, so to
say, the conviction that every political organization will, as has
often been declared, 'do as much harm as it can and as much
good as it must'. People who consider such an estimate cynical
are people who do not appreciate the implications of that
'must'. It is an imperative to whose force everyone can contribute. Malcolm, for his part, was surrounded in childhood by
people who held true almost everything that my own elders
considered dangerous nonsense. And they – those Edwardian
and early Georgian socialists – had at least as respectable a
justification for the beliefs as did the particular brand of dedicated Tory imperialists who educated me. The only thing all
those people could be said to have had in common was a
passionate belief in something.

People alleged that Muggeridge was 'unconstructive', that he
'hated everyone'. One might observe that in the editor of a supposedly independent satirical magazine these are desirable qualities, and leave it at that. But in reality a successful satirist, or, in
this case, an organizer and director of satire cannot run on the

fuel of hate alone. He has to have something of the quality of Dante in Browning's description – 'Dante who loved well, because he hated, hated wickedness that hinders loving.' And although a lot of television viewers and *Punch* subscribers claimed they saw no signs of it, it was a quality very marked in Malcolm's make-up. He positively loved people unless he thought them fraudulent or cruel. He, too, appreciated the full positive meaning of the aphorism about political organizations doing 'as much harm as they can and as much good as they must'. It was this which made the early days of his editorship exhilarating and gave hope, it seemed, that something new and positive – in the widest sense of the word – was going to develop in British journalism. And it was the fact that the abortive negotiations about the Toronto edition caused him to start seriously wondering whether all such hopes were not, after all, stupid illusions which seemed to me the saddest thing about that little fiasco. After working with him for only a month I had given it as my opinion that the only thing that could go seriously wrong with the new *Punch* was that he would become suddenly bored with it. 'With you,' I told him, 'the tendency to become bored has the quality of a vice.' Being not much subject to it myself – though there have been times now and then when I have suffered desperately – I find it difficult to understand. But I have seen enough of it in other people to conclude that boredom is a factor in life and behaviour which most people underestimate, refusing to take it as seriously as they should. A few years ago I was at a dinner-party at Lord Beaverbrook's, and – as is inevitable and natural – I was assailed with questions from fellow-guests on the subject of what finally had caused me to quit the Communist Party. Truthfully, but perhaps foolishly, I said that although there were all sorts of motivations, I felt bound to admit that probably the most cogent of all was the fact that I was becoming horribly bored. To my perhaps naïve surprise the company was unanimously offended. They felt, quite apparently, that such a reply was in the nature of an insult. I suppose they had consciously or subconsciously desired something that would have seemed to them more grandiose by way of motive for such behaviour. They could not appreciate the compelling force of boredom. And they were left, as I could see, with the impression that I was being either outrageously frivolous or else slyly deceptive. On this subject Edward Crankshaw makes, somewhere, an illuminating point about what might be called the role of boredom as a factor in international affairs. Discussing Russian political attitudes to the West, he suggested – and supported the suggestion with some convincing illustrations – that from time to time the men in the Kremlin get purely and simply bored with the whole business of pretending to think as though they were West Europeans. They find the strain tedious. And when boredom finally overcomes them we witness one of those disconcerting shifts of attitude which the diplomatic commentators find so difficult to interpret. It is certainly, I should judge, part of the truth. And it is related to Professor Wright Mills's exposition, in *The Origins of World War III*, of how, whether in the Pentagon or the Kremlin, the eternal preparation for a war which does not actually happen, the endless preoccupation with an eventuality which is not realized, can produce a state of mind in which those responsible, though they know the war will be suicidal, may be subconsciously longing for war to break out.

Malcolm unreservedly agreed with my early prognostication about *Punch*, and, in a sense, I was astonished that this vice of boredom did not overcome him earlier. But after the Toronto fiasco, I noted that he became increasingly a prey to it. At that time I wrote for *Punch* almost every week – mostly from Youghal. I would telephone him every Monday morning to get from him some proposal for the subject of the article, or to make a proposal myself. We would mull over these proposals for twenty minutes or so, and I would mail him the article on Monday night or Tuesday morning. For a long time these conversations were, as they say, 'constructive', in the sense that I could feel the whole thing coming to life as we talked. Indeed, as often as not, it seemed to me that the piece in its final form owed at least as much to Malcolm as to me. Gradually, however, he showed less and less inclination to talk about material for *Punch*, entertaining me instead with scandalous gossip or Christianity or television. Often, particularly if the long-distance line from Ireland was in poor shape as a result of tempest or other interruption, I would suggest that since we might get abruptly cut off at any minute, we ought perhaps to turn to practical discussion of my next article. 'Hell, my dear boy, I leave all that to you. Write anything you like.' Once, having mailed my weekly piece, I had a little *arrière pensée* and rang him up on a Thursday morning to suggest some small improvements. He sounded bewildered. It then transpired that it had become his habit simply to send the articles over to the printers without reading them. 'It's perfectly all right. I'll read it in galley proof.' Later still he once confessed to me that he found it nearly impossible to start reading any of the articles in *Punch* until the paper was actually in page proof. He had to postpone until the last possible moment paying attention to a matter which had come to bore him so cruelly.

31

PLAGUE

ONE night in London I heard one of my children calling for help. My wife being out at the time I ran to his bedroom, and found that he was calling in his sleep; an effect of nightmare, no more. Yet the immediate impression was frightening. Although there was, as the saying goes, nothing to it, it was an incident which seemed to give a sharply horrid reality to the fears everyone has about children – fears that they will have to call for help and there will be no help one can give, or one will not think of the right help to give until it is too late.

The alarm and depression I then felt continued through some hours, as though it were I that had had the nightmare and, waking, could not erase its impression. Nobody knows quite enough about extra-sensory perception or precognition to be perfectly assured on the subject. But it is a fact that people do have what used to be called a 'premonition of disaster'. I did not think of this as a premonition of anything, but the state of seemingly unmotivated depression was as marked as it would have been if I had actually supposed myself to have received a warning of unpleasant things to come.

We were living at that time in Hampstead because *Punch*

wanted me to be in London for a half year or so, available for production of topical articles and reportage such as could not be written from Youghal. The house was commodious enough and full of convenient mechanical gadgets, including two TV sets and a labour-saving bar in a big semi-basement room at the back. For some reason I had taken an unreasoning dislike to the place on first seeing it from the street, and, once inside I was vexed by a meaningless sense of uneasiness. It was annoying, because I had looked forward to this time in London. I was eager to experiment with numerous projects for *Punch*, and I thought, too, that, being at close quarters, I could sell articles to other papers more easily than I could from Ireland, and should be able to shore up, even perhaps establish on sound foundations, our always tottering financial structure. Nevertheless, I was no sooner in that house than I felt mysteriously less happy than I had expected and intended to be, and this *malaise* continued right through the summer.

Despite the TV which, living normally in the south of Ireland, they had never seen before, and other amusements of London life, the three boys either actively hated London or could make it tolerable for themselves only by spending money like drunken little sailors. My wife, too, though she briefly enjoyed a series of parties, and visits to the theatre, was irksomely cut off from all the creative activity involved in the development of farm and garden, the breeding of horses, the raising of sheep. Also her upbringing had been such that she instinctively imagined that to be in London in August was to indulge a perverse masochism. 'No one', she had always been led to believe, is in London in August, and although, rationally, she agreed that the statement is nonsense, she could not help feeling horror at the prospect, and a conviction that to stay there deliberately in that month would be foolish and injurious to us all. For all these reasons we arranged that at the beginning of the school holidays – the eldest boy was at school in Perthshire, the second one at a preparatory school near Dublin, and the third (then six years old) at a day school beside Hampstead Heath – we should all go to Youghal, and that I, by agreement with *Punch* – would fly back to London for one week in three.

At the last moment we hesitated because of news that a

somewhat abnormal number of cases of polio had been reported in Cork City. We reflected, however, that there were certainly a good many cases in London, too, and that whereas, if things got worse, we could, at home, virtually isolate the children on the farm, in London they must be daily exposed to whatever risks of infection might exist. There was no reason why things should get worse. We set off. It was true that on the boat I heard several conversations among people who were sailing to Cork with the sort of apprehensions you encountered among people travelling to London from the country during the bombing. I thought this the talk of people trying to make life more exciting. Men who always got drunk in the bar of the *Innisfallen* said, that night, that they were drinking as a prophylactic against polio.

The boat docked late, and it was mid-morning before we loaded all the luggage – mountains of it, as there always are when one travels with young children – into a van and packed ourselves into the hired car for the thirty mile run to Youghal. We had to visit a shop in St Patrick Street, the centre of the city, and I was suddenly surprised – pleased, at first – by the ease with which we found parking space in a street where normally it is nearly impossible to park at all. The shop, too, was agreeably empty of pushers and jostlers. I remarked that we seemed to have hit on a lucky day. The driver of the car looked at me with astonishment. 'People are afraid,' he said. 'They're afraid to come into Cork. Business is going to hell. If the epidemic goes on, in a few weeks half the shops on this street will be bankrupt.' Not lingering to buy anything but essentials we drove out into the countryside and home.

Our house stands about one and a half miles outside the town of Youghal. The land – walled garden and four fields – measures a little over thirty-five acres. The Mount Uniac road – a lane, really – passes the gate a hundred yards from the house. There are three farmhouses within a half-mile or so. The house itself is partly encircled by a fast-running stream. We immediately agreed that, for the time being at least, the boys would not visit Youghal at all, which in itself was going to be a small hardship because children, especially if they have spent the term at boarding-school, have a great lust to go into shops and buy things. They feel it the way I used to feel it when I came out of beleaguered Madrid during the Spanish war and reached Barcelona or Toulouse where there were actually goods in the stores. Nearly as vexatious for them was the fact that they were going to be forbidden to bathe in the sea – even, we decided, from the huge expanse of nearly deserted sands a couple of miles over the hill south of the house. I have never found out whether there truly is any connexion between sea-bathing and the incidence of polio, but there was supposed to be, and it is not the kind of thing a person cares to take a chance on. In any case, I believe children are not so excited about sea-bathing as older people think they must be. It is thought, by elders, to be a nearly ideal occupation for boys and girls. This, quite possibly, is a hang-over from the days of 'Doctor Brighton'. Personally, I love to swim in the Mediterranean or on the southern coast of California. Children, told that swimming anywhere, anytime, is a high achievement and bliss, are apt to take a more realistic view of Old Debbil Sea. The sea is at the best cold, and at the worst brutally rough and dangerous.

Under our circumstances at Youghal that horrible summer, the boys could at least ride horses about, or bicycle in the neighbourhood. But here again I could note that there is perhaps a discrepancy between what the elders think the youth must be longing to do and the true facts of the case. The elder boys did like to ride, but they did not care to ride much. What they liked was to build hidden huts or tree houses, to lie motionless on their backs in their tents, or find a dangerous way to the roof and sit there reading, with emotion, *The Waste Land*.

In these pursuits the summer seemed to be passing away harmlessly enough. I went to London two or three times for a few days on each visit, motoring to Cork, travelling by train from there to Dublin and thence flying. One day I had a headache and the tips of my fingers pricked with pins and needles. I am unused to headaches and thus noticed this one. And the pricking in my finger-tips was so queer that I made myself tedious about it, mentioned this pricking until everyone was much bored with the information. My eldest son also felt this pricking. We thought it was either meaningless, or else he had perhaps picked it up psychosomatically from me.

Much later, several doctors confirmed to me that this combination of unusual – baseless – headache with the prick of the finger-tips is a common, almost an infallible sign of polio. At the time we knew nothing of that. In reality, it appears, I had picked up the bug somewhere along the line between London and Cork. Even then, inevitably, Cork people had to travel in trains on their business. I recall that on the last of those journeys there was a clearly perceptible atmosphere of fear, suspicion, or perhaps simply high-grade caution on the train. Already things were at the point where Dubliners returning from some necessary trip to Cork felt that they could at least lessen the risk they had been compelled to run by not associating with Cork people longer than was absolutely necessary. We Cork people found ourselves, without the slightest word being said – and perhaps with not much of a conscious thought being thought – sitting at one end of the bar and buffet car, with the Dubliners at the other.

As the situation deteriorated in Cork, the Cork people defensively spread terrifying stories about what was happening elsewhere. It was said, and absolutely believed by very many people, that in Dublin the epidemic was worse still than in Cork. People were dying like flies in every fever hospital in the city. But, due to the savage wiles and intrigues of the Dubliners, the newspapers had been, as the Irish saying goes, 'brought to see' that it would not be in their interests to report the state of affairs in Dublin. Instead they should concentrate on ruining poor Cork.

And in Cork itself the owners of some of the biggest stores in the city made a *démarche*. In deputation to the newspapers they threatened to withdraw advertising from such newspapers as might continue to report regularly and in detail on the polio epidemic there. They were intent on bringing the newspapers to see the justice of their viewpoint. As always, too, in the sordid backwaters of panic, there were people made to suffer by the frights of others. Some nearly bedridden people nearly died in various parts of the city because it was thought that all bedridden people must be polio victims, and in consequence nobody would go to their houses to deliver the milk and meat and vegetables they needed. The Gardai had to be called in to make the deliveries to those houses which were supposedly so dangerous but in reality – not that the delivery men had any means of knowing that – were no more dangerous than the air you breathed at the railway station or the General Post Office. And that was dangerous indeed.

Things were apparently going along well enough, and I was in London, at this increasingly hateful house in Hampstead, working fast to make enough money to take us all, I thought, to Mexico for a while; a place I much wanted to visit. I came down, one late summer night, the crooked road that led to this big squat house and heard the telephone ringing. It just chanced that I had dined early and alone, and was coming back to sleep at nine-thirty in the evening. No one with good news ever rings you at that hour. How could, or would they? They are eating and drinking, and if all your affairs were in proper order you would be eating and drinking too. A call at that time can only be an act of desperation, a signal of emergency.

This was such a call. My wife had been trying to call me from Youghal and finding me from home had telephoned Malcolm at his home in Sussex, and he had kept on calling me every ten minutes with a message.

The message was to say that the youngest child was ill. I had no doubt what the message meant. My wife is no alarmist. With Malcolm's help – there has never been a man on God's earth who would do more for you when the chips are down, and he has seen a number of chips down in his life – I flew free to Dublin and hired the needed car at three o'clock in the morning to go the couple of hundred miles to Youghal. The message had meant just what I had supposed. The youngest boy was in bed with suspected polio. In a couple of hours the doctor was coming to confirm or nullify the diagnosis. He confirmed it. Two hours later the child was in the ambulance on his way to St Finnbarr's fever hospital in Cork.

By a trick of the mind, when grief and anxiety are at, you think, their imaginable height, some factor intrudes itself to give the screw an extra turn, heighten the grief and anxiety a little more. In this case, in the agony of her distress, my poor wife conceived the idea that she, because of her love of Ireland and boredom of London, had selfishly overlooked the dangers to the children involved in a return to County Cork, and was thus actually responsible for what had happened. I recalled this, many months later, when I was talking with Kitty Muggeridge about the death of their youngest son – he was eighteen or nineteen years old – in an avalanche of snow in the French Alps. She herself had been a ski champion once, and it seemed to her, after the event, that when he had mentioned to her that he was going ski-ing in that particular place at that particular season of the year, she should have remembered, over all those years, enough about conditions there to warn or discourage him, saying that at such a season there was danger of avalanches. And from this, by afterthought, it had been only a small step to the conviction that she had not only not tried to dissuade him from making the trip but, by some kind of implication, had actually encouraged him. She knew, when she talked about it, that all this was untrue or irrelevant. The young man had made his plans, he knew all that anyone needed to know about the possibilities and risks, and he would have taken those risks whatever anyone might have said. Just possibly – it is at least a possibility worth considering when grievous things happen to loved people – some people experience a compulsive need to assume guilt for what has happened, and this in reality is only an expression of a desire to become closer to them by involving oneself in their fate, rather than assume that they have been struck at by impersonal forces far beyond one's control.

Other than a compulsive need of that kind, there was no reason for Patricia to feel this bitterness of remorse, but she did feel it. And – again just possibly, although it did not look to me like that at the time – it may have been that what seemed to me an additional affliction for her was in reality a kind of aid; it could be that a sense of being in some way involved in the child's disaster, rather than a passive spectator of it, provided in its tortuous way a kind of balm in this gloomy Gilead. Yet in general remorse is both futile and debilitating.

Immediately after they had taken Patrick away in the ambulance I telephoned the school near Dublin where Andrew – then nine – was at work. For this had all happened at the very end of the holidays, and Andrew had been back at school for three or four days. He returned. I really thought all might still be well up to the very last moment when the diesel train pulled into the station and Andrew got out. I then saw that his body was bowed slightly forward in an awkward way and that he was moving his legs sluggishly. But this was the more terrifying because I had learned, by now, that the most dangerous period of polio is the period between the incidence of the infection and the moment of its diagnosis. The longer a person goes on leading a normally active life after the infection has struck, the more probable it is that he will quickly die of the disease or be permanently maimed by it.

By the following morning he, too, was in St Finnbarr's fever hospital.

A woman who had been a victim of polio in the Rhodesian epidemic some years ago pointed out to me that one is lucky to get polio when there is an epidemic rather than at some other time. Just because of the life-and-death importance of the period between infection and diagnosis, it is lucky to be infected at a time when every doctor in town has learned to recognize the preliminary symptoms – a recognition which is by no means easy unless the epidemic has alerted you so that you know what you are looking for. Had I, at the height of the Cork epidemic, mentioned to a doctor my mysterious headache and finger-pricking, he certainly would have known that I was having a mild case of polio. The consensus among doctors was that about seventy-five per cent of the population of Cork and surrounding territory had polio at that time. Whether it would have done any good for anyone to know that I had it is doubtful. The children must already have been infected by me.

In the fever hospital, necessarily, the patients are totally incommunicado. There is even a notice at the door asking relatives and friends not to seek to peer in through the windows. There are double doors, and you can go to the outer one, and a person can look out of the inner one, take your question, relay it to someone within, and give you the answer. This is an absolutely correct procedure. Or you may telephone. The people at St Finnbarr's, run nearly ragged by the epidemic, showed great humanity in this respect. They were able and willing to answer the telephone three and sometimes four times daily.

At an earlier date our telephone at the house had blown down in a financial blizzard. When we asked for it to be re-connected, they wanted a down payment of £70 with no guaranteed date for the installation. I had told them that when they guaranteed a date they could get the money. They replied that until they had the money they would not even consider the date. So what we had there was an *impasse*, and we did all our telephoning from my favourite bar in town, which was called, at that time, the Wright House. The Wrights were English and, by a queer coincidence Mr Wright senior – as suddenly emerged when the Muggeridges first visited us – had been at school with Malcolm in south London nearly forty years before. He told me he had a clear recollection of their schoolmaster monotonously repeating 'That'll be quite enough from you, Muggeridge. Be *quiet*, Muggeridge! *Sit down*, Muggeridge!' It seemed likely enough.

A fearful thing about polio, at any rate the type of polio that was loose in County Cork, is that for at least a fortnight there is no certainty at all that the patient will not, quite suddenly, die. There is, that is to say, no let-up in the attack during all that time. The fact that the victim has survived for, say, ten days is no indication that he is going to survive eleven. And for at least a fortnight, usually a few days longer, there is apparently no way of telling how badly he will be crippled if he survives at all. There is no knowing how much muscle has been actually 'killed' for ever. So it happened every day that when I went down to the Wright House at ten in the morning and put through my first call of the day to St Finnbarr's, the news could be that one or both of the boys had died in the night and would be buried that evening. And when the report was, comparatively, favourable, 'no change', that did not make it any less probable that the victims would die while I was sitting there waiting to call again at noon. Vexatious too was the inevitable fact that I had never seen the people I was talking to at the other end of the line. One could suppose that to be irrelevant. It is not quite easy to explain how important, and how frustrating, it actually was. For one thing it seemed to widen the gap between the children and oneself, to put them hopelessly beyond one's help. In a more practical sense, too, it cut them off because, having no mental picture of the person one was talking to, one felt helpless to assess their reports correctly – it was as though all these conversations were being conducted on a broken-down wire. Every nurse and doctor has, naturally, a slightly different way of formulating such a report, and usually a different person answered each of the three or four calls of the day. At nine, perhaps, the voice at the other end would say, 'They seem to be doing well.' And then at noon another voice would say, 'They're doing as well as can be expected.' In fact the two reports meant exactly the same thing, but to the straining ear of the inquirer the little shift of words seemed to mean that in the past three hours things had taken a terrible turn for the worse. Why else should they use that cautious 'as well as can be expected'? I would stand at that telephone for minutes on end, making senseless conversation, repeating what was in effect the same question in a half-dozen different ways, in the futile and unreasonable hope of luring the nurse into giving out some piece of information which in reality she could not have.

At the end of it all I would come away from the telephone with a total of about ten words of news to pass on to my wife, and the danger then was that we might sit there for the next three hours just twisting and mulling over those ten words, trying to worry more meaning out of them than could possibly be in them. After the first couple of days we understood the deadly futility of that. We forced ourselves to discuss the news only for a few minutes and then talk of other things. In these hours we were a good deal sustained by the kindness and tact of the Wright family whose role must have been a very difficult one.

For me things were probably a little easier than for my wife, because, since I did not want to waste a lot of time travelling back and forth between our house and the bar, I used to borrow the Wrights' typewriter and spend the interval between the calls working in the café-bar. People used to remark that they supposed it must be particularly difficult, even offensive, to have to write satirical and humorous articles in such circumstances, and one can see how an onlooker might imagine that. But in reality it makes no difference, at least it makes no difference to me, what the subject of the writing is. I should think that if a carpenter were at work while waiting for news of his sick children, it would make no difference to him whether he was making a kitchen table or a roulette board. Or it may even be that to be working on something so small and intricate as a short article which is designed to make people laugh is a superior therapy, requiring a maximum concentration of attention on itself, so that even the most intrusive of other cares are excluded from the mind.

This went on for three weeks. At the end of that time, Andrew – of whom, at one time, they had said on the telephone that he probably would be permanently and totally bed-ridden, unable ever even to sit upright – was discharged without any ill-effects at all. Patrick was, as things turned out, the one who suffered. Almost totally paralysed at the end of the three weeks, he had to go from the fever hospital to the Orthopaedic hospital, and he remained there for nearly six months.

Like most Irish hospitals it was finely equipped, and I was told by experts that the doctors and the physiotherapists (some of whom had been loaned by English hospitals for the emergency) were as good as any to be found anywhere. The trouble was that, as a result of this same emergency, there seemed to be a serious shortage of nursing staff with any special training in the nursing of young children. And a considerable part of the everyday care of the children seemed to be largely in the hands of maids – young country girls with no special training at all. There were almost no arrangements for the entertainment or education of the children, who were provided with beds and expert medical attention, and nothing else. There were not even arrangements for the proper care of the children's toys, with the result that toys which we and our relations and friends sent in for Patrick to share out among the other children, and which could have kept the whole ward supplied for a month, were customarily broken in a few days and thrown on the rubbish heap.

The majority of the patients came from miserably poor families. I met one mother who lived in the far west of County Cork and was able to visit her paralysed son only once in four months – on the day when there was a big football match in Cork City and the railway ran a very cheap day excursion from her village. I had the impression that the hospital people, aware of this extreme poverty, subconsciously treated it as a partial excuse for the failure to give the unhappy children the kind of psychological amenities they should have had. It was felt that they were lucky to have a fine room and good food. And the result was that to me this period was in many ways even more of a nightmare than the time when the boys had been in St Finnbarr's. Twice a week we were allowed to visit Patrick, and twice a week one could note a gradual and sometimes startling deterioration in his mental and spiritual condition. At first it seemed that one had to disregard this because there was equally no doubt that his physical condition was improving just as steadily. By the end of four months or thereabouts, he could actually move about the ward on crutches, with his legs in irons and his body in a surgical waistcoat. But all the time he, who had been so gay, so alert, inquisitive and talkative seemed to be sinking into a kind of voiceless apathy. I began to feel that the point was being approached where the psychological harm that was occurring would outweigh the physical good. There came a week when throughout our visit he never raised his voice above a whisper, and much of the time lay in total silence on his bed, not bothering, even, to try to show what progress he had made in his capacity for physical movement. And yet, in one's total ignorance, to exert the slightest pressure for his release from the hospital at a date earlier than the doctors apparently had in mind, seemed perilous, too.

In the end I thought we had better take the risk. For I had in mind the poverty of the majority of the patients which, in turn, must tend to make the hospital authorities humanely incline to prolong the sojourn in hospital, since the alternative is grim. I did, therefore, begin a small agitation – asking the authorities for a clear answer to the question whether there was any absolutely definite physical reason for Patrick to stay where he was rather than return home. After two or three weeks of frustrating uncertainties they agreed there was not. He came out. Within a fortnight he was as cheerful and mentally active as he ever had been before he was struck by the disease.

Even in such melancholy matters, there are some things which turn out a little better than one feared. I had thought that Patrick, back in the home and surroundings in which he had spent almost all of his short life, would be even more aware of his disabilities than he had been in the strange world of the hospital. He had never run across the hospital lawn, or climbed a tree there, or ridden a pony on its driveway. I feared that at home the lawn, the trees, the pony and a lot besides would savagely jog his memory of things past. Nothing of the kind happened. First he was so happy to be at home that his escape from the hospital, for he had – as he later admitted – been convinced that the hospital was going on for ever, was seen by him as in itself an exhilarating achievement. And then, being now alert and eager again, he became preoccupied not with the big range of things he could no longer do, but with the tiny extension, day by day and week by week of things he was learning to do again. To crawl from the bed to the floor, to walk a few more steps today than he could yesterday – these were a continuous, ascending series of triumphs, as uplifting as a succession of victories leading to membership of the team for the Olympic Games.

And, fortunate within the misfortune, was the fact that being so young he had developed no habitual patterns of life which must now be broken, and could occupy himself, too, with the speedy development of novel activities. My wife now taught him to read, and I began to teach him chess. In a week or two he had mastered the principles of the game, and thereupon a new field opened to him, since now he could, by himself, without need of an opponent, play over book-games, championship matches and so on, which is the easiest, perhaps the only, way to learn chess properly. I did not encourage him to play with other children. For children playing chess together are apt to play it like a game with toy soldiers. However many games they play they are hardly nearer than at the outset to understanding chess as a movement of calculable yet fluid forces, nor to appreciating that aspect of chess by which it is related simultaneously to music and to mathematics. Three years after I had started to teach Patrick the game we had reached a situation in which to play with me, a merely moderate player, was hardly more interesting for him than it would have been, at the beginning, to play with a child.

In the first weeks after his return home I was merely astonished and relieved by his vigour, determination and evident happiness. In my own mind, the dominant fact was the blow that had struck him. Gradually, under the influence of his attitude to these facts of life, I was aware of a shift in my own. It became possible to see the present, and the future that was now being constructed, as being of greater importance than the past.

In the harsh days after Patrick's return from hospital, the particular character of our town was a continual solace and stimulant. I think I should have found London or Paris intolerable at such a time.

32

TABOO

OURS is an abnormally, strangely beautiful town. But physical beauty is not enough. It is too, a more than usually interesting town. For instance, on the night we heard the news that Stalin was dead, a man in this town remarked to me that people were saying that there was a leprechaun that had been sighted, sitting on the roof of the garage of the Marine Hotel. Crowds had gathered to view the creature, with an eye, naturally enough, to the crock of gold which, if you believed in leprechauns, the leprechaun would have.

'Isn't it amazing,' said this man who spoke to me in the bar while I was thinking about the death of Stalin. 'Isn't it simply astounding that in this time, this day and age, and considering all we spend on public education, there still would be people prepared to believe in the existence of such a thing as a leprechaun? What kind of people do they think we are at all?' I said it was amazing. 'On the other hand, Mr Cockburn,' said he, 'if it chanced to be – well now, I know it couldn't be, but some people don't – if it chanced to be a leprechaun with a crock of gold, wouldn't it be insensate, absolutely insensate, for a man that thought so not to go down and see it?' So we went down to have a look. By the time we got there some kind of riot had occurred. Naturally nobody believed in the leprechaun – there may just possibly be people in Ireland who do, but we live a long way farther east on the south coast than they do. In our area a man needs all the faith he can concentrate to believe in

God, let alone leprechauns. On the other hand, there is always 'the Grand Perhaps', and a considerable crowd of non-believers gathered to see possible believers looking at a leprechaun, and to do them out of any profit that might thereby accrue to them.

That, it seemed, had been the consensus: namely, that there is no leprechaun but that people who claim to have seen a leprechaun have some profitable thing in mind, and ought to be trailed. And this it was that had caused the small riot or disturbance. The word had gone about that the leprechaun had dashed suddenly from the roof of the garage of the Marine Hotel up the rocky hill behind and was streaking across the flat fields at the top of the bluff. In our town the most improbable suggestions are welcomed as a reasonable occasion for drama and action. In consequence a number of people, many of whom had been drinking about the leprechaun for an hour or so, dashed, laughing and jostling, up the hill in pursuit of the creature. Somewhere on top of the hill further trouble occurred, it being alleged that someone had – while pretending to chase the leprechaun – deliberately opened a gate or broken down a fence in the interests of farmer A, whose cattle thereby gained a night's feed off the pastures of farmer B.

The drama, therefore, took a practical turn, one likely, it was thought, to conclude in the law court. And this possibility caused more people than before to go to see what about the leprechaun on the following night. But by now the Gardai were alerted, and warned off the observers. So on the following day it was reported that the leprechaun, after a brief return to his garage, had been seen to dash across the broad estuary of the Blackwater River where it flows into the Atlantic, and had settled itself down on the primeval jumble of rocks littered around the feet of the low cliffs of Monatrae. This, if the leprechaun – or the people who were anxious, in the interests of the drama, to make its actions credible – were serious in suggesting it was seeking a little solitude, was a logical move. The currents at just that point are deadly, and numerous people had, quite recently, been drowned at just that spot.

Only a few weeks earlier a man who had taken part in the rescue of one or two members of a bathing party there had described to me the horror of the scene as the under-tow dragged them out, one after another. He personally had dragged out a corpse, and told me in detail how it looked. I said it was a horrible thing. 'And there's worse than that,' he said. 'D'you realize, Mr Cockburn, that man was earning more than £9 a week at the time? Wasn't that a terrible time to die now?'

Despite these dangers a number of people did pile into the ferry-boat to cross the estuary – a service originated in the time of King John of England as a military measure and continued until a couple of years ago. But others recalled that we had at that time in Youghal a British helicopter, on loan from the Admiralty to the Irish Government, and engaged on some kind of photographic survey of the Irish coasts. Some genius conceived the idea that the definitive thing to do would be to have this helicopter fly over those rocks and take a picture of the leprechaun, which would settle disputes and controversies about this kind of phenomenon for good. The people operating the helicopter got in touch with the relevant Department of the Irish Government, which thought it only proper to contact the Admiralty in London. They felt that, having borrowed the machine for purposes of coastal mapping, they ought to consult with the British Admiralty as to whether it was permissible for it to be used for taking pictures of leprechauns. The Admiralty, it seems, said it had no objection to that use of its machine, and a couple of hours later the helicopter took off and hovered, with its powerful camera, over the rocks at Monatrae.

The picture was taken, the film developed. And the news as the man told it to me in the bar seemed depressing. Absolutely no sign of the leprechaun was discernible on the developed film taken by that helicopter. It looked as though the dramatic story was over, and I said as much to the man. 'And yet,' said he, 'come to think of it now, if you understand me, Mr Cockburn, isn't it a fact that a ghost can't be photographed? Isn't that a quality possessed by ghosts?' That is certainly true, and I admitted as much. 'Well then,' said my man, 'seeing that a leprechaun's a kind of a ghost, and quite obviously to you and me doesn't exist at all, isn't it a fact that if a leprechaun had been there on those rocks at Monatrae, he wouldn't ever have showed up on the film? So if there's nothing on the film, couldn't a certain class of person take it as an indication, just an indication at least, that the leprechaun was surely there?'

Nobody but some very old-fashioned English or Anglo-Irish person of the period of the Ascendancy would suppose that anyone in my town really thought there was a leprechaun there – a leprechaun, that is, in the sense in which thousands of effigies of the little creatures are manufactured in Yokohama for the Killarney trade. On the other hand, the conception of a leprechaun, and a leprechaun sitting on the roof of a garage, can bring pleasure and interest to people in a town. As I say, it is a dramatic conception, and can temporarily fill the place of a theatre. In our town we have the best local theatre in the south of Ireland. But evidently it cannot put on performances every week of the year. When it does, everyone pays money to see it, and our local theatre group makes a little money. But when it is not in a position to do so, then what, people naturally tend to think, would be wrong with news of a leprechaun, and there just might, they think, be some to believe it, too, otherwise where would be the drama? And the drama is sometimes what you cannot help seeing, sometimes what you have to peer hard at before you see it.

Brendan Behan, in black depression, was talking to me once about those times when a writer feels not merely that he cannot write today, or this week, but that he will never be able to write again; the whole craft seems as far beyond him as the craft, say, of the man who can engrave the Lord's Prayer on the head of a pin. Those, we agreed, are times when you sit there surrounded by unresponsive words like an eager woman in a room full of pansies. Perhaps I was suffering from some kind of delayed shock produced by the children's illness; whatever the cause, I felt that way right through that summer, and – as always happens in such a condition – positively welcomed extraneous interruptions, even disagreeable events, provided they offered an excuse not to keep sitting at the typewriter. I took to inventing excuses to go over to London – often to discuss projects of manifest futility.

On one of these expeditions I went down to stay with Malcolm Muggeridge at Robertsbridge, ostensibly to lay before him some scheme for the 'improvement' of *Punch*. He had expressed enthusiasm for the general idea, and I had even written out a long memorandum on the subject. But on the evening of my arrival he said we should talk about it in the morning, and in the morning, as we sat on the lawn in deck chairs drinking whisky and soda he said it was really too hot to talk about anything like that, and we had better await the afternoon. By the evening of the second day, when we had talked about everything under the sun except my project, I became aware that the boredom which had from the first threatened to extinguish his interest in the paper had finally got the better of him. It emerged, too, that his relations with the management had been deteriorating sharply.

He had become convinced, and – temporarily at least – convinced me too that all the ideas we had shared a few years before about the possibility of creating an entirely new type of satirical journal in modern England had been so many illusions. The public wanted nothing of the kind; or, if there were a public which wanted the sort of thing we had had in mind, then it was not the sort of public that would provide a market for the wares the most profitable of the *Punch* advertisers were advertising. I gathered that the pressures and complaints from the advertising department were increasing vexatiously, and that Malcolm, for his part, had lost the will to resist them doggedly and vigorously week by week as he had in the past.

I left Robertsbridge without bothering to discuss the business I had come about, and was not surprised, a couple of months later, to hear that Malcolm – with mutual recriminations – had broken off relations with the paper. For me the situation was at once alarming and stimulating. For the past few years I had been earning a regular fifty guineas weekly from *Punch*, and it did not require much perspicacity to foresee that this arrangement was not likely to continue in the circumstances. Not that I anticipated any ill will on the part of the future editor – and indeed the contrary was in fact the case. But it was obvious, too, that there would be changes in editorial policy and that one of them – particularly since I had been so closely associated in the mind of the advertising department with the Muggeridge régime – was likely to be a sharp reduction in the demand for the kind of thing I most liked to write for the paper. On the other hand I had been feeling for some time that the ease with which this basic fifty guineas could be earned was in fact a mental or spiritual hazard – it blunted, somewhat, the goad necessary to compel one to look for new fields, new roads.

Just how incompatible Malcolm and *Punch* had become I discovered some weeks later when I went into the *Punch* office just after the extraordinary explosion which greeted publication in the *Saturday Evening Post* of Malcolm's critical article on the state of the British monarchy. The management looked like mountaineers who have that minute seen the path they have just crossed being overwhelmed by an avalanche. 'If this had happened when Malcolm was still Editor,' one of them said to me, 'I believe it really would have killed the paper.' (We talked for some minutes at cross-purposes, because when he said 'paper' I thought he was referring to his 'pater' – and it did, indeed, seem possible that a shock of that kind would have been too much for the good old man.)

At the outset I thought the whole affair a ridiculous storm in a teacup – particularly since I, in Ireland, had read the text of the article without reading the astonishing distortions of it published in the London newspapers, at least two of which had for years been engaged in a more or less continuous feud with Malcolm. Also, being of a republican turn of mind, my first instinct was one of surprise that a man of Malcolm's ability should have thought it necessary to devote so much attention to the monarchy, or to consider it worth his while to exert himself to save it from what he believed to be potentially fatal dangers. (For that was, in reality, the purpose of this supposedly 'anti-monarchial' article.)

But gradually, as the affair developed, I began to realize that what we had here was an event of the highest political and social significance. Part of this significance was pointed out by Malcolm himself in an interview with Mike Wallace, which was conducted and televised in the United States but never published in this country. (And the interview itself was blacked out in Washington D.C. because the Queen was visiting there at the time.)

'One of the hazards of popular monarchy as I see it,' Malcolm said, 'is that it does evoke a sort of hysteria, and unquestioning adulation, which in my opinion is socially harmful. Of course, that is no reflection on the Queen. It's not her fault. It is the fault of the people who present her with this unquestioning adulation. In other words, it's their lack of a large faith which makes them fasten on to a purely earthly symbol.'

Wallace then asked him if he believed that in England he lived in a free society. 'Well,' Malcolm said, 'I wish to believe so.'

'Under those circumstances,' asked Wallace, 'how is it that just this week you were fired as a columnist for the London *Sunday Dispatch* and prohibited from even discussing the Monarchy on the British Broadcasting Company's show *Panorama*?' 'Both these things are episodes for which I blush, not because they affect me personally, but because I think they do reflect on the freedom of British society.'

Nothing could possibly have demonstrated better the truth of Malcolm's statement about hysterical adulation and its unhealthy effects than the consequences of his own article. (In this connexion the fact that the article was distorted in the British Press is irrelevant – relevant is simply people's reaction to what they believed was a criticism of the Queen.) I wished that Malcolm at the time had made an analysis of the mail he got – the ultimate, one might say, in non-fanmails. Quite a number of the envelopes dispatched by these gallant royalists proved, when opened, to be filled with human excrement. Another type of letter came from people who said they were so delighted to hear of the recent death of his youngest son in a ski-ing accident – it made, they said, one Muggeridge the less. Some people, not content with letter-writing, came to his house in the country and smeared it with filth and slogans – including 'God Bless Our Queen'.

I hope Malcolm has kept enough of that mail – the stuff that would bear keeping – to have it analysed; it would tell one a lot more than the newspapers or even the sociologists commonly do about the real state of mind of the British public. That it indicated the existence of a deep disease is beyond doubt. The question that arises in the mind is whether the disease is, so to say, caused by the existence of the Monarchy or whether, if there were no Monarchy, the diseased minds would find some other occasion, or trigger, that would loose off their outbursts of hatred and obscenity. Malcolm, I think, was inclined to believe that the fault lay with the institution of Monarchy as it is operated in modern England. I could wish, too, to believe that; but I cannot. Yet it is a fact, and this seems to me of some importance, that in all the years I was a Communist writer – even in the period of the Nazi-Soviet Pact and the Communist opposition to the war during the first year and a half of that war – I never, either at *The Week* or the *Daily Worker* was the victim of that kind of an outburst. Naturally people attacked me continually, and very occasionally people spat at me in public places or otherwise expressed themselves with a certain physical vehemence. But that is the natural, and, one might nearly say, proper reaction of people who do not have any great facility with the spoken word, and are, therefore, at a disadvantage – which they feel to be unfair – with the man who chances to have that facility. I can write. They can spit. Let us see which is more effective at the game. It could seem, therefore, that, even at the height of a desperate conflict in which people (wrongly, I believe, but justifiably I admit) supposed one to be on the side of the enemy, they felt less vehemently about that than they do when someone impugns the institution of the Monarchy or speaks, without notably bated breath, about the personality and entourage of Her Sacred Majesty.

All this would suggest – and it seems important to look at the question – that, as Malcolm thought, the Monarchy itself (as an institution) is in some way responsible for the stinking midden of foul emotions which are seen to pullulate verminous or fungoid when it is attacked.

Kingsley Martin, in a book which ought to be more widely read, called *The Magic of Monarchy*, drew attention – apropos of the Abdication Crisis – to the fact that in the fifty years or so before the event, the British had, mysteriously, become more mystical, more politically insane in their attitude to Monarchy rather than less. They were even prepared to believe – and I mean *believe* – in 'the King's weather' (a fine day for some royal occasion), and to accept the view that the anointing of the King with sacred oils in the course of the Coronation ceremony actually does set him, his mind and his spirit, apart from, and above, other men. If anyone were to write today the type of criticism of the Monarchy – and the Monarch – written in *The Times*, no less, in the 1860s, he would, on the analogy of the reaction to Malcolm Muggeridge, be publicly lynched.

Possibly, in this compilation by Kingsley Martin, we have a clue to what really has happened and is happening – not an explanation, but a clue. It would seem, that is to say, that in the days when the British middle classes flourished and were confident of their power and prosperity, they were without that need of a reverential symbol which they have today. The upper classes in Britain have never reverenced either the monarchy or anything else except (among the best of them), independence of mind, and (among the worst), money. But the working class attitude of the late nineteenth century was different, too. After the famous Tranby Croft case – when the Prince of Wales was forced to bear witness in a trial which showed that he had been present at a card party where it was possible for the guests mutually to suspect one another of cheating – he went down to Bethnal Green to open a Boys' Club or some other institution of the kind. There was a banner right across the street with the words 'Welcome to Our Prince – but no gambling please.' Try and put a banner like that across some road about to be traversed by the Duke of Edinburgh today and see what you get from the police. You would be lucky just to have your banner torn down without yourself being charged with some criminal offence and probably roughed-up in the police station in the interval.

It could be that the change occurred because all classes of that imperialist society became aware that their security was evaporating. For the working class of Britain lived, no less than the upper class, on the exploitation of the out-gunned millions of India and Africa. The importance of the Monarchy, as a mystic security symbol, increased.

Malcolm thinks, or he thought when he wrote that absurdly notorious article, that what had happened was that people who had lost their faith in God, had latched this faith-need on to the Monarchy – and that, I think, is what transpires from Kingsley Martin's book too. And if this be true, we have to accept some rather peculiar thoughts about our materialistic, damn-you-Jack society. We have to accept that the toughies, the damn-you-Jacks are really a gang of sentimentalist mystics, groping for a father (or mother) figure in the gloom of the espresso bars. And I think this is about the way things really stand.

Which brings us to another awkward corner. Numerous intellectuals today – rightly sickened by a number of the things that have happened, and are supposed to be the responsibility of the intellectuals of yesterday – are looking for a way of escape from ideologies into a day-by-day, practical acceptance of life and way of dealing with it. Anyone who proclaims an ideology is, intelligibly, suspect as a man who the day after tomorrow is going to proclaim a crusade, and the day after that will have to draw up his casualty list. Many are bored and nauseated by these proceedings. But, in their revolt against ideologies – which is to say a revolt against mythologies, which is to say a revolt against beliefs in anything but the visible and palpable – they are, inevitably, forced to revolt against a number of suppositions and assumptions which, in the common parlance, 'keep a man going'. To keep going is what people want. But the ideologies, suppositions and assumptions which kept the intellectuals going between the wars were for the most part assumptions of 'the Left'. In consequence it is those that have suffered most severely in the climate of today. And as a further consequence, the intellectuals who, only a few years ago, would have been more or less actively republican in attitude, more or less actively critical or contemptuous of the institution of Monarchy, today subconsciously reject such a position, since to adopt it is to move back, they imagine, towards the Left. All of which leaves the robustly old-fashioned critic of the Monarchy in a singularly isolated situation.

Viewed from Ireland, the British uproar over Malcolm's article was the more interesting for its bearing on the entire question of censorship which is a matter of such continual concern and controversy among the Irish. What we seemed to be seeing was a remarkable demonstration of both the similarities and the contrasts between censorship on the one hand and taboo on the other. And there are occasions, as for instance in the business of the Muggeridge article, when one has the impression that, so far as freedom of expression is concerned, a taboo can be more dangerous than a censorship. There is, in Ireland, in reality, a kind of double censorship. The censorship of books, for example, is exercised by a Board of Censors who, when left to themselves, appear to act in a reasonably sensible manner, seeking to ban only those books which, in their opinion at least, are deliberately pornographic. But as any country librarian could tell you, the difficulties begin when some fanatic or bigot finds on the shelves of the public library a book to which he takes exception. He demands its withdrawal. The librarian argues, in defence of the book, that had it been objectionable it would have been banned by the censors. The complainant then avers that obviously the censors have never read the book, and insists that it be withdrawn until their attention has been drawn to it. The librarian has no alternative – he submits the book to the censors. And the censors are then in the position of not merely 'passing' the book, but of having positively, so to speak, to give it their blessing, which is rather a different thing. For they are well aware that if they do 'pass' the book after complaint has been made at the public library, the next thing that is likely to happen is that the complainant will rush round to the local Deputy and there will be a question in the Dail – the worst of all the bugbears that trouble the sleep of Government appointees or other public servants.

This, evidently, is a case where censorship and taboo intermesh and interact. And it is true, too, that in the numerous cases of stage plays being either castrated or withdrawn by the management of the theatres concerned, the pressure has been the result not of any official censorship but of outcries from a section (often very small) of the audience, sometimes supported or even provoked by the ecclesiastical authorities.

These incidents cause a good deal of excitement in Dublin, and occasionally provide the play with a sort of publicity that is of some use when those concerned are trying to sell it to a London management. And, partly as a result of this publicity, one finds in London a cosy assumption that London is in this respect 'freer' than Dublin, supposedly strangling in the grip of the 'hierarchy'. The misleading absurdity of this assumption would be clear to anyone who saw, at the Gate Theatre, Dublin, the delicious play *Aisling* – a complex and often uproarious satire, in which the most savagely satirized character is that of a Roman Catholic priest. And this priest is presented not simply as an individual priest, with the evil qualities of a single individual, but also as a symbolic figure, representative of an entire trend in the Roman Catholic Church and its policies in Ireland. The play was received with respectful interest, amusement and frequent applause by crowded audiences. There were no protests from the playgoers and none – so far as I know – from outside sources. I tried, as I watched it, to imagine what would happen to a British playwright who trod so heavily and so uncompromisingly as that on the toes of British taboos – in particular on taboos relating to the Monarchy. One has only to imagine it for a moment to realize just how violent and restrictive those particular taboos are.

The discussion of the matter is usually bedevilled from the beginning by an almost wholly irrelevant issue – the issue, that is to say, of whether one is in favour of the Monarchy, or against it, or indifferent to it, considering it, perhaps, in the nature of a harmless charade on the lines of the Lord Mayor's Show. On these matters there can be dozens of opinions, but none of them affect the central point, which is the existence of the taboo itself – the fact that if a man speaks about the Queen in the same tone of voice that he would use to comment on the Prime Minister or the Archbishop of Canterbury, a big section of the population goes hog-wild, squealing as though an attempt had been made to rape it.

I think the distinction between censorship and taboo important because a censorship is a lot easier to evade or abolish than a taboo. I know of no civilized country which has any taboo corresponding to the one Britain has about the Monarchy. Though (as the Muggeridge case showed) it is risky, it is certainly still safer to criticize the Queen in England than to proclaim yourself a Communist in the United States or an anti-Communist in Russia. The difference is that in Russia and the United States these risks are, so to speak, legalistic, or Governmental, whereas in Britain they result from an attitude of mind in the populace as a whole.

The excremental letters, the defilement of his house, and the cries of pleasure over the death of his son, were to Malcolm shocking and, in the fullest sense of the word, depressing, since they all seemed to confirm an estimate of the human condition which one half of his mind had always suggested to him was a correct one, and the other had hopefully claimed to be exaggerated. He had often berated or derided me for what he claimed was my ludicrously over-optimistic view of human nature. Equally, he had always, as I repeatedly noticed, himself grabbed hold of, and held up for inspection and perhaps exaggerated admiration, whatever instances of human kindness or nobility might present themselves in history or day-to-day living. To what is called 'the detached observer' – if there is such a creature – it could seem obvious that for every person capable of writing letters of that kind there must be scores of thousands to whom such an act would be a thing of abhorrence. But that is not just the way it strikes the man who gets the letters. When the sewer bursts right in front of his home he is apt to be thinking less about the general excellence of the municipal system of sewage control than of the fact that this powerful mass of filth is there under our feet and, given certain conditions, can break out.

A person's feelings on such an occasion are close to the Chinese feelings about 'face' – so often and so crudely misunderstood in the West. The Westerner in general supposes that 'loss of face' means simply loss of your own 'face' and that the conception is equivalent to the idea of loss of prestige, or of strictly personal humiliation. But the Chinese notion is that for someone *else* to behave in a bestially disgraceful manner can cause 'loss of face' to all humanity.

I found the atmosphere personally and politically depressing, and this depression was increased by the fact that during that particular visit to England I chanced, quite incidentally, to meet on various social occasions numerous prominent figures in the Labour and Conservative Parties. I returned to Ireland with a sense of relief and release – a hostile critic could call it a sense of escape. I am not one whose heart is uplifted by the sight of priests and nuns parading the streets, or of crowds packing off to Mass on a Sunday morning. But on moving from England to Ireland at that time I was reminded of a couple of sentences of Ezra Pound in his essay on *The Serious Artist*. 'Even this pother about Gods,' writes Pound, 'reminds one that something is worth while. Satire reminds one that certain things are not worth while. It draws one to consider time wasted.'

I grew weak and lethargic, and since I had a great deal of work to do kept myself active by taking daily increasing doses of whisky and dexedrine. These, it goes without saying, are deleterious to anyone suffering from advanced tuberculosis, which was, as presently emerged, my condition. I dare say any-one with any experience of the disease in friends or relatives could have diagnosed my symptoms at once. But neither my wife nor I had any such experience, so that I thought my troubles were due to the pressures of modern life on the creative writer, or some other mumbo jumbo as one hears of, and my wife thought they resulted from excessive drinking. Twice I fainted at the typewriter, and soon after began running a temperature all the time. I took for granted that what I had was Asian flu, of which there was at the time an epidemic.

When my temperature subsided, I concluded that what I was really in need of was gaiety. We took off through a fierce snow-storm for a Christmas Party at Luggala which lasted for ten days and nights and was gay indeed, with such animated and animating characters as Sean MacBride, John Huston, the Wood-row Wyatts, Brendan Behan, a palaver of diplomats, and a cohort of racing men – of which latter one may say, like the old-time drama critics of provincial newspapers, all were excel-lent but were too numerous for individual mention. There were mornings when I found myself awaking, after a long night of song, dance and passionate conversation, feeling a little below par. But I well knew that a long drink of vodka before breakfast is a sure means of putting oneself a little above par again. It is not, however, a means of arresting the onslaughts of myco-bacterium tuberculosis, and as the day wore on, longer and longer drinks became necessary to ward off the fainting fits. I went for little walks with Patrick swinging along on his crutches, to the lakeside, where we would stand between the precipitous granite of the surrounding hills and he would ask that we should wait there a little 'to listen', as he said, 'to the quiet'. I too like listening to quiet (although I enjoy a lot of noise also), but I was a little disconcerted to find that apart from that, I – after just that quarter mile walk to the lake – was actually glad of an occasion to sit down on one of the enormous granite boulders which rolled off the hills in the ice-age, and rest. And on the way back to the house I, supposed to be looking after an invalid, had several times to beg Patrick to go a little more slowly on those crutches.

It was a long party, and I can recall but few that I have enjoyed more. So hospitable was it, that a number of us stayed on for a couple of days after our hostess had to fly to New York. Apart from the songs and dances, there were a good many conversations to be completed. Finally, in another snowstorm, we drove back to Youghal, and by the time we got there it was apparent that whatever I had it was something more debilitating than Asian flu. There came a morning when I was incapable of the exertion required to get my legs off the bed and on to the floor. We drove through another blizzard to Cork, had me X-rayed, and – when they showed me those queerly intimate pictures – I could see that there was little indeed left of either lung which had not been invaded by the tiny, tubercular creatures.

I had never been ill for more than a few days at a time, and when the specialist at the Cork hospital told me I would have to go into hospital for 'perhaps four months' – he, of course, knowing full well that it would be nine months at least, but merely softening the blow – I felt such a shock as I think I never had experienced in my entire previous life, which, nevertheless, was a life with many shocks in it. What, when I came to meditate on the matter, truly shocked me was the sense simply of confinement – of being in the power of others. I remained in the glass house I have described, eight months.

33

THE WORST POSSIBLE TASTE

A MAN came angrily back to Youghal from a trip to London and stamped about the quays complaining that whether you wanted to talk about selling Irish lobsters, or the present and future state of the theatre, both subjects which interested him, nobody in London would talk about anything but the Profumo case. I agreed, it must get tedious, especially as 40 per cent of the talkers were only quoting the newspapers, 20 per cent were drooling a dream fantasy, and of the rest 25 per cent were the most bare-faced, though clumsy, liars since Ananias, or at least Stanley Baldwin. All the same, I said, it was probably hard for the people on the Ark to stop talking about the weather.

Personally at that time I was temporarily letting myself off the British newspapers altogether. I read the Irish newspapers and the invaluable *Le Monde* of Paris. It was a practice which seemed to me to freshen the mind; shift, in a healthy way, one's angle of vision. This produced occasionally tricky situations. I was at that time writing a weekly column for the *Sunday Telegraph*. The Editor, Donald McLachlan, had arranged with me that we should have, around noon on Wednesdays, a short telephonic consultation about the general lines of next Sunday's piece. Like most dwellers in the world's big conurbations, Londoners are somewhat provincial in outlook. They believe, for instance, that everyone within reach of London publications is reading what they are reading. Donald would say to me, 'Don't you think that first paragraph in the *New Statesman* Diary gives you an excellent peg upon which to hang a satirical comment?'.

Not having seen the *New Statesman* for months, I had to think fast. 'Donald,' I said, 'the most appalling thing has happened. There has been an almighty flood here and the van bringing the copies of the *New Statesman*, and, I may say, the *Spectator*, has been either held up on the Cork road or utterly submerged.'

'Oh bad luck. Look . . .'

Another day Donald remarked that obviously I would be doing something about a big, significant letter in *The Times* from some Bishop whose name I was unable to catch. I had to tell him there had been a hurricane at Cork Airport. Before its precious freight could be unloaded, the plane with *The Times* – and, I hastened to assure him, all the other British daily newspapers – aboard, had been blown off the tarmac to hellangone; no one knew whether and when they might be salvaged and delivered.

'Good God!'

Later, Donald was supposed to be coming to stay with me.

but suddenly cancelled the trip. A mutual friend told me that Donald had explained that he had only a short holiday, and did not dare have it ruined by the climate of County Cork. 'Floods, hurricanes every other week – I can't risk it.'

Among the publications I had heard of but never read, was *Private Eye*. I was thus baffled to receive, that summer, an invitation to go over to London and, as 'guest Editor', take over production of a single special issue of the magazine. Having informed myself as well as I could in the circumstances – *Private Eye*, one need hardly say, was not available in Ireland – I decided, for many good reasons, to decline. Just for a start, I was approximately twice the average age of the men who had conceived the paper, were running it, and were giving it its unique character. A person of my generation would probably, I thought, even in a single issue, seriously damage its 'image'. Also, England appeared to me, just at that time, as Czechoslovakia did to Neville Chamberlain – a far-off country of which I knew little. Also, when the invitation came, I was sitting on a hot rock by the blue water of Ardmore Bay in a rare, wonderful heatwave, and I wanted to go on doing that.

I sat there thinking about satire, and its functions. With the ruins and Celtic myths of Ardmore all around, I naturally reflected on that thing that happened to prehistoric Irish King Bres, whose father was a Formorian and mother one of the People of the Goddess Danu. He was elected King, and married one of the People of the Goddess Danu, in the expectation that peace would thus be brought about between these latter and the Formorians.

In those days nobody could be a King in Ireland who suffered from any physical blemish. Bres was in good physical shape, but he was arrogant, inefficient, and vexatious. So vexatious, indeed, that the people went to the Satirist Cairbre and begged him to do some Satires on Bres. Cairbre complied. Bres stood it for a while, but in the end these savage satires got, literally, under his skin. Boils burst out all over his face. As a result of this blemish he was forced to resign, and a war broke out between the Formorians and the People of the Goddess Danu which lasted seven years. I recalled, too, that the Celtic hero Cu Chulainn, who was so agile in battle that he could 'turn round in his skin so that his feet and knees were to the rear and his calves and buttocks to the front', was ultimately brought low by a poet who threatened to satirize him unless he complied with certain demands. Cu Chulainn did not dare face satire. He acceded to the demands and was ruined.

These were stimulating recollections.

I got off my rock and went home to write a letter to *Private Eye* saying 'Yes'. I did, fortunately, manage to come out of my exhilarating haze of thoughts about satire long enough to stipulate that I must be paid a sum – huge in relation to their tiny financial resources as they then stood – sufficient to assuage the fears of any Irish creditors who might be alarmed at my leaving the jurisdiction. I also made it a condition that I must have at least three weeks in London, before assuming the temporary editorship, in order to inform myself of the state of affairs; to see some men who knew some men. This was to be at the expense of *Private Eye*. But by a nice coincidence the *Sunday Telegraph* people got the idea they would like to have me within easy reach for a bit, so they paid these expenses instead, relieving *Private Eye* of quite a burden. It is always agreeable to see the rich helping the poor. Still, I could see I was going to be busy. For despite Donald McLachlan's eager anxiety to cut what he called the 'Umbilical Cord' supposed to be spiritually linking the *Sunday Telegraph* to the Tory orthodoxy of its rich Mama, the *Daily Telegraph*, it was still going to be quite a trip, involving sharpish changes of climate, from the *Telegraph* office in Fleet Street to the bottom of Greek Street, Soho, where – between a strip-tease and a betting-shop, into which some gangster had recently thrown a more or less abortive bomb – was located the office of *Private Eye*.

The barker for that strip-tease has a claim to be classed with the top ten of the world's optimists. As I approached the office for the first time very early on a bright Friday afternoon he spoke to me urgently, begging me to view the naked women. Since I was a stranger, that was intelligible. I certainly hope that I am not the only man who looks as though he might want to spend a sunny afternoon in that way. But I have entered the *Private Eye* office several hundred times since then, and when I have been alone, the barker has never failed to look me in the face and repeat the invitation with the same hopeful urgency. On this first occasion, before going up to the office I stepped into the betting-shop and placed the type of bet known as a 'Yankee' on four of the races still to be run that day. By the evening I was able to collect a little over £72 for the twenty-two shillings I had bet. That was agreeable in itself, and could be deemed a good omen. That betting-shop was certainly an amenity. In the old days, a person briefly visiting London from Ireland with its very numerous legal betting-shops, had found it a frustrating, sometimes nearly agonizing, task to find a place to get his money on in a hurry. With betting now legalized in Britain, I used often, when editorial problems became harassing, to drop down to this place next door and enjoy, for a half-hour or so, the mingled excitement and relaxation of betting a little money, and listening to the races being broadcast from the course. Other *habitués* included many heavily razor-scarred but, for the most part, infectiously cheerful Maltese Negroes. They were obviously poor, and I cannot imagine what they had to laugh about. Nor did I ever find out, because they were notably stand-offish with Whites. But, as a tiny contribution to study of the Social Scene, I noted that their nerves seemed in better shape than were those of the White gamblers. These latter would often twitch and swear and even gnash their teeth as the loud-speaker reported the failure of their fancy. The Negroes from Malta – who must have guessed wrong just as often as anyone else – smiled through it all, only occasionally letting go with a guttural sigh.

Greek Street, like so much of Soho, is soothing in its architectural charm. It is not always easy for a sane man to appreciate the charm because he is rightly nagged by the thought that there must be something perhaps dangerously wrong with a society which can daily produce enough customers to support so many strip-tease joints. Brothels are less unseemly. The best, though certainly not the 'peak' Viewing Time for Soho is a shining Sunday mid-morning. (At night the neon lights are pretty, though they could often be a lot prettier, but they obscure or distort the building structures.) On Sunday morning the streets are almost free of traffic. The poor strippers are at rest. So are the rich club owners and the protection racketeers.

Behind a closed door here and there, the coshed and the burgled are for the most part still unaware of what happened to them in the dark early hours. There is so little noise that you can hear the church bells calling the faithful to prayer. Sunday is press day for *Private Eye*, and on the first such Sunday I was there I was standing on the doorstep of *Private Eye*, waiting for the Coach and Horses public house to open, when the customary hush was shattered by a rising roar of motor-cycle engines. From Soho Square, a cohort, led by a uniformed policeman, was coming slowly and rowdily down Greek Street. It just crossed my mind that we were being raided, possibly for seeking to raise boils on the already red faces of Government men. Just as the leading policeman drew level with us, he turned to shout over his shoulder at the cohort behind.

'And that,' he said, with a big hand-signal, 'is *Private Eye*.'

We ascertained that the cohort was composed not of policemen but of aspirant taxi-drivers. On Sunday mornings Scotland Yard takes a score or so of them on conducted tours of London, teaching them the geography of the city and the location of the most notable buildings and institutions. It was gratifying to realize that we were up there among the worthwhile sights and tourist attractions along with St Paul's and the White City dog-track.

I taxied and telephoned for the stipulated three weeks, working at meeting – or re-meeting – the men who knew the men. The experience reminded me of the days of *The Week*. Under certain stimuli, the normally taciturn or discreet members of the British Establishment can become quite astonishingly talkative. The reek of the political mess of that year provided such a stimulus for many. A surprising number seemed to feel that the best way for all good men and true to come to the aid of the country was to spill whatever beans they might have to an uninhibited satirical magazine. (Naturally, a lot of the beans were mouldy, or phoney – made of plastic gossip. But, as I have said before, even the existence of a particular rumour can be a significant fact.)

Nevertheless, as the time approached when I was to take over sole editorial charge, while the regular editors took off for foreign parts, I was daunted, and often wished myself back on that sun-warmed, lonely rock. But the charm, the ebullient confidence, and the tireless assistance of all concerned in the enterprise reduced any natural alarms. Also the ululations against satire and satirists now to be heard on all hands seemed convincing evidence that the satirists were achieving something useful, and might achieve more.

In this belief I was notably encouraged by the personality of Richard Ingrams, Editor. He had been a progenitor of the magazine – a bold notion in itself. Perhaps more important and remarkable was the fact that as Editor he had kept the little boat afloat in storms – external and internal – which would certainly have wrecked a craft less ably skippered. (I speak of 'internal' storms because obviously people working enthusiastically for such a magazine are not likely to be the most placid of men.)

Even Malcolm Muggeridge at *Punch* had no more tricky a job than Richard. Anyone who thinks the regular editorship of *Private Eye* requires other than nearly magical – black magical some will say – qualities, should try his hand at, for example, paddling a canoe across the Bay of Biscay in a Force 10 gale with a crew, some of whom are keen to get to Oporto while others are seeking to set the course for Staten Island.

'"Daddy's on the engine",' says the old music-hall song, '"don't be afraid. Daddy knows what he is doing," said the little maid. "Daddy's on the engine, there's no need for fear. *My* Daddy's on the engine, and my Daddy's an engineer."' Such reassurances were being loudly voiced from Westminster, Whitehall and Elsewhere, as always in Times of Crisis, whatever Government chances to be in power. I have forgotten whether, in the song, the little maid's faith was justified, or whether the train was wrecked with carnage. In real life (and I am not speaking principally or even mainly, of the farcical, yet unpleasantly ominous, events of 'Profumo year', a year in which the Profumo affair can be seen by hindsight as one of the least of the nation's troubles), it is customarily hard to believe that more than a very few of the numerous people on the engine are engineers at all.

At this point we get one of the main divisions in political thinking. Granted that the man on the engine has very little idea what he is doing, ought we or ought we not to apprise the passengers? There are those on the one hand who say, 'Absolutely not. People would panic and start pulling the communication cord. They might even surge up the corridors and try to get on the engine themselves, whereupon the whole vehicle would be brought into greater peril than ever. Leave the men on the engine alone. With a large hatful of luck they might get us somewhere without a smash-up. And if not, well, that just goes to show that journeying through the world is a hazardous business and it is a mistake to look for too much security.' The people who take this view exist everywhere – in Communist countries no less than in others. It was one of the reasons why Stalin got left on the engine a long time after he was visibly unfit to run the train. Others, and they, too, exist in millions everywhere, are all for spreading the dire news among the passengers as speedily as possible. They think these unfortunates have the right at least to know what is going on up there at the head of the train. Some of them think that just spreading that news, and pointing with derision at the way the driver is acting, is all that they can usefully do. They are satirical and unconstructive. They admit they probably could not operate the engine any better themselves, while claiming as credit to themselves that at least they are not even pretending to. Some others are firm in the belief that once the passengers know what is happening they will somehow find ways and means to avert the threatened catastrophe – perhaps, somewhere in the second-class coaches, there are some real engineers. These call themselves democrats, but as they have never yet got full control of the footplate, nobody knows what their large claims amount to.

What arouses the indignation of the honest satirist is not, unless the man is a prig, the fact that people in positions of power or influence behave idiotically, or even that they behave wickedly. It is that they conspire successfully to impose upon the public a picture of themselves as so very, very deep-thinking, sagacious, honest and well-intentioned. You cannot satirize a man who says 'I'm in it for the money, and that's all about it.' You even feel no inclination to do so. In the 1930s it was easier, or perhaps simply more stimulating, to satirize the leaders of the British Government than to go to work on Hitler or Mussolini. For these latter, at least in the eyes of other peoples than their own, were creatures who roared out in public their bestial thoughts and intentions. Hitler in particular, because he had the enthusiastic support and spiritual concurrence of the vast majority of Germans, had no need of that hypocrisy which Wilde described as the tribute vice pays to virtue. He said he was going to persecute and murder the Jews, and no sooner was it said than it was done. He proclaimed his delinquent's contempt for civilization, and, to ensure that nobody misunderstood him, organized such fêtes and galas as the 'burning of the books'. He lied certainly – lied continuously. But his lying was of a special kind – it did not, and could not by him have been expected to, deceive anyone who did not secretly wish to be deceived. In this he resembled the great confidence tricksters.

The confidence tricksters, it seems, consider it axiomatic that no wholly honest man can be regarded as a likely victim of the confidence trick. It is not the mere fools that the confidence men successfully delude. It is, in their pregnant phrase, the 'larceny in the blood' of the victim which results in his victimization. And that was how Hitler operated – exploiting and using as his leverage the 'larceny in the blood' of innumerable politicians in every country who wanted to believe that here was a man who really had found a way of making diamonds out of plastics; a way, that is to say, of making a quick profit out of an illicit sale of the Western soul. You cannot satirize a confidence trickster – the best you can do is expose him, send for the police. But when you find a respectable citizen – the victim – who, beneath his air of solid good sense and goodwill is secretly hoping to turn a dishonest political profit by getting a flashy-looking collection of goods labelled 'peace' or 'security' or 'the end of Bolshevism' for some minimal down-payment in the way of a betrayal of the Jews, or the sacrifice of a couple of small nations, then you have a subject which invites and excites the attention of the satirist.

The satirist, as I have remarked, is certainly among those who cannot bear that the passengers should be left for a moment longer in ignorance of the incompetence or malignancy of the engine driver. He is also likely to feel that having done that much his particular function has been accomplished, and he is not apt to pay much heed to those who keep asking him for his 'solution'. He will reply that while he may, in some other capacity – as, say, a voter or a magistrate or Trade Union secretary – feel able and bound to propose and work towards 'solutions', as a satirist this is not his job.

With such thoughts in mind I started to get my special issue together. About lay-out I know scandalously little. Nothing, in fact, or just enough to be a nuisance to experts who do. (It is characteristic of our educational system that when I was young nobody told journalists just graduated from Oxford that it was their business to know at least the elements of all the processes of their trade, including some manual labour at the linotypes. By the time I had grasped that this was important, there never seemed to be a spare moment in which to learn. As in so many other areas of life, one regrets, too late, not anything one has done, but all the things one might have done but never got around to doing.)

Fortunately, I had the almost imperturbable Tony Rushton to take total charge of that part of our operation. I say 'almost' because at times my notions of the technically feasible must certainly have perturbed him to the point of madness. But he remained cheerfully sane, and helped to keep me sane, I think, too.

The front cover of the special issue was attractive enough to be described by many as pictorially and textually nauseating. That seemed to indicate that it bore at least some serious relation to the political situation. The issue also 'broke' – in the journalistic sense of the word – the scandal of the Harold Wolfe case, which as a result later became the subject of defensive statements from Scotland Yard, Home Office inquiries, and finally a very white White Paper. (I had for long hammered away at the point that a satirical paper cannot justify its existence only by satirizing what is already known. It must disclose news, too. The indispensable *Canard Enchainé* of Paris could not have lived and more or less prospered – without ever accepting a paid advertisement – on its jokes and cartoons alone.)

That press day was an unexpected strain, and sometimes a nightmare, for both myself and Tony Rushton. For Dr Stephen Ward, having in fact attempted suicide, was still hanging between life and death in the hospital. We had to have two cartoons ready, one for use in case he seemed to be going to survive, the other in case of his death. We rang up the hospital every half-hour, and every half-hour the printers rang us to ask why the copy was so late, and warn us that if we hung on much longer the magazine would not appear that week at all. However, it did punctually appear, and the circulation shot up to a record figure. This, of course, was in large part due to the special circumstances of that particular fortnight, the super-heated political atmosphere. All we did – all any publication could have done – was to make sure that we were giving the fullest possible expression to the true mood of the period; were reflecting what a lot of people who were inarticulate in public were muttering in the clubs and pubs and on their way to church, or to University lectures. In addition, numerous items of 'inside news' which nobody else could publish because of the libel laws, and an 'exposure' such as that of the Wolfe affair, positively added some new ingredients to the atmosphere. A small-scale inquiry into the number of people who read each single copy of the issue – not buying it, unfortunately, but borrowing or stealing it from buyers – indicated that its actual readership must have been pushing the half-million.

I stayed on in London for a while in case of trouble. Men who knew men kept ringing me up saying we were going to be arrested for this or that vexing misdemeanour committed in the issue. They said that, as was natural enough MI5 and the Special Branch, on learning that the ex-editor of *The Week* had suddenly appeared out of the deep green yonder of Ireland to do this *Private Eye* job, were keeping a particularly sharp lookout. There was, in fact, a bit of trouble, because I had disclosed as a matter of current interest, the name and address of the head of MI5. This was supposed to be a deep State secret. One could be, it seemed, heavily penalized – presumably under the Official Secrets Act – for disclosing the man's identity and function. Except that I thought one might have been hustled off to jail after a trial of which the vital parts were conducted *in camera*, with no chance to put one's case before the general public – a danger never to be quite disregarded when official secrets are involved – I would not have found such a case wholly unwelcome. Since there was no doubt at all that the Russians, the French, the Chinese and the Americans all were familiar with the name of the official concerned, it seemed to me ludicrous that the British public should be kept in ignorance. Why should so important and powerful a functionary remain faceless and nameless to the democratic citizenry of the land? This same citizenry was being not only insulted but deceived, to the extent, at least, that it believed, as it was supposed to believe, that our top anti-spy man was genuinely under wraps; a personage unbeknown to frustratedly inquisitive and potentially hostile foreigners, a valuable secret weapon. Even the Americans, supposedly so much more obsessed with 'security' (the current term for insecurity) than the British, freely published the name of the heads of the F.B.I. and of the C.I.A., organizations a good deal more important in their activities and ramifications than MI5 and MI6 put together.

A source I had good reason to consider well-informed, arranged to meet me in an agreeably open space without microphones – not that I believed that there really were any in the *Private Eye* office – and told me there was a terrible row going on about the naming of this man. Some important people, it seemed, were insisting that I must be arrested, not because they seriously supposed the name was not known to every major Embassy in London, but 'on principle'. It might be well known to everyone who might possibly make improper use of such knowledge, but it was still officially secret. To let *Private Eye* get away with publishing it would create an evil precedent. One big thinker had, too, taken the view that to disregard *Private Eye*'s behaviour would 'cause jealousy' in Fleet Street and thus injure MI5's secret public relations. My informant urged me to go back to Ireland, while the going was still, possibly, good.

I was eager to get back to that rock beside the bay. But I thought that to slink away – it would be the phrase used – just then might make myself and the magazine appear either ridiculous or guilty of some genuine crime. Also it seemed to me that, provided I was allowed to make it, my defence was unanswerable. Above all I believe there are a lot of people with at least ordinary common sense everywhere – even, despite all the jokes and the Memoirs, at MI5. (This estimate, in case anyone is becoming over-optimistic, does not apply at times of panic, which the Lord knows are frequent enough everywhere from Washington to Peking and back through Moscow to Paris and London.) But this was not such a moment, and although I hung about London for a while I thought they would sensibly do nothing, and nothing is what they did. To their credit, the *Sunday Telegraph* and Donald McLachlan – who had certainly been hearing some harsh things about me and *Private Eye*, behaved with impeccable *sang froid* and courtesy throughout. They seemed to take the view – happily not uncommon in Fleet Street, yet so rare in the U.S. – that unless and until the roof actually fell in on me, the attitude of 'the authorities' was no business of theirs. I recalled how, years before, an agent of the U.S. Government called very confidentially on Malcolm Muggeridge and pointed out how undesirable and potentially dangerous it was for *Punch* to employ a man with a past such as mine. That agent presently went staggering out into Bouverie Street in a state of shock.

34

THE LOVED ONE

WHILE I still loitered in London, Mr Donald McLachlan confided to a Mutual Friend that he felt the paper was not 'making enough use' of me.

'Send him,' said the Mutual Friend, 'to New York.'

Naturally enough, McLachlan demurred – not to say recoiled.

'But surely,' he said, 'with his Left wing opinions, his general attitude to what he calls capitalist society, he would hardly be inclined to . . .'

'My dear fellow,' said the Mutual Friend, 'there are Europeans who fear and detest America. There are Europeans who rather like America. Claud is the only real European I know who for more than thirty years has been passionately – and often besottedly – in love with America. Send him to see how the loved one is getting on.'

The paradox was, nevertheless, a reasonable assessment. Perhaps it is nonsense to talk of being 'in love' with a country. (Albert Camus certainly did not think so. In his story *La Femme Adultère*, the chief character – Janine – falls so much in love with the North African desert that she, lying alone on the roof of the house, listening to the silence of the desert broken only by 'the muffled cracking of the stones which the cold was splitting up into sand', and watching the stars, has a complete orgasm.)

Personally, although I have never quite duplicated Janine's experience, I believe Camus was on the right track with that story. Certain places, certain scenes, do produce in some people reactions easily comparable to the experience of sexual love. The Danube valley has this effect upon me, and so does North America.

I thought it prudent not to attempt to explain this theory to Donald McLachlan. Such ideas can easily be misunderstood. One could be classified as unbalanced. Or else an unseemly story could percolate through the office to the effect that 'they're sending Claud to New York to have an orgasm.'

Still less, naturally, did I seek to explain myself in these terms to the United States Consul-General. In view of my past, and the American present, I had to explain a good deal else to him.

Without the assistance of McLachlan and the *Sunday Telegraph* I would hardly have got to first base. The Consul General was exceedingly kindly and cooperative. But, the United States laws on the subject being what they are, it was quite impossible for him to grant a visa to a formerly prominent member of the Communist Party without careful interrogation. The results of the interrogation had to be sent by him to the State Department, and by the State Department to the Department of Justice. Then, if the Department of Justice were satisfied, it could issue a 'waiver', permitting the State Department to inform the Consul General that a visa could be issued.

On the steps of the Embassy in Grosvenor Square, as I went in for my interview, Patricia had given me a last, percipient, warning. 'For God's sake,' she said, 'don't try to be funny. They won't like it.' I promised, but there were moments when it was a hard promise to keep. In fact I nearly broke it in the first quarter of an hour of the interview.

The Consul General courteously explained to me that, had I been a more or less anonymous member of the Communist Party, sitting like a bump on a log with my mouth open through months and years of meetings, and then just checked out of the organization, the matter of the 'waiver' would be simple enough. But not, very regrettably, so. I had been diplomatic correspondent, foreign editor, political correspondent, of the *Daily Worker*. I had written hundreds of thousands of Communist words. I had agitated on public platforms. I had fought in Spain. Therefore, what the Department of Justice would be looking for was some evidence of what was called 'commensurate counter-activity'.

I said, 'You mean like Arthur Koestler and Douglas Hyde?'

He maintained diplomatic silence and immobility.

Breaking my promise to Patricia I said, 'If there's still time, I might with your assistance, rush out and write an article for *Encounter*.' This was in the days – now past – when *Encounter* was supposed to benefit – directly or indirectly – from the special interest of the State Department and the C.I.A. As Patricia had predicted, the Consul General was not amused. But despite this he went right ahead doing his best for me.

Towards the end of the interview he asked, more or less perfunctorily, what 'front organizations' I had been a member of in my time. I said 'None', and then recalled that I had been, for a matter of two months, the Press Officer of an organization called The People's Convention. I told him that, and he said he knew that already. But what other 'front organizations' had I belonged to?

'None.'

He looked very grave. It was an answer, he conveyed to me as diplomatically as possible, that would not satisfy the Department of Justice. Indeed it would make them very suspicious. From his explanation emerged the fact that the American

414

Establishment had become the prisoner of its own propaganda to the extent of believing that since the cunning Commies are known to operate through front organizations, all genuine Communists must have been members of a lot of these, and a Communist – claiming to be ex-Communist – who denies that he was a member of such, must still be a cunning Commie, not 'ex' at all.

I racked my brains to think of some such organization, some-where, that I might have at some time joined. Restrained by my promise to Patricia, I prevented myself listing a lot of impeccably Tory or Labouristic or religious organizations which, had I named them, would have found themselves under laborious surveillance by the F.B.I. and the subject of interesting reports from the C.I.A.

At length I said, 'Sir, I can only tell you that being a full-time, hard core, all down the line, red Red, was a full-time job. I just did not have the time to go out and join anything else. Besides, I never got on very well with the front members of front organizations.'

He sighed resignedly and made some notes. But he must have been as honestly friendly as he seemed, for in a couple of weeks my visa came through. In duty bound, he had to put some little marks on it, but at the time I failed to notice them, certainly did not ask what they meant. That emerged some weeks later in Kingston, Jamaica.

In the middle of my stint in my much-loved New York, I had gone down to Jamaica for a couple of weeks to join Patricia. We were staying in the south-east part of the island, forty-five miles south of Montego Bay, with an old friend who, incident-ally, first introduced marlin fishing to Jamaica. Subconsciously I must have had, on leaving New York for Montego Bay and points south, the not quite irrational notion that the whole of the Caribbean was part of the United States. On realizing that this was, at best, an anticipation of history, I telephoned to the American Consul in Kingston, explaining that I had a 'one shot' visa, and asking how long it would take to get it re-stamped so that I could get back to New York.

He said, 'Bring it in in the morning and we'll have it stamped by afternoon.'

415

But when I got there things looked different. The Vice-Consul said, 'Mr Cockburn, you have misled me as to the situation.'

I had no notion of what situation he was speaking about, and said so.

He then opened my passport and ran his finger along a hand-written couple of lines which said – now I came to look at them – 212 (d) d i (3) (A) 28 F K G 2 12.

I said I felt like the man in the fairy stories who takes a message to the King and the bit of small print on the back of the message says 'Hang messenger'.

He said, 'Well, you see . . . it's The Party.'

Remembering Patricia, who was sitting in an outer room expecting the worst, I clenched my teeth and forbore to ask whether it was the Republican or Democratic Party to which he referred. It is nevertheless a curious fact that when a British or American authority refers to 'the Party' he almost always means the tiny Communist Party. It is one of those areas in which the devil-propaganda has boomeranged. Khrushchev once pointed out that, although there are almost no Communists in Iran, if the Shah were suddenly overthrown the Western press would immediately declare the Communists responsible. And this, as Khrushchev noted, would do a lot of good to the Communists without trouble or expense on their part.

The Vice-Consul then partially decoded for me the signs and signals on my visa. They indicated, among other things, my lack of 'commensurate counter-activity', and my refusal to admit membership of front organizations.

'I will do,' he said, 'what I can for you. But I shall have to send for your entire dossier from Frankfurt.'

It was hot and horribly humid and I thought I might be having hallucinations. 'Frankfurt?' I said. 'I haven't been in Frankfurt for forty years.'

'Your dossier,' he said, 'will be in Frankfurt. That's where dossiers in your category get processed.'

I said, 'If I could have a quick strong drink I believe I might be able to focus on this entire situation more clearly than I seem to be able to just at the present time.'

The kindly man immediately gave me a big drink. And after some talk he took me to see the Consul – a very able woman from New York who offered to telephone the State Department and ask the State Department to telephone the Department of Justice, and see about the 'waiver'.

She did that, and by the time Patricia and I came back from the neighbourhood bar she had everything fixed up, and we left for New York that evening.

If New York really resembled the image of itself it projects on the moving pictures and through other media it would certainly be hell – or, at the best, Dortmund. A cliff-dwelling Megalopolis, smooth and shining, and whizzing around the clock with inhuman precision.

On the contrary, the essential quality of that city is that it simply refuses to tick over in that fashion. It is a rich museum of ramshackle inefficiency. Only those Europeans who have been willingly brain-washed by the films fail to notice its true, and truly endearing characteristics. It is, one must remember, a city created by fanatics and extremists: the original Dutch and English refugees from religious and political conformity; the German Liberals on the run; the starving Irish; and the Jews who, even when they are most active and successful in their service of Mammon, never omit to remind themselves and everyone else of the pervasive existence of things unseen. In New York, a rich Anglo-Saxon can lull you into the belief that being rich and Anglo-Saxon is about as far as you can get. But the rich New York Jew almost always gives one the impression of a man with a mask that keeps slipping. The mask twitches and slips, and has the effect of caricaturing the whole set-up, the whole of the values according to which he purports to live.

And if the reader now thinks he is observing simply the effects of the love affair, let me say at once that if you take another close look at that haggard old bag, New York, you will not have to look or go far to see its casual cruelty, the callous wickedness of man's inhumanity to man. In fact, when you feel you may be falling fatuously in love with New York, the thing to do is to take a walk through Harlem, if you, as a white person, dare do that. The fact that a lot of white people would, quite rightly, not dare walk through much of Harlem is sufficient comment on the state of the city. It is a supreme example of social inefficiency triumphing, temporarily at least, over all the advantages provided by riches and technology.

This is the far from endearing aspect of New York's ramshackle way of life. On the other hand, that way of life – product of all those fanaticisms which New York fought and cherished turn by turn – has produced in large areas of New York life a kind of genial permissiveness, a shirt-sleeved *je m'en foutisme*, an acceptance of the fact that the next man may look mad to you but may seem sane to himself, which is the antithesis of everything that is meant by 'McCarthyism' or 'Goldwaterism'. It is no great wonder that Goldwater once expressed the view that it would be a good thing if New York just broke off from the continent and floated away into the Atlantic Ocean, joining, I suppose, the wrecked ships of the world in the Sargasso Sea.

You can relax in New York because people there freely and openly admit what is going on to an extent in London the people who know do, as I have said, only under special stimuli. You do not have to contend with either hypocrisy or complacency. In New York even a banker will tell you that, in his opinion, the 'system' makes less and less sense, and may have to be defended with the sub-machine-guns of the police. He may be wrong. But he says it. What London banker would allow such thoughts to pass the barrier of his lips? Only the newspapers even hope to be believed when they claim that napalm versus peasant is 'democracy's last hope'.

An engineering executive said to me – showing a Japanese gadget in every way superior to anything his firm was producing – 'If only we too could become Americanized.' On the other hand a patriotic New Yorker in whose presence I had been, perhaps rather too freely, expounding my view of the colossal, wambling, money-wasting, energy-wasting mess of that city, said to me, 'I just want to tell you that in New York a hell of a lot of things really work a hell of a lot of the time.'

I could agree that far. And I told him that to me New York, even when I was first there, had always appeared to me as a kind of reflection of what – if the history books and memoirs are correct – St Petersburg had been like around the beginning of World War I. A city blazing with banks, with millions of more or less imaginary roubles floating amid the chandeliers and run, so far as the main body of the personnel was concerned, by barely-reconstructed mujiks.

The most intelligent men and women in the world were probably to be found in New York. And that had probably been true of St Petersburg, too. But the chores – like actually running the banks – were done by people from the steppes of, say, Siberia or Nebraska, or the savannahs of Turkestan or Louisiana. After waiting an hour and a half in a big bank on Fifth Avenue to complete a transaction which in London would have taken about five minutes, I said to the man sitting on the other side of the enormous, executive-type desk, under the concealed lighting and surrounded by costly murals, that I enjoyed sitting there in his huge chair but felt badly about the bank's shareholders, whose time and money I could not but feel I was wasting.

He said, 'Trouble is, it's the computer.'

It seemed that practically everything that went on in that bank had to be fed through a computer before it made sense. We had so much time to spare that I had the opportunity to question the man about his background and found, not at all to my surprise, that he had arrived only twenty-five years or so earlier from a bog-town in County Kerry, Ireland.

'But there,' I said, 'you could have put through my little bit of business in ten minutes.'

'I could, Mr Cockburn,' he said, 'of course I could. But would they have paid me a tenth of what they pay me here? Of course they would not have, Mr Cockburn. Of course not. D'you understand me now?'

All this time, as everyone now sadly knows, a time bomb was ticking.

Adlai Stevenson went to Texas and was there spat upon and otherwise physically assaulted. And in the atmosphere of those days – electric with hatred – the episode was not regarded as a major national scandal. Naturally I had no notion of what was really going to happen next, but I did remark to a number of people that there was something dangerously sinister about a situation in which a man of Mr Stevenson's eminence – United States Ambassador to the United Nations – could be thus treated without the newspapers raising more than a perfunctory, routine-type outcry and protest.

Then Mr Stevenson came back to New York and talked very seriously to two people I knew – two people hardly known to one another – about the menacing situation in Texas and the unlimited capacities for violence of the extreme Right Wing forces there.

Like all confidential conversations, those conversations leaked – at least in part – through New York. But then Stevenson had the reputation of a liberal, a softish type of man – what was termed at the time a 'dove' as opposed to the 'hawks' around the Kennedy administration. He was said to have 'over-reacted' to being spat upon by those Texans; he was seeing burglars under the bed.

Stevenson then did a thing which, in his position, was courageous. He warned President Kennedy that in his, Stevenson's opinion, it would be a dangerous thing for the President to go to Texas – an intention of which Stevenson had just learned. I was told of this warning on the following day in the very greatest confidence. I have sometimes wondered since whether it was, perhaps, one of those confidences one is supposed to break. Just possibly someone had the idea that if the fact of such a warning were published somewhere (whereupon it would be likely to be picked up and published everywhere), the grim course of events might be changed.

But that was not what I thought at the time. What I thought then was that the story, though really creditable to Stevenson, could do him nothing but harm. More burglars under more beds, and now he was trying to put his own scare into the President of the United States.

But with the confidential knowledge of that warning in mind, I began to be just aware, at the back of my mind, of the possibility of a tragedy moving as though written by Sophocles, an ineluctable conclusion. On the day I returned from the United States, I tried to explain some of these thoughts to people in Fleet Street, and elsewhere.

It was not easy. And the difficulties of so doing were expressive of the basic difficulties of Anglo-American relations. For in the United States people had been inclined to regard me as typically Anglo-tepid in my supposed underestimation of the power of the political dynamite that might at any moment – this year, next, some time, but not never – explode. In London I was treated as a sensationalist.

However, I am used to being so treated by English people, and I plugged ahead, seeking to set out my view. It was an error, I told them, to suppose – as most of them did at that time – that President Kennedy was so universally popular and loudly acclaimed as to be politically omnipotent. On the contrary, his necessary effort to keep the South in line for his re-election of 1964 – and he absolutely needed the South – had at this time produced a mood of disappointed scepticism about him (and still more about his brother, the Attorney General) among many Liberal and Negro leaders. They were not by any means against the Kennedys. But the impetus of their enthusiasm for them was lagging and sagging.

The Southern Right was as well aware of this as anyone else. The Southern Right understood very well the capacity for blackmail which it now had in its hands. Naturally, it intensified its pressures, its threats. A situation was reached in which it became essential for President Kennedy to mend his fences in the South, and – at least for a start – in Texas.

He was forced to do something to prove to waverers in Texas that the Kennedy band-wagon down there was still the band-wagon to get aboard if you wanted to be the man with the votes and the patronage and the dams, and other Federal Government projects, in 1965.

That was the background of the Sophoclean situation.

So – come hell and high water, and despite the warnings of Adlai Stevenson – he had, physically, to go to Texas. Show that he, this Irish Bostonian, was also one of them.

That, in other circumstances, might have been arranged in a quiet way – a meeting with political and business leaders in a hotel here, and a mansion there. But, in the real circumstances, such tactics would not suffice. There had to be a public demonstration. Some act that looked democratic as well as Democratic.

Thus it was decided. But in the meantime an annoying thing had happened. The President had gone to Pennsylvania for a triumphal motorcade. The weather had been bad. The turnout of the populace had been meagre. Apart from the weather, the reasons were those mentioned: the Kennedy image – it is hard to remember this now – was not compelling such public enthusiasm as it had only a few months before. The demonstration in Philadelphia was rated by the experts as a flop.

Well, whatever about Pennsylvania, there must be no risk of such a flop in Texas.

What, in physical fact, did that mean? It meant that the President must present himself to the public in the most public possible way. No protection of bubble car. Standing up for all to see.

It meant more still than that – and this was the fatal factor. It meant that, if adequate crowds were to be assembled, his route had to be announced in advance.

People at that time were admiring, or deploring, the audacity of General de Gaulle who, at a moment when skilled assassins pullulated in the streets of France, used, on passing through some village, to spring suddenly from his car and stride into the crowds, embracing chosen peasantry. But as nobody knew more than a half-hour or so in advance which village was to be the scene of these amenities, the assassins were at a loss. The only occasions upon which they very nearly got him in their sights were those when he was following a route which, if not pre-announced, could at least be reasonably predicted.

This was a fundamental difference between the political requirements of General de Gaulle and President Kennedy. It preserved, at that time, the one, and destroyed the other.

All through a horrible November day in London I tried to clarify to myself and others – I had left New York only the night before – the atmosphere in which it seemed to me these things must be regarded as important. I was aware of boring a lot of people a lot of the time. Finally came that moment of defeat, so common in England, when the editor I was lunching with, said, 'Well, well that's all terribly interesting, and I'd like to talk about it some more next week. There might be a piece in it. Meantime, you've been flying the Atlantic half the night, so why don't you go back to your hotel and have a nice rest? Relax.'

422

I did that. And around six the telephone was ringing and the Editor was saying, 'Can you get down to the office right away? The President has been shot dead in Dallas.' The fact that you have had a feeling, as the old saying goes, 'in your bones' that a particular appalling thing might happen, makes it no easier to realize that it actually has happened. And there is, in all such circumstances, the odious sensation that someone is going to accuse you of saying 'I told you so.' When, in reality you did not – absolutely could not – have 'told them so'.

Months later, a Committee of distinguished people who were investigating the assassination and were very much dissatisfied with the findings of the Warren Report asked me – on the strength I suppose of what I had written immediately after the event – to join my name to theirs in denunciation of the Warren Report.

I sympathized with their sense of outrage. But I had to decline. I thought, to put it in a nutshell, that they were barking up the wrong tree. It was at that time my opinion that Oswald was guilty of firing the shot that killed President Kennedy. And I thought that by seeking to prove Oswald guiltless, the Committee was in effect deflecting the lightning from the real culprits – that is to say those people (there is not much need to name names) who had created that state of mind in Texas which had caused the late Stevenson to dare to warn the President of the United States not to venture into that murderous territory.

Any nut-case in Texas, I thought, might – under those influences, in that atmosphere – have pulled the trigger. (With, it goes without saying, some assistance somewhere along the line.)

So I thought by trying to prove that Oswald was innocent, they would be moving up a blind alley. (Things heard and read since have not modified my opinion. I still believe that Oswald, though he may have fired the fatal shot, was a mere tool of the Texan rightists and was all along cast as the 'patsy', the 'fall guy'.)

At the time what deeply interested me was the depth and violence of the passions aroused by the mere fact of the Warren Report being questioned. The questioners – Mark Lane, Bertrand

Russell, Trevor Roper, for example – were attacked in that note of shrill exasperation which is heard when people feel that some sort of sacrilege has been committed; the profanation of some rite sacred to those people.

This 'over-reaction' to what were, to say the least of it, quite reasonable queries and doubts, was psychologically very revealing – in some of its tones recalling the original reactions to Malcolm Muggeridge's criticisms of the Queen. And going a long way farther afield, it was not psychologically irrelevant to remember the fury stimulated against themselves by the Gnostics, in the second century A.D., who sought to impugn the orthodox account of the Crucifixion. Basilides asserted that in point of fact Jesus Christ was not the person who died on the Cross. It was a ringer – namely Simon of Cyrene. Basilides and his fellow Gnostics had their own reasons for attempting to undermine at every point the orthodox Christian views of everything. They were trying, for their own purposes, to re-open a case which the orthodox Christians, like the authors of the Warren Report, had declared closed. So were those 'liberal elements' at the Vatican Council of 1965 who – to the rage and terror of Roman Catholic ecclesiastics trying to maintain themselves in Moslem lands – insisted that the Jews were not responsible for the killing of Christ. From the Gnostics to Nasser, those who supported and those who opposed the official theory, had profound ulterior motives for so doing. The sophisticated opponents of the Gnostics suspected their long-term spiritual and political aims. The true believers in the Warren Report also suspected unavowed political motives among those who questioned it. But among the Americans and, to an extent which was sometimes astonishing, the British, there was evident another element in the outcry against the questioners. People seemed, in the face of that horror in Dallas, to long, above all things, for the thing to be accounted for, filed away – put officially into a category where it no longer could nag at the public mind and conscience. For if the act was simply the act of a lunatic, then that could put an end to the terrifying sense of collective guilt, of general social responsibility for a state of affairs in which such a thing could by any means come to pass.

As Henry Miller says in *The Colossus of Maroussi*:

We are all involved, all participating, willy-nilly. The earth is our creation. As long as we refuse to think in terms of world order, world peace, we shall murder and betray one another. We can go on until the crack of doom, if we wish it to be thus. Nothing can bring about a new and better world but our own desire for it. Man kills through fear, and fear is hydra-headed. Once we start slaying, there is no end to it. An eternity would not suffice to vanquish the demons who torture us. *Who put the demons there?* That is for each one to ask himself. Let every man search his own heart. Neither God nor the Devil is responsible, and certainly not such puny monsters as Hitler, Mussolini, Stalin *et alii*. Certainly not such bugaboos as Catholicism, Capitalism, Communism. Who put the demons there in our hearts to torture us?

In the months after the assassination, the demons were working overtime in millions of hearts, and millions longed chiefly for the demons to be put under heavy sedation.

After what seemed, in moments of depression, the nearly demonic world of New York and London, it was a relief to return for the time being to Ireland. When one says that, people in New York and London think you are talking in terms of relaxation, some sort of 'escape'. I have never thought of Ireland in that sense. Indeed I can hardly imagine anyone in his right mind and having some knowledge of Ireland, supposing anything of the kind.

But there is, in my experience, a genuine qualitative difference between small countries and big ones. This is not based on any sentimental or semi-mythical notions about the virtues of the small in contrast to the big. The difference consists in the fact that in a small country – I have no idea how relatively small it has to be to achieve this effect – less people, less of the time, experience that sense of being helpless in the grip of forces that they, with all their votes and arguments and lobbies and polemical articles in the newspapers and statements on the TV, have no real capacity to affect, let alone control.

In big countries, the complexities of society are such as to produce that kind of defeatism. They accentuate man's alienation from his politico-social environment. It becomes impossible – or at least is felt to be impossible – even to count correctly or effectively. The Chancellor of the Exchequer – any Chancellor of the Exchequer – says that so and so many score million pounds spent or saved on this or that will affect so and so many million people in this or that way. And you know, and he knows, that neither he nor his computers can be anywhere near sure of the real answer. This induces cynicism. It down-grades the citizen.

It need not do so. The citizen still has the capacity to take a grip on his own destiny and – whatever the outcome – at least wrestle with it to some effect. But in the big countries it is harder and harder to believe that this is so.

Even in Ireland it is hard enough. I have sympathy with the remarks of an elderly Irish police official who was talking to me once beside a lake in Wicklow in the grey of a dawn which for him was critical and might be disastrous. He said to me, 'Mr Cockburn, do you know what it takes to deal with modern life?'

I said I did not.

He searched his historical memory for a figure of speech which would convey the ultimate in terms of physical and intellectual achievement. 'It takes,' he said, 'the brains of Glad-stone and the balls of a Munster Fusilier.'

Professor E. H. Carr, in his Trevelyan Lectures of 1961, re-marks on the 'observed fact that the effect which is needed to drive civilization forward dies away in one place and is later resumed in another,' and suggests that

the group – call it a class, a nation, a civilization, what you will, which plays the leading part in the advance of civilization in one period is unlikely to play a similar part in the next period, and this for the good reason that it will be too deeply imbued with the tradi-tions, interests, and ideologies of the earlier period to be able to adapt itself to the demands and conditions of the next period.

One is reminded of the remarks which I have already quoted of Saint-Beuve on the desirability of keeping our watches up to time.

It can be done. Animals – even horses – can do it. Only the other day Patricia told me about three Australian hunters im-ported to Ireland. In the first year of their sojourn in the island, they grew – these Antipodeans – heavy winter coats in summer,

426

and nearly died of sweaty heat. In the winter they had only their thin coats, and nearly died of cold.

But at the end of three years they started growing the right coats at the right time.

35

UP GREEK STREET

ONE hilarious night at his Establishment Club in New York Peter Cook, majority shareholder in *Private Eye*, had spent some time between the cabaret acts urging me to join the editorial board. I told him it was impossible. I adduced all the arguments about my advanced age-group; explained that I was going to spend the next year or so sitting among green fields writing two books. I got to the green fields and remained among them for a while. And whenever the greenery became monotonous I could walk and sit about in the strange loveliness of Youghal.

Then in the early spring letters came from Greek Street with the same suggestion Peter Cook had made. There was a lot of correspondence. In this all agreed that with the end of 'Profumo year' the wind before which we had run so easily, with only an occasional comber threatening to poop our little craft, had first dropped, leaving the magazine in the doldrums, and was now showing signs of shifting alarmingly. The type of people which regards any satirist junior to Dean Swift as a dirty fellow, and a menace to national virtue and well-being, was again ululating, spraying the correspondence columns of the newspapers with the smug eagerness of a skunk imagining that the defensive jet from its behind is a wholesome disinfectant. It was the sort of situation which the public orators term 'a challenge'. So, having said 'No' several times, I said 'Yes' and went to London.

I should add that I had also run myself into some more than usually grievous financial trouble. The Irish Inland Revenue were breathing very hotly on my neck, and I thought a spell in London might give me time and opportunity to calm, if not fully satisfy, the Commissioners. How morally satisfactory it would be to have an unearned income of £100,000 per annum post-tax, so that the motive of one's actions would always be absolutely pure, quite free of sordid considerations.

The magazine, as appeared when I got back to Greek Street, was in no better financial state than myself. There had been some costly libel actions here and there. (It is a squalid fact of British law that you cannot even start to defend yourself against a libel suit without spending a lot of money. Even if you have the cash you are gambling it on the chance that the Judge will see things your way and, if you win, make the other side pay all the costs. One could not be at all sure that there were many Judges who would, to that extent, see eye to eye with our magazine.) Also it was becoming evident that a lot of people had bought the magazine during the Profumo affair and its aftermath simply in the hope of finding in it stuff about the case which they could enjoyably consider as obscene. (Critics, claiming to be alarmed at my association with such a paper, used to tell me that much of it was made up of 'the sort of stuff you see written up in public lavatories'. I said I had often seen some very funny stuff there. I also quoted Maurice Richardson who once remarked to me with characteristically perceptive pessimism, that if Fleet Street newspapers and magazines went on folding up or amalgamating at the rate they were going 'there'll soon be nothing left to write on but the lavatory walls'.)

The people who had bought the paper for its obscenity value had apparently used up their whole sex potential in Profumo year, were mentally shagged out. Or else they thought that with that business over, life was going to be so clean from then on that it was not worth while trying to spell out printed words (for many of them, sufferers from our educational system, a gruelling task at the best of time). For whatever reason, they were ceasing to buy in thousands.

Still, in these superficially gloomy conditions, there were also good grounds for hope. If we could survive the immediate crisis, then the loss of the semi-literate sections of our public, people that are disappointed when they go to the theatre and find it is not always the same as a strip-tease, would in the longer run be beneficial. (They were going to drop off anyway when they found the magazine devoting – like *Le Canard Enchaîné* – valuable space to news and satire concerned with politics, finance, the 'mass media' and other aspects of the social scene.) Also, this was going to be an election year, and if that failed to put a bit of breeze into the sails of a satirical magazine, it might as well scuttle itself, and the crew sign on with the nearest millionaire-owned tanker. Furthermore, we very soon found that the loss of the strip-tease addicts was beginning, very slowly, to be compensated by a steady growth of circulation among a wide range of intelligent people who were irked by the muffled tones of Fleet Street, and liked the uninhibited manner of a magazine which would print significant information, however 'unfit for print' it might be thought to be by people who would rather be drugged than shocked. They enjoyed the disturbance of stagnant waters by cartoons and satirical observations in the worst possible taste. They were also, so their letters told us, relieved to find there were people who at least tried to put those things in print which occur in conversation – including the pungent obscenities which so often enliven the conversation of the ordinary man, even on his way to a funeral.

There were times when, despite the agreeably increasing gaiety of London's streets, cafés, and pubs, and the brilliance of its theatres, the basic situation gave one an unpleasant feeling that we might all be on our way to the funeral of the country. But in the meantime we had to exert ourselves to avert or postpone a funeral for our magazine. I myself made some attempts at fund-raising which were quite futile. An enormously rich member of a former Labour Government, an old friend, spoke earnestly and with sincere disapproval of the frivolity of *Private Eye*. He, too, mentioned the *graffiti* of the public lavatories. He also thought the paper politically irresponsible. He said, meaning to be helpful, 'I understand that you are only one of three members of the editorial board. You could be out-voted on any issue of principle.'

I started to say that we never took a vote on anything – at the worst just went on arguing till someone collapsed or had to get to Lime Grove for a TV show. But he pursued his line of thought. 'Now if,' he said, 'I and some of my friends in the

Labour Shadow Cabinet were convinced that you, and you alone, were in charge, we might be prepared to . . .'

Neither he, nor the other people in the House of Commons tea-room where we sat, could understand why this kindly-meant remark jerked me into a coarsely unseemly guffaw. Getting it quickly under control, I explained that this same guffaw had been caused by the thought of how, not so many years ago, a majority of the present Labour Shadow Cabinet used, whenever I drew myself, or was drawn, to their attention, to denounce me as very evil. They would certainly have shunned, and occasionally did urge others to shun, any enterprise with which I had any connexion. I now found it nearly disquieting to find myself such a worthily respectable character. ('How little one knows oneself' – as General de Gaulle remarked when he heard himself described, in three successive speeches in the Assemblée as Joan of Arc, Robespierre, and Napoleon Buonaparte.) A little later I was dining at the House with another member of the Shadow Cabinet who had heard of *Private Eye*'s search for funds, and – though by this time I had almost given up even trying very hard to raise money – asked about the magazine's political position. I said, rather thoughtlessly perhaps, but seeking goodwill, that on the whole the people in Greek Street thought nobody could do worse than Sir Alec Douglas-Home and that Harold Wilson's heart was probably in the right place.

This time the guffaw came, with a loud explosion, from my host. When he recovered himself, he asked, referring to his colleague and leader, 'What in God's name makes them think he has a heart at all, let alone in the right place?' The thought amused him so much that he kept calling over Labour M.P.s as they entered the dining-room to tell them, amid renewed laughter from all, that he had just heard of some people who thought Harold had a heart and it was in the right place. I was one of them, he said. So now I had a reputation not only for respectability but also for extreme naïveté.

Matteradam, as the great Flann O'Brien often puts it, about these usually futile efforts to raid the vaults where the big money is. The truly interesting point, one of a general significance much greater than the struggles of this one little magazine, is the extent to which, whenever the paper started sending out S.O.S. signals, people from the most varied strata of British society, rushed to the rescue with donations of whatever amount they could afford. This happened at the time I have been describing. It happened again in 1966, after Lord Russell of Liverpool got huge damages and the paper had to pay £3,000 in costs as well. Those who, with donations large and small, kept the pumps of the imperilled ship going, very often gave anonymously, sending postal orders, or hurrying in with cash and hurrying out again, leaving no addresses. Once when I chanced to be in the office early on a Monday morning, a little man whom I recognized from a news photograph as a member of the House of Lords noted for taciturnity and absenteeism, came puffing up the stairs and into the office, his face ravaged by anxiety. He handed the editorial secretary a fattish bundle of five pound notes. 'Was in the North,' he gasped (he lived not far south of the Scottish border). 'Only saw your appeal late Saturday. Afraid to send cheque. Posts very unreliable. Government's fault. Anyway would have taken couple of days to clear. Thought it might be too late. Took overnight train last night. Went my bank in London soon as it opened this morning – God knows why banks can't open at a reasonable time, like shops. Don't wonder country's going to pot. Got cash. Here it is. Hope to God not too late.' We told him it was not too late. 'Thank God,' he gasped. 'Couldn't do without *Private Eye*. Think what things would be like.' So saying he stumped out of the office, fluttering a hand in refusal of a receipt.

Some of those who contributed to, as many of them put it, 'save the Eye', were schoolboys. In some schools they passed the hat round and sent the takings collectively in the name of the school. A lot of teachers, including a Headmaster here and there, and many University dons, also participated. So did a large number of post-graduate students and research workers. The City was pretty well represented, along with a fair number of Trades Union officials. I was not surprised at the number of M.P.s who found they could not bear the thought of life without *Private Eye*, but a similar feeling, expressed in terms of cheques, seemed to exist in the House of Lords. (I was thus less astonished than I would otherwise have been when, in the mid 1960s,

the Lords sometimes seemed to be running quite a way ahead of
the Commons when the course required vigour, freshness and
independence of mind in jumping the social hurdles.) Less surprising, but matter, all the same, for very good cheer, was the
response from the professionals – famous or still struggling
upwards – of show business, journalism, fiction, the 'visual
arts', and the advertising business. (These last were doing their
best in their private capacity. But, as an executive of one of the
major publicity agencies sadly told me: 'Whenever we've
nearly persuaded one of our client companies to take space in
Private Eye there's always one little squirt on their Board who
ups and says he'd rather be found dead in a whorehouse or
soliciting a Guardsman in Birdcage Walk than see his firm using
that frightful rag as an advertising medium.' I said it certainly
took all sorts to make a world. It seemed we should have to
wait until all that sort actually were found dead in whore-
houses, or arrested for assaulting, in public, some unconsenting
male.

It seems of some importance to disclose and draw attention
to this social phenomenon. It is difficult to do so without
apparent pomposity – an absurd exaggeration of its significance.
For although the paying customers of *Private Eye* are, at the
moment of writing, more numerous than those of the *Spectator*,
their numbers are minuscule in comparison with those of
Woman's Own or the weekly colour supplement of *The Daily
Telegraph*. Also, some financial disaster, or grave political
mishap, might eliminate it abruptly. (In this latter case it would
be necessary to launch another magazine of the same type,
fulfilling the same needs, with the least possible delay. And if
that proved unfeasible it would mean that there were even
more things rotten in the State of Denmark than there are at
this moment.) Looking fixedly on the brighter side, as I always
sought to do while we held lunch-time editorial conferences in
the Coach and Horses, I used to point out that at the peak of its
influence during the last century, the purchasers of *The Times*
formed a scarcely larger percentage of the literate and mentally
active population than did ours today. (When I said this my
colleagues, I believe, thought I was suffering from euphoria.
I am subject to that condition. All the same, though not

susceptible of statistical proof, it is a better guess, founded on a good deal of research, and nearer the probable truth, than a lot of people imagine.) Certainly nobody can deny that *The Times* was in those days quite often moving along a financial queer street, which sometimes looked unpleasantly like the blind alley of bankruptcy. One would not, of course, wish to press any analogies between *The Times* and *Private Eye*.

It was cheering, both spiritually and financially, to contemplate the particular type of support *Private Eye* was shown to have. It was also somewhat dismaying in the sense that we were aware of perpetually falling quite a long way short of giving these people all they deserved by way of instructive entertainment, and the desirable whizz-bang of a well-run firework display. No one was so vain as to suppose that the addiction to *Private Eye* of this cross-section of citizens, their certainty that they would suffer dire withdrawal symptoms if deprived of it, were wholly the result of the properties of the product itself. The demand was created not by any means simply by what *Private Eye* did, but by what the rest of the British Press either could not, or would not, do. *The Week* became the addiction of many for the same reason. (If I refer rather often to *The Week* it is because it is one of those few phenomena about which I know all that is worth knowing.)

The Week benefited from the fact that a big section of the Press of the thirties suffered from lockjaw, or, at the best, chronic constipation. The condition – diagnosed by friendly quack doctors as an 'exercise in discretion, keeping to oneself knowledge which might be harmful if generally released' – resulted, in part, from an over-dose of advertising. Wickham Steed, a former Editor of *The Times*, has described how, in October 1938, 'certain large advertising agents warned journals for which they provide much revenue that advertisements would be withheld from them should they "play up" the international crisis and cause an alarm which was "bad for trade". None of the newspapers thus warned,' Steed noted, 'dared to publish the names of these advertising agents or to hold them up to public contempt.' In the sixties, the trouble with a large part of the Press seemed to be that it was a martyr to verbal diarrhoea, much of it caused by that very same diet; something has to be written on the back of the washing machine advertisement, just as in commercial TV something has to fill the big spaces between the commercials which make the whole enterprise possible in the first place. Their supposed expertise in divining the mind and mood of 'the masses' had promoted a lot of people to near the top echelons of the 'popular' Press who believed what the public, roughly speaking, wants is to know less and less about more and more. The essential, they opined, was to talk quick, talk loud, and never mind the hiccups. Other thinkers were haunted by the notion that if TV touched on this or that topic briefly, their business, especially on Sunday, was to write on these or closely kindred subjects at enormous length. Much of the garrulity was funny and even informative. Some of those daunting 'treatments in depth' were informative and even funny. But all that still left a gap. A lot of brisk-minded democrats around the country had a well-founded suspicion that a lot of facts it would interest them to know were being passed over in silence. They felt that in words and pictures a lot of punches were being pulled, that they were paying their money to watch a fixed fight, and as for getting a bit of a laugh, they could hardly not notice that the Bowdlers – 'can't put that in a family newspaper' – were on the job everywhere, swabbing down the lavatory walls. To hear a really pungent joke in public, you had to pay out good money at a night-club cabaret.

Private Eye did not, could not, with its existing resources, by any means fill this gap – a gap almost literally yawning. But people could see that it was at least trying to do that thing – and given its limitations of money and manpower it did pretty well at it. I found participation in this endeavour exhilarating. For one thing, as for instance when we were looking more closely than others thought it prudent to do, into the Protection Racket, or into where the money went on 'Defence' contracts, one met, as they say, such interesting people. But after a time I left the Editorial Board, largely because I am unsuited by temperament to be a member of the board of anything. At such discussions – and I have been, very very briefly, a member of many committees – I can occasionally fall into a coma and suffer aphasia. More often, particularly at the sort of meetings

434

held at *Private Eye*, I find the atmosphere euphoric, and enthusiastically propose, or support, projects which an hour later are seen to be ludicrously ill-conceived and impracticable. I devoted myself instead to news gathering and, at the time when it became both desirable and necessary to go back to Ireland, writing a fortnightly article for the magazine.

I had left a country which had just held a General Election and, in view of the tiny Labour majority of 1964, was evidently soon going to have another. In such circumstances, the political consciousness of the citizens might be assumed to be more than averagely sharp. Perhaps it was. But on reaching the other island, the tiny Republic with a population of less than three million, I was jolted – not for the first time – into an awareness of the extent to which the difference between a large nation State and a little one is qualitative as well as quantitative. Hemingway was wrong when he told Scott Fitzgerald that the difference between us and the very rich is simply that the very rich have more money. And it is wrong to suppose that the only – even the principal – difference between a little State and a big one is that the big one has more people in it, more money, more factories, more bombs, more tractors, neon tubes, and universities. Of at least equal importance in the conditions of our civilization is the fact that in a small State a larger percentage of people at least believes that what they themselves say and do is really going to have some effect on what happens. There is, that is to say, a larger percentage of hopeful 'political animals' than in the huge State, where, except in times of war and extreme crisis, a much smaller proportion truly believes in its own power to affect or effect anything much beyond a radius of a couple of miles from the Town Hall. That 'alienation' of man as individual from man as citizen, by being visibly less extreme in the small State, sharply illuminates the extent to which it has developed in the big one. Lord knows the Irish speak cynically enough of politicians. But they do not so speak, or think, of politics. Naturally this is in part due to the relative youth of the Republic, and the short space of time separating the citizens of today from the period when the political clash, first between the Irish and the British, then between the opposing views existing among the Irish people themselves, became so serious that

435

it could be resolved only by gunfire. The man who in those days failed to 'take politics seriously' – even careful hedging is in itself a sordid way of recognizing that politics were a matter with which a person must seriously concern himself – was liable to suffer the dreary fate of the eternal 'innocent by-stander' who becomes the victim of a row in the street.

But even allowing for Ireland's particular and immediate political past, the small size of this State would still produce a condition of affairs in which a majority of the men in the street are more aware of their own individual weight than they are in an England where the sheer size and complexity of the political and economic apparatus, the bewildering, inhuman hugeness of the whole box of tricks, induce illusions of impotence – resulting as is often physically the case, in impotence becoming a reality. You can, evidently, find plenty of people in Ireland who will pretend to be 'bored with politics'. But not many really are and a majority would find it obscurely shameful to be taken seriously even if they said such a thing. It would be like a Manchester man at a football match saying it made no difference to him whether United won or lost. In England it is often almost *de rigueur* to pretend to be bored by politics – even at election time. And unfortunately this is often not a pretence but a truth. One must give thought to the case of Mrs Wight, mother of the fourteen-year-old boy who, in the election of 1966, hit the Labour Prime Minister in the eye with a stink bomb. She was by no means depressed by the fact that this schoolboy was still – at fourteen – a total political ignoramus. On the contrary, she proclaimed the fact in an interview, and seemed – perhaps rightly – to assume that friends and neigh-bours in the so modern township of Slough would see this dis-tressing disability as natural and even, perhaps, laudable. She said to an interviewer, 'My son doesn't know the difference between the Labour and Conservative Parties.' I am afraid the context of the remark made clear that she did not mean that the lad, having studied the record and the declared aims of the parties had, after due consideration, concluded that there was very little to choose between them. Few would positively have censured the boy for that conclusion, mistaken or not as it might be. As though clearing herself and son of some

436

disgraceful charge, she said, 'We have no political feelings.' And as, apparently, some sort of ultimate proof that the two of them were at heart respectable and responsible citizens she added, 'We do not have newspapers.' Max Beerbohm remarked of an observation by some complacently moronic critic, 'It would be interesting to see the man who wrote that.' It is certainly interesting, but a long way from exhilarating, to go about England and see whole families of Wights, or names to that effect, not just on the edge of the Slough factory belt, but from Kent through Kensington to Cumberland, and in any income-tax bracket you care to take a look at.

Wights are not a common phenomenon in Ireland, and although the event is not, according to the form book of the Western world, probable, it is not entirely absurd to speculate as to whether the Irish may not find a way of preventing the multiplication of Wights and Wightism – of defeating, in fact, this enfeebling type of alienation. If civilization is to keep going, a start in this direction has to be made somewhere, and perhaps a rather new, very small nation is the place where it could be made. Even so, it could be no more than an object lesson from which the big States pick up a few tips. For although Mr Morganthau, the American statesman and Cabinet member, wanted after World War II to make Germany a better, more democratic place by chopping it up into its little old constituent States, the idea came to nothing, and the dismaying size of their total apparatus is something the big States are stuck with. Their problem of alienation has to be solved by means other than shrinkage. On the other hand, we cannot afford to have a war every so often just to give people a sense of – in the American phrase – 'belonging'; a sense above all that what they are doing as citizens and workers is necessary otherwise than as merely a way of making a living for themselves; is effective as a means towards a communal objective; and is something which – given those most undesired circumstances – they basically will and desire to do.

It is not the 'fault' of the Wights that they live in a state of civic alienation. One of the troubles (or, as some think, amenities), of an unplanned society, or a society which is partly planned and partly jungle, is that hardly anything that goes wrong can be said, with absolute assurance and precision, to be anybody's fault. Hardly anyone can be packed off to some social equivalent of the Russian 'virgin lands' for lousing things up, because almost every louser-up can convincingly claim that he was not really responsible for the thing that happened. 'Circumstances beyond his control' were responsible. An incompetent tycoon has to make a really enormous blot on his copybook, and leave his finger-print on the mess, before he can be sufficiently identified to qualify for a golden handshake and returned to store in Sussex or the East Riding. And a society which produces Wights must address its complaint not to them but to itself. Or, if that be seen as a possible cause of unpleasantness, the matter may be referred to History, which is the fault of no living being, or, if so desired, to God Almighty, who is not held to be any particular person's fault either.

Those who deem it subversive to indict our society, our 'way of life', who read no history, and are dubious about the role of the One Above in the whole imbroglio, have from time to time produced other alleged culprits such as the Press, the cinema and television. It can be argued, in a back-handed kind of defence, that these mass media in their existing form, are a result rather than by any means a cause of our social malaises and potentially fatal sickness. However you weigh that up, the mass media certainly provide a kind of 'blown up' photograph of our general condition. They do so not in the sense that they report it fully and accurately, providing comprehensive documentaries, but in the sense that their own character is a reflection of the state of the society which has produced them, just as a sadistic, obviously moronic or, say, good-hearted God reflects the mind of his human creators. The Press has been longest on the job and is still the best reflector. It bulges with good stuff. But the best friends of the Press have to tell it what too much of it too often smells like. (In moments of depression or on reading of sage proposals for improving the tone of our Press, I recall a time when the promoters of some breath-sweetener or over-all stink-reducer, were displaying advertisements picturing a man whose halitosis, or his body-reek, was so bad that he was utterly without friends of either sex and had to spend his evenings playing solitaire. The New Yorker immediately reported the case of a man who, wearying of solitaire, gargled the breath-sweetener daily, soaped himself continually with whatever the stink-antidote was, cured his halitosis and exhalations, and then found that nobody liked him anyway.)

The people right on top of the British Press live in a state of perpetual apprehension. They are frightened – perhaps not much more, certainly not less, than in the thirties – of the advertising agencies. This is a masochistic fear – they enjoy being tied up by the big advertisers and occasionally lashed for bad behaviour. The pay for submitting to the peculiar lusts of advertisers is good. They are frightened, in a quite different way, of the public – frightened of saying anything that could disastrously offend anyone who might otherwise buy their paper. Naturally a Tory newspaper will not be afraid of offending militant socialists – they are not potential customers, unless the paper's racing experts can come up with an exceptionally successful run of racing tips. To this extent politics can be seen as setting a limit to circulation.

And to this extent circulation-hungry men visibly rejoice in the existence among the populace of a-political attitudes. The less people hold any serious political opinions, the less difficult it is for a newspaper to find the 'highest common factor' among many millions of readers. This is one reason why the political power of the Press is a great deal less than it was before World War I, when though circulations were relatively tiny, it was yet worth while for Governments to try to bribe or ruin any paper from *The Times*, to the little green *Westminster Gazette*, and Northcliffe's *Daily Mail*, with a circulation which now would appear puny, terrified the Cabinet and made such an impact that it was ceremonially burned on the Stock Exchange. Which of today's papers risk such a fate?

The frustrating failure of Lord Beaverbrook's political campaigns is often cited in this connexion. To his political sermons, it was apparent, hardly anyone listened. Ironically, the techni-coloured haze of irrelevance and frivolity in which his newspapers enveloped their readers, obscured the figure of the preacher from their view. But it is a mistake to regard Beaverbrook as in this sense unique. The 'mass' Press envied and imitated him. The results were similar. They had helped to create attitudes of mind which made it as difficult for people to take them seriously – in case they wanted to be so taken – as for a slapstick comedian to hold his audience with a short commentary on the Book of Revelations.

The American newspapers frequently point to the British as an example of the most irresponsibly sensational Press in the world. (As often as not, this merely means that someone has inadvertently or even on purpose written something unpleasing to the world strategists in the White House or Pentagon.) The British Press, meantime, prides itself on its responsible attitude to 'serious issues'. Unfortunately what it calls responsibility is often identical with what Oscar Wilde defined as 'presence of mind'. He instanced the case of the man sitting in the stalls when the theatre went on fire. With the greatest presence of mind he rose, and shouted confidently 'Keep your seats. There's no immediate danger.' People who had been going to make an ugly rush for the doors relaxed. The man with presence of mind was thus able to reach the exit unimpeded before the roof fell in on the rest of the audience. Unless great chunks of the roof are actually falling, the newspapers, when they have to mention fire at all (which they often do, because look at all that smoke), prefer to indicate that it is only an expendable part of the scenery that is burning, and that will soon be brought under control.

Even those newspapers which from time to time see fit to act a little bit radical, are liable to turn coy when it comes to the point of saying that the Emperor is totally naked and needs a complete new outfit. They claim they can see his loin cloth.

All these fears and calculations existed in the thirties. The newspapers of the sixties are more amusing, and usually better written – except when they fall victims to that dreadful back-slapping 'mateyness' of style which is supposed to persuade the Wights that there is nothing egg-headly un-Wightish about a jolly old newspaper. Outside contributors, politicians, bankers, clergymen and the like, are often more sinful in this respect than professional journalists. 'Mateyness' apart there are too many people about who seem never to have been told that the power to employ language effectively is, for the moment, one of the characteristics distinguishing man from the apes. Those talking dolphins at Annapolis would be amused to learn how little many supposedly educated Englishmen are concerned with the structure and capabilities of their own fine and flexible language.

In arranging shows for the amusement and occasional edification of our affluent public, with its 'growing problem of leisure' the newspapers of the sixties are certainly more sophisticated than their forerunners. (They do not, however, always make entirely clear that for a large proportion of industrial workers, 'affluence' and the 'problem of leisure' are seen as linked together in the question of how much overtime you have to sweat out in order to make enough money to get a few hours relaxation with a sound roof to spend them under.) But something new has been added to the newspapers' preoccupations. It is the spectre of TV. Despite the good money some newspaper proprietors draw from TV, the Press as such has shown, in face of what is so repeatedly described as 'this challenge', many of the symptoms of nervous breakdown.

It is aware that part of its occupation's gone. The news – certainly most of the news that even distant relatives of the Wights want to hear – has been on TV before the morning newspapers can get to the doormat. (Mrs Wight said, 'We do not have newspapers' – no more, it seemed, than they had leprosy. But it is a reasonable bet that most Wights have TV.) All an enterprising newspaper proprietor could do about that new fact of life would be to pay out good, big money to prominent people to make frightfully startling statements, or to students to burn down some American Embassy, on condition they did so in the couple of hours between the final TV news and the latest possible newspaper deadline.

The clamour of conflicting advice offered on the question of what to do about TV is hard on every newspaper's nervous system. Since any question of principle, moral or political, is but rarely a factor in discussions of how Fleet Street is not merely to avoid the fate of the moving picture industry, but go on making as much money as before, the field for suggestions is wide open. There are those who aver that TV is really a blessing – even though very heavily disguised. Viewers, they say, see a snippet of something on the box, and become avid to read more and more about it in print. This theory often results in journalists being compelled to pad out the simple facts with a lot of fluff and wool, or to construct 'angles' which may be new, but may be also irrelevant.

Others maintain that newspapers should pluckily face the facts about 'news', and turn themselves into a sort of magazines. This sometimes makes for a lot of very informative reading. But it is extremely hard to fill acres and acres of newsprint with fresh magazine material daily and weekly. And in the nature of things there is nobody around with more than a few years' experience in even trying to do it. This must be why the newspapers are frequently, and quite obviously, in the condition Patrick Campbell once described to me when I asked how a novel he was thought to be writing was coming along. 'Not badly,' he said, 'except that now I've finished Chapter Three, I can't think what to put.'

The silver lining for the newspapers is attached to the dark cloud by the fact that TV faces many of the same problems, and often finds even more inept 'solutions'. Even more than the newspapers, TV is dominated by the need to find the 'highest common factor' in an enormous and disparate public, which it cannot afford to antagonize too often or too long. When TV audaciously sets out to risk giving offence to these or those, its brain-children are liable to be short-lived, strangled at, or soon after, birth by people who think their taboos should be everyone else's taboos, too. TV's handling of allegedly basic and even 'dangerous' topics can also be fraudulent, corresponding to some of the 'hard-hitting exposures' in newspapers. In such cases nothing is exposed which is not either unimportant, or common knowledge.

Pessimists hold that with supreme control of TV in the power either of multi-millionaires or a State corporation, and the control of fewer and fewer newspapers being concentrated in fewer and fewer hands, the brain-washing of the public has increased, is going to go on increasing for ever, and cannot be diminished. But it seems to me probable that the ingenious and resilient human race still has some surprising cards up its sleeves. There are those, and the devil knows they have some grounds for alarm, who have for many years pointed to the immense extension of the power of dictators provided by, first the radio, later TV. It is true enough. But it is also true that this same technical achievement has been used in a quite different way. It is certain that a larger proportion of people in German-occupied France during World War II heard British propaganda from the BBC than the proportion of the population of Napoleonic France which, by broadsheets or the mouths of secret agents, heard the propaganda of those who were giving the British line from the office of William Pitt. And since the penalty for listening secretly to the BBC could be torture and death, the listeners were apt to be more serious and effective than were those in England who freely listened to Lord Haw-haw.

To this point it may be cogently objected that this was, after all, merely an instance of one immensely powerful, immensely expensive apparatus battling another. That is certainly so. But the development did not stop there. In the years since that war, the 'clandestine' or 'rebel' radio has played an important, sometimes a major role, in the education and organization of resistance to apparently invulnerable Establishments in, for instance, Latin America and the Middle East. Naturally, one of the first acts of rebels against a condition of affairs which they consider intolerable is to seize the official radio station from which to broadcast home truths or blatant lies as the case may be. But where that is impossible, and in any event for a long time before it becomes possible, relatively cheap, mobile transmitters have been at work. The mere seizure of the official radio transmitter, like the arrest of the Cabinet and the installation of another, is not a qualitative change in the apparatus of power. The development of the little secret transmitter is.

People who, at this point, cry out that this is not Iraq or Ecuador, and it can't happen here, even if enough people want it to, are looking at the wrong point. (Though one should not forget the relative success of the Welsh Nationalists who had quite a run for their risks with their secret transmissions damning the Government.)

The real point is that, contrary to a general, defeatist, belief, things such as the improvement and exploitation of technical advance, do not have to go on and on for ever in the same direction they have followed over, say, the past forty years or so. The skills which produced the first radio transmitters and, long before that, the rotary press, basis of the mass circulation newspaper, are already capable of partially negating the social effects of these achievements. The invention of the mimeograph machine is a primitive example. It has for many years been the secret weapon of every group which cannot afford to put up the huge money needed to run a conventionally printed newspaper or magazine, and is unwilling to put itself – even if offered the chance – in pawn to the advertisers. (It is often the indispensable vehicle of candidates at election whose expenditure is limited by law.)

The old jingle says, 'Small as I am, and big as you are, I'm bigger than you are, small as I am.' It is already, under certain conditions, true of the little transmitter and the mimeograph. Those who find it hard to imagine that the big are not going to go on and on getting bigger, and the small smaller, and more helpless – that we are condemned, in fact, to the 'dull calamity' of a continuously increasing uniformity – underestimate the fruitful contradictions inherent in the technical capacities of man. In terms of 'real money', of comparative purchasing power as distinct from the nominal cost in inflated or depreciated currency, a good motor-car today is dirt cheap. (The fact that it is often a pretty 'cheap' job in the other sense of the word is here irrelevant.) Similarly, it is about as certain as anything in the future can be, that technicians will find cheaper and cheaper ways of producing radio, and even television, transmitters, and also written words. (You could already produce an entire newspaper on microfilm and show it in the homes of friends and fellow-thinkers.)

In 1964 the Verholme shipyard at Cork was busy building what was to be the world's first 'pirate' TV station. It was an artificial island to be anchored, outside territorial waters, off the Dutch coast. The project was quashed by the Dutch Government and the political parties who shared between them the time on the official Dutch TV, and were alarmed by the threat of competition. It is significant that the Dutch 'pirate' radio was already so popular that the Government realized it was now too late to try to suppress it. But before the TV 'island' could be got into position the authorities announced they would send

444

troops to invade and occupy it. Thereupon, the big advertising money took fright and pulled out.

Certainly the TV island was terribly expensive. Certainly the money behind it was as nervous as big money always is. The whole enterprise was a swallow that made no summer. But as the technical possibilities of producing all such sources of mass communication more and more cheaply are discovered and exploited, minority groups – groups without much money and not interested in making any more -- will find instruments ready to hand. They will be able (and this is something the British are thought to be particularly good at) to do it themselves. And it is not necessary to think simply in terms of political minorities. It could cause giggles to evoke a picture of people in Slough or Coventry gathered in the living-room to hear or view exhortations from cheap, secret transmitters to rush out and arrest the local Council, and hang delinquent industrialists. (People who, in the words of the poet Browning, 'paint the future from the past' do have that sort of picture in mind when they think of 'revolutionary change'.)

The essential point here is not the content and purport of what might be transmitted through the ether or by written word. The 'revolutionary change' which may be nearer than most people suppose, consists, in this context, simply in the technical possibility of a reversal of past trends in the control of the 'mass media', the opening of opportunities for minorities to express vigorous opinions as they did through the newspapers after the repeal of the Stamp Act made distribution of newspapers cheap, and before the compulsion to attract advertising money and earn high dividends made the creation of a newspaper so dauntingly expensive.

If we have to rely on protesting letters to the newspapers, or the Press Council or the Independent Television Authority to make truly radical improvements in the character of the mass media, God help us, for certainly nothing else will. And this is a matter of the greatest possible social significance because, as I have said, the character of our mass media is a 'blown up' photograph – a little caricatured as hopeful observers believe – of our own. (It is no good people saying it is not their fault that X Y and Z, mass media controllers, are avaricious orang-outangs

445

for whom they are not responsible. So who buys their product?)

I find many people surprised that a person such as myself who, with longish intervals for relaxation or for different activities – has been sometimes up to the neck, and usually up to the waist, in politics in the widest sense of the word, should continue to hope. Some of them, modern chiliasts, almost happy in the certainty that the end of the world is due any day now and cannot be averted, resent my attitude. Others think it means I suffer from some kind of mental cataract blurring my vision of human crimes such as the German massacre of the Jews, the bombing of the Vietnamese, and the fact that the vast majority of the world's population suffers grievous privation and oppression as a result of the greed or incompetence of those who could control the world's riches. To my astonishment, I saw a friend of mine quoted in the *Sunday Times* as saying of me that I was 'the most profound cynic' he had ever known. Had he accused me of being absurdly starry-eyed I should have understood him better. For despite the fact that those ancient Greeks thought so ill of Hope, as being illusory and dangerous, luring men to doom, I am hopeful amid the reek of blood and disaster because I am hopeful about man's power and his will – sluggish though it often be – to change the conditions from which these horrors are born.

However strong the evidence to the contrary, I find it almost impossible to believe that we are stupider than those Australian horses.

INDEX

INDEX

449

450

MORE ABOUT PENGUINS

If you have enjoyed reading this book you may wish
to know that *Penguin Book News* appears every
month. It is an attractively illustrated magazine
containing a complete list of books published by
Penguins and still in print, together with details of
the month's new books. A specimen copy will be
sent free on request.

Penguin Book News is obtainable from most
bookshops; but you may prefer to become a regular
subscriber at 3s. for twelve issues. Just write to
Dept EP, Penguin Books Ltd, Harmondsworth,
Middlesex, enclosing a cheque or postal order, and
you will be put on the mailing list.

Some other books published by Penguins are
described on the following pages.

Note: *Penguin Book News* is not
available in the U.S.A., Canada or Australia

THE AGE OF ILLUSION:
ENGLAND IN THE TWENTIES AND THIRTIES

Ronald Blythe

It was the age of Lloyd George, Baldwin, Ramsay Mac-
Donald, 'Jix', Lansbury, Chamberlain, and Winston
Churchill; the age of Sir John Reith, T. E. Lawrence, the
Prince of Wales, T. S. Eliot, Amy Johnson, Kate Meyrick,
the Rector of Stiffkey, and Colonel Blimp; the age of the
Charleston, Bodyline Bowling, Jarrow, the Spanish Civil
War, the Left Book Club, the Brighton Trunk Murder,
Abdication, and Munich. It was the age of illusion, by
depression out of inaction – the age of a nation in
mourning.

High-lighting fifteen typical episodes and personalities,
Ronald Blythe evokes in *The Age of Illusion* the brittle
atmosphere of the two decades between the wars with
clipped and pungent precision.

INSIDE ROBERT ROBINSON

Presenting Robert Robinson of T V's 'Points of View'

Robinson of the *Sunday Times*, the *Observer*, *Punch*

Robinson . . . Crusoe on an island of clowns

Robinson . . . fly on everyman's wall

Robinson in the world of song-pluggers, pigeon-fanciers, undertakers, disc-jockeys, pig-race bookmakers, body-builders, pawnbrokers . . .

Now pinned down in print and twice as droll.

HATRED, RIDICULE OR CONTEMPT

A BOOK OF LIBEL CASES

Joseph Dean

'It cannot be said that chastity is a necessary qualification for the management or ownership of a garage.'

Such a measured and memorable conclusion (from *Ralston v. Ralston*, 1930) suggests that the law of libel can at times be as quaint as a Cornish lane. Consider the case of Mr John Canning, who received a postcard telling him to 'get back to his ruddy cage'. It transpired that in a recent book there had been a Mr Canning who ran from cage to cage in the Zoo to escape the police. Mr John Canning took action for libel. As did an actress, Mrs Porteous, who was said in a review to have performed like 'a raging, frothing epileptic, rolling on the floor and biting her toe-nails'.

Many familiar figures take their place in the witness box in this curious and fascinating collection of libel cases – Lord Alfred Douglas, Winston Churchill, Horatio Bottomley, Prince Youssoupoff, Aleister Crowley, Harold Laski, and even the sons of W. E. Gladstone, fighting to expunge a charge of lechery against the G.O.M. of the Liberal tradition.

A PAINTER OF OUR TIME

John Berger

For twenty years Janos Lavin, a refugee from pre-war Hungary, has lived, thought, and worked as an artist in London. Suddenly, a week after the successful opening of his own exhibition, he disappears. Why?

John Berger, the well-known critic and painter, reconstructs the tormented conflicts of an émigré in an England whose security seems almost hostile to him. Gradually, in Lavin's diary, the daily problems and preoccupations of an artist – rarely presented with such exactness and conviction – give way to an upsurge of revolutionary memories, as the crisis in Eastern Europe approaches.

Berger's subtle account mirrors the crisis of art and politics in our time, while Lavin's diary acquires the same kind of absorbing interest as the letters of Van Gogh. 'The feeling of urgency and passion communicates itself to the reader . . . an enthralling book' – *Cambridge Review*

Claud Cockburn has written a piece in

THE INCOMPATIBLES

TRADE UNION MILITANCY AND THE CONSENSUS

Edited by Robin Blackburn and Alexander Cockburn

Britain is in economic crisis, and the unions are more and more being nailed as the culprits. They are accused of pricing Britain out of world markets with their inflationary claims and restrictive habits: costs are forced up, but production pegged. As unemployment rises, the unions seem to be busy bickering over trivialities like demarcation.

How much truth and how much prejudice is there in this picture? Have the unions, like the rhinoceros, outlived their age? And what about shop stewards and wildcat strikes? And the 'go-it-alone' strike of the seamen – was that engineered by Communists, as the Prime Minister suggested?

The contributors to *The Incompatibles* include Philip Toynbee, Jack Jones (Assistant Secretary of T.G.W.U.), Ken Coates, Michael Frayn, Perry Anderson, Paul Foot, and Clive Jenkins (General Secretary of ASSET). From varying standpoints they re-examine the roots of Trade Unionism, and their appraisal of the present functions and purposes of unions and of their relationship with the Labour Movement raises fundamental questions concerning the unions and Socialism.

a Penguin Special

THE PENGUIN PRIVATE EYE

'These outrageous libels are not in the public interest' – *Edward Martell*

'I enjoy Private Eye more than I can say' – *Baroness Asquith*

'When are you going to develop a point of view?' – *Kenneth Tynan*

'Long may you flourish' – *Anthony Wedgwood Benn*

'God rot the lot of you' – *Dr Jonathan Miller*